12.95

AN INTRODUCTORY
HEBREW GRAMMAR

WITH

PROGRESSIVE EXERCISES IN READING, WRITING AND POINTING

AN INTRODUCTORY
HEBREW GRAMMAR

WITH

PROGRESSIVE EXERCISES IN READING
WRITING AND POINTING

BY THE LATE

A. B. DAVIDSON, Litt.D., LL.D.

PROFESSOR OF HEBREW AND OLD TESTAMENT EXEGESIS,
NEW COLLEGE, EDINBURGH

REVISED THROUGHOUT BY

JOHN MAUCHLINE, D.D.

PROFESSOR OF OLD TESTAMENT LANGUAGE AND LITERATURE,
UNIVERSITY OF GLASGOW, AND
PRINCIPAL OF TRINITY COLLEGE, GLASGOW

(TWENTY-SIXTH EDITION)

Edinburgh: T. & T. CLARK, 38 George Street

PRINTED IN SCOTLAND BY
MORRISON AND GIBB LIMITED

FOR

T. & T. CLARK LTD., EDINBURGH

0 567 01005 8

FIRST TO EIGHTEENTH EDITIONS .	*A. B. Davidson*	1874-1913
NINETEENTH EDITION	*J. E. Mc Fadyen*	1914
TWENTIETH EDITION	*J. E. Mc Fadyen*	1916
TWENTY-FIRST TO TWENTY-FOURTH EDITIONS	*J. E. Mc Fadyen*	1921-1960
TWENTY-FIFTH EDITION	*J. Mauchline*	1962
TWENTY-SIXTH EDITION	*J. Mauchline*	1966
LATEST IMPRESSION		1978

PREFACE TO THE TWENTY-FIFTH EDITION

The late Professor A. B. Davidson's *Hebrew Grammar* ran through 18 successive editions, the first one being published in 1874. The 19th edition, which was published in 1914, was thoroughly revised by the late Professor John E. McFadyen, and the Davidson-McFadyen *An Introductory Hebrew Grammar* has now run to the 24th edition. The fact that the plates are now so worn that further use of them has become impracticable provided an occasion for another revision of the Grammar, and I have undertaken this task at the invitation of the Society for Old Testament Study, whose advice on the matter was taken by the Publishers.

It was the wish of the Publishers that whereas the reviser should have considerable liberty in doing his work, yet certain characteristics of the Grammar as known and used should remain, so that the new Grammar should have some of the lineaments of its predecessor and should be recognisable as a descendant. A statement, therefore, ought to be given of the main ways in which alteration and revision have been made:

1. TRANSLITERATION. It will be noticed that the transliteration of צ into ç has been dropped and the sibilants are represented by the signs ס s, צ ṣ, שׁ š, שׂ ś,which is now the common practice. The aspirate or fricative use of the *Bᵉghadhkᵉphath* letters is represented by <u>bh</u>, <u>gh</u>, <u>dh</u>, etc. (as formerly) and not by ḇ, g̱, ḏ, etc. (as is now sometimes done); the former usage may look clumsier than the latter, but surely must be continued in use, especially for learners, so long as terms like Kᵉthibh, Methegh, Maqqeph, Nipḥʿal, Hiphʿil, etc. are used in these forms.

2. THE ORDER OF TREATMENT has been much altered in some parts of the Grammar. The first ten sections, for instance, have been rid of all tautology, shortened and recast, because, as they were, they presented a daunting introduction

to the study of the Hebrew language. It was considered preferable, however, to continue to place much of the content of these sections at the beginning of the book rather than to introduce it incidentally, in an unsystematic manner, because they contain much which is of fundamental importance for the intelligent study of the later sections. The study of them may entail some initial drudgery, but the time of tribulation has been reduced as far as possible.

The other large alteration is in the part of the Grammar dealing with the various types of verbs. Those which are commonly in use, *Pē Yôḏh* and *Pē Wāw*, *'Ayin Wāw* and *'Ayin Yôḏh*, and *Lāmeḏh Hē* verbs, are treated at a much earlier point than was formerly the case in order that the student's working vocabulary may be significantly increased at a correspondingly earlier stage, and that he may gain thereby much greater facility in reading simple prose passages.

There are, of course, many minor changes also; e.g. the study of the verb is not introduced incidentally in a section which professes to deal with the conjunction (cf. § 15), but is now explicitly introduced in § 11; the prepositions are treated more systematically, and cross references are given to aid the study of them; the contents of § 45, which, as it was, covered a wide range, have now been divided among three sections; the section on the Numerals has been largely recast, and the statement on Accents is no longer an appendix but is included as the final section in the Grammar proper.

3. THE VOCABULARIES used in the exercises have been confined as far as possible to common words. That has had its effect upon the choice of material for the sentences or passages for translation. It was the practice in the Grammar to use sentences taken more or less word for word from the Old Testament; that had the advantage of giving students samples of the *ipsissima verba*, but it had the effect of bringing in uncommon words and forms which were often disturbing for a learner, and made footnotes essential. That practice has been abandoned in the new Grammar, and in many cases sentences

have been constructed to illustrate the use of the chosen vocabulary, although they are often based on passages from the Old Testament. Formerly the exercises were based largely on short sentences which tended to have the appearance of utility models. A few of these short sentences have normally been retained, since they have the advantage of giving the student quick and easy illustrations of the forms and uses with which a section is concerned, but it has generally been the endeavour to make the remainder of the exercises consist of longer (and, in consequence, more interesting) sentences, and, at least in the later sections, of series of sentences in narrative sequence. It will also be noted that in the later sections passages from the Old Testament for additional reading have been suggested. These a student may read with the help of a dictionary (e.g. Langenscheidt's) for the unknown words if he chooses. But even that can be dispensed with, and he can use a modern translation to fill out the meaning, because the purpose of suggesting such passages at this stage is that the student should get experience of reading connected passages in Hebrew prose rather than that he should add to his vocabulary.

4. FOOTNOTES. It will be noted that few footnotes are used. An overdose of these in a grammar, especially in one intended for learners beginning their study of the language, can be disturbing and even annoying. Sometimes such notes contain comments on, or explanations of, forms which should never have been used; also their multiplication may simply be a sign of the need for a complete revision of the material.

5. GENERAL VOCABULARIES. The references in the General Vocabularies at the end of the Grammar are to the sections of the Grammar and not to the pages. That should make it possible to retain these references with little, if any, change, even when parts of the Grammar come to be altered in the light of experience and advice.

6. PARADIGMS. These have been considerably extended in scope in response to a request which has often been made by

many teachers who use this Grammar. In the case of the Verb Tables, the sign '&c.' has been used only when it was deemed clear that the student could reasonably be expected to complete the conjugation of the form indicated. There have been added tables of the various classes of nouns and prepositions, and it is hoped that these will be found helpful.

7. INDEXES. The Index of Subjects has been retained; that of Hebrew words has been dropped, the Hebrew-English vocabulary being made to serve the purpose which it formerly served.

8. ABBREVIATIONS. The abbreviations which are to be found in the Grammar are those which are commonly in use, but mention should be made here of two related symbols whose use has been found to be most advantageous for certain purposes. These symbols are > and <, the first meaning 'leading to', 'developing into' or 'becoming' (e.g. thorough > through, bittacle > binnacle) and the second meaning 'developing from', 'derived from' (e.g. sheriff < shire reeve, shammy < chamois).

I wish to take this opportunity of thanking many who have given me helpful comments and suggestions with regard to the revision of the Grammar. I should especially mention Professors G. R. Driver, C. J. Mullo Weir, Cyril S. Rodd and Sidney Jellicoe, Mgr. J. M. T. Barton and Dr. William McKane. Not all which they advised could be put into practice in the Grammar; their unanimity was not such as to ensure that. To accept some suggestions entailed the rejection of others; but even where suggestions have not been accepted, their proposal often occasioned a salutary rethinking of many questions.

I acknowledge with gratitude my indebtedness to the Rev. H. St. J. Hart, Dean of Queens' College, Cambridge, and to Dr. William McKane, a colleague in Glasgow, for their laborious, but invaluable, work in assisting me with the reading of the proofs. And I have pleasure in expressing my appreciation of the unfailing courtesy and skilled craftsmanship of the printers, E. J. Brill, of Leyden, and the great interest and generous co-operation of the publishers, T. & T. Clark, of Edinburgh.

To write a Hebrew Grammar is to essay a difficult task; to revise a Hebrew Grammar which has been in use for many years is an unenviable one. Every experienced teacher is tempted to think that his way of handling the material is the only one which a sensible, practical teacher would ever use; and he has often composed his own Hebrew-English and English-Hebrew exercises and believes that they serve his purpose better than any others which he has encountered (or is likely to encounter). To determine what should be included and what left out is never easy and seldom, in the end, wholly satisfactory. To define the limits of the syntactical instruction which should be included in a grammar is likewise difficult; yet to add some such instruction is essential; it introduces a flavour of the living language into the dry roots of grammatical forms. It may, indeed, be that occasionally more has been added than some teachers consider advisable. Beyond such decisions upon particular topics, the general aim was to keep the Grammar as a whole about the same size as its predecessor.

It is true that I have introduced many changes and modifications, great and small, in this edition of the Grammar, but these imply no criticism of the work of the two scholars, Professor A. B. Davidson and Professor J. E. McFadyen, who were responsible for the earlier editions. The fact that so many editions have been called for gives ample evidence of the esteem in which this Grammar has been held for a period of over eighty years and of the extensive use which has been made of it in classroom and study. It is hoped that the changes and modifications which have now been made will not detract from the worth of the Grammar and that it will continue to find acceptance and to be used as widely in days to come as it has in the past.

PREFACE TO THE TWENTY-SIXTH EDITION

A second printing of the recently revised form of the Grammar has provided the opportunity to make the necessary corrections of author's and printer's *errata* and to rectify sins of omission and of commission. But more than this has been done. Some footnotes have been added to the Exercises to aid students with Hebrew forms and usages which, occurring where they do, students may find difficult. In addition, certain paragraphs have been recast for simplification or for greater clarity, of which the most significant are these: § 7. 4; § 20. 1 (first part); § 23. 1b. I have also accepted a suggestion made to me by one of my former students that there might with advantage be inserted in the Grammar a summary of §§ 2–7 which, in some circumstances, students might be advised to regard as providing a sufficient introduction to these sections until they have completed their study of §§ 8–25. That completed, they might then return to §§ 2–7 for a study of them in full form.

The complaint has been made by some teachers using the Grammar that the Exercises are too long for the purposes of classroom instruction. The aim in providing enlarged exercises was twofold: to offer to teachers a field of selection from which they can take what is most suitable for their own conditions of classwork, and to provide material for students who want to pursue further study on their own.

With gratitude I record my indebtedness to many scholars who have sent to me intimations of detected *errata* or have suggested certain modifications and amendments in the printed text. I must make special mention of the Baroness de Ward, Mrs. R. B. Edwards, Miss Miriam Ettisch, Professor C. J. Mullo Weir, Professor D. Winton Thomas, Professor P. R. Ackroyd, the Rev. L. H. Brockington, the Rev. H. St. J. Hart, the Rev. Barnabas Lindars, Dr. P. Wernberg-Möller, Dr. William McKane and the Rev. William Johnstone.

CONTENTS

INTRODUCTION

INTRODUCTION

It should be stated at once that this Grammar is concerned with the Hebrew language as it is used in the Old Testament and not with post-Biblical Hebrew at all. One remarkable fact about the Hebrew of the Old Testament is that while the dates of the written documents in which it is used range in time over a period at least as long as that from Chaucer to the present in English literature, the differences in word-forms, vocabulary and style between the earliest period and the latest are not nearly so extensive or notable as might be expected. That is doubtless owing to the amount of editorial revision of the Old Testament documents which has taken place and which has given to them a uniformity of form and usage which otherwise they would not possess.

It is commonly true that non-Jewish students of Hebrew begin their study of the language at a later age than they do in the case of most other languages to which they give their attention; in fact most of them do it in terms of the demands of a theological curriculum. That often means that they are not particularly interested in Hebrew as a language, but hope (or have been more or less persuaded to hope) that by some understanding of this language they will enter more fully into the thought of the Old Testament. Unfortunately they have commonly inherited an oral tradition to the effect that the language itself is absurdly difficult, and that the drudgery of learning it ought not to be tolerated by theological students at the age when they undertake such studies.

But the beginner should enter upon his study of Hebrew with the assurance that it is not more difficult, but in some important respects easier, to acquire a working knowledge of it than of most other languages. With a reasonable amount of intelligent application he will more quickly learn to read a piece of ordinary historical narrative in Hebrew than in Latin, Greek or German.

Hebrew, however, has difficulties of its own which must be frankly acknowledged and faced. Of these, the three which meet the beginner at once are (i) the strangeness of the alphabet, (ii) the fact that the language is read from right to left, and (iii) the unlikeness of the sounds represented by some of the signs to any in our own language. The first two difficulties cause only temporary concern, the third is more serious. There are, e.g., two *k* sounds and two *t* sounds, one in either group having no equivalent in English. Thus the word *kōl,* read with one of these *ks*, means *all,* but, read with the other *k,* means *voice.* These two *ks* are represented quite differently in writing. The student must learn, therefore, from the beginning to pronounce them differently in reading, otherwise he will be in continual danger of confusing totally diffeıent words. (iv) Another difficulty is that the roots, whatever may have been their original form, are in the Old Testament almost entirely triliteral, with the result that at first the verbs especially all look very much alike—e.g. *malak, zakar, lamad, harag,* &c.— thus imposing upon the memory a very heavy strain. Compound verbs are not found: there is nothing in Hebrew corresponding to the modifications of verbal meaning which can be made in Latin, Greek or German by prefixing prepositions as in *exire, inire, abire, redire,* &c.: ἐκβαίνειν, ἐμβαίνειν, ἀναβαίνειν, καταβαίνειν, &c.: *ausgehen, eingehen, aufgehen, untergehen,* &c. Every verb has to be learned separately: the verbs *to go out, to go up, to go down* are all quite different, having nothing in common with one another and being quite unrelated to the verb *to go.*

Over against these difficulties have to be set certain counterbalancing factors: (i) the working vocabulary of Hebrew is comparatively small. It is true that many rare words occur in certain books of the Old Testament, such as the Book of Job, but to know thoroughly a dozen chapters is to acquire a vocabulary which has a wide usefulness; (ii) the so-called irregular verbs are for the most part strictly regular, and the features, which they illustrate, which are not found in the regular verb, are due to the presence of a guttural or a weak letter as one of the radicals. Their forms are intelligible to a student who understands the fundamental principles of the Hebrew language. It is therefore of primary importance that the learner should take care to understand those principles from the very beginning. If he does not neglect this advice, his progress in learning Hebrew will not be unduly slow, and he will find in grammatical forms a system which he will come quickly to understand, and in syntactical usage a flexibility which may at first seem excessive and lead to uncertainty concerning the meaning or nuance which is to be conveyed, but which in the end will be found to be very effective; (iii) the noun has no case endings and the verb has only two tenses or forms. The contrast with the complexities of Latin and Greek, for instance, in this respect will at once be obvious; (iv) Hebrew syntax has the appearance of great simplicity; an ordinary narrative passage from the Old Testament with its recurring use of the word *and* illustrates that at once. In Latin or Greek the practice is to relate subsidiary clauses to the main one, so that a sentence may be quite an elaborate structure; in Hebrew, clauses tend to be laid together or co-ordinated, even if in English translation some of them may require to be made subsidiary that the meaning may be made perfectly plain. By the use of particles, participles, relative and other subordinate clauses, a number of thoughts are expressed in those languages in their perspective and in their relation to one another and are presented as a correlated whole, sometimes with the one principal verb; the habit of Hebrew is to co-ordinate rather than to subordinate. A piece of idiomatic Greek, such as the introductory words of St. Luke's Gospel, does not readily go into Hebrew. Even a simpler form of Greek would become simpler still in Hebrew. Take, *e.g.*, Mat. 27, 28-30: καὶ ἐκδύσαντες αὐτὸν χλαμύδα κοκκίνην περιέθηκαν αὐτῷ, καὶ πλέξαντες στέφανον . . . ἐπέθηκαν ἐπὶ τῆς κεφαλῆς αὐτοῦ . ., καὶ γονυπετήσαντες . . . ἐνέπαιξαν αὐτῷ . . . καὶ ἐμπτύσαντες εἰς αὐτὸν ἔλαβον τὸν κάλαμον, &c. These participles would in Hebrew be most naturally rendered by finite verbs, and the passage would run as follows: "and they stripped him and put a scarlet robe on him and plaited a crown . . . and put it upon his head and knelt . . . and mocked him . . . and spat on him and took the reed," &c. This indeed makes for syntactical simplicity. These being the characteristics of the Hebrew language, it often exhibits an altogether extraordinary regularity. It is methodical almost to the point of being mechanical.

The language of a people is the product of its history, its geographical position and its resultant cultural contacts. The basic importance of the verb and the derivation of nouns from it, which is a characteristic of Hebrew, is not peculiar to it alone; it is to be found in many languages. But the notable absence of abstract words, the practice of using a metaphor from everyday life in place of an adverb of manner, the use of an auxiliary verb rather than an adverb to describe how an action was done repeatedly, or quickly, or slowly, etc., and the significant fact that not a few nouns have a primary and a secondary meaning, such as those which mean nose and anger, heat and wrath, weight and honour, height and pride, smoothness and flattery, etc., and other characteristics which might be noted, give a colourfulness, a directness and a concreteness to Hebrew which make it a vigorous and effective instrument of communication and make it difficult for anyone using the language to wrap his thought in verbal obscurities or to darken it with complicated modes of expression of uncertain intent. It has a brevity which is arresting, a clarity which is often challenging and, as used in rhythmic form, sonorities which are deeply impressive.

§ 1. HEBREW ALPHABET

Name	Form	Final.	Sound and Sign	Signification of the Name	Numerical Value
ʾĀ́-leph	א		ʾ	Ox	1
Bêth	ב		b, bh	House	2
Gî́-mel	ג		g, gh	Camel	3
Dā́-leth	ד		d, dh	Door	4
Hē	ה		h	Air-hole *or* Lattice-window ?	5
Wāw	ו		w	Hook	6
Zá-yin	ז		z	Weapon	7
Ḥêth	ח		ḥ	Fence	8
Ṭêth	ט		ṭ	Snake ?	9
Yôdh	י		y	Hand	10
Kaph	כ	ך	k, kh	Bent hand	20
Lā́-medh	ל		l	Ox-goad	30
Mêm	מ	ם	m	Water	40
Nûn	נ	ן	n	Fish	50
Sā́-mekh	ס		s	Prop	60
ʿÁ-yin	ע		ʿ	Eye	70
Pē	פ	ף	p, ph	Mouth	80
Ṣā-dhê	צ	ץ	ṣ	Fish hook ?	90
Qôph	ק		q	Eye of needle *or* back of head ?	100
Rêš	ר		r	Head	200
Śîn, Šîn	שׂ שׁ		ś, š	Tooth	300
Tāw	ת		t, th	Sign *or* cross	400

1. *The Shape of the Letters.* The Hebrew alphabet, as given in the table on the page opposite, consists of 22 letters which are all consonants and is in the square script which came into use among the Jews, probably not earlier than the time of Ezra, and possibly later. It was a stylized development of the old Phoenician script which remained in use at least until the Samaritan schism (4th century B.C.). In the Phoenician script the shapes of a number of the letters represent, more or less, the objects denoted by their names; e.g. *Šîn* W, *ʻÁyin* 0 or o, and *Tāw* × or †, whose names mean *tooth, eye* and *sign* or *cross* respectively, may be regarded as being reasonably representative of the objects denoted. But such representative value has been almost wholly lost in the letters of the square script.

Hebrew is read from right to left.

Observe carefully how the following letters are distinguished: (a) גנכב. כ *k* is rounded, ב *b* has a *tittle* (Mat. 5.18) at the lower right-hand corner, נ *n* is square-cornered, while ג *g* is broken at the foot; (b) ךרד. ד *d* is square at the top right-hand corner, ר *r* is rounded, ך final *k* is like ד *d* with the down stroke elongated below the line; (c) תחה. ה *h* is open at the top left-hand corner, ח *ḥ* is shut, and ת *t* has a foot on its left limb; (d) ןזוי. י *y* is wholly above the line, ו *w* reaches down to it, ז *z* has a cross-stroke at the top and is wavy, while ן final *n* is extended under the line; (e) םס. ס *s* is round in shape and ם final *m* is square; (f) מט. ט *ṭ* is open at the top and מ *m* open at the bottom left-hand corner; (g) ץצע. ע (transliterated by ʻ) has its tail turned to the left, צ *ṣ* curves to the right and then to the left, while ץ final *ṣ* droops its tail straight down.

The five letters צפנמכ, when they occur at the end of a word, have the forms ץףןםך. All these final forms except ם have an extension below the line; no other letter except ק has such an extension.

ל begins above the top of the other letters.

2. *The Sound of the Letters.* (a) תפכדגב (mnemonically,

the bᵉghadhkᵉphath) have a double pronunciation. They can be hard and explosive, and they can be aspirate and fricative, as is shown in the Table. In the latter use, ב is *bh* or the English *v*, ג is *gh* as the sound is heard in N. German *Tage*, ד is *dh*, as *th* is heard in *father*, כ is *kh*, as in the place-name Kharkov, פ is *ph* as the English *f* unvoiced, and ת is *th* as in *thin*.

(b) The Labials are פמוב. Of these ו must be noted, since it can have vocalic as well as consonantal value (see (g) below).

(c) Of the Palatals (or Velars) קכג, care must be taken to distinguish the sounds of כ and ק. The sound of the latter is much stronger than that of כ and is pronounced at the back of the palate.

(d) The Dentals are טתד. ת is the English *t* as in *ten*, but ט is pronounced by pressing the flat of the tongue to the top of the mouth, and so is a palatal rather than a dental.

(e) The Sibilants are שׂשׁצסז. ז *z* (as in *zebra*) and שׁ *š* call for no comment; ס and שׂ were doubtless originally distinguishable, but are not so now and are sometimes used interchangeably in the Old Testament; e.g. סכר for שׂכר *to hire*; צ is a strong *s* and may be said to bear the same relation to ס as ט does to ת.

(f) The Gutturals are עחהא. ר is for certain reasons associated with these gutturals (cf. § 7. 3b, 7), but that is not to be taken as evidence that the letter had a rolling, throaty sound (a so-called burr). א, transliterated by a smooth breathing ʾ, expresses simply the emission of breath, and may be exemplified in the emission of breath which occurs at the beginning of the second syllable, following the initial open one, in *reaction* or in the German *beachten*. Its appearance and effect at the beginning of a Hebrew word may be roughly compared to that of the letter *h* in the word *hour*. ע is a sharp, guttural sound, caused by a sudden opening of the glottis; it is transliterated by means of a rough breathing ʿ. The fact that the letter represents two originally different sounds is now shown only in the semantic range of some words in Hebrew (cf. ענה *to answer* and *to sing*). [1] ה corresponds to the English *h* as in *hat*, but ח is a deep, guttural sound as in the Scottish pronunciation of *loch* or in the German *machen*.

(g) ו and י, as consonants, have the sound of *w* in *water* and of *y* in *year* respectively (but they have also the vocalic values of *u* and *i*; cf. § 2. 2).

(h) The phonology of the letters of the Hebrew alphabet is difficult to determine in certain particulars, but the following table may be an aid towards the understanding of it:

	Bilabial	Labio-dental	Inter-dental	Post-dental	Palato-alveolar	Palatal	Velar	Glottal or Guttural (Laryngal)
Explosive	p, b, w			t; d		ṭ	k, g, y	', ', q
Fricative or Aspirate		ph bh	th dh		š		kh gh	h, ḥ
Sibilant			s, ś, z			ṣ		
Lateral				l				
Vibrant				ṛ				
Nasal	m			n				

---

[1] Greek renders this consonant in several ways: it transliterates it sometimes by a smooth breathing (עמלק = Ἀμαλήκ), sometimes by a rough breathing (עלי = Ἡλί, also Ἡλει), sometimes by a γ (עזה = Γάζα).

Note—(i) p, p̲h̲, t, t̲h̲, s, ś, k, k̲h̲ are voiceless.

(ii) b, b̲h̲, d, d̲h̲, z, g, g̲h̲ are voiced.

(iii) ṭ, ṣ, q, ' are emphatic consonants.

(iv) ṣ is described in the table as a palatal sibilant, but if the sound of it is correctly represented by the conventional *ts*, it should be described as a post-dental explosive.

3. The vowels were not originally written in the Hebrew mss. but eventually came into use in them in the manner which is explained in §§ 2-4. The absence of vowels in any written tradition of the Hebrew text of the Old Testament might be considered to be a serious defect and to cause uncertainty of meaning; e.g. the consonants דבר can be read to mean *speak* or *speaking* or *he spoke* or *word* or *pestilence*. The context usually removes any such uncertainty, except occasionally in the choice between a verb and a noun from the same stem, just as, in an English sentence, it would normally be clear whether *btr* should be read as *batter, bather, beater, better, bitter* or *butter*. An experienced reader finds little difficulty with unvocalized texts in Hebrew, which is no more remarkable than the parallel circumstance that a trained stenographer today can read with ease a modern system of shorthand which almost wholly dispenses with vowel signs.

EXERCISE

Write the following in English and Hebrew

בית, דבר, ירד, ירך, גנב, זקן, ימט, טעם, מעט, עצה, החשך,
קצף, כפים, מגן, מים, רצח, כנען, אתה, אזן:

bh, b, l, lm, ml, sṭ, šn, lk̲h̲, gd̲h̲, dg̲h̲, qwm, rṣ, kp̲h̲, ṣw,
hm, mṣ, mṭ, 'ṣ, r', 'm, yyn, ngn, mym, 'wp̲h̲p̲h̲, ḥms, ṣyṣ,
tmm.

N.B.—The forms *b̲h̲*, *g̲h̲*, &c., represent ב, ג, &c., without the dot; *b*, *g*, &c., the dotted letters בּ. גּ. &c.

§ 2. VOWEL SOUNDS—VOWEL LETTERS

A summary of §§ 2–7 will be found on pages 314–319. A study of this summary may, in some cases, be regarded as a sufficient introduction to the contents of these sections until the study of §§ 8–25 has been completed, when §§ 2–7 may be studied in their full form.

1. Only the general principles of the Hebrew vocalic system can be dealt with at this stage. There are in Hebrew, as in other languages, short vowels, long vowels and diphthongs. But in Hebrew there is, besides the ordinary short vowels, a vowel so short as to be almost indistinct; the long vowels may be either pure long or tone-long; and the diphthongs have passed, for the most part, into long vowels.

2. *Vocalization.* (a) All the Semitic alphabets consisted originally of consonantal signs only (§ 1. 1). The first use of vocalic letters probably arose when ו י and ה, falling at the end of a syllable, lost consonantal value and formed with the preceding vowel a diphthong which became modified to a long vowel; e.g. *a* before ו (i.e. *aw*) would pass through *au* to *ô*; so *uw* to *û*; *ay* (*ai*) to *ê*; and *iy* to *î*. Thus ו would come in time to stand for long *o* and *u*, י for long *e* and *i*. ה likewise came to have a vocalic usage and the three letters are often termed vowel-letters or vocalic consonants (also *matres lectionis*). They represent long vowels and, broadly speaking, the pure, unchangeably long rather than the tone-long (see 7 below). We may summarize their vocalic use thus:

ה represents the long *a*, but also short *e* and long *o*.

י represents the long *i* and the long *e*.

ו represents the long *u* and the long *o*.

Thus independently of the special system which was later devised for the accurate representation of the vowels, we know that מה is *mā*, *me* or *mō*, לי is *lî* or *lê*, סוסי *sôsî*, *sôsê*, *sûsî* or *sûsê*.

(b) When ה ו י occur at the beginning of a syllable, they are necessarily consonantal; e.g. יום *yôm* (*day*), וכסף *wᵉkheseph* (*and silver*), הוד *hôdh* (*glory*). When ו י occur within a syllable (as the vocalic *waw* does in יום and הוד above) or at the end of it, they are always vocalic; e.g. לִין *lîn*, קוּם *qûm*, לִי *lî*, לוֹ *lô*. ה is vocalic only at the end of a final syllable, and even in that position it can be used as a consonant (§ 6. 8).

3. So long as Hebrew was a living language, the helps to vocalization described above, though scanty, might be found sufficient. But when the language ceased to be spoken and became unfamiliar, fuller representation of the vowels was needful for correct reading. The proof of this is that the vowel-less text was frequently read in one way by the Greek translators, and in another by the later Jewish scholars who added the vowels. *E.g.*, Gen. 47. 31, "Jacob bowed upon the head of the *bed*" (*miṭṭā*); but in LXX, "of the *staff*" (*maṭṭe*). (Cf. Heb. 11. 21). The consonantal form is the same for both words, המטה. So in Amos 9. 12 the *Edom* of the original becomes *men* (Hebr. *'ādhām*) in the translation Acts 15.17).

4. During the time when there were no written vowel signs, a tradition of pronunciation of the words of the Scriptures was handed down. It was this tradition, named the *Massora*, which Jewish scholars, the Massoretes, in the early centuries of the Christian era, sought to preserve by the introduction of a system of vowel signs which received the name of the Massoretic System of Points. Its purpose was to preserve and to transmit with accuracy the textual tradition and to remove ambiguities concerning the reading and interpretation of the consonantal text. Theirs was not the only system which was devised; there were two others, an older Palestinian and a Babylonian, which employed a supralinear system of vocalization; but the Massoretic or Tiberian system became dominant. It probably dates from the sixth and seventh centuries; the signs are not regarded as integral parts of the words but are placed above or below so that they are *outside* them. The names given to the vowel signs probably have some reference to the action of the mouth in uttering the sounds. These sounds are contained in the first syllable of most of the names.

5.	First Class *a* sound	Second Class *i* and *e* sounds	Third Class *o* and *u* sounds
Long Vowels	*qāmeṣ* ָ *â ā* calf	*ḥîreq* ִ *î* ravine	*šûreq* וּ } *û* true
	e.g. קָם *qâm*	e.g. חָסִיד *ḥāsîdh*	*qibbûṣ* ֻ }
	דָּבָר *dābhār*	*ṣērê* ֵ *ê ē* pain	e.g. קוּם or קֻם *qûm*
		e.g. חֵק *ḥêq*	
		כָּבֵד *kābhēdh*	*ḥôlem* ֹ *ô ō* bone
			e.g. דֹּר *dôr*
			חֹק *ḥōq*

N. B. See the note at the foot of the Table in § 3.1.

6. (a) *Pure Long Vowels.* The essence of a pure (or naturally) long vowel is that it cannot under any circumstances be modified. For example, the *ô* in *qôṭēl* is a pure long vowel; if, for instance, there were added to *qôṭēl* an inflectional addition which altered the position of the tone, that would not affect the pure long *ô*, which would remain unchanged. Again, the vowels *ê* and *ô*, when they represent original diphthongs *ai* (*ay*) and *au* (*aw*) respectively, are unchangeable. Thus the pure long vowels are *â ê î ô û*, all unchangeable, and indicated in transliteration by the circumflex. The pure long *â* is much the least common in Hebrew.

(b) *Tone-long Vowels.* In contrast to the pure long vowels which are long by nature and unchangeable, there are the so-called tone-long vowels which are long only because of their relation to the tone and which are subject to modification when that relation changes. The tone syllable in a word is that upon which the stress or accent falls—in Hebrew, as a general rule, it is the final syllable. Thus in *dābhār* (דָּבָר, *word*) the second *a* is tone-long because it is the vowel of the tone syllable; the long *a* of the first syllable illustrates the fact that in certain classes of nouns the vowel of the pretonic syllable may be long by position. But if an inflectional ending is added to *dābhār* so that the tone falls on it, the vowels of *dābhār* undergo modification in consequence (cf. § 5. 2b, (c)i).

7. *Rules of Writing.* (a) Motives of reverence made the Massoretes leave intact the sacred text, including the vocalic consonants; their own vocalic system was complete in itself. It thus happens that in all those cases where a textual vowel already existed, there is now a double vocalization, the textual and the Massoretic. Thus on the older system *qôl* would be קול (*voice*) and *šîrā* שירה (*song*); with the Massoretic vowels alone, these words would be written קֹל and שִׁרָ respectively. But in actual fact the vowels were added to the existing consonantal text, in which the pure long were, to a large extent, already consonantally represented. Therefore, we have the forms קוֹל and שִׁירָה in which the vowels are practically written twice.

(b) The long vowels *e i o u*, at the end of a word, are pure-long and are regularly represented by a *mater lectionis*; e.g. קמי =*qâmê* or *qâmî*, קמו =*qâmô* or *qâmû*. When any of these four vowels occurs at the end of a syllable which is not final, a distinction is usually drawn between the pure long and the tone-long vowels. The general rule is that in the case of the tone-long vowels no *mater lectionis* is used, while in the case of the pure long it is; e.g. in לֵבָב *lēbhābh* (*heart*) the *ē* is tone-long, while in שִׁירָה *šîrā* (*song*) the *î* is pure long; in בֹּקֶר *bōqer* (*morning*) the *ō* is tone-long, while in כּוֹכָב *kôkhābh* (*star*) the *ô* is pure long. It is an almost invariable usage that, as above, the tone-long vowel should not have a *mater lectionis* written; occasionally a pure long vowel does not have one written; e.g. קִיטוֹר *qîṭôr* (*thick smoke*) is also found written as קְטוֹר or even קִטֹר; and קוֹטֵל *qôṭēl* may be found as קֹטֵל.

(c) A vocalic consonant, used as a *consonant*, is not usually followed by the same consonant used as a vowel: in such a case only the vowel sign is written; e.g. מִצְוֹת *miṣwôth* (*commandments*), in which the ו must be consonantal (cf. sing. מִצְוָה *miṣwā*), is better than מִצְווֹת (in which the first ו must be consonantal and the second vocalic).

(d) There is a disinclination to use vocalic consonants in each of two contiguous syllables; therefore, the form שִׁרִים is preferred to שִׁירִים (*songs*), and קְטָלֻהוּ to קְטָלוּהוּ (*they slew him*).

(e) When the consonantal letter is present (as in חֵיק *ḥêq*, *bosom*) the syllable is said to be written fully (*scriptio plena*); when it is absent (חֵק) the syllable is said to be written defectively (*scriptio defectiva*).

(f) When such vowels are written fully, i.e. with the vowel sign and the vocalic consonant, the Massoretic point stands in its proper place under the consonant which it follows, except *ḥôlem*, which is placed over the *wāw* and *šûreq* which is placed in the bosom of the *wāw*; e.g. חִיל (not חיִל) *ḥîl* (*to writhe*); חֵיל *ḥêl* (*rampart*); יָדִי *yā<u>dh</u>î* (*my hand*); but חוֹל (not חוֹל) *ḥôl* (*sand*); סוּס *sûs* (*horse*).

(g) When the vowel preceding a vocalic consonant is not of the class homogeneous with it, the vocalic consonant has consonantal value; e.g. יָדַי *yā<u>dh</u>ay* (*my hands*); עָנָו *ʿānāw* (*humble*), הוֹי *hôy* (*ah!*), גָּלוּי *gālûy* (*revealed*), עַוְלָה *ʿawlā* (*injustice*), זִו *ziw* (*April-May*). The suffixal form (to be explained in § 16) ָיו is sounded *āw*, as סוּסָיו *sû-sāw* (*his horses*).

EXERCISE

Write these words in English letters

מה, מי, מימי, לי, לו, לין, לון, שירו, קומה, לולי, שירות, היניק, הושיעה, סוסים, הוריתי, קול, קולותינו, עוף, הובישו, הילילי, הוליכו, נא:

Write these Hebrew words, expressing the vowels by vowel letters:

qûm, qôm, šîr, šîrîm, sûs, sûsô<u>th</u>ênû, qôṣ, lî, lô, lû, mê, mêšî<u>bh</u>, mô<u>th</u>, hêlîl, ḥûl, ḥîlā, hôṣî', ṣî<u>ph</u>, mêqîṣ, ṭô<u>bh</u>ê, nîrî, hôšî<u>bh</u>û, hôlî<u>kh</u>û, lûlê, mênîqô<u>th</u>ênû.

§ 3. EXTERNAL VOWEL SIGNS
THE MASSORETIC POINTS

1. *Table of external vowel signs or Massoretic points.*

		First Class *a* sound	Second Class *i* and *e* sounds	Third Class *o* and *u* sounds
Short vowels		*páthaḥ* ַ *a* fat *e.g.* בַּד *badh*	*ḥîreq* ִ *i* pin *e.g.* מִן *min*	*qibbûṣ* ֻ *u* put *e.g.* מֻשְׁלָךְ *mušlākh*
			s^{e}ghôl ֶ *e* pen *e.g.* חֶלְקָם *ḥelqām*	*qam. ḥaṭûph* ָ *o* on *e.g.* חָדְשָׁם *ḥodhšām*
Long vowels		*qắmeṣ* ָ *â ā* calf *e.g.* קָם *qâm* דָּבָר *dābhār*	*ḥîreq* ִ *î* ravine *e.g.* חָסִד *ḥāsîdh*	*šûreq* וּ, *qibbûṣ* ֻ *û* true *e.g.* קוּם or קֻם *qûm*
			ṣērê ֵ *ê ē* pain *e.g.* חֵק *ḥêq* כָּבֵד *kābhēdh*	*ḥôlem* ֹ *ô ō* bone *e.g.* דֹר *dôr* חֹק *ḥōq*
Indistinct vowels	*simple sh^{e}wa* [1]	ְ *e.g.* דְּבַר *d^{e}bhar*	ְ *e.g.* סְפָרָם *s^{e}phārām*	ְ *e.g.* בְּקָרִם *b^{e}qārîm*
	composite sh^{e}was or *ḥatephs* ...	ֲ *e.g.* חֲכָמִם *ḥ^{a}khāmîm*	ֱ *e.g.* יֶחֱזַק *yeḥ^{e}zaq*	ֳ *e.g.* חֳדָשִׁם *ḥ^{o}dhāšîm*

N.B.—In the above illustrations I have intentionally written words involving the pure long *î* without the vocalic letter י which usually accompanies them, in order to exhibit the vowel signs by themselves. The customary spelling will be explained in § 4.

---

[1] The term *sh^{e}wa* will be used in the Grammar in this form and not as Š^{e}wa, since it has to be adopted into the English vocabulary for the purposes of the Grammar.

2. As the Table indicates, the vowel signs designate a quality of sound as well as the quantity, long or short. In the pronunciation of the vowels the two modes which are known in Europe are the ashkenazi and the sephardi; the latter, which is that of the Spanish Jews, is normally adopted in modern grammars, as it is in this one.

The fact that the sign ◌ָ is used to represent two vowels, not only of different classes (first and third) but of different quantity (long *ā* and short *o*), is notable. The reason for the usage was doubtless the approximate similarity of sound of the two vowels concerned; cf. the sound of ***a*** in man, cat, etc. as contrasted with its sound in ball, swan, etc. Nevertheless, it is true that the short vowel of the first class is ◌ַ *pat͟haḥ*, while ◌ָ *qāmeṣ ḥaṭûp͟h* is a short vowel of the third class. The position of the vowel within a Hebrew word in terms of its relation to the tone will usually make plain whether ◌ָ signifies an *ā* or an *o* in any particular case.

3. (a) *Pat͟haḥ* appears to be always short, whether it occurs in an open or a closed syllable, but it must be carefully noted that it can occur under the tone; e.g. נַעַר *náʿar*, בַּיִת *báyit͟h*, הִקְטִילַנִי *hiqṭîlánî*.

(b) *Ṣērê* is normally long; it is doubtful if it can ever be a short vowel (as, e.g., in the verbal form קִטֵּל, which has a common variant קִטַּל).

(c) *Ḥîreq* can be long or short, as the examples in the Table show.

(d) *Seg͟hôl* is short and is closely related to *pat͟haḥ*; in fact, in the other systems of vocalization mentioned above, the two were indicated by the same sign. Like *pat͟haḥ*, *seg͟hôl* can be used under the tone (cf. מֶלֶךְ *mélek͟h*), and, when it is used in conjunction with the vocalic consonant *yôd͟h*, it can indicate a pure long vowel (cf. תִּגְלֶינָה *tig͟hlênā*).

(e) *Ḥôlem* is long; it is often a modification of an original *â* or of the diphthong ***au***; e.g. קוֹטֵל *qôṭēl*, מוֹשָׁב *môšāb͟h*.

(f) *Šûreq* and *Qibbûṣ* were originally used as two signs for *u* without distinction of quantity, the signs being · and ֻ. But owing to the fact that the sign · was liable to be misinterpreted when used with any consonant, its use became confined to *wāw*, written וּ. Long *û* was usually represented in the Hebrew text by *wāw*, in which case the point was placed in its bosom, as in קוּם. When *wāw* was not in the text, *û* was represented by *qibbûṣ* so that *qibbûṣ* was used to represent short *u* and long *û*.

4. *Indistinct Vowels.* (a) The name *sh*e*wa* was given to that indistinct, hurriedly pronounced vowel which resembles the swift *e* in *the* or the second *e* in *benediction.* Its sign is ְ, and it was sounded so indistinctly that the class of vowel was not clearly enunciated, so that the same sign is used for the in- distinct vowel of each of the three classes.

(b) In the case of the four guttural letters an indistinct sh^e^wa following them acquired a certain degree of distinct pronunciation which was expressed by the Massoretes by the use of composite sh^e^was, signs compounded of simple sh^e^wa and one of the short vowel signs: ֲ, ֱ, ֳ. They are also specifically named *ḥaṭeph-paṯhaḥ*, *ḥaṭeph-s*e*ghôl* and *ḥaṭeph-qāmeṣ*; e.g. חֲמֹר *ḥ*a*môr*, *ass* (not חְמֹר), אֱמֹר *'*e*mōr*, *say* (not אְמֹר), חֳלִי *ḥ*o*lî*, *sickness* (not חְלִי).

5. The sign of simple sh^e^wa ְ is also put under every consonant without a vowel of its own, if it be sounded and not final. The sh^e^wa in this position is called *silent*, having no sound. *E.g.* in נִקְטָל *niqṭāl* (*killed*, ptc.), the ק has ְ under it, because, unlike נ and ט, it has no vowel of its own; on the other hand, ל, though, like ק, it has no vowel of its own, is written without ְ, because it is final.

6. Thus the same sign is used to indicate both an indistinct vowel and merely the end of a syllable. But it must be noted that the exigencies of pronunciation in Hebrew cannot tolerate two vocal sh^e^was in collocation; the first of the two must

become a full vowel, commonly *ḥîreq*; e.g. דְּבְרֵי >[1] דִּבְרֵי. This phenomenon is not peculiar to Hebrew. A helpful parallel may be cited from French. In the phrase *de ce que je ne te le dis pas*, there are not two but seven vocal shᵉwas or muted *e*'s in collocation. The rhythm of utterance demands that some of these vowels should be given more vocalic value and in practice the pronunciation is something like this: dis/ kᵉ/ jin/ til/ dī/ pa. That is, some of the muted *e*'s are so lightly touched in pronunciation as to be almost, if not wholly, inaudible, while others are strengthened in sound.

When two shᵉwas are found together, as in יִקְטְלוּ, the first must be a silent shᵉwa ending the syllable *yıq* and the second a vocal shᵉwa beginning the next syllable *ṭᵉlû* (or perhaps even constituting by itself the syllable *ṭᵉ*; cf. § 4. 5).

7. *Position of the Vowel Sign.* (a) The vowel sign stands under the consonant after which it is pronounced, as מַר *mar, bitter,* נָמֵר *nāmēr, a leopard*; with the exception of (i) *ḥôlem,* which stands over the left hand corner of the consonant which it follows, as חֹק *ḥōq, statute,* קָטֹן *qāṭōn, little*; (ii) *šûreq*, which is set within the *wāw*, as סוּס *sûs, horse*; and (iii) *pa<u>th</u>aḥ furtive* (cf. § 7. 4), which stands below the consonant before which it is pronounced. Only *qāmeṣ* is found as a final vowel without a final vocalic consonant; e.g. לְךָ, קָטַלְתָּ are the common forms although לְכָה, קָטַלְתָּה are occasionally found.

(b) When *ḥôlem* precedes an א, if the א is at the end of a word or syllable, the *ḥôlem* is placed on its right apex, as בֹּא *bô'* (*enter*); but if the א begins a syllable, the *ḥôlem* occupies its proper place, as בֹּאָם *bô'ām* (*their entering*). When *ḥôlem* follows א, it is placed on its left apex, as אֹב *'ô<u>bh</u>* (*ghost*).

(c) A *ḥôlem* preceding שׁ coincides with its diacritical point, as מֹשֶׁה *môše, Moses,* not מֹשֶׁה. There is no ambiguity; since no vowel sign following the מ is visible, it must be concluded

[1] The sign > is used in the Grammar to indicate 'becoming' or 'developing into' and < to indicate 'derived from' (e.g. Eng. has not > hasn't, hasn't < has not).

that its vowel is a *ḥôlem* coinciding with the diacritical point of the שׂ. Similarly a *ḥôlem* following שׁ coincides with its diacritical point, as שֹׂנֵא, *śônē’*, *hating*. The sign שׁ will be *šo* at the beginning of a syllable and *oś* elsewhere; e.g. שֹׁמֵר, *šô-mēr, keeper*, and יִרְפֹּשׂ, *yir-pōś, he treads*. In the first case the initial consonant could not be שׂ, because in that case the other point above the consonant would have no significance; in the second the final consonant could not be שׁ, for that would leave the preceding פ without a vowel.

EXERCISE

Transliterate the following Hebrew words into English, and English into Hebrew with Mass. vowels

יָד, גֵּר, חֵן, חֹק, גַּם, עַל, שׁוּם, אִם, אַף, עֲבֹד, בְּךָ, דֹּב, צַר,
צָרָה, עִיר, אֱכֹל, חֲזַק, אֲשֶׁר, רְפֹשׂ, שֹׁפֵט, קֻם, רָץ, רוּץ, הֲגַם,
וָו, דְּבַר, אֱמֶת:

gam, bôr, bôš, šûbh, šîr, šôr, šām, ḥōq, ’im, ‘im, kōl, qôl, ‘am, har, rōbh, rûṣ, h^{a}rōgh, ṣēl, ḥêq māšāl, m^{e}šal, qôṭēl, šālôm, yārûṣ, qômām, po‘^{o}lô, ’^{e}sōph, heḥ^{e}zîq.

§ 4. PRINCIPLES OF THE SYLLABLE. READING

1. (a) Hebrew is a strongly accented speech, and the Accent or Tone to a great extent rules the various vowel changes in the language. It is important to know where the accent falls, as the same word, differently accented, may have two widely different meanings; *e.g.* נָ֫חָה *náḥā, she rested,* but נָחָה *nāḥá, he led*; so (בָּנוּ) *bānû', they built,* but *bánû, in us. Usually, however, the accent falls on the last syllable of the word, e.g.* יָשָׁר *yāšár, upright,* זָקֵן *zāqḗn, old*; in certain cases it may fall on the penult, *e.g.* קֶ֫רֶן *qéren, horn*; אֹ֫זֶן *’ózen, ear* (§ 25).

(b) If the accent be on the penult, either the accented

penult or the unaccented final must be open; e.g. סֵ֫פֶר *sēp̱her, book*; קָטַ֫לְתָּ *qāṭáltā, thou hast killed.*

2. *Kinds of Syllable.* Every syllable in Hebrew must begin with a consonant; such a word as *ore,* if transliterated, would have to begin with a prosthetic א. But no syllable can begin with more than one consonant; if words like *dream* and *impress* were to be transliterated, a vocal shᵉwa would have to be intruded between the *d* and the *r* of the first (i.e. *dᵉream*) and the *p* and the *r* of the second (i.e. *impᵉress*).

A syllable ending in a vowel is termed *open,* as קָ *qā*; one ending in a consonant is termed *shut,* as קַל *qal.*

3. *End of the Syllable.* A syllable may end in a vowel or a consonant. None but a final syllable can end in more than one consonant, and a final in not more than two; e.g. יַשְׁקְ *yašq* (*he waters*); it cannot end in a doubled consonant (cf. §§ 39, 40).

Silent shᵉwa is placed under the consonant which ends the syllable, provided that it is sounded and not the last letter of a word; e.g. נִקְטָל *niq-ṭāl* (*killed*). A consonant which is not sounded does not take shᵉwa; e.g. רֵאשִׁית *rêšîṯh* (*beginning*), not רֵאְשִׁית, the א being quiescent; and a single consonant at the end of a word does not take it, except *kap̄h,* which takes it in its bosom, probably to distinguish final *kap̄h* ךְ from final *nûn* ן (thus לָךְ *lāḵh, to thee,* not לָךְ). Words ending in two consonants are rare. But two sounded consonants at the end of a word both take shᵉwa; e.g. קֹשְׁטְ *qōšṭ,* (*truth*). If, however, the first is quiescent and not sounded, and, in consequence, drops the shᵉwa, the second drops it also; לִקְרַאת *liq-raṯh* (cf. § 7. 6). If it is the second which is quiescent, the first retains the shᵉwa; e.g. גַּיְא *gay* (*valley*).

4. (a) *Vowel of the Syllable.* The vowel of an open syllable is commonly long; e.g. חָ in חָכָם *ḥāḵhām* (*wise*), לֵ in לֵבָב *lēḇhāḇh* (*heart*), כּוֹ in כּוֹכָב *kôḵhāḇh* (*star*). The vowel of a

shut syllable is commonly short; e.g. מִדְ in מִדְבָּר *midhbār* (*desert*), and יַלְ in יַלְדָּה *yaldā* (*girl*).

But the vowel of an open syllable may be short if it has the accent, e.g. מַ in שָׁמַ֫יִם *šāmáyim* (*heaven*) or בַּ in בַּ֫יִת *báyi<u>th</u>* (*house*); the vowel of a shut syllable may be long if it has the accent, e.g. כָם in חָכָם *ḥā<u>kh</u>ām* (*wise*) or טָל in נִקְטָל *niqṭál* (*killed*), in which the vowel of the first syllable נִק, which also is shut, is short because that syllable is not accented.

(b) the vowels *î* and *û* cannot stand in a shut syllable before two consonants, even with the accent (cf. § 30. 5a).

5. *Half-open Syllable.* Every syllable must contain a vowel. The question, therefore, arises: 'Does a consonant followed by vocal shᵉwa constitute an open syllable?' The answer must be No. E.g. יִקְטְלוּ must be divided syllabically into *yiq-ṭᵉlû* and בִּקְטֹל into *bi-qᵉṭōl* or *biqᵉ-ṭōl*. A syllable like *biqᵉ*, which appears in the last form, has sometimes been described as a half-open syllable.

(a) Such massoretic pointing as מַלְכֵי and בִּנְפֹל, in which the כ in the first and the פ in the second have no *daghesh lene*, shows that the shᵉwa in each case must be treated as vocal (cf. §§ 5. 2d; 6. 2a, b).

(b) Such a shᵉwa is usually the reduced form of an originally full vowel, so that, by treating it as vocal, we retain an evidential trace of the original full vowel.

But it must be noted that there are certain cases in which the shᵉwa has lost vocalic value and become silent, probably because of the rapid pronunciation of a form commonly in use; e.g. קְטֹל *qᵉṭōl*, but לִקְטֹל *liq-ṭōl* (§ 18. 2a. iii); with this may be compared the pronunciation of *family* in English as *fam-ly*, etc.

Examples of the Syllable:

קָטַ֫ל *qā-ṭál*, קָטַ֫לְתִּי *qā-ṭál-tî*, קְטַלְתֶּ֫ם *qᵉṭal-tém*, כְּרֻבִ֫ים *kᵉrû-*

bhî'm, יִשְׁקְלוּ *yiš-qᵉlû'*, הַבְדִּיל *habh-dî'l*, מַמְלֶכֶת *mam-lé-kheth*, עֲבָדִים *ʿᵃbhā-dhî'm*, אֱלֹהֶיךָ *ʾᵉlô-hê'-khā*, יְלִידֵי *yᵉlî-dhê'*, יַשְׁקְ *yašq*, יֵאָמֵר *yē-ʾā-mḗr*, חֲלָיֵינוּ *ḥᵒlā-yê'-nû* (or חֲלָיֵנוּ (cf § 2. 7c)).

EXERCISE

Write the following words in English,
dividing them into syllables

אֱלֹהִים, חֳלִי, חֲמוֹר, אֲרִי, מֶרְחָק, הֲלָהֶן, נִשְׁקְלוּ, מְצַפְצְפִים, קַמְנוּ, קְצִיר, לָאֲנָשִׁים, הָקְטְלָה, הִקְטִיל, יַפְתְּ:

Write these Hebrew words

qôṭēl, qâm, ʾekhtōbh, māqôm, wlô, mizmôr, qiṭlû, šāmáyim, qû'mû, lmînēhû, ûlyāmîm, yéreq, lilqōṭ, mamlākhā, lšālôm, šmônîm, šnê, mqômî, yôršîm, nilḥam, yiśrāʾēl, šmô, náʿar, ḥᵃmôrîm, leʾᵉsōph, ʿāmálnû.

Note.—In the above English words simple shᵉwa, silent or vocal, is not expressed: the exercise is set partly for practice in placing it. The accent, unless marked, is on the last syllable, both in the Hebrew words and English transliterations.

§ 5. THE VOWEL SYSTEM AND THE TONE

1. It has already been stated that the pure long vowels *â, ê, î, ô, û*, are unchangeable (§ 2. 6) and in consequence are unaffected by their relation to the tone in a word. A short vowel in a closed syllable may become long under the tone (§ 4. 4a) but it cannot be reduced to vocal shᵉwa because a closed syllable must retain a full vowel. This section is concerned with tone-long vowels. These, not being long by nature, but in terms of their relation to the tone, may undergo change when that relation is changed.

2. (a) There are only three tone-long vowels, ָ ֵ ֹ, *ā, ē, ō*, one for each class; a short *ḥireq* (ִ), when tone-lengthened, becomes not long *ḥîreq* but *ṣērê* ֵ, and a *qibbûṣ* (ֻ), when tone-lengthened, becomes not long *qibbûṣ* but *ḥôlem* (ֹ).

(b) Tone-long vowels are found in the open syllable immediately before the tone and in the shut syllable, chiefly the final, under the tone. In יָשָׁר *yāšār, upright,* e.g., the last syllable שָׁר is closed and has a long vowel under the tone; the first syllable יָ is open and has a long vowel before the tone (§ 2. 6b); so also, e.g., זָקֵן *old,* and לֵבָב *heart,* and קָטֹן *small.* When the syllable before the tone is closed, as, e.g., in מַזְלֵג *mazlēgh. fork,* its vowel is short and unchangeably so.

(c) i. When the vowel of the final syllable is long under the tone and that of the penultimate is long in an open pretonic syllable, the rhythm of pronunciation demands that the vowel of the antepenultimate, if it is open, should be as hurriedly pronounced as possible, i.e. should be reduced to vocal shᵉwa in the case of changeable vowels. Thus in יְשָׁרִים *yᵉšārî'm* (plur. of יָשָׁר) the final syllable רִים has a long vowel, the open penultimate שָׁ has a pretonic long vowel (the *qāmeṣ* which follows שׁ in the sing. יָשָׁר) but the vowel following the י, which was a pretonic *qāmeṣ* in the sing. יָשָׁר, is in the plural removed two places from the tone in the antepenultimate syllable and is reduced to vocal shᵉwa. Note that the plural of כּוֹכָב *kôkhābh, star,* is כּוֹכָבִים *kôkhābhîm,* the long *ô* in the antepenultimate syllable of the plural remaining unchanged because it is pure long; likewise the vowel of the antepenultimate syllable remains unchanged when it is in a closed syllable; e.g. מִשְׁפָּט *miš-pāṭ, judgment,* plur. מִשְׁפָּטִים *mišpāṭîm.*

ii. The indistinct vowel arising from the reduction of a vowel of any class because of its distance from the tone is simple shᵉwa vocal under ordinary consonants; thus יְשָׁרִים from יָשָׁר, לְבָבִי, *my heart* from לֵבָב, רְמָחִים *spears* from רֹמַח [1].

---

[1] This word, accented on the penultimate, in seeming contravention of the rule, will be explained in § 25, and should be accepted without question here and now.

Under gutturals (§ 3. 4b) it is one of the *ḥaṭephs*, generally *ḥaṭeph pathaḥ* for vowels of the first and second classes (§ 3. 1; not *ḥaṭeph sᵉghôl* for the second class) and *ḥaṭeph qāmeṣ*[1] for vowels of the third class; thus חֲכָמִים from חָכָם *wise*, חֲלָבִים (not חֱלָבִים) from חֵלֶב[2] *fat*, חֳדָשִׁים from חֹדֶשׁ[2] *new moon, month*.

(d) i. Two vocal shᵉwas cannot stand together (§ 3. 6). When, therefore, through processes of inflection (e.g. יְשָׁרִים plur. absol., יְשְׁרֵי plur. constr.; § 14. 3b) or composition (as when, e.g., the prepositions בּ *in*, כּ *as*, ל *to* precede a word beginning with shᵉwa, לְמְשִׁיחוֹ (§ 12. 1) *to his anointed* from the absolute form מָשִׁיחַ), this would happen, the first becomes a full, short vowel, commonly *ḥîreq*. Thus יְשְׁרֵי >[3] יִשְׁרֵי *yišᵉrê*; and לְמְשִׁיחוֹ > לִמְשִׁיחוֹ *limᵉšîḥô*.

ii. If the first of the shᵉwas be a composite (as will happen when the first consonant is a guttural; cf. § 3. 4b), the short vowel arising is not *i*, but is generally the full, short vowel corresponding to the composite shᵉwa. Thus חֲכְמֵי (from חָכָם *wise*) becomes not חִכְמֵי but חַכְמֵי *ḥakhᵉmê*. That is, the class of the original vowel is retained; and this occasionally, but rarely, happens with other letters than gutturals; e.g. כְּנְפֵי (from כָּנָף *wing*) becomes not כִּנְפֵי but כַּנְפֵי *kanᵉphê*.

(e) In יִשְׁרֵי and חַכְמֵי the shᵉwa is vocal (cf. § 4. 5). To consider the first syllable of יִשְׁרֵי as closed and the shᵉwa as silent would obliterate the fact that originally a full vowel (*ā*) stood between *š* and *r* (cf. plur. absol. יְשָׁרִים and sing. יָשָׁר). But it is one of the fundamental principles of Hebrew to conserve, in whatever way possible, the ultimate elements of words. The only way to conserve evidence of the original *qāmeṣ* following the שׁ is to treat the shᵉwa as vocal in יִשְׁרֵי

---

[1] This *ḥaṭeph* would be more correctly named *ḥaṭeph qāmeṣ ḥaṭûph*.

[2] See page 26 note 1.

[3] See note on p. 21.

so that it should be transliterated as *yiš^{e}rê*, not as *yiš-rê*. This principle covers examples such as these: חַכְמֵי *ḥakh^{e}mê* derived from the absol. plur. חֲכָמִים; קִטְלוּ *qiṭ^{e}lû* (2 m. plur. Imper.) from the sing. קְטֹל (*kill*); similarly בְּרָכָה *b^{e}rākhā* (*blessing*) with a suffix becomes בְּרָכָתִי > בִּרְכָתִי i.e. *bir^{e}khāthî* (*my blessing*).

(f) The principles stated in sub-paragraphs (b) and (c) are carried out both in nouns and verbs. There are, however, two remarkable exceptions:

First, the law in (b) regarding the tone-long vowel in the final accented shut syllable has not been carried out fully in the case of the vowel *a*. *Verbs* always write *á* for *ā́* (except in pause; cf. § 11, footnote to the Heb.-Eng. Exercise). Thus קָטַ֫ל he killed, not קָטָל—that is, the final syllable, though accented, has the short vowel, if it be *a*. This *á*, when it occurs in an open syllable in a form of קָטַל with a suffix, has the same scheme of vocalic modification as if it were *ā* (cf. § 27. 3a).

Second, in opposition to the law in (c), in the case of *verbs*, the sh^{e}wa stands not in the second place from the tone but immediately before it. Thus, while the noun (or adjective) inflects יָשָׁר, יְשָׁרָה (fem.) *y^{e}šārā* (*upright*), the verb inflects יָשַׁר, יָשְׁרָה *yāš^{e}rā* (*he, she, was upright*), the sh^{e}wa being sounded to represent the original vowel *a*. So adj. חָכָם (*wise*), חֲכָמָה; vb. חָכַם (*he was wise*), חָכְמָה. (But see § 9, Note 2 to the Exercise.)

EXERCISE

Correct the following words

לֵבָבִי, מִדְבַּרִים, זַקְנִים, חֹדָשִׁים, כּוֹכַבִים, קָטַלוֹ, קָטַלְתֶּם,
קָטָ֫לְנוּ, קְטַ֫לְנוּ, סֵפָרִים, עֵנַבִים, צִדְקַ֫תֵנוּ, דָּבָ֫רֶיךָ, גַּדוֹלִים,
הָקִימוֹתֶם, שְׁמַ֫יִם, חְכַמָה, אָלָפִים, תַּשׁוּב, יַקִים:

Note.—The accent falls on the last syllable, unless otherwise indicated.

§ 6. DAGHESH—THE LETTERS B^{E}GHADHK^{E}PHATH—MAPPIQ

1. The word *Daghesh* [1] is from a root which possibly expressed the idea of *hardness*. The sign of *Daghesh* is a point in the bosom of a letter, and this point was used (i) with the ב ג ד כ פ ת letters to denote their hard or explosive use (בּ, *b*, &c.); and (ii) with consonants generally (but not universally) to denote a strengthening of them which is best indicated by duplication. The former is called *Daghesh lene*, the latter *Daghesh forte*.

2. *Daghesh lene*. (a) The letters בגדכפת have two pronunciations (cf. § 1. 2a); used with *Daghesh lene* they are hard or explosive (i.e. *b*, *g*, *d*, *k*, *p*, *t*); without that sign they are aspirate or fricative <u>*bh*</u>, <u>*gh*</u>, <u>*dh*</u>, <u>*kh*</u>, <u>*ph*</u>, <u>*th*</u>).

When these letters stand at the beginning of a syllable following upon a closed syllable, they take *Daghesh lene*; but when they immediately follow a vowel sound, they do not take it. Thus זָכַר *zā-<u>kh</u>ár, he remembered*, יִזְכֹּר *yiz-kōr, he remembers*. The first כ follows a vowel (*ā*) and, therefore, has no *daghesh*; the second כּ follows upon a closed syllable, and, therefore, has a *daghesh*. Also these letters take *daghesh* when they stand at the beginning of a sentence or clause, and at the beginning of a word unless the word is closely associated with the preceding one and it ends in a vowel. That is to say, Hebrew is not pointed mechanically, but account is taken of the relation of words to one another in a sentence. Where two words are closely associated so that they are read together, they are treated as one unit, so that, if the first ends in a vowel, the first letter of the second, if it is one of the *B^{e}<u>gh</u>a<u>dh</u>k^{e}<u>ph</u>a<u>th</u>* letters, does not take a *daghesh*. Contrast, e.g., וַיְהִי־כֵן *and it was so*, Gen. 1. 7 (where the connection is very intimate and further indicated in the Hebrew by the hyphen; cf. Note 1 to the Exercise in § 9) with וַיְהִי כִּי *and it*

---

[1] For the form of the term Daghesh (not Da<u>gh</u>eš) cf. the note on sh^{e}wa in § 3. 1.

came to pass when etc., Gen. 6. 1 (where the connection is broken and a new start is made with כִּי).

(b) For this purpose vocal shᵉwa, simple or composite, has the same effect as the full vowels; e.g. זְכֹר *zᵉkhōr, remember,* חֲכַם *ḥᵃkham, wise* (cf. § 4. 5). This being so, it is at once clear whether a shᵉwa which appears before a *bᵉghadhkᵉphath* letter in a written form is vocal or silent; e.g. in בִּלְבָבוֹ *in his heart,* the shᵉwa under the ל must be vocal because the ב immediately following has no *daghesh lene*; the pronunciation is, therefore, *bilᵉbhābhô.*

3. *Daghesh forte.* (a) Hebrew does not write a double consonant. To indicate that a consonant is doubled, or strengthened, it inserts in it a point, as קַלּוּ *qal-lû* (*they were swift*). When so used the point is called *Daghesh forte. Daghesh forte* can be inserted in the letters י and ו when they are used consonantally; thus צִיָּה *ṣiyyā* (*dryness*), חִיָּה *ḥiyyā* (*he preserved alive*), צִיּוֹן *ṣiyyôn* (*Zion*), צִוָּה *ṣiwwā* (*he commanded*), צַוּוּ *ṣawwû* (*command,* imper.), קַוָּם *qawwām* (*their line?*). There is no danger of this duplicated *wāw* being confused with *wāw* carrying the vowel *šûreq*, because, in the nature of the case, a duplicated letter must be preceded by a vowel, and, conversely, if there be a vowel before the וּ, then the וּ must=*ww* and not *û*. If, e.g., in קַוָּם we gave וּ the value of *û*, there would be no consonants with which to read the vowels ַ and ָ. The word is therefore=קַוְוָם, i.e. *qawwām.*

The duplicated consonant should be distinctly and firmly enunciated.

(b) When, by processes of inflection, a form is developed in which the same consonant occurs at the end of a syllable and at the beginning of the one immediately following, the practice is to write the consonant once with *daghesh forte*; thus נָתַנְנוּ *nāthannû, we gave,* becomes נָתַנּוּ. But if vocal shᵉwa follows the first occurrence, *daghesh forte* cannot be used; thus קִלְלַת *qilᵉlath* must not be written קִלַּת *qillath,* because the shᵉwa is sounded, representing as it does an original *ā* (קְלָלָה, *q·lālā, curse,* noun).

(c) A word cannot end in a doubled letter (cf. § 4. 3). Therefore, whereas the word for *peoples* is עַמִּים, the sing. is עַם, not עַםּ.

(d) It is important to note that the gutturals (i.e. א ה ח ע) cannot be doubled, and therefore cannot take *daghesh forte.* Thus we cannot write בִּעֵּר (*he burned, consumed*), or שִׁחֵּת (*he destroyed*). See § 7. 7.

4. The *B·ghadhk·phath* letters, which alone can take *daghesh lene,* can also take *daghesh forte*; thus שִׁבֵּר *šibbēr* (*he broke in pieces*). In these cases it is the hard sound of the consonant that is doubled: i.e. we say *šibber,* not *šivver*; so סַפֵּר *sappēr* (*relate,* imper.), not *saffēr.*

Daghesh forte and *daghesh lene* need never be confused, because *daghesh forte,* as we have seen, is always preceded by a vowel; *daghesh lene,* never. Thus in מִדְבָּר *midh-bār, wilderness,* the daghesh in the ב is necessarily *d. lene*; it cannot be *d. forte,* because the latter requires a full vowel before it; even if the sh·wa could be vocal, that would not be enough, because it is not a full vowel. On the other hand, the daghesh in the *beth* of the word מְדַבֵּר *m·dhabbēr, speaking* (part.) is necessarily *d. forte,* because it is preceded by a vowel.

5. *Omission of Daghesh forte.* In the case of the consonants ו, י, ל, מ, נ, ק, when followed by vocal sh·wa, the *d. forte* is very frequently omitted in writing where usage would lead us to expect it; e.g. הַיְאֹר (not הַיְּאֹר), *the Nile*; עִוְרִים (not עִוְּרִים; sing. עִוֵּר), *blind*; הַלְלוּ (not הַלְּלוּ; sing. הַלֵּל), *praise ye*; הִנְנִי (not הִנְּנִי; absolute form הִנֵּה), *behold me*; מְבַקְשִׁים (not מְבַקְּשִׁים; sing. מְבַקֵּשׁ) *seeking*; יִקְחוּ (not יִקְּחוּ; sing. יִקַּח), *they will take.* This also applies to sibilants, especially when they are followed by a guttural; e.g. כִּסְאוֹ (not כִּסְּאוֹ) *his throne*; so יִשְׂאוּ (not יִשְּׂאוּ), *they will lift up.* Since, in most of these examples, the sh·wa represents an originally full vowel, it is to be regarded as vocal.

6. *Insertion of Daghesh forte. D. forte* is sometimes inserted in a consonant to secure the more audible enunciation of the shᵉwa under it; e.g. עִנְּבֵי *ʿin-nᵉbhê* for עִנְבֵי *ʿinᵉ-bhê* (*the grapes of . . .*). This is known as *D. forte dirimens*. In certain cases two words, of which the first ends in ָ, ָה or ֶה, and the second is monosyllabic or almost so (like שְׁמוֹ), may be closely connected by the insertion of a *D. forte* at the beginning of the second word; e.g. עָשִׂיתָ זֹּאת *thou hast done this*. This always happens when זֶה (*this*) or מָה (*what*) is joined by *maqqēph* to the following word; e.g. זֶה־שְּׁמוֹ *this is his name*, מַה־לְּךָ *what to thee? what aileth thee?* This is known as *D. forte conjunctivum*.

7. The short unaccented vowel of the *third* class in syllables ending with a doubled letter is *u*. E.g. הָקְטַל, but הֻגַּד (not הָגַּד) *it was declared*. (Rarely—and chiefly under gutturals—it may appear as *o*; e.g. עָזִּי, also עֻזִּי *my strength*.)

8. *Mappîq* (extender).—A point is inserted in the letter *Hē*, when final, to indicate that it is to be pronounced, and is not a mere sign of a vowel. When so used the point is called *Mappîq*, as אַרְצָהּ *arṣā́h* (*h* sounded), *her land*, whereas אַ֫רְצָה = *ā́rṣā*, *towards* (*the*) *land* (cf. § 14. 5).

EXERCISE

Daghesh lene and *forte*

Write these Hebrew words

1. gam, kōl, dām, bēn, ʾēt, môt, pat, kap, keleb, tiktōb, kātabtā, bkû, lbad, dābār, mišpāṭ, midbār, btôk, malkî, yabdēl, kôkābîm, kbadtem, tikbdî, kaspkā, ḥelqkā, lārédet, yirb, yēbk, gdôlîm.

2. mbaqqšîm, ḥallôn, hammáyim, wayyinnāgpû, limmadt, dibbēr, mdubbār, sappdû, mispēd, bkaspkem, šabbāt, mibbnê, ṣippôr, ykattēb, bqiṣrkem, baddām, bôdēd, yittnû, lbaddô.

Note.—In this exercise the *Bᵉghadhkᵉphath* are expressed by ordinary hard letters, and *shᵉwa* is not expressed, as the exercise is set for practice on the syllable.

§ 7. THE GUTTURALS AND REŠ

1. The letters א ה ח ע are called Gutturals. ח and ע are much more strongly sounded than א and ה (cf. § 1. 2f). The gutturals have the following peculiarities:

(a) They take composite shᵉwa in place of simple shᵉwa vocal (cf. § 3. 4b); e.g. פְּרִי *pᵉrî, fruit,* but אֲרִי *ʾᵃrî, lion;* קְבֹר *qᵉbhōr, to bury,* but עֲבֹר *ʿᵃbhōr, to cross.*

(b) By far the most common *ḥaṭeph* is ֲ. Initial ח ה ע commonly take ֲ, but initial א ֱ: e.g. (קְטֹל) עֲמֹד *stand,* אֱמֹר *say;* but when further from the tone א may take ֲ; אֶל (also אֱלֵי) *to, towards,* but אֲלֵיהֶם (not אֱלֵיהֶם).

(c) Since two vocal shᵉwas cannot stand together (§ 3. 6), a simple shᵉwa vocal before a *ḥaṭeph* becomes the full, short vowel corresponding to the *ḥaṭeph*; e.g. בְּקְטֹל *bᵉqᵉṭōl* becomes בִּקְטֹל *biqᵉṭōl,* but לְעֲבֹר *lᵉʿᵃbhōr* becomes לַעֲבֹר *laʿᵃbhōr, to cross.*

2. The short *i*, falling before gutturals not final, is usually depressed to *e*; thus יִכְבַּד *he is heavy,* but יֶחְדַּל *he ceases* (not יִחְדַּל). This depression of *i* to *e* may also take place *after* a guttural; thus סִפְרִי *my book,* but עֶזְרִי (not עִזְרִי) *my help.*

3. (a) The gutturals tend to have associated with them the *a* vowels; e.g. פֹּעַל (type בֹּקֶר) *work;* נַעַר (type מֶלֶךְ) *young man;* and עֲמֹד *to stand,* שָׁחֲטָה *she slaughtered,* מֵאֲנָה *she refused,* and כֹּהֲנִים *priests,* in each of which the ֲ is in place of the simple shᵉwa vocal of a similar form without a guttural.

(b) It should be noted that ר, which has affinities with the gutturals, has frequently, but not invariably, the vowel *a* before it; e.g. וַיָּסֹר *wayyāsor* (*and he turned aside*) and וַיָּסֶר *wayyāser* (*and he removed*) both become וַיָּסַר *wayyāsar;* מִהַר (type קִטֵּל) *he hastened.* But יְמַהֵר *he will hasten;* and סֵפֶר *book,* בֹּקֶר *morning,* &c. (cf. § 25).

4. A final guttural, except quiescent א, must be preceded by *pathaḥ* or *qāmeṣ*. Therefore:

(a) A short vowel, other than *pat͟hah̩*, before such a guttural becomes *pat͟hah̩*; e.g. מֶלֶךְ *king*, but מֶלַח *salt* (not מֶלֶח).

(b) A tone-long vowel often becomes *pat͟hah̩*; e.g. יִשְׁמֹר *he will watch*, but יִשְׁלַח *he will send*, and יְבַקֵּשׁ *he will seek* but יְשַׁלַּח *he will let go*.

(c) Between a pure-long vowel, other than *qāmeṣ*, and a final guttural there steals in, in utterance, the sound of a short *a*; this vowel is represented in writing by the so-called *pat͟hah̩ furtive*; e.g. הִשְׁלִיךְ *he threw*, but הִשְׁלִיחַ (*hišlîaḥ*) *he sent*, גָּבֹהַּ (*gābhôah*) *high* (ה with *mappîq* being consonantal, § 6. 8). This *pat͟hah̩* furtive, as the two last illustrations make plain, is written *under* the final guttural but pronounced *before* it; it disappears when the guttural, with which it is associated, ceases to be final; e.g. רוּחַ *rûaḥ* (not *rûḥa*) *spirit*, but רוּחִי *rû-ḥî*, *my spirit*; הִשְׁלִיחַ *he sent*, but fem. הִשְׁלִיחָה.

Pat͟hah̩ furtive is never written to a final א, which is quiescent (cf. 6 below); thus נָבִיא *nābhî*, *prophet*, not נָבִיאַ.

5. (a) When a guttural is not final, but falls at the end of a syllable, it sometimes takes a helping vowel; e.g. רַגְלִי *ragh-lî*, *my foot*, but נַעֲרִי *naʿᵃrî*, *my lad* (not נַעְרִי *naʿrî*), *and* פָּעֳלִי *poʿᵒlî*, *my work* (not פָּעְלִי *poʿ-lî*), the helping vowel in each case being the *ḥaṭeph* corresponding to the preceding short vowel. Similarly, in verbal forms, helping vowels may be found: e.g. הִאְרִיךְ (*he prolonged*) >[1] הֶאְרִיךְ *heʾrîkh* (cf. 2 above) > הֶאֱרִיךְ *heʾᵉrîkh*; יַעְמִיד *yaʿ-mîdh* (*he sets*) > יַעֲמִיד *yaʿᵃmîdh*; הָעְמַד *hoʿ-madh* (*he was set*) > הָעֳמַד *hoʿᵒmadh*. Either the short vowel before the guttural (as *a* in the original בַּעְלִי) or the composite shᵉwa under the guttural (as ᵃ in עֲבֹר; cf. 1b above) is determined, and then the combinations ַ ֲ, ֶ ֱ, ָ ֳ follow as a matter of course.

---

[1] See note at foot of p. 21.

(b) But in some cases ע and, more so, ח do not require such a helping vowel (cf. Intro. para. above); e.g. פַּחְדּוֹ *paḥ-dô, his fear* (not פַּחֲדוֹ *paḥᵃdhô*); רָחְבָּהּ *roḥ-bāh, its breadth* (not רָחֳבָהּ *roḥᵒbhāh*); יַעְצֹר *ya'-ṣōr, he restrains* (not יַעֲצֹר *ya'ᵃṣōr*); נֶעְלָם *ne'-lām, concealed* (not נֶעֱלָם *ne'ᵉlām*); יֶחְסַר *yeḥ-sar, he will suffer need* (not יֶחֱסַר *yeḥᵉsar*).

6. ה and, even more, א require some separate treatment.

(a) These letters, occurring at the beginning of a syllable, are consonantal; e.g. אָמַר *'āmar, he said,* הָלַךְ *hālakh, he went,* מֵאֵן *mē-'ēn, he refused,* and טָהוֹר *ṭā-hôr, clean.*

(b) Occurring at the end of a syllable their use is as follows:

i. ה at the end of a syllable not final remains consonantal; e.g. נֶהְפַּךְ *neh-pakh* (type נִקְטַל; cf. 2 above), *he turned himself*; there are very few examples of consonantal ה at the end of a final syllable; e.g. גָּבֹהַּ *gābhôah, high,* שְׁלָחָהּ *šᵉlāḥāh, he sent her* (cf. § 6. 8). In forms like פָּרָה, שָׁלְחָה, &c., the ה is vocalic (§ 2. 2a, b).

ii. א at the end of a syllable not final is rarely consonantal; e.g. נֶאְדָּר *ne'-dār, glorious,* where its consonantal value is indicated in writing by the silent shᵉwa written to it and by the daghesh lene in the *daleth*; likewise יֶאְמַץ (type יִכְבַּד) has consonantal א (cf. הֶאֱרִיךְ in 5a above). But usually in such a case, and always at the end of a final syllable, א is quiescent; e.g. יֹאמַר *yō-mar,* רֵאשִׁית *rē-šîth*. When א thus becomes quiescent, the syllable in which it stands is open and its original vowel is usually lengthened; e.g. מָצָא (type קָטַל) *he found.* Cf. also the letter *yôdh* in יוֹם *yôm day* and in בִּימֵי (< בִּיְמֵי < בְּיְמֵי) bîmê *in the days of.*

7. The gutturals cannot be doubled (§ 6. 3d); ר shares this characteristic with the gutturals. Hence in forms of the types בִּקֵּשׁ, בַּקֵּשׁ, גַּנָּב, &c. (§ 6. 3d), if the middle letter is a guttural, it cannot take daghesh forte and the effect of that upon the preceding vowel has to be noted:

(a) Commonly the vowel is now regarded as falling in an

open syllable and receives compensatory lengthening, becoming the corresponding tone-long vowel (§§ 4. 4a; 5. 2a); e.g. בִּקֵּשׁ *biq-qēš, he sought,* but שֵׁרֵשׁ *šē-rēš, he uprooted,* מֵאֵן *mē-ʾēn, he refused;* קֻטַּל *quṭ-ṭal,* but בֹּרַךְ *bō-rakh, he was blessed, ō* being the tone-long form of the short *u;* הַדֶּרֶךְ *had-dérekh, the way,* but הָעֶבֶד *hā-ʿébhedh, the servant.* Such a vowel, lengthened by compensation, remains unchangeable, since it is the lengthened form of a vowel which, in forms in which the middle letter is neither a guttural nor a *rêš,* is in a shut syllable and, for that reason, unchangeable.

(b) This compensatory lengthening of the vowel takes place practically always with א and ר, and commonly with ע; e.g. מֵאֵן (type קִטֵּל) *he refused,* הָרָעָה (type הַפָּרָה) *the evil,* הָעָם (type הַפָּר) *the people.* Usually with ה, and very frequently with ח, the preceding vowel remains short; the consonant is thus considered to be virtually doubled, so that the presence and effect of the daghesh forte is implied and it is known as *daghesh forte implicitum;* e.g. מַהֵר (type קַטֵּל) *hasten,* הַחֶרֶב (type הַמֶּלֶךְ) *the sword,* הַחֹדֶשׁ (type הַבֹּקֶר) *the month.*

EXERCISE

Correct the following words

הִשְׁמִיע, פֶּשֶׁע, עְבֹד, לְאֲרִי, שָׁמֹע, אְמֹר, יִשְׁחְטוּ, שַׁרִים, נִאְמַר,
חְזַק, שָׁלוּח, יִאְהַב, יַעְמֹד, טַעְמוּ, בְּחֲמֹר, גָּלַה, יְהָפֵךְ, יִמְצַא,
יַעֲמְדוּ, מָצַאְתָּ, גָּבוֹהַ, יֹאכַל, הִאְרִיךְ, רוּחַו, נָקִיאַ:

Write the following in Hebrew

ʿ^{a}mōdh, yišḥ^{a}ṭû, beʾ^{e}meth, lāʿebhedh, neʿ^{e}madh, šērēš, šôlēaḥ, yēʿābhēr, yeḥdal, baʿ^{a}lî, paḥdô, mēʾ^{a}nā, nāqî, ʿezrî, poʿ^{o}lî, šākhûaḥ, š^{e}khûḥîm, kôh^{a}nîm.

§ 8. THE ARTICLE AND THE ADJECTIVE

Hebrew has no *indefinite* article; e.g. יוֹם *yôm, a day,* אִישׁ *'îš, a man.*

1. The definite article is not a separate word but an inseparable, prefixed particle which shows no difference of form for number or gender. Its form before ordinary consonants is ·הַ, i.e. *ha* with the following consonant bearing dagh. forte. It was originally a demonstrative pronoun, and something of this force attaches to it in one or two phrases; e.g. הַיּוֹם *the day,* i.e. *today,* and הַלַּיְלָה *the night,* i.e. *tonight.*

2. The primary form of the article may have been *hā* (as in Arab. *hāḏhā, this,* and Syr. *hāḏhā, hālein. this, these*) which appears in Hebrew as הַ with the following consonant doubled; or it may have been *hal* (cf. Arab. *al, the*) or *han.* In the latter case, as happens with prefixed particles in other languages, the *l* or *n* is assimilated to the following consonant; e.g. הַקּוֹל *haq-qôl, the voice*; הַשֶּׁמֶשׁ *haš-šemeš, the sun.* Sometimes the daghesh forte is elided when the opening consonant of the following noun has a vocal shᵉwa written to it (cf. § 6. 5).

3. When the article is used with a noun whose opening consonant is a guttural or *rêš,* the principles laid down in § 7. 7 apply. Since these letters cannot be doubled, *either* the *paṯhaḥ* of the article, falling in an open syllable, is lengthened to *qāmes, or,* in the case of certain of the gutturals, there is implicit doubling of the guttural and the *paṯhaḥ* of the article commonly remains unchanged. The former takes place regularly before א and ר, and commonly before ע; e.g. הָאוֹר *the light*; הָאִישׁ *the man*; הָרֶגֶל *the foot*; הָרָשָׁע *the wicked*; הָעִיר *the city*; הָעַיִן *the eye*; the latter takes place usually before ה and ח; e.g. הַהֵיכָל *the palace*; הַחָכְמָה *the wisdom.*

4. But certain variations to the rule given in 3 must be noted in the pointing of the article before ח ה ע pointed with *qāmeṣ* or *ḥaṭeph qāmeṣ*:

(a) before accented הָ, the article, falling in the pretone, takes *qāmeṣ* (cf. § 5. 2b); e.g. הָהָר *the mountain*.

(b) before unaccented עָ and הָ, the article, falling *before* the pretone, takes *seghôl*; e.g. הֶהָרִים *the mountains*, הֶעָמָל *the trouble*.

(c) before חָ, accented or unaccented, and חֳ, the article takes *seghôl*; e.g. הֶחָכָם *the wise*; הֶחָג *the festival*; הֶחֳלִי *the sickness*.

The following will serve as a useful summary of the vocalization of the article. It should not be mechanically committed to memory but read in the light of the principles which govern it, and then it will be remembered without serious difficulty.

Before ordinary conss.		הַ·	הַקּוֹל
Before gutturals	א, ר, ע	הָ-,	הָעָם, הָעִיר, הָרֹאשׁ, הָאִישׁ
	ה, ח	הַ-,	הַהֵיכָל, הַחֶרֶב
But before	הָ,	הָ-,	הָהָר
	עָ, הָ	הֶ-,	הֶהָרִים, הֶעָמָל
	(חֳ), חָ	הֶ-,	הֶחֳלִי, הֶחָכָם

אִישׁ man [1]	אִשָּׁה *f.* woman	בֹּקֶר morning
יוֹם day	לַיְלָה *m.* night	עֶרֶב evening
חֹשֶׁךְ darkness	רָקִיעַ firmament	אוֹר light
מַיִם *pl.* water, waters	גָּדוֹל great	עָפָר dust
רָם high	עַל־ upon	טוֹב good
שָׁמַיִם *pl.* heaven	כֶּסֶף silver	חָכָם wise
	זָהָב gold	וְ and

Note.—The conjunction וְ is a particle inseparably prefixed to words; e.g. וְאִישׁ *and a man.*

[1] Throughout the vocabularies, *feminine* nouns are marked *f.*, those unmarked are *masculine*.

5. *Rules of usage of the article and the adjective*:

Rule 1. The article defines an individual thing or person within a group; it is not used if the individual thing or person is otherwise defined; e.g. it is not used with a proper name (as in English). Cf. also §§ 14 and 16.

Rule 2. For the generic use of the article, cf. § 12. 2. b.i.

Rule 3. The adjective, when it qualifies a noun, stands after it; e.g. *a good man* אִישׁ טוֹב. If the noun is definite, the adjective, as well as the noun, has the article; e.g. *the good man* הָאִישׁ הַטּוֹב, i.e. *the man, the good* (one). If two or more adjectives qualify the same noun, each of the adjectives has the article; e.g. *the great and good man* הָאִישׁ הַגָּדוֹל וְהַטּוֹב.

Rule 4. The adjective, when used predicatively, does *not* take the article. It may come before or after the noun—usually before; e.g. *the man is good* הָאִישׁ טוֹב or טוֹב הָאִישׁ (lit. *good is the man*); in neither case does the adjective take the article. The copula *is, are* etc., is not usually expressed. This, however, occasions no ambiguity; הָאִישׁ טוֹב could not be mistaken for *the good man*, which would require הַטּוֹב.

EXERCISE

Translate

הַלַּ֫יְלָה וְהַיּוֹם׃ 2 הָאִישׁ וְהָאִשָּׁה׃ 3 הַחֹשֶׁךְ הַגָּדוֹל׃ 4 רָם הָרָקִיעַ׃
5 טוֹב הַכֶּסֶף׃ 6 הָעֶרֶב וְהַבֹּקֶר׃ 7 גָּדוֹל הַחֹשֶׁךְ עַל־הַמָּיִם׃
8 טוֹב הָאִישׁ׃ 9 היום הגדול׃ 10 האור על־השמים והחשך על־המים׃

Today. 2 The morning. 3 The night. 4 The light (is)[1] good. 5 The good light. 6 The lofty firmament. 7 The man and the woman. 8. The darkness (is)[1] great. 9 The good man. 10 The great and good man. 11 A great day. 12 The gold (is)[1] good. 13 The dust (is)[1] upon the waters. 14 A good man.

---

[1] Throughout the Exercises, bracketed words are not to be translated.

§ 9. THE FORM OF THE SENTENCE IN HEBREW—MAQQEPH—METHEGH

1. Sentences are of two kinds: (a) verbal—having a *finite* verb for a predicate; e.g. *the angel cried*; and (2) nominal—having any other kind of predicate, such as noun, adjective, participle; e.g. *Thou art God, God is good*, etc. The order in a verbal sentence is commonly verb, subject; e.g. קָרָא הַמַּלְאָךְ *the angel cried*; but the subject may be placed first for emphasis; e.g. וְהָאִישׁ אָמַר *but the man said*. The order in a nominal sentence is commonly subject, predicate; e.g. יהוה מַלְכֵּנוּ *Yahweh*[1] *is our king*; but the predicate, if emphatic, can be placed first, e.g. עָפָר אַתָּה *dust thou art*, and frequently also, as we have seen (§ 8. 5, Rule 4), if it be an adjective, e.g. צַדִּיק אַתָּה יהוה *righteous art Thou, Yahweh*.

In sentences of the type *the people is wise* (cf. § 8. 5, Rule 4), the predicate is sometimes followed by the third personal pronoun (in the appropriate number and gender); thus הָעָם חָכָם הוּא *the people is wise*. Sometimes, especially when subject and predicate are co-extensive, this pronoun precedes the predicate; e.g. יהוה הוּא הָאֱלֹהִים *Yahweh is the God*. In such cases it is resumptive in force—in the former case, without emphasis, *as for the people, it* (הוּא) *is wise*; in the latter, with emphasis, *Yahweh, he* (and no other) *is the God*, or *Yahweh Himself is the God*.

2. The subject is placed first in circumstantial clauses, which describe, not an action or a development, but a situation or a circumstance; commonly they are introduced by the connective וְ, sometimes they stand asyndetically; e.g. בָּא הָאִישׁ וְהַיֶּלֶד יוֹשֵׁב עוֹד *the man came in while the boy was still sitting*; בָּא הָאִישׁ וְדָוִד לֹא יָדַע *the man came in, but David did not know it*; וְאַבְרָהָם זָקֵן *now Abraham was old*.

---

[1] יהוה is thus translated in the Grammar, not by *the Lord*, and it is left unpointed. The name Jehovah is derived from a misunderstanding of the vocalized form יְהוָֹה (cf. Note in § 15).

3. The negative stands immediately before the verb or predicate; thus, in a verbal sentence, the order is (negative), verb, subject, object, e.g. לֹא שָׁמַע הָאִישׁ אֶת־הַקּוֹל *the man did not hear the voice.*

4. (a) The *definite* object in nouns and pronouns, when directly governed by an active verb, is in prose usually preceded by the particle (itself a worn down noun; cf. § 12. 1, 3) אֵת, or rather אֶת־ (see note 1 after Exercise), as in the above illustration [1]. But the noun must be definite; *a voice* would have been simply קוֹל, not אֶת־קוֹל. A noun is definite: (i) if it is preceded by the definite article or is in a Genitive relation with a following noun which is definite (cf. § 14. 4, Rule 1); (ii) if it is particularized by a possessive pronoun (which is expressed in Hebrew by means of a pronominal suffix (§ 16), e.g. *God* heard *his voice,* אֶת־קוֹלוֹ; and (iii) if it is a proper name, e.g. he smote *David,* אֶת־דָּוִד.

(b) אֶת־ is repeated before each noun, if there be more than one; e.g. Abraham took *Sarah and Lot,* אֶת־שָׂרָה וְאֶת־לוֹט.

מֶ֫לֶךְ king חֶ֫רֶב *f.* sword	עַם people	אֶ֫רֶץ *f.* earth, land
יֶ֫לֶד boy	אֱלֹהִים God	יהוה Yahweh
הֵיכָל palace, temple	רָעָב famine	בָּרָא to create
קָרָא to call	שָׁפַךְ to shed	לָקַח to take
שָׁמַע to hear	אָמַר to say	בָּא to come
יָשַׁב to sit	יָדַע to know	מְאֹד very
רַע מְאֹד very bad	רַע bad, evil	עָצוּם strong, powerful
כָּבֵד heavy	אֶל־ unto	לֹא not

Note—(i) The nouns הַר *hill,* עַם *people,* חַג *festival,* פַּר *ox,* when preceded by the article, lengthen the *paṯhaḥ* to *qāmeṣ*;

[1] Thus הַקּוֹל is ideally in the Genitive; cf. § 14. 1.

הַפָּר, הֶחָג, הָעָם, הָהָר. So also אֶרֶץ (original form אַרְץ) becomes הָאָרֶץ with the article.

(ii) רַע (*f.* רָעָה) can mean *bad*, both in the sense of unfortunate and even disastrous, and in the sense of morally bad.

(iii) The verbal form which is quoted in the vocabulary is not the Infin. but the 3rd sing. masc. perf. active, which is, for all classes of verbs, with one exception, the basic and simplest form and the one quoted in reference. It might seem right and proper, therefore, to give the meaning of בָּרָא, for example, as *he created*, rather than *to create*, as is the common practice; but בָּרָא has a considerable range of meaning (Perf., Preterite, Fut. Perf., Pluperf. etc.; cf. § 11. I, 5), so that to say בָּרָא *to create* intimates simply that בָּרָא is a verb and gives its meaning.

EXERCISE

Translate

יהוה הוּא הָאֱלֹהִים׃ 2 כָּבֵד הָֽרָעָב עַל־הָאָֽרֶץ׃ 3 בָּא הַיֶּלֶד אֶל־
הַֽהֵיכָל וְהַמֶּלֶךְ לֹא יָדַע׃ 4 לָקַח הָאִישׁ אֶת־הַזָּהָב וְאֶת־הַכֶּסֶף׃
5 בָּרָא אֱלֹהִים אֶת־הַשָּׁמַיִם וְאֶת־הָאָרֶץ׃ 6 קָֽרָא הַיֶּלֶד אֶל־
הָאִישׁ הֶֽחָכָם וְהָאִישׁ לֹא שָׁמַע׃ 7 בָּרָא אֱלֹהִים אֶת־הָאוֹר וְאֶת־
הַחֹשֶׁךְ׃ 8 שָׁפַךְ הַיֶּלֶד אֶת־הַמַּיִם עַל־הָאָרֶץ׃ 9 הָעָם הֶֽעָצוּם
וְהַגָּדוֹל׃ 10 לָקַח הַמֶּלֶךְ אֶת־הַחֶרֶב׃

The good man. 2 The palace (was) very high 3 The good king heard the woman and did not take the silver and the gold. 4 The wise man sat upon the dust and did not hear. 5 Darkness (was) upon the morning and the evening and famine (was) upon the land, and it (was) very serious. 6 Yahweh is God. 7 The good man is the wise man. 8 The good and great people. 9 The boy called the people to the mountain.

Note 1. The *maqqēph* or hyphen, which is illustrated in the exercise above, joins together two or more words so that they are pronounced as a rhythmical unit and are treated in writing as an accentual unit; e.g. אֶת־כָּל־אֲשֶׁר־לוֹ *all* (accus.) *that was to him*, i.e. *all that he had*. The occurrence of two accented syllables in collocation, which is contrary to the rhythm, is thus avoided by the use of *maqqēph*, since all the words joined together by the sign lose their accent except the last, and, in consequence of this, their long vowels, if changeable, become short (§ 2. 6b); e.g. כֹּל אִישׁ becomes כָּל־אִישׁ, *kol-'îš*, *every man*, the vowel of כָּל־ being now short because it is in a closed syllable before the tone. *Ṣērê*, followed by *maqqēph*, is usually reduced to *sᵉghôl*; thus הִשָּׁמֵר *hiššāmēr*, but הִשָּׁמֶר־נָא *beware*; so תֶּן־לוֹ תוֹדָה וְהַגֶּד־נָא *give praise to him and tell*, &c.

The *maqqēph* is used almost invariably with אֵל *to* (thus אֶל־), כֹּל *all* (thus כָּל־), אֵת sign of the definite object (thus אֶת־), and a few other common words (e.g. מִן־ *from*, פֶּן־ *lest*).

Note 2. The main accent or tone falls generally, but not invariably, upon the last syllable of a word (e.g. דָּבָ֫ר *dābhā́r*, *word*; but דֶּ֫בֶר *débher*, *pestilence*, and קָטַ֫לְתִּי *qāṭáltî*, *I killed*). According to the natural rhythm of the language the syllable immediately before the Tone has a fall, but the syllable second from the Tone a certain emphasis or accentual rise. Especially if this syllable is open and, in consequence, more liable to be slurred, it is marked with a מֶתֶג, *methegh*, *bridle* (a small perpendicular stroke to the left of its vowel [1]) in order to preserve its secondary emphasis. In fact, *the second full vowel from the tone, if open, is uniformly marked by methegh*, both when its vowel is long (הָֽאָדָם *the man*) and when it is a short vowel before a guttural with dagh. forte implicitum (הַֽהֵיכָל *the palace*, הֶֽחָכָם *the wise*); e.g. אָֽנֹכִי *I*, וְזָֽכַרְתָּ֫ *and thou shalt remember*, הֶֽעָפָר *the dust*. The *methegh* is rarely used with the vowel of a shut syllable, since it is

[1] Under the consonant, if the vowel is *ḥôlem*; e.g. כּֽוֹכָבִים *stars*, כֹּֽהֲנִים *priests*, אֽוֹיְבִים *enemies*.

in little danger of being slurred (therefore, *not* מְֽדַבְּרִים), nor with a vocal shᵉwa (therefore, *not* דְּֽבָרִים). But it is used when the open syllable is separated from the tone even by vocal shᵉwa only; e.g. אָֽכְלָה *ā-khᵉlā* (accent on last syllable) *she ate*, חָֽכְמָה *ḥā-khᵉmā, she is wise*. *Methegh* in such cases clearly indicates that the shᵉwa is vocal, and thus serves to distinguish between *ā* and *o* and between *î* and *i*. Thus אָכְלָה and חָכְמָה without *methegh* are to be read as *'okh-lā, food* and *ḥokh-mā, wisdom*. Similarly יִֽרְאוּ *yî-rᵉ'û, they will fear* (open syllable, long *i*) but יִרְאוּ *yir-'û, they will see* (shut syllable, short *i*).

If the vocal shᵉwa in this case be a *ḥaṭeph*, the preceding vowel, though short, has that distinctness that requires to be preserved by *methegh*; hence the combination referred to in § 7. 5a always appears in the form ֲ-ַ-, ֱ-ֶ-, ֳ-ָ-; e.g. יַֽעֲמִיד *he stations*, הֶֽעֱמִיד *he stationed*, הָֽעֳמַד *he was stationed*.

§ 10. PERSONAL, DEMONSTRATIVE, INTERROGATIVE AND OTHER PRONOUNS

1. *The Personal Pronouns.*

	Sing.	*Signif. part.*	*Plur.*	*Sig. part.*
1 *pers. c.*	אֲנִי, אָנֹכִי[1] I	*i, ni, ki*	אֲנַ֫חְנוּ we	*nu*
2 *pers. m.*	אַתָּה[2] thou	*ta*	אַתֶּם[2] ye	*tem*
f.	אַתְּ[2] thou	*t*	אַתֵּ֫נָה,[2,4] אַתֶּן[2,4] ye	*ten*
3 *pers. m.*	הוּא he[3]	*w, hu*	הֵ֫מָּה, הֵם they	*m*
f.	הִיא she[3]	*y (ha)*	הֵ֫נָּה they	*n*

[1] אָנֹכִי is composed of two demonstrative elements, *'anô* from *'anā* (cf. Arab. *'anā, I*) and *kî*. אֲנִי and אָנֹכִי have the same value in Hebrew; אֲנִי is more commonly used, but considerations of rhythm sometimes give the preference to אָנֹכִי.

[2 3 4] See footnotes on following page.

The above forms of the Pers. Pronouns are used only to express the Nominative: they must not be put as *oblique cases* after a verb or preposition: therefore *I-buried him* is not קָבַרְתִּי הוּא (§§ 11.6; 27); *declare to* (לְ) *me* is not סַפְּרוּ לְאֲנִי (§ 12. 1 f). When, as in these cases, the Pers. Pronouns do not express the Subject, they become attracted in a fragmentary form, to be explained later (§§ 16; 27; 12. 1f; 12. 3d, &c.), to the end of other words. These fragments (the *significant parts* in the preceding table) are named *Pronominal suffixes*.

2. *Demonstrative Pronouns.*

	Sing.	*Plur.*	*Sing.*	*Plur.*
mas.	זֶה this		הוּא that	הֵ֫מָּה, הֵם those
f.	זֹאת this		הִיא that	הֵ֫נָּה those
c.		אֵ֫לֶּה these		

The demonstratives may be used predicatively or adjectivally. Like adjectives when used predicatively they do not take the article, and the order is as in English: e.g. *this is the man*, זֶה הָאִישׁ; *this is the good man*, זֶה הָאִישׁ הַטּוֹב. When used as adjectives their noun is definite, and they are written, with the definite article, after the noun—exactly like adjs. (§ 8, Rule 3); e.g. הָאִישׁ הַזֶּה *this man* (i.e. *the man—this one*), הַתּוֹרָה הַזֹּאת *this law*, הַיּוֹם הַהוּא *that day*, הַדְּבָרִים הָאֵלֶּה *these words*. With another adj., the demonstr. stands last: *this good man*, הָאִישׁ הַטּוֹב הַזֶּה.

Note that though, with the art., the sing. is הַהוּא, the plur. is הָהֵם.

[2] אַתָּה is from an original *ʾantā*; similarly with the other 2nd pers. pronouns.

[3] In הוּא *hû* and הִיא *hî* the א which is silent, points to an earlier stage in the history of the word when it was consonantal (*hûʾa* ? *hîʾa* ?).

[4] Both forms are very rare.

3. *Interrogative pronoun.* The interrogative is מִי *who*? for persons, and מָה *what*? for things, both words indeclinable.

The emphasis of the question, not being on the interrogative particle, falls forward on the next word (§ 6. 6), and מה assumes a *pointing quite like the Article* (§ 8).

Before non-gutturals	*path. and dag.*	מַה־זֶּה	what is this?
before א and ר	*qāmeṣ*	מָה־אֵלֶּה	what are these?
before other gutturals	*pathaḥ*	מַה־הִיא	what is it?
but before gutt. with qam.	*sᵉghôl*	מֶה עָשָׂה	what has he done?

(a) מִי is also used to express the indefinite *whoever, whosoever* and מָה *whatever, whatsoever*; e.g. מִי לַיהוה אֵלָי *whoever* (is) *for Yahweh,* (let him come) *to me.* Note that מִי יִבְטַח בַּיהוה means: *Who will trust in Yahweh*?, whereas אֲשֶׁר יִבְטַח בַּיהוה means: *He who will trust in Yahweh.* (Cf. 4c below).

(b) *Whom*? is expressed by אֶת־מִי; e.g. אֶת־מִי עָשַׁקְתִּי *Whom have I oppressed*? *Whose*? is expressed by לְמִי; e.g. לְמִי הַיֶּלֶד הַזֶּה *Whose boy is this*? (§ 12. 1a) or by the use of מִי in the Genitive; e.g. בֶּן־מִי אַתָּה *Whose son are you*? (§ 14. 1). אֶת־ is never used before מה; cf. above מֶה עָשָׂה, *What has he done*?

(c) מָה is also used as the exclamatory *How!* e.g. מַה־טּוֹב הַמֶּלֶךְ *How good the king is!*

4. *Relative Pronoun.* (a) There is no relative pronoun in Hebrew. אֲשֶׁר is a general word of relation and is invariable for all genders, numbers and cases; and, as it is used to introduce clauses beginning not only with *who, whom, whose, which,* but also with *where, whence, whither,* it has sometimes been likened to the *wh* in these words. The Hebrew way of turning such relative sentences is to place the relative particle at the beginning and to define the relationship by the use of the appropriate complement within the relative sentence; e.g. *the man to whom I spoke* is rendered as *the man* אֲשֶׁר (*wh*) *I spoke to him*; *the house in which I lived* as *the house*

אֲשֶׁר (*wh*) *I lived in it.* So *whose* = אֲשֶׁר followed by *his*; הָאָדָם אֲשֶׁר נְשָׁמָה בְּאַפּוֹ *man in whose nostrils* (אֲשֶׁר .... בְּאַפּוֹ) *is* (but) *a breath.* So *there* is שָׁם, *where* שָׁם .... אֲשֶׁר; *thither* is שָׁמָּה, *whither* שָׁמָּה .... אֲשֶׁר; *thence* is מִשָּׁם (מִן *from*; *n* assimilated), *whence* מִשָּׁם .... אֲשֶׁר.

(b) Almost always, however, when the English relative pronoun is in the nominative, and frequently also when it is in the accusative, אֲשֶׁר is used alone, i.e. without the need being felt for a word within the relative sentence to define the relationship; e.g. the king *who pursued* אֲשֶׁר רָדַף (the אֲשֶׁר is not followed up by the pronoun הוּא (*he*)); he put there the man *whom he had formed,* אֲשֶׁר יָצַר (אֲשֶׁר in such a case may not be followed by a word for *him*). It is doubtless this familiar usage which has led to the statement that אֲשֶׁר is a relative pronoun.

(c) אֲשֶׁר can also be a compound relative = *he who, him who, that which,* and, as such, may take a preposition before it; *that which* (אֲשֶׁר) he had done pleased Yahweh; he said *to the man who* (לַאֲשֶׁר) was over his house.

(d) Occasionally the particle is omitted at the beginning of a relative clause, and the relative relationship of the clause is left to be understood; e.g. בָּא הָאִישׁ אֶל־אֶרֶץ לֹא יָדַע the man entered a land he did not know.

5. *Other pronominal expressions. Each* אִישׁ; e.g. kings were sitting *each* (אִישׁ) upon his throne. So *any*; e.g. if *any one* (אִישׁ) can number, &c.

Every, all, כֹּל (which is strictly a noun = *the whole*); e.g. *every day,* כֹּל יוֹם; *all the day,* כָּל־הַיּוֹם (§ 9, Note 1 to the Exercise).

No, none, אִישׁ ... לֹא or אִישׁ לֹא (lit. *not a man*): כֹּל ... לֹא or לֹא ... כֹּל (lit. *not every,* i.e. *not any*); e.g. *none living* is just before thee, כָּל־חַי ... לֹא; *no work shall be done,* כָּל־מְלָאכָה לֹא־יֵעָשֶׂה.

The one, the other, זֶה ... זֶה: *the one called to the other,* קָרָא זֶה אֶל־זֶה.

For other forms of reciprocal and reflexive usages, see §§ 22. 3; 23. 3b; 33. 4, 5.

עַ֫יִן *f.* eye	יָד *f.* hand	הַר mountain
חֳלִי disease	רֹאשׁ head קָדוֹשׁ holy	אֶ֫בֶן *f.* stone
עֶ֫בֶד servant	עָשָׂה to do, to make	יָלַד to bear

EXERCISE

Translate

הָהָר הוּא רָם מְאֹד: 2 אַתָּה הוּא הָאֱלֹהִים: 3 הַחֶרֶב הִיא עַל־
הֶעָפָר: 4 הָעָם הוּא עָצוּם מְאֹד: 5 אֲנִי הָאִישׁ הֶחָכָם: 6 מִי
אַתֶּם: 7 רָם מְאֹד הָהָר הַזֶּה: 8 זֶה הַיּוֹם אֲשֶׁר עָשָׂה אֱלֹהִים:
9 הָעָם הֶעָצוּם הַזֶּה: 10 זֶה הַיֶּלֶד אֲשֶׁר שָׁמַע אֶת־הַקּוֹל: 11 בָּא
הָאִישׁ אֲשֶׁר שָׁפַךְ אֶת־הַמַּיִם עַל־הָאָרֶץ: 12 מַה־טּוֹב הַיּוֹם הַזֶּה:
13 קָרָא זֶה אֶל־זֶה [1]וְאָמַר קָדוֹשׁ יהוה: 14 לקח המלך את־
החרב: 15 זה המלך העצום:

The mountain is very lofty. 2 The dust is upon the waters. 3 I (am) the man. 4 We (are) the people. 5 The good and powerful people. 6 The great and lofty mountain. 7 Who (are) these? 8 What (are) they? 9 Who (is) this woman? 10 I (am) the great king who (is) over the land. 11 That great day. 12 This (is) a good head. 13 This head (is) good. 14 This good head. 15 This (is) the bad boy who spilt the water upon the earth. 16 These (are) the heavens and the earth which God created this day. 17 How great (is) that palace!

---

[1] Cf. § 20. 5b.

§ 11. THE SIMPLE FORM OF THE VERB THE PERFECT—THE CONJUNCTION—PAUSE

I *The Verb*

1. *Root.* The root of a verb is considered to be the 3rd *sing. masc. perf.* of the simple form, e.g. שָׁבַר *he broke* (cf. Note iii to Voc. § 9). This form is called *Qal* (קַל) "light", in distinction from all the other forms, which are heavy, being loaded by additional inflectional letters, e.g. נִשְׁבַּר *he was broken,* or by the duplication of a radical, e.g. שִׁבֵּר *he broke in pieces.*

2. *Inflection.* Inflection to express person takes place by the connection, in most cases, of the significant parts of the personal pronoun with the stem (§ 10. 1); and the third sing. as simplest is taken first, then the second, and finally the first. In the perfect the pronominal element is attached to the stem as an afformative, in the imperfect as a preformative.

THE PERFECT

3 sing mas.	קָטַל	*he killed,* &c.	
3 sing fem.	קָֽטְלָה	*she killed,* &c.	*ā* = fem. ending
2 sing. mas.	קָטַלְתָּ	*thou didst kill,* &c.	*tā* of אַתָּה
2 sing. fem.	קָטַלְתְּ	*thou* (*f.*) *didst kill,* &c.	*t* of אַתְּ
1 sing. com.	קָטַלְתִּי	*I killed,* &c.	*tî*=*kî* of אָנֹכִי, with *k* assimilated to *t* of 2 sing.
3 plur. com.	קָֽטְלוּ	*they killed,* &c.	-*û*=masc. pl. ending
2 plur. mas.	קְטַלְתֶּם	*ye killed,* &c.	*tem* of אַתֶּם
2 plur. fem.	קְטַלְתֶּן	*ye* (*f.*) *killed,* &c.	*ten* of אַתֶּן
1 plur. com.	קָטַלְנוּ	*we killed,* &c.	*nû* of אֲנַחְנוּ

Thus these are not arbitrary forms: קָטַ֫לְתָּ is really *killed thou,* and קָטַ֫לְנוּ *killed we.*

3. Note carefully where the accent falls—usually on the טַל. The first syllable is pretonic and open, therefore has a tone-long vowel, קָ (§ 5. 2b), e.g. קָטַ֫לְתִּי (not קְטַלְתִּי). The heavy terminations תֶּם, תֶּן, draw the accent upon them, so that the first vowel, being now no longer pretonic but two places from the tone, vanishes into shᵉwa (§ 5. 2c), e.g. קְטַלְתֶּ֫ם (not קָטַלְתֶּם)

4. Note carefully the verbal inflection: *m.* יָשַׁר, *f.* יָֽשְׁרָה (cf § 5. 2f) In other words, in *verbal* inflection with vocalic additions—e.g. *ā* of 3rd sing. fem. (ה) or *û* of 3rd pl. (וּ)—the vowels *á é ó*[1] in the tone-syllable become vocal shᵉwa thus: *m.* קָטַל, *f.* קָֽטְלָה (not קָטְלָה), *m.* כָּבֵד, *f.* כָּֽבְדָה (not כְּבֵדָה), *m.* יָכֹל, *f.* יָֽכְלָה. In the 3rd sing. fem. and the 3rd plur. the first vowel has *methegh*—קָֽטְלָה, קָֽטְלוּ, because the shᵉwa, representing as it does an original full vowel (*á*), is sounded (§ 5. 2e, § 9. Note 2 to Voc.). This preserves the *a* sound: without *methegh,* the words would be *qoṭlā, qoṭlû.* Naturally, if the third radical were a *bᵉghadhkᵉphath,* it would not take daghesh lene; e.g. כָּֽתְבָה *she wrote,* כָּֽתְבוּ *they wrote.*

5. *Uses of the perfect.* The Perf. expresses:

(a) The Aorist (Past), *he killed.*
(b) The Perfect, *he has killed.*
(c) The Pluperfect, *he had killed.*
(d) The future Perfect, *he shall have killed.* (See § 43).

6. אֵת or אֶת־, the objective particle (§ 9. 4a), when used with the pronominal suffixes, appears as follows: אֹתִי *me,* אֹתְךָ m. אֹתָךְ f. *thee,* אֹתוֹ *him,* אֹתָהּ *her,* אֹתָ֫נוּ *us,* אֶתְכֶם m. אֶתְכֶן f. *you,* אֹתָם m. אֹתָן f. *them.*

The *scriptio plena* is also common: אוֹתִי, &c.

---

[1] Most regular vbs. have their second vowel in *á*, many in *é*, a few in *ó* (§ 19. 1).

II. *The Conjunction*

The inseparable conjunction ו *and,* is pointed very much like the inseparable prepositions in § 12.

(a) Its ordinary pointing is shᵉwa, וְאַתָּה *and thou,* וְדָבָר *and a word.*

(b) Before the *ḥaṭephs* it takes the corresponding short vowel (§7. 1c), וַאֲנִי *and I,* וֶאֱמָץ *and be strong.* חֶסֶד וֶאֱמֶת *kindness and faithfulness.*

ו with אֱלֹהִים gives וֵאלֹהִים (not וֶאֱלֹהִים).

(c) Its pointing is וּ before simple shᵉwa, וּדְבָרִים *and words.* וּשְׁמַרְתֶּם *and ye shall keep,* and before the Labials (בומפ), וּבֵן *and a son,* וּפָרָה *and a cow.*

(d) Note that before *yôdh* with shᵉwa the pointing is *ḥîreq*; e.g. with יְמֵי it is neither וּיְמֵי nor וִיְמֵי, but וִימֵי, in which the *yôdh* is quiescent, so that no shᵉwa is written under it (cf. יֹאמַר and רֵאשִׁית in § 7. 6b, ii).

(e) Before the accent, especially if disjunctive (see § 47), it often takes *qāmeṣ* (§ 5. 2b): טוֹב וָרָע *good and evil,* פָּרָה וָדֹב *a cow and a bear,* דֹּר וָדֹר *generation after generation*; especially with words that go in pairs: יוֹם וָלַיְלָה *day and night,* זָהָב וָכֶסֶף *gold and silver,* תֹּהוּ וָבֹהוּ *waste and void* (וָ in spite of Labial; cf. אֱלֹהִים וָמֶלֶךְ *God and king*).

(f) When the conjunction precedes a noun with the definite article, the vocalization of the article remains unchanged and the conjunction is simply prefixed; e.g. *and the people* וְהָעָם (contrast § 12. 1e).

דָּוִד David	יְהוֹנָתָן Jonathan	מֹשֶׁה Moses
מִרְיָם Miriam	יִשְׂרָאֵל Israel	יְהוּדָה *f.* Judah
מִלְחָמָה *f.* battle, war	בְּהֵמָה *f.* cattle	יַבָּשָׁה *f.* dry land
מִצְרַיִם Egypt	מִצְרַיְמָה to Egypt	אָדָם man, humanity
שְׁבִיעִי seventh	צָעַק, זָעַק to cry, cry out	שָׁבַת to rest
סֵפֶר book		

מָכַר to sell
שָׁמַר to keep, watch
מָחָה to destroy, blot out
מְעַט a little
כָּתַב to write
רָאָה to see
הִנֵּה, הֵן behold
שָׁפַט to judge, rule over

EXERCISE

Translate

אָמַר יהוה אֶל־הָֽאִשָּׁה׃ 2 אֱלֹהִים וּמֹשֶׁה׃ 3 אֶל־אֱלֹהִים זָֽעֲקוּ
וְהָֽרָעָב עַל־הָאָֽרֶץ׃ 4 דָּוִד וִיהֽוֹנָתָן׃ 5 יִשְׂרָאֵל וִֽיהוּדָה׃ 6
כָּֽבְדָה הַמִּלְחָמָה עַל־הָעָם וְהֵם מָֽכְרוּ אֶת־הַבְּהֵמָה׃ 7 אֲנִי
הָאִישׁ אֲשֶׁר מְכַרְתֶּם אֹתִי [1]מִצְרָֽיְמָה׃ 8 רָאָה אֱלֹהִים אֶת־אֲשֶׁר
עָשָׂה וְהִנֵּה טוֹב מְאֹד׃ 9 והיום ההוא כתבתי את־הספר׃ 10
משה ומרים׃ 11 יום ולילה׃

I said to (אֶל־) the man. 2 We rested (on) the seventh day. 3 We cried out to God and He (וְהוּא) heard us. 4 God destroyed man and cattle upon the earth. 5 People and king. 6 Who spilt the water upon the ground? 7 Thou hast said, Holy (is) Yahweh. 8 Night and morning. 9 Thou hast ruled (f.) over this people. 10 We sat upon the dry ground and there we rested a little. 11 The cattle which David had sold, the boy took into the city. 12 God made day and night. 13 The king saw what he had made and it was very good.

[1] *Note.—Sillûq* ◌ֽ marks the last tone syllable in a sentence, while *'athnāḥ* ◌֑ marks the main pause within the sentence:

בְּרֵאשִׁית בָּרָא אֱלֹהִים אֵת הַשָּׁמַיִם וְאֵת הָאָֽרֶץ׃

The strong emphasis on the tone syllable at the end of a sentence or at the main division, or divisions, within it produces so-called pausal forms which are characterized by alterations of vocalization and sometimes by movement of the tone within the word in pause:

(a) A short vowel in the tone becomes long, as מַיִם *water*, pause מָיִם; שָׁמַר *he kept*, pause שָׁמָר; שָׁמַרְתִּי *I kept*, pause שָׁמָֽרְתִּי.

If the short vowel has been modified from another, it is the long of the *primary* sound that appears, אֶ֫רֶץ *earth,* p. אָ֫רֶץ (from a primary אַרְץ *'arṣ*).

(b) Occasionally the tone is shifted from the last syllable to the penult, which is lengthened if it was short; עַתָּ֫ה *'attā* (*now*), pause עָ֫תָּה *'ắttā* (not, of course, *'ottā*, which would be the pronunciation of עָתָּ֫ה).

(c) When the original tone-syllable in a verb loses the tone and undergoes modification of its vowel in inflected forms, both are restored in pausal forms; e.g. שָׁכַ֫ן *he dwelt,* fem. שָׁ֫כְנָה, in pause שָׁכֵ֫נָה; עֲמֹ֫ד *stand* (imper.), pl. עִמְד֫וּ, in pause עֲמֹ֫דוּ.

Similarly the composite sh^ewa under a guttural is raised, in pause, to the corresponding long vowel; thus אֲנִ֫י *I*, in pause אָ֫נִי; חֳלִ֫י *sickness,* in pause חֹ֫לִי.

§ 12. THE INSEPARABLE PREPOSITIONS

1. Prepositions and similar words in Hebrew are usually nouns, sometimes entire, but oftener worn down and fragmentary. The following three fragments used as prepositions are, like the Art., inseparably prefixed to words:

ב *in, by, with*; local and instrumental.
כ *as, like.*
ל *to, at, for*; sign of *dat.* and *infin.*

(a) The usual pointing of these light fragments is simple sh^ewa; e.g. בְּשָׁלוֹם *in peace,* בְּיָד חֲזָקָה *with a strong hand,* כְּפַרְעֹה *like Pharaoh,* לְמֹשֶׁה *to Moses.*

(b) Before another sh^ewa this becomes *ḥîreq*, by § 5. 2d, i, forming a half-open syllable לְבַב, בִּלְבַב (< בְּלְבַב) *in the heart of*; the sh^ewa is here sounded, because it was (necessarily) so in the original לְבַב (cf. § 5. 2e); therefore not בִּלְבַּב. If the consonant be י, it quiesces and the shᵉwa is not written (§ 11. II d); e.g. יְמֵי, but בִּימֵי *in the days of*; יְהוּדָה, לִיהוּדָה *to Judah*.

(c) Before a *ḥaṭeph* the shᵉwa becomes the corresponding short vowel, by § 7. 1c, אֲרִי, כַּאֲרִי (< כְּאֲרִי) *like a lion*; אֱכֹל, לֶאֱכֹל *to eat*.

But with the very frequently recurring words אֱלֹהִים *God*, and אֱמֹר (in the phrase לאמר *saying*), the vowel under the guttural is swallowed up in a long vowel under the preposition; thus, not בֶּאֱלֹהִים but בֵּאלֹהִים *in God*, לֵאלֹהִים *to God*, כֵּאלֹהִים *as God*, לֵאמֹר (cf. § 11. II b).

(d) Before the tone, the prep., falling in the *pretone*, often has tone-long *qāmeṣ* (§ 5. 2b), as לָמַ֫יִם *to water* (for לְמַ֫יִם). This is found chiefly in one or two familiar expressions לָעַ֫ד *for ever*, לָבֶ֫טַח *securely*, and with a certain kind of infinitive; e.g. לָלֶ֫כֶת *to go* (§ 34. 2a, 3c, § 29. 2, 2b iii, § 30. 1a, § 39. 3a, α).

(e) In words with the Art. the weak *He* almost always surrenders its vowel to the prep. and disappears (cf. the weak *h* in English words such as *hour*, *honest*, etc., and in French words such as *homme*, *heureux*, &c.). E.g. בְּהַשָּׁמַ֫יִם, הַשָּׁמַ֫יִם > בַּשָּׁמַ֫יִם *in the heavens*, לְהָעָם, הָעָם > לָעָם *to the people*. לֶהָרִים (§ 8. 4b) *to the mountains*. To express it summarily, the Article disappears, but its vowel is written under the preposition.

(f) Prepositions cannot be used immediately before pronouns; therefore *to me* is not לַאֲנִי, nor is *in you* בְּאַתֶּם (cf. § 10. 1). Instead, the significant parts of the pronouns (§ 10. 1) are appended to the prepositions in more or less modified forms; thus—

Sing.

לִי *to me*, לְךָ [1] (m.) לָךְ (f.) *to thee*, לוֹ *to him*, לָהּ *to her*.

---

[1] Pause, לָֽךְ.

Plur.

לָ֫נוּ *to us,* לָכֶ֫ם (m.) לָכֶ֫ן (f.) *to you,* לָהֶ֫ם (m.) לָהֶ֫ן (f.) *to them.* בְּ is inflected like לְ, but it also takes בָּם in 3rd plur. masc.. כְּ uses the poetic form כְּמוֹ as the base for *light* suffixes, with which the accent is on the penult, with pretonic *ā*; and the base כְּ for *heavy* suff., with which the accent is on the last syll., with pretonic *ā*. Thus: כָּמ֫וֹנִי, כָּמ֫וֹךָ, כָּמ֫וֹךְ, כָּמ֫וֹהוּ, כָּמ֫וֹהָ, כָּמ֫וֹנוּ, כָּהֶם, כָּכֶם.

2. Note the following usages:

(a) בְּ

i. *in spite of*; e.g. בְּכָל־זֹאת *in spite of all this.*

ii. בְּ *pretii*; e.g. עָשָׂה זֹאת הַמֶּ֫לֶךְ בְּנֶ֫פֶשׁ הַיֶּ֫לֶד *the king did this at the cost of the boy's life.*

(b) כְּ

i. with an idiomatic use of the generic article; e.g. כַּשֶּׁ֫לֶג *like snow,* כַּצֹּאן *like sheep,* כַּמִּדְבָּר *like a wilderness.*

ii. כְּ repeated in comparisons; e.g. כַּצַּדִּיק כָּרָשָׁע *the righteous is as the wicked*; כָּמוֹךָ כְּפַרְעֹה *thou art as Pharaoh.*

(c) לְ

i. *Dativus Commodi*; e.g. בָּרַח לוֹ lit. *he fled for himself,* i.e. *he fled for his life.*

ii. מַה־לְּךָ פֹּה *What are you doing here?* מַה־לָּךְ lit. *What is to you? What have you?* i.e. *What is the matter with you?* מַה־לִּי וָלָךְ lit. *What is to me and to you?* i.e. *What have I to do with you?*

3. The short word מִן, used as a prep. in the sense of *from, out of,* is also a worn down noun, and generally used as an inseparable particle.

(a) The weak *n*, as in other languages, is assimilated to the next consonant, which is doubled, מִמַּ֫יִם *from water.* (מִן־מַיִם > מִם־מַיִם > מִמַּיִם).

Dagh. f., with certain consonants, may be omitted (§ 6. 5); e.g.

מִקְצֵה (for מִנְקְצֵה) *at the end of*. When the consonant is י, it quiesces (§ 11.II d); e.g. מִן־יְמִינִי *at my right hand* > מִיְּמִינִי > מִיְמִינִי > מִימִינִי.

(b) Before gutturals, the short vowel expands in the open syllable into the corresponding tone-long, מֵעֵץ *from a tree* (מִן־עֵץ > מִע־עֵץ > מֵעֵץ), by § 7. 7; but occasionally, with ח, *ḥîreq* remains, by § 7. 7; e.g. מִחוּץ (not מֵחוּץ), dagh. f. implicit., *outside*.

(c) Before the Art. either (b) is followed, or oftener the prep. is prefixed entire to the word with help of *Maqqeph*, מֵהָעֵץ or מִן־הָעֵץ *from the tree*. This fuller form is also common in poetry. With these exceptions, the usual form is the assimilated.

(d) מִן appears with the pronominal suffixes as follows:

Sing.: מִמֶּנִּי *from me*, מִמְּךָ (m.), מִמֵּךְ (f.) *from thee*, מִמֶּנּוּ *from him*, מִמֶּנָּה *from her*.

Plur.: מִמֶּנּוּ *from us*, מִכֶּם *from you*, מֵהֶם *from them*.

The forms מִכֶּם (מִן־כֶם) and מֵהֶם (מִן־הֶם) are intelligible, but the others seem to postulate a reduplicated form *minmin* > *mimmen*; מִמֶּנּוּ (*from him*) is a modification of מִמֶּנְהוּ (*mim-men-hû*) and מִמֶּנָּה of מִמֶּנְהָ (*mim-men-hā*).

4. Note the following usages:

(a) local; e.g. בָּא מִן־הַהֵיכָל *he came from the temple*.

(b) temporal; e.g. מִן־הַיּוֹם הַשְּׁבִיעִי *from* (*i.e.*) *after the seventh day*.

(c) partitive; e.g. יָצְאוּ מִן־הָעָם *there went out* (*some*) *of the people*.

(d) causative; e.g. מִן־הַקּוֹל אֲשֶׁר שָׁמַע *because of the voice which he had heard*.

(e) privative; e.g. מִגְּבוּרָה *without strength*.

(f) for the use of מִן to express the comparative degree, cf. § 44. 1.

(g) מִקָּטוֹן וְעַד־גָּדוֹל lit. *from small and up to great,* i.e. *both small and great, small and great alike.*

קָטֹן, קָטוֹן	small, little	גַּן	garden	מָקוֹם	place
עֵץ	tree	אֲדָמָה	*f.* ground, land	מְלָאכָה	*f.* work
אֲרִי	lion	חֲמוֹר	ass	דָּם	blood
שְׁמוּעָה	*f.* report, rumour	רָשָׁע	wicked	כָּתַב	to write
		נָתַן	to give	אָכַל	to eat
מָשַׁל בְּ	to rule over	שָׂרַף	to burn	אֵשׁ	*f.* fire
קָרָא	to call, to recite	קָרָא לְ	to name	הָיָה	to become, to be
		עַד	up to, as far as		
בָּרַח	to flee			כִּי	for, because, that

EXERCISE

Translate

קָרָא אֱלֹהִים לָאוֹר יוֹם וְלַחֹשֶׁךְ קָרָא [1]לָֽיְלָה׃ 2 שָׁבַת אֱלֹהִים
בַּיּוֹם הַשְּׁבִיעִי מֵהַמְּלָאכָה אֲשֶׁר עָשָׂה׃ 3 שָׁמַע הָאָדָם אֶת־הַקּוֹל
[1]בַּגָּֽן׃ 4 מָשַׁל הַמֶּלֶךְ בָּעָֽם׃ 5 יָשַׁב הַיֶּלֶד בַּמָּקוֹם הַזֶּה׃ 6 מָחָה
יהוה אֶת־כֹּל אֲשֶׁר עָשָׂה מֵאָדָם וְעַד בְּהֵמָה׃ 7 עָשָׂה אֱלֹהִים
אֶת־הָאָדָם עָפָר מִן־הָאֲדָמָה׃ 8 הָאֱלֹהִים הוּא בַּהֵיכָל׃ 9
שָׁפְכוּ דָם [1]כַּמָּֽיִם׃ 10 שָׂרַפְתֶּם אֶת־הַהֵיכָל בָּאֵשׁ׃ 11 [2]בִּימֵי דָוִד
הַמֶּלֶךְ׃ 12 בָּֽרְחוּ הָעָם מִקָּטוֹן וְעַד־גָּדוֹל מִן־הָאָֽרֶץ׃ 13 מִן־
הַשְּׁמוּעָה אֲשֶׁר שָֽׁמְעוּ בָּֽרְחוּ לָהֶם מִן־הַמָּקוֹם׃ 14 נתן את־החרב
למלך׃ 15 כתב הילד בספר׃

1 To a lion. 2 God gave the woman to the man for wife. 3 In the morning. 4 In these heavens. 5 In the earth. 6 In that day. 7 In the lofty palace. 8 The lion cried like an (the) ass. 9 God called the firmament heaven, and the dry land called he earth. 10 Man is dust out of the ground.

[1] Pausal form (cf. § 11. Note to Ex.). [2] Cf. § 12. 1. b.

11 He ate of the tree. 12 The wise people rested on the seventh day. 13 To the dust. 14 On (בּ) the high mountain. 15 One called to the other[1] and said,[1] Yahweh is good. 16 The people, righteous and wicked alike, ate upon the mountains while (and) the famine was in the land. 17 He spilt the blood upon the ground like water.

§ 13. THE NOUN—INFLECTION

1. Stems in Hebrew, as it has come down to us, commonly contain three root letters; e.g. כבד, שמר. In most cases the verb seems to have been the root from which the other related parts of speech were derived, although there are examples of nouns which are primitive, i.e. not traceable to extant verbal stems. On the other hand, there are examples of verbs which are presumably denominatives (i.e. derived from nouns); e.g. שָׁבַר *to buy corn* (שֶׁבֶר *corn*), שֵׁרֵשׁ *to uproot* (שֹׁרֶשׁ *root*), מָלַח *to salt* (מֶלַח *salt*); cf. English *to skin, to dust, to poison*.

2. *Types of Nouns*. Only the common types will be catalogued and illustrated here; no attempt should be made to learn them all in a first study of this section of the grammar:

(a) There are various types of monosyllabic nouns which should be noted; e.g. דָּג *fish*, יָד *hand* (§ 15); שֵׁם *name*, בֵּן *son* (§ 26); עַם *people*, אֵם *mother* (§ 40); טוֹב *good*, רוּם *height* (§ 31); and אָב *father*, אָח *brother* (§§ 33. 3c; 42).

(b) The majority of nouns are from stems containing three root letters; the main types are as follows, the type being indicated in brackets after the word:

i. with one originally short vowel after the first root letter: e.g. מֶ֫לֶךְ (qaṭl[2]) *king*, סֵ֫פֶר (qiṭl) *book*, בֹּ֫קֶר (quṭl) *morning* (§ 25); בַּ֫יִת (qaṭl) *house*, עַ֫יִן (qaṭl) *eye* (§ 31); אֲרִי (qaṭl) *lion*, פְּרִי (qiṭl) *fruit* (§ 33).

[1] . . . [1] וְאָמַר (or וְאָמְרוּ according to the Hebrew form of the first clause), cf. § 20. 5b.

[2] As קָטַל is commonly used as the paradigm verb (cf. § 11. 2), its root letters may be conveniently used in naming the various types of nouns.

ii. with two originally short vowels; e.g. דָּבָר (qaṭal) *word*, זָקֵן (qaṭil) *old man*, יָתוֹם (qaṭul) *orphan*, לֵבָב (qiṭal) *heart* (§ 15).

iii. with a pure long vowel after the first root letter; e.g. שׁוֹמֵר[1] (qâṭil) *watcher*, עוֹלָם[1] (qâṭal) *age, eternity* (§§ 15, 26).

iv. with a pure long vowel after the second root letter; אָדוֹן[1] (qaṭâl) *lord*, פָּקִיד (qaṭîl) *overseer*, בָּחוּר (qaṭûl) *a young man* (§ 15).

v. with a preformative *m*, e.g. *of place*: מִדְבָּר, *wilderness* (a place for *driving* cattle), מִזְבֵּחַ *altar* (a place for *sacrifice*), מִזְרָח *east* (the place of the sun's *rising*); *of instrument*: מַפְתֵּחַ *key* (an instrument for *opening*), מֶלְקָחַ֫יִם *tongs* (an instrument for *taking up* embers, etc.); other examples: מִשְׁפָּט *judgment, sentence,* &c., מַמְלָכָה *kingdom*, מִזְמוֹר *melody, psalm*.

vi. with preformative *t*: e.g. תַּלְמִיד *scholar, learner*, תּוֹשָׁב *dwelling*, תְּפִלָּה *prayer*, תַּחֲנוּנִים *supplications*.

vii. with afformative *ān* or *ôn*; e.g. שֻׁלְחָן *table*, קָרְבָּן *gift, offering*, קִנְיָן *possession* רִאשׁוֹן *first*, זִכָּרוֹן *memorial*.

3. *Inflection of Nouns* Inflection in Hebrew takes place after two modes, an outside and an inside mode. These modes are to be observed in most languages; e.g. *boy, boys* by outside inflection, *man, men* by inside inflection (so *fear, feared*, but *tread, trod*; *facio, feci* and *brechen, brach*). The Semitic languages have a preference for inner inflection. This is used to distinguish the various conjugations of the Hebrew verb. The *personal* inflection is done by the use of the outside mode, which is commonly used also for the inflection of the noun. Alterations do occur within the noun in Hebrew, but these are due to movements of the tone, e.g. דָּבָ֫ר *word*, דְּבָרִ֫ים *words*, דִּבְרֵיכֶ֫ם *your words*, and differ altogether from such changes as appear in *foot, feet*. At the same time, as the accentual changes take place to a certain extent on various principles,

[1] The long *o* vowel in these words in Hebrew comes from an original pure long *a*.

they afford means for classifying nouns into several *Declensions*. The external changes may be called Inflection.

4. *Inflection, external modifications in Nouns and Adjectives.*

(a) In Hebrew there are:

i. *two* genders, *masc.* and *fem.*

ii. *three* numbers, *sing.*, *dual* and *plur.* The sing. is commonly a *nomen unitatis*, but sometimes it is a collective; e.g. אָדָם *mankind*, צֹאן *sheep*. And occasionally a noun with a plural ending is sing. in meaning; e.g. חַיִּים *life*, זְקוּנִים *old age*.

iii. *two* states, *absolute* and *construct*. A noun is said to be in the absolute state when by its own form and use it expresses the intended idea; e.g. *the man, a dog*, etc.; it is said to be in construct state when it requires to be read in close association with a following noun in genitival relationship for the full definition of the intended idea; e.g. in the phrase *the dog of the man, the dog* is in the construct state (§ 14).

iv. no case endings, apart from some residual forms and uses (cf., e.g., § 14. 5).

(b) The *masc. sing.* has no distinctive ending; the same is true of some fem. sing. forms; e.g. יָד *hand*, אֵם *mother*, אֶרֶץ *earth*.

(c) The *fem. sing.* of an adjective is formed by adding ָה to the *masc. sing.*; e.g. טוֹב, טוֹבָה. It is likewise the case with some nouns; e.g. פַּר *ox*, פָּרָה *cow*; סוּס *horse*, סוּסָה *mare*. Besides, the majority of fem. nouns have the ending ָה in the *sing.*

The original *fem.* ending was *a̲t̲h̲* ַת. This is used in the construct (§ 14. 3d) and sometimes is found as simple ת (cf. מוֹאָבִית *Moabitess*, from מוֹאָבִי).

(d) The *masc. plur.* is formed by adding ִים (*îm*) to the *sing.*, e.g. טוֹבִים; and the *fem. plur.* by changing ָה (*ā*) into וֹת (*ô̲t̲h̲*), e.g. טוֹבָה, טוֹבוֹת, or by adding *ô̲t̲h̲* to the *sing.* if it has no *fem.* termination, e.g. רוּחַ *wind*, רוּחוֹת.

(e) The *dual* is formed by adding ַיִם (*áyim*: ׳ consonantal) to the *masc. sing.* for the *masc.*, and to the original *fem. sing.*

(which was ־ַת *ath*) for the *fem.* Thus: from סוּס, סוּסַ֫יִם; from סוּסָה (orig. סוּסַת), סוּסָתַ֫יִם (*a* under ס lengthened to *ā*, because pretonic, § 5. 2b).

	masc.		*fem.*	*masc.*		*fem.*	
sing.	טוֹב	*good*	טוֹבָה	סוּס	*horse*	סוּסָה	*mare*
plur.	טוֹבִים	,,	טוֹבוֹת	סוּסִים	,,	סוּסוֹת	,,
dual				סוּסַ֫יִם	,,	סוּסָתַ֫יִם	,,

5. *Classes of nouns feminine.* (a) Words ending in ָה or ת; e.g. צְדָקָה *righteousness,* בְּרָכָה *blessing,* מִצְרִית *an Egyptian woman* (from מִצְרִי *an Egyptian*), עִבְרִיָּה *a Hebrew woman* (from עִבְרִי *a Hebrew*).

(b) Words of any termination that are names of female creatures, as אֵם *mother,* רָחֵל *ewe..*

(c) Names of cities, countries, &c., which may be considered *mothers* of their inhabitants; e.g. צִיּוֹן *Zion,* אַשּׁוּר *Assyria.*

(d) Names of organs of the body of men or animals, especially such organs as are double, as יָד *hand,* אֹ֫זֶן *ear,* קֶ֫רֶן *horn*; but רֹאשׁ *head,* אַף *nose,* פֶּה *mouth* and לֵב *heart* are *masc.*

(e) Names of things productive, the elements, unseen essences, &c., as אֶ֫רֶץ *earth,* אֵשׁ *fire,* נֶ֫פֶשׁ *soul,* רוּחַ *spirit.*

In all these classes, however, there are numerous exceptions; and many words are of both genders, though in general where this is the case one gender is largely predominant in usage over the other; e.g. דֶּ֫רֶךְ *way,* masc. (less often fem.), שֶׁ֫מֶשׁ *sun* fem. (less often masc.).

(f) Words *fem.* usually assume the distinctive *fem.* termination in the *plural*; e.g. צְדָקָה, צְדָקוֹת; כּוֹס, כֹּסוֹת *cup.* Some *fem* nouns, however, have the *masc. plur.* ending, e.g. שָׁנָה *year,* regular pl. שָׁנִים (in poetry sometimes שָׁנוֹת), and on the contrary some *masc.* words have the *fem.* termination in the *plur.*, e.g. אָב *father,* pl. אָבוֹת, especially if they incline towards a *fem.* sense by (d) or (e); e.g. לֵבָב *heart,* pl. לְבָבוֹת, קוֹל *voice,* pl. קוֹלֹת or קֹלוֹת (§ 2. 7d).

As a rule, the plur. takes the gender of the sing.; e.g. אָבוֹת טוֹבִים *good fathers,* שָׁנִים טֹבוֹת *good years.*

(g) The *fem.* often corresponds to the Greek or Latin neuter; e.g. טוֹבָה *welfare,* רָעָה *misery,* זֹאת *this* (τοῦτο).

6. *The Dual.* (a) The *Dual* is confined to substantives (and the numeral שְׁנַיִם *two*); it is no more found in the adjective, pronoun or verb. It is not used to express two in general; e.g. two horses would not be סוּסַיִם, nor would two songs be שִׁירַיִם (cf. § 45. 1). It is used of things which are found in pairs, both of organs of the body and of things made in pairs; e.g. *eyes* עֵינַיִם, *ears* אָזְנַיִם (*'oznáyim*), *hands* יָדַיִם, *feet* רַגְלַיִם, *lips* שְׂפָתַיִם (from שָׂפָה), *horns* קַרְנַיִם, *shoes* נַעֲלַיִם, *tongs* מֶלְקָחַיִם; and with one or two other common words, e.g. יוֹמַיִם *two days,* שְׁנָתַיִם *two years.*

(b) Verbs and adjectives, having no dual, use the plural with a dual noun, עֵינַיִם רָמוֹת וְיָדַיִם שֹׁפְכוֹת דָּם *haughty* (high) *eyes and hands that shed blood.*

(c) When terms denoting members of the body are used to express inanimate objects, the *fem. plur.* is used; e.g. קַרְנוֹת *horns* of the altar.

(d) The vowel before the dual termination, if open, is long, being pretonic (§ 5. 2b), e.g. שְׂפָתַיִם *ś·phāth※áyim.*

(e) מַיִם *water,* and שָׁמַיִם *heaven,* are not duals, but plur. from unused sing. forms (מַי and שָׁמַי).

פַּר [1] ox	פָּרָה *f.* cow	גִּבּוֹר hero, mighty man
סוּס horse	סוּסָה *f.* mare	
כּוֹכָב star	שַׂר [1] prince, officer	שָׂרָה *f.* princess

[1] The words פַּר, שַׂר, have, for etymological reasons (§ 40), *a* (*path.*); with the Article, פַּר has ָ *ā* (cf. § 9, Note (i) to Voc.), the other has ַ *a.*

בְּאֵר	*f.* well	שִׁיר	song	שִׁירָה	*f.* song
דָּם	blood	נָבִיא	prophet	חֲלוֹם	(*pl.* חֲלֹמוֹת) dream
לֶ֫חֶם	bread	נָתַן	to give, to set	הָרַג	to slay
סָפַר	to count				
זָכַר	to remember	שָׁתָה	to drink	חָדָשׁ	new

EXERCISE

Translate

אֵלֶּה הַפָּרוֹת הָֽרָעוֹת אֲשֶׁר רָאָה הַמֶּ֫לֶךְ בָּעִיר׃ 2 מָשַׁל הָֽאָדָם
בַּבְּהֵמָֽה׃ 3 הֵמָּה הַשָּׂרִים וְהַגִּבּוֹרִים אֲשֶׁר נָתַן הַמֶּ֫לֶךְ עַל־הָעָֽם׃
4 אָמַרְתִּי אֶל־הָעָם הַזֶּה צַדִּיקִים אַתֶּֽם׃ 5 הֶֽהָרִים הָאֵ֫לֶּה רָמִים
מְאֹד׃ 6 סָפַרְתָּ אֶת־הַכּוֹכָבִים׃ 7 מָה רָמִים הַהֵיכָלִים הָהֵם
בָּעִיר׃ 8 רָאָה הַמֶּ֫לֶךְ כִּי [1]חֲכָמִים הַדְּבָרִים אֲשֶׁר אָמַר הַשַּׂר
הַצַּדִּיק לָעָֽם׃ 9 טוֹבֹת הַשִּׁירֹת אֲשֶׁר שָׁמַעְתִּי בַּֽהֵיכָֽל׃ 10 עֵינַ֫יִם
רָמוֹת וְאָזְנַ֫יִם כְּבֵדוֹת וְיָדַ֫יִם אֲשֶׁר שָֽׁפְכוּ דָֽם׃ 11 ראה המלך
בחלום את־הפרות הטבות על־ההיכל׃ 12 זכר יהוה כי עפר
אנחנו׃

I remember (*perf.*) the songs which I heard in the temple. 2 Those heavens (are) very lofty. 3 These (are) the asses which we slew. 4 Who (are) these princes and heroes? 5 Thou hast heard the cows. 6 God remembers the just (*pl.*). 7 We sat on the hills two days. 8 Bread he ate and water he drank. 9 The just are as the stars which (are) in the firmament. 10 He took oxen and cows and horses and asses. 11 I counted the stars which God has set in the heavens. 12 Water from the wells. 13 God gave me a new song. 14 Thou (*f.*) hast spilt blood (*pl.*). 15 Two days we rested in the temple and there we remembered the good things which God had done for us.

[1] In the Old Testament חָכָם is used only of persons.

§ 14. CASES—THE CONSTRUCT STATE—CASE ENDINGS—*HE LOCALE*

1. *The Construct State.* There is reason to believe that Hebrew, like Arabic, once had three cases, the nominative, accusative and genitive, ending respectively in *u*, *a*, and *i* (see 5 below). In such a phrase as *the palace of the king*, the close genitival relationship between the governing noun (*nomen regens*) and the governed (*nomen rectum*) is expressed in Hebrew in a way which demands special attention; it has no analogy in the corresponding Latin or Greek construction. The first noun *palace* which is dependent for its full definition upon the noun in the genitive which follows is said to be in the *construct state* before that genitive; the second noun *king*, being independent, is in the *absolute* state (§ 13. 4a, iii).

2. (a) The cstr. relation corresponds most nearly to the relations expressed by *of* in English, in all its many senses: e.g. *the palace of the king, the son of the father, a ring of gold, the fear of God, a song of Zion.* This relation is usually, not invariably, expressed by *of*: when the first word is, as it may be and often is, an adjective or participle, it may be expressed by *in*, &c.; e.g. in "great in power, fair in appearance, broken in heart". *Great, fair*, and *broken* would be in the construct, *power, appearance*, and *heart* in the absolute.

(b) The point is that the whole phrase in each case must be uttered before the idea or subject of reference is fully defined. In consequence, the word in the construct and the following word in the genitive relationship are conceived to be, and are treated as, one unit of speech with one main accent which falls inevitably upon the noun in the absolute, the noun in the construct being hurriedly pronounced. The effect of this upon the noun in the construct is to shorten, as far as possible, any tone long vowels in it.

3. *Forms of words in the construct.* (a) Abs. דָּבָר (both vowels tone long, cf. § 5. 2b) has constr. דְּבַר, which is the shortest form it can assume (the final syllable בַר, being

closed, requires a full vowel, while in the preceding דְּ the vocal shᵉwa represents the minimum of vocalic sound).

(b) In the case of the *plur.* in *îm* and the *dual* in *áyim*, the *m* is elided in each case in the construct and the ending becomes *ê*. The construct of דְּבָרִים is דִּבְרֵי (the בָ of the absolute form, when hurriedly pronounced, being reduced to בְ, and דִּ being required instead of דְּ of the absolute because two vocal shᵉwas cannot come together (§ 5. 2d, i)). In דִּבְרֵי the shᵉwa is vocal because it represents an original full vowel; consequently, if the third root letter is one of the *bᵉghadhkᵉphath*, it does not take dagh. lene; e.g. abs. plur. כְּבֵדִים, constr. כִּבְדֵי (not כִּבְדֵּי).

(c) The dual cstr. is similarly formed; e.g. abs. קַרְנַ֫יִם *horns*, cstr. קַרְנֵי; abs. יָדַ֫יִם *hands*, cstr. יְדֵי. So from שָׂפָה *lip*, dual abs. שְׂפָתַ֫יִם (§ 13. 6), cstr. שִׂפְתֵי.

(d) In *fem. sing.* the original ending ־ַת (§ 13. 4c) is resumed; e.g. abs. סוּסָה *mare*, constr. סוּסַת; abs. צְדָקָה *righteousness*, constr. צִדְקַת (צִדְ < צְדָ; *ṣidhᵉqath*); abs. אֲדָמָה *ground*, constr. אַדְמַת (אַדְ < אֲדָ; cf. § 5. 2d, ii).

(e) *Fem. pl. cstr.* ends, like abs., in וֹת, but is shortened, like all constructs, as much as possible; pl. abs. צְדָקוֹת, cstr. צִדְקוֹת.

4. סוּס, with its unchangeable vowel, illustrates the endings in their simplest form: the other illustrations show how the changeable vowels are affected—יָשָׁר *upright*, יָד *hand*, שָׂפָה *lip*.

	Mas.			*Fem.*		
	Abs.		*Cstr.*	*Abs.*		*Cstr.*
sing.	סוּס	horse	סוּס	סוּסָה	mare	סוּסַת
plur.	סוּסִים	horses	סוּסֵי	סוּסוֹת	mares	סוּסוֹת
dual	סוּסַ֫יִם	horses	סוּסֵי	סוּסָתַ֫יִם	mares	סוּסְתֵי

	Masc.	*Fem.*		*Masc.*[1]	*Fem.*
abs. sing.	יָשָׁר	יְשָׁרָה	*abs. sing.*	יָד	שָׂפָה
cstr. sing.	יְשַׁר	יִשְׁרַת	*cstr. sing.*	יַד	שְׂפַת
abs. plur.	יְשָׁרִים	יְשָׁרוֹת	*abs. dual*	יָדַ֫יִם	שְׂפָתַ֫יִם
cstr. plur.	יִשְׁרֵי	יִשְׁרוֹת	*cstr. dual*	יְדֵי	שִׂפְתֵי

Rules of Usage.

Rule 1. The construct *never* has the article; the absolute, when it is definite, has it according to normal usage (cf. §§ 8. 1; 9. 4a, i); and the construct is definite or indefinite according to the definiteness or indefiniteness of the absolute standing in the genitive relationship to it. If the absolute is definite, the construct also is definite; if it is indefinite, the construct also is indefinite; thus *the king's horse* (never in this order in Hebrew, but always *the horse of the king*), סוּס[2] הַמֶּ֫לֶךְ (not הַסּוּס הַמֶּ֫לֶךְ); *the man of war, the warrior,* אִישׁ הַמִּלְחָמָה; *the word of the prophet,* דְּבַר הַנָּבִיא; *the righteousness of the people,* צִדְקַת הָעָם; *the lips of the girl* שִׂפְתֵי הַנַּעֲרָה; but *a warrior,* אִישׁ מִלְחָמָה; *a word of a prophet,* דְּבַר נָבִיא.

Note that מִזְמוֹר דָּוִד is *the psalm of David,* because David, being a proper name, is definite; similarly הַר יהוה is *the mountain of Yahweh.* Such a phrase as *a psalm of David* is expressed in Hebrew as מִזְמוֹר לְדָוִד.

So with adjs.: *a good-looking girl,* נַעֲרָה טוֹבַת מַרְאֶה (lit. *good in appearance*), *a woman of good understanding* (אִשָּׁה טוֹבַת שֶׂכֶל lit. *good of understanding*); and with participles, (*the*) *broken-hearted,* נִשְׁבְּרֵי־לֵב (lit. *those who are broken* (pl. cstr. of נִשְׁבָּר) *in heart*).

[1] יָד is *fem.*, but may be used here for illustration's sake, as it has not the fem. ending.

[2] Since the student has now had some experience of nouns such as יָדַ֫יִם, שָׁמַ֫יִם, מַ֫יִם, אֶ֫רֶץ, מֶ֫לֶךְ etc. which are accented on the penultimate syllable, they will no longer be marked with the accentual sign < in the text.

Rule 2. The cstr. must immediately precede the noun to which it is related; therefore two (co-ordinate) constructs cannot precede the same noun; e.g. *the hands and lips of the man* would *not* be יְדֵי וְשִׂפְתֵי הָאִישׁ, because יְדֵי being construct must precede הָאִישׁ. Hebrew writes therefore *the hands of the man and his lips,* יְדֵי הָאִישׁ וּשְׂפָתָיו; *the prince's sons and daughters,* not בְּנֵי וּבְנוֹת הַשַּׂר, but בְּנֵי הַשַּׂר וּבְנוֹתָיו. Similarly in phrases like *the God of heaven and earth,* the cstr. is, as a rule, repeated: thus אֱלֹהֵי הַשָּׁמַיִם וֵאלֹהֵי הָאָרֶץ rather than אלהי השמים והארץ (in which אֱלֹהֵי is separated from הָאָרֶץ and, in consequence, can strictly be in the cstr. before הַשָּׁמַיִם alone).

Such a *succession* of constructs, however, as דֶּרֶךְ עֵץ הַחַיִּים *the way of* (i.e. *to*) *the tree of life*; יְמֵי שְׁנֵי חַיֵּי אֲבוֹתַי *the days of the years of the life of my fathers,* constitutes a unity and is perfectly normal.

Rule 3. An adj. qualifying a noun in the cstr. must stand after the compound phrase, and, if the noun in the cstr. is definite, the adj. takes the article; e.g. *a good warrior,* אִישׁ מִלְחָמָה טוֹב; *the good horses of the king,* סוּסֵי הַמֶּלֶךְ הַטּוֹבִים (i.e. *the horses of the king, the good ones*; סוּסֵי הַמֶּלֶךְ הַטּוֹב would be *the good king's horses*); *the king's good mare,* סוּסַת הַמֶּלֶךְ הַטּוֹבָה (with הַטּוֹב for הַטּוֹבָה, it would mean *the good king's mare*).

If the gender and number of the cstr. and abs. happened to be identical, a certain ambiguity would arise: סוּסַת הַמַּלְכָּה הַטּוֹבָה *the queen's good mare, the good queen's mare*; but these cases would be obviously few, and the context would usually decide. Ambiguity may be definitely avoided by the use of a relative clause; e.g. *the queen's good mare,* הַסּוּסָה הַטּוֹבָה אֲשֶׁר לַמַּלְכָּה; i.e. *the good mare which* (*belongs*) *to the queen.*

The above illustrations show that, though an adj. agrees with its noun in gend. and numb. it does not agree in state. Even when a noun is in the cstr. its adj. is in the abs.

5. *Case Endings.* In some Semitic languages the cases are

marked by these terminations: nom. *-u*, accus. *-a*, gen. *-e* or *-i*. Of these, little trace remains in classical Hebrew; the *û* in שְׁמוּאֵל, and the *ô* of בְּנוֹ as in בְּנוֹ צִפּוֹר, (Num. 23, 18) may illustrate residual nom. terminations, the *ā* as in חָלִ֫ילָה an accus., the *i* of בְּנִי as in בְּנִי אֲתוֹנוֹ (*his ass's colt*; Gen. 49, 11) a gen. The commonly-held view that the ־ָה as in צָפ֫וֹנָה *northwards*, the so-called *He Locale*, or *He* of direction, was an accus. ending is now questioned; it is probably a distinct usage, and there is evidence that the *He* was originally marked with a *mappîq*. This use of the ending ־ָה, the *He Locale*, to indicate direction, does not take the tone; so הַבַּ֫יְתָה *homewards*, הָהָ֫רָה *towards the mountain*. It even admits a preposition prefixed to the word with which it is used; e.g. לִשְׁאוֹלָה *to Sheol*. It may be affixed to the plural; e.g. הַשָּׁמַ֫יְמָה *heavenwards*, and even to a noun in the cstr. state, e.g. בֵּ֫יתָה יוֹסֵף *to the house of Joseph*.

It is used occasionally even with reference to time; e.g. מִיָּמִים יָמִ֫ימָה *from year* (lit. *days*) *to year*. It may not be used with reference to persons; *to* (*towards*) *David* would not be דָּוִ֫דָה but אֶל־דָּוִד.

צָפוֹן	*f.* north	יְאֹר	river, Nile	אֶבְיוֹן	poor
רוּחַ	*f.*[1] wind, spirit	חַ֫יִל	valour, force, army	יְשׁוּעָה	*f.* salvation, deliverance
מִצְוָה	*f.* command	עִיר	*f.* city	תּוֹרָה	*f.* law, instruction
מַתָּן	gift, gifts (coll.)	בָּשָׂר	flesh		
		בַּת	*f.* daughter	מַלְכָּה	*f.* queen
שְׁאוֹל	*f.* Sheol, the underworld	יָרַד	to go down	אַרְבַּע	four
		נָטָה	to stretch	הָלַךְ	to go
בָּטַח בְּ	to trust	נִשְׁבָּר	broken	שָׁבַר	to break

[1] Less often *masc.*

Note.—תּוֹרָה, being derived from a verb which meant originally *to shoot* (arrows) can mean (a) an oracle, response or ruling given by seer, prophet or priest, (b) teaching from God given through prophet or priest, instruction, and (c) the law of God, and, specifically, the Law of Moses.

רוּחַ can mean (a) breath, both as mere breath and breath of life, (b) wind, (c) animation, temper, courage, zeal, (d) spirit, the life-spirit as the gift of God, and (e) the spirit of God, the source of all the gifts of the spirit in men.

EXERCISE

Translate

תּוֹרַת יהוה טוֹבָה לְאָדָם וְרוּחַ הָאֱלֹהִים עֲצוּמָה אֶל־יְשׁוּעָה׃
2 סָפַר יהוה אֶת־כּוֹכְבֵי הַשָּׁמַיִם וְגַם יָדַע אֶת־כָּל־הָאָרֶץ׃ 3
אֶבְיוֹנֵי הָעָם הֵם צַדִּיקִים׃ 4 לֹא שָׁמַרְנוּ תּוֹרַת יהוה אֱלֹהֵי יִשְׂרָאֵל׃
5 עָשָׂה הַשַּׂר כְּמִצְוַת הַמֶּלֶךְ׃ 6 וּבְתוֹרַת יהוה לֹא [1]הָלָכְתָּ׃ 7 אֵלֶּה
מִצְוֹת אֱלֹהֵי כָל־הָאָרֶץ אֲשֶׁר כָּתַבְתִּי הַיּוֹם הַזֶּה׃ 8 בִּימֵי דָוִד
הַמֶּלֶךְ שָׁמְרוּ כָּל־הָעָם אֶת־תּוֹרַת יהוה וְהָאֶבְיוֹנִים בָּטְחוּ בוֹ׃
9 בָּא חַיִל גָּדוֹל מֵאַרְבַּע רוּחוֹת [1]הַשָּׁמָיִם׃ 10 אָכַלְנוּ מִכָּל־עֵץ
[1]הַגָּן׃ 11 וּמַלְכַּת הָאָרֶץ בַּת אִישׁ גִּבּוֹר [1]חָיִל׃ 12 הָיָה רָעָב בָּאָרֶץ
וְאַבְרָם יָרַד מִצְרַיְמָה כִּי כָבֵד הָרָעָב בָּאָרֶץ׃ 13 תּוֹרַת יהוה
טוֹבָה׃ 14 ביום ההוא עשה יהוה ישועה בישראל׃

The great day of Yahweh. 2 The day of Yahweh (is) great. 3 The good queen of the land. 4 All the people of the earth. 5 All the king's good asses. 6 The captain (prince) saw all the mighty-men of valour and all the people of war. 7 I have gone northwards. 8 We are gone down to Sheol. 9 He went towards-the-mountain. 10 We slew the man's ass. 11 The people did not drink from the waters of the river, for they (were) blood.[2] 12 Ye have not kept the commandments of

---

[1] Observe the pausal vowels in 6, 9, 10, 11 (cf. § 11, note to Exer.).

[2] In dependent clauses with כִּי *for, that,* &c., the pronoun is put last.

the God of all the earth. 13 God of the earth and of the spirits of all flesh. 14 Thou hast kept the poor of the land from all ill. 15 Thou (*f.*) hast eaten of the tree of the garden. 16 The prophet heard the word of the Lord in the temple and there he remained and did not go home. 17 The sons of the king and his daughters[1] took the gift to the man of God and he (וְהוּא) stretched his hands[2] heavenwards and to the people he gave an instruction from the God of all the earth.

§ 15. THE FIRST DECLENSION. K^E^THIBH AND Q^E^RE

Nouns may be arranged in Declensions according to their vowels and according to the internal vowel changes produced by alteration in the place of Tone occasioned by *Inflection* (§ 13. 2). Many forms of Nouns, however, contain unchangeable vowels, i.e. vowels pure long, or diphthongal (§ 2. 2, 6), or unchangeable by position, as גִּבּוֹר (*gibbôr*) *a hero,* אֶבְיוֹן (*'ebh-yôn*) *poor,* in both of which the first vowel is unchangeable by position (short, because in closed syllable, גִּבּ, אֶבְ), and the second pure long (as we might infer from its consonantal representation וֹ), and consequently unchangeable by nature. Such Nouns, as they suffer no internal change from inflection, do not seem to require classification. No additions at the end can in any way affect the vowels of either syllable; e.g. plur. גִּבּוֹרִים, אֶבְיוֹנִים; גִּבּוֹרֵי, אֶבְיוֹנֵי.

The forms that suffer change are those having *tone-long* vowels; e.g. in each of the words דָּבָר, זָקֵן (not זָקִין), לֵבָב (not לֵיבָב) both vowels are tone-long, and are therefore both subject to change. These vowels, having been rarely expressed by the so-called *Vowel-letters* (§ 2. 6, 7), may very generally be distinguished from pure long, and diphthongal, vowels, which were usually so expressed (§ 2. 6). In general only *qāmeṣ* and *ṣērê* are tone-long in nouns, as in the above illustrations; *ḥôlem* being for the most part unchangeably long, and therefore usually represented by ו; e.g. גָּדוֹל (*gādhôl*), כּוֹכָב (*kôkhābh*).

[1] Cf. § 14. 4. Rule 2. [2] יָדָיו.

In these words the *ā* is subject to change, being only tone-long, but not the *ô*.

The forms with changeable vowels seem capable of being generalized under *three* classes or Declensions.

1. *The first declension.* This declension contains words having:

ā ָ in the pretone (זָקֵן, אָדוֹן) or in the tone (כּוֹכָב, לֵבָב) or in both positions (דָּבָר, יָשָׁר).

We may conveniently include within this declension, not only nouns, but participles and adjectives which satisfy the condition concerning vocalization.

If the principles concerning the effect of the tone upon the vowels (§ 5) be clearly understood, and also the rules for the formation of the plur. (§ 13) and the construct (§ 14), no special rules for this declension are necessary. We have only to remember that when words are increased at the end (e.g. by ִים., ָה, &c.) the accent falls upon the significant inflectional addition; e.g. דָּבָר, but דְּבָרִ֫ים. The tone, falling on *bhār* in the sing., falls on *rîm* in the pl.; *bhā*, being pretonic, has the long *ā*, and the original *dā* of *dābhắr*, being now *two* places from the tone (and open), becomes *d*ᵉ. The construct, which, as we have seen, is always made as short as possible (§ 14. 2b), becomes דְּבַר (sing.) and דִּבְרֵי (pl.): the shᵉwa in pl. is vocal, hence no daghesh in *bᵉghadhkᵉphath* letters; e.g. כּוֹכְבֵי, לִבְבוֹת.

Note that the form with vocalization *ā-ē*, e.g. זָקֵן, has *a* in the constr. sing. זְקַן.

A few words have, in the construct, *sᵉghôl* in both syllables: e.g. גָּדֵר *wall*, cstr. גֶּדֶר (pronominal suffix, § 16, regularly of the type גְּדֵרוֹ *his wall*); כָּתֵף *shoulder*, c. כֶּתֶף; יָרֵךְ *thigh*, c. יֶרֶךְ; כָּבֵד *heavy*, c. both כְּבַד and כֶּבֶד.

	Sing.	Plur.	Cstr. sing.	Cstr. plur.
(1) upright	יָשָׁר	יְשָׁרִים	יְשַׁר	יִשְׁרֵי (< יְשְׁרֵי)
(2) old, old man, elder	זָקֵן	זְקֵנִים	זְקַן	זִקְנֵי (< זְקְנֵי)
(3) great	גָּדוֹל	גְּדוֹלִים	גְּדוֹל	גְּדוֹלֵי
(4) blessed	בָּרוּךְ	בְּרוּכִים	בְּרוּךְ	בְּרוּכֵי
(5) overseer	פָּקִיד	פְּקִידִים	פְּקִיד	פְּקִידֵי
(6) heart	לֵבָב	לְבָבוֹת	לְבַב	לִבְבוֹת (< לְבְבוֹת)
(7) star	כּוֹכָב	כּוֹכָבִים	כּוֹכַב	כּוֹכְבֵי
(8) desert	מִדְבָּר	מִדְבָּרִים	מִדְבַּר	מִדְבְּרֵי

Rem.—The forms 1, 2, 3 with vowels *ā—ā, ā—ē, ā—ô,* may be considered the typical forms of this declension. The forms 4, 5 are pass. participles, and 6 is a less common nominal formation.

2. *Feminine nouns* ending in ה ָ have in the constr. sing. the original ת ַ of the feminine (cf. § 13. 4c). The construct, as usual, is pronounced as rapidly as is consistent with the laws of the language (§ 14. 3a): abs. שָׂפָה *lip,* cstr. שְׂפַת.

Abs. sing.	צְדָקָה	*righteousness.*	cstr.	צִדְקַת	(< צְדְקַת)
Abs. plur.	צְדָקוֹת	*righteousnesses.*	cstr.	צִדְקוֹת	(< צְדְקוֹת)
Abs. sing.	נְבֵלָה	*corpse.*	cstr.	נִבְלַת	(< נְבְלַת)

The shᵉwa in the cstr. (sing. and pl.) is vocal. But in cstr. sing. of בְּרָכָה *blessing,* the first syllable is closed בִּרְכַּת.

Some fem. nouns retain the long *ē* under inflection: e.g. גְּזֵלָה *plunder,* cstr. גְּזֵלַת; גְּנֵבָה *thing stolen,* 3 sing. masc. suff. (§ 16) גְּנֵבָתוֹ.

3. A few monosyllables with changeable vowels (*ā ē*) in the tone attach themselves to this declension. They are probably real dissyllables, which have undergone contraction. The chief are יָד *hand,* דָּם *blood,* דָּג *fish,* עֵץ *tree.* They are inflected exactly like the last syllable of דָּבָר (or זָקֵן);

as this is in sing. abs. בָּר cstr. בַּר plur. abs. בָּרִים cstr. בָּרֵי
so we have sing. abs. דָּם cstr. דַּם plur. abs. דָּמִים cstr. דְּמֵי
עֵץ cstr. עֵץ[1] plur. abs. עֵצִים cstr. עֲצֵי

So פָּנִים *face* (plur.), cstr. פְּנֵי.

זָכָר male	קָצֵר short	תָּמִים perfect
דָּבָר word	מָאוֹר *m.* } luminary	שָׂפָה *f.* lip, shore
מָשָׁל proverb	מְאוֹרֹת *pl.* } luminary	בְּרָכָה *f.* blessing
כָּבֵד heavy	נָבִיא prophet	נְקָמָה *f.* vengeance
קָדוֹשׁ holy	בָּרִיא fat	נְבֵלָה *f.* corpse

EXERCISE

Write the *cstr. sing.* and the *abs.* and *cstr. pl.* of the above words. (The *abs.* and *cstr. dual* of שָׂפָה.)

שְׁנַ֫יִם two	חוֹל sand	אָסַף to gather
נָשָׂא to lift up	יָם sea	יִצְחָק Isaac
יַעֲקֹב Jacob	לָ֫מָּה why? (לְ מָה, for what reason?),	
שָׁם there	עֵשָׂו Esau	עֵצָה *f.* counsel

Parse and Translate

בְּרִיאוֹת, נְבִיאֵי, יִשְׁרֵי, רְקִיעַ, לְבָבוֹת, מְאוֹר, מִשְׁלֵי, כְּבַד, לְבַב,
שִׂפְתֵי, נִקְמַת, בִּרְכוֹת, יָדַיִם: וְחֹשֶׁךְ עַל־פְּנֵי הַמָּ֫יִם: 2 כָּתַב
הַנָּבִיא אֶת־כָּל־הַדְּבָרִים בַּסֵּֽפֶר: 3 הָיָה דְבַר יהוה אֶל־
הַנְּבִיאִֽים: 4 תּוֹרַת יהוה בִּלְבַב הַצַּדִּיקִֽים: 5 כָּתַבְתִּי לָעָם הַזֶּה
אֶת־כָּל־דִּבְרֵי תוֹרַת יְהוָֽה: 6 לֹא הָיָה שָׁם אִישׁ מִזִּקְנֵי יִשְׂרָאֵֽל:
7 נָתַן אֱלֹהִים אֶת־שְׁנֵי הַמְּאוֹרוֹת הַגְּדֹלִים בִּרְקִיעַ הַשָּׁמָ֫יִם: 8 אָסַף
הַשַּׂר חַיִל כָּבֵד כְּכוֹכְבֵי הַשָּׁמַיִם וְכַחוֹל אֲשֶׁר עַל־שְׂפַת הַיָּֽם:

---

[1] Same as abs.; similarly in the case of דָּג.

9 אָמַר יִצְחָק הַקּוֹל קוֹל יַעֲקֹב וְהַיָּדַיִם יְדֵי עֵשָׂו׃ 10 נָשָׂא הַנָּבִיא הַזָּקֵן אֶת־נִבְלַת אִישׁ הָאֱלֹהִים אֶל־הַחֲמוֹר׃ 11 צִדְקוֹת[1] יהוה אֱלֹהֵי יִשְׂרָאֵל גְּדוֹלָה מְאֹד 12 לְנִשְׁבְּרֵי[2] לֵב׃ 12 כבד־לשון אנכי׃
13 קרא החכם בספר תורת האלהים׃

The law of Yahweh (is) perfect. 2 The king saw the fat kine upon the bank (lip) of the river. 3 Ye have eaten the flesh of fat oxen. 4 The words of the lips of Yahweh (are) upright. 5 I (am) not a man of words. 6 Good (are) the words of the law of Yahweh. 7 The waters (are) upon the face of the ground. 8 We have heard the words of the prophets of the God of all the earth. 9 Thou hast kept the heart of this people from evil. 10 Very great (are) the righteousnesses of God. 11 Blessed (are) the upright of heart. 12 The vengeance of the people (was) great. 13 The proverbs of the wise king (are) perfect. 14 He destroyed all the fishes of the river. 15 The proverbs of the old king are very wise.

Note.—In צִדְקוֹת the consonantal text, called כְּתִיב, *K*ᵉ*thîbh* (*written*) demands the reading צִדְקוֹת, but the vowels in the text indicate that what is to be read (קְרֵי, *Q*ᵉ*rê*, *read*) is צִדְקֹת. The explanation of this is that the Massoretic scholars regarded the consonantal text as inviolable. When, therefore, for any reason, of tradition, grammar or propriety, they preferred another reading to that of the consonantal text, the vowels of this reading were attached to the *K*ᵉ*thîbh*, while the consonants of it, which could not be inserted into the text, were placed in the margin. This recommended reading in such a case is named the *Q*ᵉ*rê*. Attention is called to the margin by a small circle or obelus placed over the *K*ᵉ*thîbh* thus: הַנַּעֲרָ֯, Gen. 24, 14. The marginal note (unpointed) to which attention is thus drawn runs הנערה קרי (or simply הנערה ק׳), i.e. הַנַּעֲרָה is to be read; the vowels to accompany this recommended reading are those which are attached to the *K*ᵉ*thîbh* in the text.

[1] For this form see the note at the foot of the Exercise. [2] Cf. § 14. 4, Rule 1, final para.

In the case of יהוה and a few other words of very frequent occurrence, the *Qᵉrê* is not placed in the margin, but its vowels are simply inserted in the text. יהוה was so venerated that it was called the separated name, too holy to be uttered by the lips of men. Therefore, whenever it occurred in the reading of the sacred text, אֲדֹנָי Lord was read in its place; the vowels of אֲדֹנָי were attached to יהוה thus, יְהֹוָה (i.e. with ְ written after י instead of the ֲ which follows א in אֲדֹנָי) but the consonants were not written in the margin. (It is to be noted that in Kittel's *Biblia Hebraica* (3rd and later editions) we find יְהוָה[1], i.e. the *Qᵉrê* is שְׁמָא *šᵉmā*, *Aram.* for *the name*.)

§ 16. THE PRONOMINAL SUFFIXES

The separate Personal Pronouns are used only as nominatives to express the Subject (§ 10).

1. Hebrew has not largely developed the adjective; instead of saying *holy hill, silver idols, eloquent man*, it says *hill of holiness*, הַר קֹדֶשׁ; *idols of silver*, אֱלִילֵי כֶסֶף; *man of words*, אִישׁ דְּבָרִים, and the like. Similarly for *my horse* it says *horse-of-me*; the possessive pronouns *my, thy, his, our*, &c. are altogether wanting. In other words, what we have in such cases is—ideally—a noun in the construct, followed by a personal pronoun in the absolute, which, however, is not now written as a separate word, but attached to the noun as a suffix. There are a few words in which this process is still perfectly clear, and the pronoun is present in practically its original form; e.g. אָבִיהוּ *his father* (father-of-him, הוּא); but in all words the pronoun is really present, though not often so obvious; e.g. סוּסוֹ *his horse*. Here the original *sûs-hû* (horse-of-him) became first, by means of the helping vowel *a* (appropriate before the guttural *h*) *sûsahû*; then that was abbreviated to *sûsaû*, the *h* being elided and not written (§ 12. 1e) and *sûsaû* easily passed into *sûsô* (§ 2. 2a).

[1] But when the preposition לְ is prefixed to the name, the pointing is לַיהוָה.

All the so-called pronominal suffixes correspond, with simple modifications similarly accounted for, to the significant parts of the personal pronouns § 10, except that in the second person *k* appears instead of *t*. The slight occasional differences between the forms of the suffixes, according as they are attached to singular or dual and plural nouns, should be carefully noted. E.g. in סוּסֵיהֶם *their horses,* the ה of the original 3rd pers. pron. (הֵם) is preserved; in סוּסָם *their horse,* it has disappeared (as in סוּסוֹ).

2. (a) The suffixes are divided into *light* and *heavy*; the heavy are those containing *two consonants*—כֶם, כֶן, הֶם, הֶן (not נוּ *nû*, for the ו is a vowel); all the others are light. Before the heavy suffixes the actual construct form of the noun appears explicitly: e.g. דְּבַרְכֶם *the word of you, your word*; דִּבְרֵיכֶם *the words of you, your words*; דִּבְרֵיהֶם *the words of them, their words* (דְּבַר and דִּבְרֵי being respectively cstr. sing. and pl. of דָּבָר); so סוּסַתְכֶם *your mare,* צִדְקַתְכֶם *your righteousness,* שִׂפְתֵיכֶם *your lips* (dual.). Before the light suffixes, the regular rules of vocalization apply (§ 5), which are illustrated, e.g., in the formation of the plural—דְּבָרִים from דָּבָר. Thus, *my word* = דְּבָרִ֫י: the accent falls at the end, on the suffix; the pretonic syllable being open, its vowel is long; the vowel before that, being in an open syllable removed two places from the tone, is reduced to vocal shᵉwa. So דְּבָרוֹ *his word,* דְּבָרֵ֫נוּ *our word* (note that the accent falls on the ֵ), שְׂפָתִי *my lip*. Similarly with a plural noun: *my words* דְּבָרַ֫י; *our words* דְּבָרֵ֫ינוּ (not דִּבְרֵינוּ, because נוּ is not one of the heavy suffixes); so שְׂפָתַ֫יִךְ (*f.*) *thy lips,* שְׂפָתֵ֫ינוּ *our lips,* but שִׂפְתֵיהֶם *their lips.*

(b) For purpose of vocalization, it is obviously important to know where the accent falls; in the paradigms it is specially marked, when it does not fall upon the last syllable. It may be put thus: (a) the heavy suffixes take the accent, e.g. דִּבְרֵיכֶ֫ם *your words,* דִּבְרֵיהֶ֫ם *their words*; (b) the light suffixes take the accent, except those which are dissyllabic, in which it falls upon the penult: e.g. דְּבָרַ֫י *my words,* but סוּסֵ֫נוּ *our horse,* דְּבָרֵ֫נוּ *our word,* דְּבָרֶ֫יהָ *her words.*

NOUN WITH SUFFIXES

	Masc.		*Fem.*		
Singular noun	סוּס (horse)	דָּבָר (word)	סוּסָה (mare)	שָׂפָה (lip)	צְדָקָה (righteousness)
sing 1 *c* my	סוּסִי	דְּבָרִי	סוּסָתִי	שְׂפָתִי	צִדְקָתִי
2 *m* thy	סוּסְךָ	דְּבָרְךָ	סוּסָתְךָ	שְׂפָתְךָ	צִדְקָתְךָ
2 *f* thy	סוּסֵךְ	דְּבָרֵךְ	סוּסָתֵךְ	שְׂפָתֵךְ	צִדְקָתֵךְ
3 *m* his	סוּסוֹ	דְּבָרוֹ	סוּסָתוֹ	שְׂפָתוֹ	צִדְקָתוֹ
3 *f.* her	סוּסָהּ	דְּבָרָהּ	סוּסָתָהּ	שְׂפָתָהּ	צִדְקָתָהּ
plur. 1 *c.* our	סוּסֵ֫נוּ	דְּבָרֵ֫נוּ	סוּסָתֵ֫נוּ	שְׂפָתֵ֫נוּ	צִדְקָתֵ֫נוּ
2 *m.* your	סוּסְכֶם	דְּבַרְכֶם	סוּסַתְכֶם	שְׂפַתְכֶם	צִדְקַתְכֶם
2 *f.* your	סוּסְכֶן	דְּבַרְכֶן	סוּסַתְכֶן	שְׂפַתְכֶן	צִדְקַתְכֶן
3 *m.* their	סוּסָם	דְּבָרָם	סוּסָתָם	שְׂפָתָם	צִדְקָתָם
3 *f.* their	סוּסָן	דְּבָרָן	סוּסָתָן	שְׂפָתָן	צִדְקָתָן
Plural noun	סוּסִים (horses)	דְּבָרִים (words)	סוּסוֹת (mares)	שְׂפָתַיִם (dual)	צְדָקוֹת (righteousnesses)
sing. 1 *c.* my	סוּסַי	דְּבָרַי	סוּסוֹתַי	שְׂפָתַי	צִדְקוֹתַי
2 *m.* thy	סוּסֶ֫יךָ	דְּבָרֶ֫יךָ	סוּסוֹתֶ֫יךָ	שְׂפָתֶ֫יךָ	צִדְקוֹתֶ֫יךָ
2 *f.* thy	סוּסַ֫יִךְ	דְּבָרַ֫יִךְ	סוּסוֹתַ֫יִךְ	שְׂפָתַ֫יִךְ	צִדְקוֹתַ֫יִךְ
3 *m.* his	סוּסָיו	דְּבָרָיו	סוּסוֹתָיו	שְׂפָתָיו	צִדְקוֹתָיו
3 *f.* her	סוּסֶ֫יהָ	דְּבָרֶ֫יהָ	סוּסוֹתֶ֫יהָ	שְׂפָתֶ֫יהָ	צִדְקוֹתֶ֫יהָ
plur. 1 *c.* our	סוּסֵ֫ינוּ	דְּבָרֵ֫ינוּ	סוּסוֹתֵ֫ינוּ	שְׂפָתֵ֫ינוּ	צִדְקוֹתֵ֫ינוּ
2 *m.* your	סוּסֵיכֶם	דִּבְרֵיכֶם	סוּסוֹתֵיכֶם	שִׂפְתֵיכֶם	צִדְקוֹתֵיכֶם
2 *f.* your	סוּסֵיכֶן	דִּבְרֵיכֶן	סוּסוֹתֵיכֶן	שִׂפְתֵיכֶן	צִדְקוֹתֵיכֶן
3 *m.* their	סוּסֵיהֶם	דִּבְרֵיהֶם	סוּסוֹתֵיהֶם	שִׂפְתֵיהֶם	צִדְקוֹתֵיהֶם (תָם)
3 *f.* their	סוּסֵיהֶן	דִּבְרֵיהֶן	סוּסוֹתֵיהֶן	שִׂפְתֵיהֶן	צִדְקוֹתֵיהֶן

3. (a) Note i. that the shᵉwa before the 2nd pers. suff. sing. and plur. attached to a sing. noun is vocal; hence the *kaph* does not have the daghesh lene. דְּבָרְךָ *dᵉbhārᵉkhā* (in pause דְּבָרֶךָ), דְּבַרְכֶם *dᵉbharᵉkhem*.

ii. The suffix ָיו is pronounced *āw* (סוּסָיו = *sûsāw*). The י is ignored in pronunciation but it is properly written, since it is the י of the cstr. plur. ending.

iii. Suffixes to fem. plur. nouns, curiously enough, are preceded by י, which, appropriate with masc. plur. (because it is really the cstr. plur. ending), is, with fem. nouns, strictly speaking, neither necessary nor justified. The result is that the plural is in such cases doubly indicated; e.g. סוּסוֹתֵינוּ.

iv. The *dual* takes the same suffixes as the plural, e.g. יָד *hand*, יָדַ֫יִם *hands*, יָדֶיהָ *her hands*, יָדֵינוּ *our h.*, יְדֵיכֶם *your h.*

v. The suffixes of *sing.* nouns are sometimes joined to *fem. pl.*, particularly the 3rd pl. suffix; e.g. נַפְשׁוֹתָם *their souls* (instead of נַפְשׁוֹתֵיהֶם), דּוֹרוֹתָם *their generations*.

(b) *Rules of Usage.*

Rule 1. The noun with suffix, being already definite, does not take the def. art. (cf. § 8. 5, Rule 1), but naturally its adj. does; e.g. *my good horse*, סוּסִי הַטּוֹב (*my horse, the good one*); *your evil words*, דִּבְרֵיכֶם הָרָעִים; *thy strong hand*, יָדְךָ הַחֲזָקָה.

Rule 2. The suffix is repeated with each co-ordinate noun: e.g. *he took his sons and daughters*, לָקַח אֶת־בָּנָיו וְאֶת־בְּנוֹתָיו (cf. § 9. 4b); *son*, בֵּן, *pl.* בָּנִים; *daughter* בַּת, *pl.* בָּנוֹת.

4. (a) *face* פָּנִים (*pl.*)

my face	פָּנַי	*the man's face*	פְּנֵי הָאִישׁ
before me	לְפָנַי	*before the man*	לִפְנֵי הָאִישׁ
before thee	לְפָנֶיךָ	*before you*	לִפְנֵיכֶם

(b) Note i. לִפְנֵי can mean *before* in a temporal sense also; e.g. לִפְנֵי הַבֹּקֶר *before the morning*.

ii. מִלִּפְנֵי and מִפְּנֵי have the meaning *from before, from the presence of*; מִלִּפְנֵי הַמֶּלֶךְ *from the presence of the king*.

iii. מִפְּנֵי can also mean *because of*; יָשְׁבוּ הָעָם בָּעִיר נִשְׁבְּרֵי לֵב מִפְּנֵי הָרָעָב *the people sat in the city, broken-hearted because of the famine.*

5. Particles, such as *prepositions* and *adverbs*, are generally *nouns* in a fragmentary condition and may take suffixes which are attached to them precisely as to nouns. For בְּ כְּ and לְ see § 12. 1f; for מִן see § 12. 3d. Some prepositions take suffixes of the form attached to plural nouns. In some cases the reason is that the preposition is itself a *plural*; e.g. אַחֲרֵי *after* (pl. cstr., *hinder parts*)—hence אַחֲרַי *after me,* אַחֲרֶיךָ[1] *after thee,* אַחֲרָיו *after him,* &c.; in others, like עַל *upon, beside,* אֶל *to, into,* the yôdh is part of the original form of the root (עלי, אלי) and merely produces the impression of a plural.

עָלַי, עָלֶיךָ, עָלַיִךְ, עָלָיו, עָלֶיהָ, עָלֵינוּ, עֲלֵיכֶם, עֲלֵיהֶם

אֵלַי, אֵלֶיךָ, אֵלַיִךְ, אֵלָיו, אֵלֶיהָ, אֵלֵינוּ, אֲלֵיכֶם, אֲלֵיהֶם

Like עַל is עַד *unto, as far as.*

לוֹט	Lot	שְׁמוּאֵל	Samuel	שְׁלֹמֹה	Solomon
אֶפְרַיִם	Ephraim	טוֹב	good things, goodness	חוֹמָה	*f.* wall
אֵת (אֶת־)	with (w. suff. אִתִּי, etc., see p. 184)	דֶּלֶת	*f.* door	בֵּן	(pl. בָּנִים) son
פֶּתַח	opening, door	אֲרוֹן	(but הָאָרוֹן) chest, ark	סָגַר	to shut, close
זִכָּרוֹן	memorial	עוֹלָם	long duration, age	בְּרִית	*f.* covenant
תְּפִלָּה	*f.* prayer	עַד־עוֹלָם	for ever	חֶסֶד	mercy, love devotion
מִשְׁפָּט	judgment, ordinance, justice	כָּרַת בְּרִית	to make a covenant	מֵעוֹלָם	from of old
כָּרַת	to cut off, cut down	רָשָׁע	wicked	תָּמִיד	continually
שָׂמַח	to rejoice			יָרֵא	to fear; (as part.) one who fears
עַל	on, upon, beside			מַלְאָךְ	messenger

[1] The reason why אַחֲרֶיךָ ,אַחֲרַי, &c. has a different vocalization from דְּבָרֶיךָ ,דְּבָרַי, &c. and from פָּנֶיךָ ,פָּנַי, &c. is not certain, but is probably because the first noun is of a different type from the other two.

EXERCISE

Translate

תּוֹרָתוֹ, שְׂפָתָיו, בִּרְכֹתֶיךָ, בָּנֶיךָ, מִשְׁלֵיכֶם, מְקוֹמָהּ, מִבְּשָׂרִי,
בְּשַׂרְכֶם, לְפָנַי, לְפָנֶיךָ, שְׂפָתֶיךָ, בָּנֵינוּ, לְבָבֵנוּ, בְּנֵיהֶם, יָדַי, יָדוֹ,
תּוֹרָתָם, יְדֵיהֶן׃

יָצָא לוֹט אֶל־[1]הָאֲנָשִׁים הַפֶּתְחָה וְהַדֶּלֶת סָגַר אַחֲרָיו׃ 2 הוּא
יהוה אֱלֹהֵינוּ בְּכָל־הָאָרֶץ מִשְׁפָּטָיו׃ 3 זָכַר לְעוֹלָם בְּרִיתוֹ אֲשֶׁר
כָּרַת אֶת־אַבְרָהָם׃ 4 חֶסֶד יהוה מֵעוֹלָם וְעַד־עוֹלָם עַל־יְרֵאָיו
וְצִדְקָתוֹ לִבְנֵי בָנִים׃ 5 וַאֲנִי עָלֶיךָ בָטַחְתִּי יְהוָה אָמַרְתִּי אֱלֹהַי
[2]אָתָּה׃ 6 עִבְרוּ לִפְנֵי אֲרוֹן הַבְּרִית אֶל־הַיַּרְדֵּן וְהָעָם נָשְׂאוּ
[3]אֲבָנִים מִן־הַיַּרְדֵּן לְזִכָּרוֹן׃ 7 [4]כָּרַתִּי אֶת־בְּרִיתִי אֶת־הָעָם הַזֶּה
וּמִיָּמִים יָמִימָה[5] הָלַכְתִּי לִפְנֵיהֶם עַד־הַיּוֹם הַזֶּה׃ 8 יָצְאוּ מִלִּפְנֵי
הַמֶּלֶךְ וְאַנְשֵׁי הַמִּלְחָמָה אַחֲרֵיהֶם׃ 9 שמע יהוה אלהינו את־
תפלתנו׃ 10 ירד אל־בניו שאולה׃

Your blessings. 2 Her corpse. 3 My commandments. 4 Her lips. 5 Thy words. 6 His face; her face; my face. 7 And his words we heard out of the fire. 8 Thy law (is) in my heart, (O) my God. 9 Thou hast heard my voice out of thy temple. 10 We sat before her. 11 The words of thy (*f.*) lips (are) as the sand which (is) upon the shore of the sea. 12 He came and in his hand a sword. 13 Very good (are) the proverbs of his lips. 14 Ye (are) my sons and my daughters, saith (*perf.*) your God. 15 My heart (is) in his law continually. 16 Thou hast kept their heart. 17 We have not kept the covenant of our God with all our heart. 18 Ye have kept my law and my commands. 19 Thy perfect law. 20 By (בּ) all his great

---

[1] אִישׁ. *man*, plur. אֲנָשִׁים, cstr. אַנְשֵׁי.

[2] Pausal form (§ 11, Note to Ex.).

[3] Plur. of אֶבֶן.

[4] כָּרַתְתִּי > כָּרַתִּי.

[5] Cf. § 14. 5.

prophets. 21 The men whom David sent to us from the wilderness (have been) a wall[1] beside us day and night. 22 You rejoiced there before the Lord with all your heart, you and your prophets with you.[2]

§ 17. THE SIMPLE FORM OF THE VERB; THE IMPERFECT

1. *Tenses.* The verb has not *Tenses* strictly speaking. It has two forms, which express not time but the quality of an action as complete or incomplete; the one expresses a finished action, and is called the *perfect,* the other an unfinished action, and is called the *imperfect.* It must be clearly understood that these words are not used in the sense which they bear, e.g., in English or in Latin grammar.

The use of the perfect form covers all *perfect tenses* of other languages, such as perfect, pluperfect and future perfect, as well as the narrative aorist (§ 11, 5). The use of the imperfect covers all *imperfect tenses,* e.g. present (especially of general truths), the classical imperfect and the future (see 5 below); this range of use is examined more fully in § 43. Suffice it here to say that Hebrew is not so handicapped in defining time reference as might be assumed. Since the perfect expresses completed action, it is used to express the English past tense, e.g. רָדַף *he pursued*; likewise the imperfect, being used to express incomplete action, is used to express the English future, e.g. יִרְדֹּף *he will pursue.* But the imperfect cannot, on that account, be described as the *future*; to express the English future is only one of its uses.

2. *Moods.* The subjunctive, optative, &c., and broadly, words implying potential or contingent ideas, are generally expressed by the *imperfect* and its modifications (§ 20); e.g. of every tree *thou mayest eat*; hearken, that *ye may live*; hasten, lest *thou be consumed*; *may he judge*! *let us go*! This

[1] Idiomatically לְחוֹמָה. [2] אִתְּכֶם.

usage is thoroughly in accordance with the fundamental idea of the impf.—incompletion—as already explained. It might seem that this tense was greatly overworked, and that its use would give rise to endless obscurities and ambiguities: in point of fact, as we shall see, this is rarely so.

There are, besides, an *imperative,* which is connected in form with the imperf.; two forms of *infinitive,* called absolute and construct; and a *participle.*

3. *The Imperfect.* In the perfect (cf. § 11) the person and gender are indicated by the use of afformatives; in the imperfect it is done by means of preformatives, though not quite so obviously as in the other case; e.g. א– points to the 1st pers. sing. (אֲנִי), נ– to the 1st plur., ת– to the 2nd sing., &c. But, in addition, the imperfect uses afformatives, e.g. ו– to mark 3rd and 2nd plur. masc. (e.g. יִקְטֹל, pl. יִקְטְלוּ) and נָה– to mark 3rd and 2nd plur. fem. (e.g. תִּקְטֹל, pl. תִּקְטֹלְנָה).

4. *Imperfect*

sing.	3 *m.*	יִקְטֹל	he	*will, may,* &c., *kill; is, was, killing,* &c.
	3 *f.*	תִּקְטֹל	she	,, ,,
	2 *m.*	תִּקְטֹל	thou	,, ,,
	2 *f.*	תִּקְטְלִי	thou	,, ,,
	1 *c.*	אֶקְטֹל	I	,, ,,
plur.	3 *m.*	יִקְטְלוּ	they	,, ,,
	3 *f.*	תִּקְטֹלְנָה	they	,, ,,
	2 *m.*	תִּקְטְלוּ	ye	,, ,,
	2 *f.*	תִּקְטֹלְנָה	ye	,, ,,
	1 *c.*	נִקְטֹל	we	,, ,,

Note carefully where the accent falls.

Note further that the first syllable is closed: in other words, the shᵉwa is silent, consequently the second radical, if a bᵉghadhkᵉphath, would take the dagh. lene; thus pf. כָּתַב *he wrote*, impf. יִכְתֹּב *yikhtōbh* (not יִכְתֹב).

(a) The original vowel in first syllable of impf. of active verbs appears to have been *a* (יַ֫קְטֹל: cf. Arab. *yáqtulu*), which was later thinned to *i* (יִקְ: cf. דִּבְרֵי for דַּבְרֵי from *dābhār*, § 5. 2d). This should be borne in mind, as the *a* reappears in certain forms of guttural and other verbs to be dealt with afterwards (§§ 30, 35, 39).

(b) The termination of the 2nd *pl.m.* and 3rd *pl.m.* sometimes appears as וּן (יִקְטְלוּן), which always bears the tone.

5. *Uses of the Imperfect.* The Impf. expresses:

(a) The Present, *he kills* (especially of general truths); e.g. a bribe *blindeth* (impf.) the clearsighted. Ex. 23, 8.

(b) The Imperfect, *he killed* (particularly of repeated past acts, i.e. *used to kill*: Latin or Greek impf.); e.g. a mist *used to go up*, Gen. 2, 6.

(c) The Future, *he will kill.*

(d) The Potential, *he may* or *can kill*, *might*, *could*, *would*, &c., *kill*. (See § 43).

פָּקַד to visit, inspect	רָדַף to pursue	שְׁמוּאֵל Samuel
פָּקַד עַל to punish	שָׁכַח to forget	סָמַךְ to lean, support
עָמַד to stand	שָׁכַן to dwell	קָרָא to read, recite
יֵשׁ (יֶשׁ־) there is	עָשַׁק to oppress	זָבַח to sacrifice
מִזְבֵּחַ altar	דָּרַשׁ to seek, inquire	כֹּפֶר bribe, ransom
חֶסֶד love, kindness (pl. חֲסָדִים)	שׁוֹר ox	כֹּהֵן priest
עוֹד yet, still, again	שְׁנַיִם two (cstr. שְׁנֵי)	הֵ֫נָּה here, hither
חֻקָּה statute	מְאוּמָה anything (after a negative)	פֹּה here
		אֵיךְ how?

EXERCISE

Parse

תִּזְכֹּרְנָה, תִּזְכְּרִי, תִּפְקְדוּ, נִשְׁמֹר, יִשְׁמְרוּ, תִּשְׁמֹר, אֶשְׁמֹר:

Translate

לֹא־תִשְׁמְרוּ אֶת־מִשְׁפְּטֵיהֶם: 2 אֲנַחְנוּ נִכְרֹת עֵצִים מִן־הָהָר:
3 לֹא יִרְדְּפוּ גִּבּוֹרֵי הַחַיִל עוֹד אַחֲרֶיךָ: 4 בַּיּוֹם הַהוּא אֶשְׁפֹּךְ
אֶת־רוּחִי עַל־כָּל־בָּשָׂר: 5 יִרְדְּפוּ אַנְשֵׁי הַמִּלְחָמָה אֶת־הָעָם
אֲשֶׁר יֵרְדוּ אֶל־הָעִיר וְגַם יִשְׁפְּכוּ אֶת־דָּמָם כַּמָּיִם: 6 הִנֵּה שְׁנֵי
הַ[1]מְּלָכִים לֹא עָמְדוּ לְפָנָיו וְאֵיךְ [2]נַעֲמֹד אֲנָחְנוּ: 7 אֶת־כָּל־אֲשֶׁר
תִּכְתֹּב בַּסֵּפֶר נִשְׁמֹר בְּכָל־לְבָבֵנוּ: 8 יִסְמֹךְ הַזָּקֵן עַל־הַחוֹמָה
וּבְסֵפֶר הַתּוֹרָה [3]יִקְרָא לִפְנֵי הָעָם וְהֵם יִשְׁמְעוּ אֵלָיו: 9 אָמַר
שְׁמוּאֵל אֶל־הָעָם אֶת־שׁוֹר מִי לָקַחְתִּי וַחֲמוֹר מִי לָקַחְתִּי וְאֶת־מִי
עָשַׁקְתִּי וּמִיַּד מִי לָקַחְתִּי כֹפֶר: 10 וְכָל־הָעָם אָמַר לֹא־עֲשַׁקְתָּ
אִישׁ וְלֹא־לָקַחְתָּ מִיַּד אִישׁ מְאוּמָה: 11 נרדף את־האנשים
מן־המדבר אל־ההרה[4] ושם נשמר אתם כי רשעים מאד
הם: 12 יכרת יהוה לפניכם את־יאר מצרים:

I will pursue after her. 2 Yahweh will judge this people. 3 Ye shall keep the commandments of your God with all your heart. 4 His commandments and his words will we keep. 5 His children (sons) will keep his covenant. 6 But I would seek unto God. 7 He will burn your city with (in the) fire. 8 We will remember thy kindnesses, O Lord, for they have been of old. 9 He said to the elders of the city, These men are wise and upright in heart; let them keep the law of the Lord [5]and we[5] will keep our covenant. 10 I have heard your

---

[1] plur. of מֶלֶךְ king.

[2] 1st plur. Imperf. of עָמַד.

[3] 3rd sing. masc. Imperf. of קָרָא.

[4] Note how direction is doubly indicated, by אֶל־ and by *He Locale* (cf. § 14. 5).

[5] . . . [5] וַאֲנַחְנוּ (pron. used for emphasis).

prayer; the priest shall keep the fire upon the altar[1] and the people shall remember[1] my law. 11 Who am I that (כִּי) I should judge this people and what is my honour that (כִּי) they should listen to me? 12 Today you shall remember before Yahweh your God all the great things which he did for you in the wilderness and you shall not forget.

§ 18. THE IMPERATIVE, INFINITIVE AND PARTICIPLE

1. *The Imperative* (cf. § 20. 3)

2 *s.m.*	קְטֹל *kill* thou	2 *pl. m.*	קִטְלוּ *kill* ye
2 *s.f.*	קִטְלִי *kill* thou	2 *pl. f.*	קְטֹלְנָה *kill* ye

(a) The imper., being used to express commands, consists of hurriedly pronounced verbal forms. These appear to correspond closely to the imperf. forms related to them in number and gender, with the difference that the preformatives have been elided; e.g. imperf. תִּקְטֹל, imper. קְטֹל. But whereas the sheʷa in תִּקְטֹל is silent, in קְטֹל it is vocal; cf. imperf. תִּכְתֹּב, imper. כְּתֹב. This correspondence *in form* between the imper. and the imperf. is not to be taken as evidence that the former is derived from the latter; rather the imper. should be regarded as of independent origin.

(b) Note the fem. sing and masc. plur. with afformatives; קִטְלִי (< קְטְלִי) and קִטְלוּ (< קְטְלוּ), in each case the first of the two vocal sheʷas becoming a full vowel, *ḥîreq* (§ 5. 2d, i).

2. *The Infinitive.*

Inf. cstr. קְטֹל *to kill* (admitting inseparable prepositions before it and pronominal suffixes after it).

Inf. abs. קָטוֹל (also קָטֹל) *to kill* (admitting neither prefix nor suffix).

---

[1] . . . [1] Keep this order in the Hebrew translation for emphasis.

(a) *The infin. cstr.*

i. is the same in form as the 2nd sing. masc. Imper. It may be used as a verbal noun, corresponding to the English verbal noun in *-ing*; e.g. as subject: שְׁמֹר אֶת־מִשְׁפְּטֵי הַסֵּפֶר הַזֶּה טוֹב בְּעֵינֵי יהוה *to keep the judgments of this book is good in the eyes of Yahweh,* דְּרשׁ אֶת־אֱלֹהֶיךָ בְּכָל־לְבָבְךָ לִבְרָכָה *to seek thy God with all thy heart brings* (lit. is for) *blessing*; or as a genitive: עֵת סְפֹד *a time for mourning.*

ii. may be used with pronominal suffixes; e.g. בְּכָתְבוֹ[1] (*b*ᵉ*kho̲th*ᵉ*bhô*) *in his writing,* i.e. when he wrote.

iii. is very frequently used with the preposition לְ in the same way as the English infin.:

(α) after such verbs as *begin, continue, cease,* &c.: *e.g.* חָדַל לִסְפֹּר he ceased *to count* (occasionally in such cases without לְ), and (β) to indicate purpose: *e.g.* I have come *to sacrifice* (לִזְבֹּחַ) to Yahweh. This ל joins so closely with the inf. that the first syllable is regularly closed; לִכְתֹּב *to write,* not לְכְתֹב. (Contrast § 12. 1b). It is used with לְמַעַן also to express purpose; e.g. לְמַעַן סְפֹר *in order to count* (cf. § 20. 5a).

iv. may be used with a pronominal suffix and, at the same time, govern a noun or pronoun in the accus.; e.g. בְּשָׁמְרוֹ אֶת־הַבַּיִת *when he kept the house* (§ 27. 8b).

v. may be negatived by means of לְבִלְתִּי; e.g. שָׁאַל מִן־הַמֶּלֶךְ לְבִלְתִּי שְׂרֹף אֶת־הָעִיר *he asked the king not to burn the city.*

(b) *The Infin Absol.* To the infin. absol. nothing can be prefixed or added; it stands alone.

i. It has a wide range of use, but is most often used in close association with a finite form of the same verbal stem to emphasise the verbal idea. To give this emphasis it is placed before the finite form; e.g. שָׁמֹר שָׁמַרְתִּי אֶת־מִצְוֹתָיו (lit. keep I kept)

---

[1] For the use of the infin. constr. with pronominal suffixes cf. § 27. 8.

I earnestly kept his commandments. It is often rendered by an English adverb, such as *surely, utterly,* e.g. פָּקֹד יִפְקֹד *he will surely visit*; מָלֹךְ תִּמְלֹךְ *thou shalt certainly be king.* Less frequently the infin. absol. is placed after the finite form, when it may convey the idea of continuity; e.g. שִׁמְעוּ שָׁמוֹעַ may mean *hear ye continually, go on hearing,* but it may also mean *listen attentively*; and יֵצֵא יָצוֹא is probably an emphatic way of saying *he shall go out.*

ii. It may be used by itself with the value of a finite form of the verb, especially an imperative: e.g. זָכוֹר אֶת־יוֹם הַשַּׁבָּת *remember the Sabbath day.*

3. *The Participle.*

Act. Part. *m.s.* קוֹטֵל or קֹטֵל *killing* (participial use)
or *killer* (substantival use)

f.s. קֹטְלָה[1] or (more often) קֹטֶ֫לֶת[2]

m.pl. קֹטְלִים[1] *f.pl.* קֹטְלוֹת

Pass Part. *m.s.* קָטוּל } *being killed* (participial use) or *killed,*
f.s. קְטוּלָה } i.e. *one who is* or *has been killed* (substantival use).

m.pl. קְטוּלִים *f.pl.* קְטוּלוֹת

(a) The shewa in fem. and pl. of act. ptc. is vocalic, *qô-ṭe-lā, -lîm,* as it represents an original full vowel. The *ḥôlem* is unchangeable, whether written with or without *wāw.*

The act. partic. denotes continuous action or circumstance; e.g. הוּא יֹשֵׁב *he is, was sitting* (not *he sat*); נָפַל הַבַּיִת וְהוּא עוֹד יוֹשֵׁב

---

[1] For the change of ‥ (ē) into : (vocal shewa) in *f. s.* and *m.* and *f. pl.*, see § 26. 2.

[2] When the *fem. ptc.* has the force of a substantive, it tends to retain the long *ē* of the masc.; e.g. יֹלֵדָה *a woman in travail* (יָלַד *to bear*).

שָׁם *the house fell while he was still sitting there*; הָאִישׁ הַשֹּׁמֵר *the man who is watching* (or *was watching*).

(b) Of the *passive* voice there are few remaining traces besides the participle. [1]

שָׁפַט	to judge	גָּנַב	to steal	רָמַשׂ	to creep
שֹׁפֵט	(*ptc.*) judge	שָׁמַר	to watch	אִיזֶבֶל	Jezebel
שָׁבַר	to buy (grain)	שֹׁמֵר	(*ptc.*) watchman	דְּבוֹרָה	Deborah
חָלַם	to dream			מָצָא	to find
תָּמָר	a palm tree	קָבַר	to bury	אָכַל	to eat
קֶבֶר	grave	אֲבִימֶלֶךְ	Abimelech	אֹכֶל	food
תָּמִים	perfect, complete	חָדַל	to cease	צָבָא	(cstr. צְבָא) host, army, service
פָּעַל	(*poet.*) to do	אֱמֶת	*f.* faithfulness, truth	הַכַּרְמֶל	Carmel
לָשׁוֹן	tongue	מֵאָה	*f.* hundred	שֻׁלְחָן	table
גּוֹי	nation	עֵת	*f.* time	דֹּבֵר	[2] speaking
קָבַץ	to gather	עַל	on account of	כִּסֵּא	throne
		עַתָּה	now	תַּחַת	under

Note the range of meaning of מִשְׁפָּט:

(a) act of judgment, decision, ruling; a case (as presented to a judge); a sentence of a judge.

(b) custom, use (the administration of justice being according to precedent and established custom.)

(c) justice, right (the judge who seeks God's guidance being led to just and right decisions).

(d) an ordinance (as promulgated by a judge); the ordinance or law of the LORD (which states the demands of His service).

---

1 For other traces see § 34. 3d.
2 In Qal the verb דבר *to speak* is used only in *act. ptc.*

EXERCISE

Parse

גָּנוֹב, לִשְׁמֹר, שִׁמְרוּ, שְׁמֹר, גְּנוּבִים, תִּזְכְּרִי, זְכֹר, כֹּרְתִים, דֹּרְשֵׁי,
רֹמֶשֶׂת:

Translate

רִדְפוּ אַחֲרָיו: 2 אָמַרְתִּי לִשְׁמֹר דְּבָרֶיךָ: 3 מֹשְׁלֵי הָעָם הַזֶּה:
4 מִי יִשְׁכֹּן בְּהַר יְהוָֹה: הוֹלֵךְ תָּמִים וּפֹעֵל צֶדֶק וְדֹבֵר אֱמֶת
בִּלְבָבוֹ: 5 בָּא יוֹסֵף מֵאֶרֶץ מִצְרַיִם לִקְבֹּר אֶת־יַעֲקֹב: 6 קִבְרוּ
אֶת־נִבְלַת הַנָּבִיא הַזָּקֵן בַּקֶּבֶר אֲשֶׁר אִישׁ הָאֱלֹהִים קָבוּר שָׁם:
7 יָרְדוּ בְּנֵי יַעֲקֹב מִצְרַיְמָה [1]לִשְׁבָּר־אֹכֶל: 8 וְעַתָּה קְבֹץ אֵלַי
אֶת־כָּל־יִשְׂרָאֵל אֶל־הַר הַכַּרְמֶל וְאֶת־נְבִיאֵי הַבַּעַל [2]אַרְבַּע
מֵאוֹת[2] אֹכְלֵי שֻׁלְחַן אִיזָבֶל: 9 וּדְבוֹרָה אִשָּׁה נְבִיאָה הִיא שֹׁפְטָה
אֶת־יִשְׂרָאֵל בָּעֵת הַהִוא: וְהִיא יוֹשֶׁבֶת תַּחַת־תֹּמֶר דְּבוֹרָה בְּהַר
אֶפְרָיִם: 10 אָמַר אֱלֹהִים אֶל־אֲבִימֶלֶךְ בַּחֲלוֹם הַלָּיְלָה הִנֵּה
אַתָּה עָשׁוּק בְּיַד־הָאִשָּׁה אֲשֶׁר לָקָחְתָּ: 11 אַתָּה עוֹבֵר הַיּוֹם אֶת־
הַיַּרְדֵּן לִמְצֹא גּוֹיִם גְּדוֹלִים מְאֹד: 12 וַיהוה אֱלֹהֶיךָ הוּא הָעֹבֵר
לְפָנֶיךָ לִכְרֹת אֶת־הָעָם בָּאָרֶץ אֲשֶׁר אַתָּה הוֹלֵךְ שָׁם: 13 חָלַמְתִּי
חֲלוֹם וְהִנֵּה יהוה יוֹשֵׁב עַל־כִּסֵּא כְבֹדוֹ וְכָל־צְבָא הַשָּׁמַיִם עוֹמֵד
לְפָנָיו:

I promised (said) to pursue after them. 2 Pursue after him. 3 He set the stars in the firmament of the heavens to rule over the night. 4 A city shedding blood like water. 5 Keep thy tongue from evil. 6 They left off counting the proverbs of his lips, for they (were) as the sand which (is) upon the shore of the sea. 7 Hands shedding blood. 8 He came to shed blood. 9 Bury my corpse in the grave where the prophets (are) buried (*ptc.*). 10 We remember that our God is a great God and great judge; he remembers that we are dust and flesh

---

[1] Cf. § 9, Note 1 after Ex. [2] . . . [2] Cf. § 45. 1g.

that goes down to the grave. 11. He commanded (said to) them not to dwell in the city where the people did not keep his ordinances. 12 When he judged[1] Israel, the people ceased to steal and the judges ceased to watch from the city walls.

§ 19. INTRANSITIVE VERBS (OR STATIVE VERBS)

(See Paradigm of Regular Verb, p. 263)

1. (a) There were originally three classes of verbs, designated the a, i and u classes in terms of the vowel following the second root letter; in Hebrew the corresponding vowels are a, ē and ō and the classes are illustrated by קָטַל, כָּבֵד, קָטֹן. For קָטַל see §§ 11, 17, 18. Normally Hebrew verbs of the first of these three classes are transitive and of the other two intransitive. The range of intransitive verbs is very wide, embracing words which describe the *condition* of the subject (as מָלֵא *to be full,* צָמֵא *to thirst,* יָרֵא *to fear,* אָהֵב *to love*), although some of them take an object after them. Sometimes they have been termed by grammarians stative verbs, because they indicate a state or condition, which may be physical (גָּדֵל *to be great,* זָקֵן *to be old*) or mental (שָׂמַח *to rejoice,* שָׂנֵא *to hate*). But it must be noted that not all intransitive verbs belong to the ē or the ō class (cf. מָשַׁל *to rule,* שָׁכַן *to dwell*), nor are all verbs belonging to these two classes intransitive (cf. לָבֵשׁ *to put on* (clothes), אָהֵב *to love,* חָצֵב *to hew, cleave*). Neither intransitive nor stative, therefore, is a wholly satisfactory term.

2. *The Perfect.* (a) Of intransitives in *é*, which are numerous, only a few have *é* invariably, *á* frequently occurring instead; e.g. קָרֵב and קָרַב *to draw near.*

(b) In the perfect, vbs. in *ē* are inflected exactly like vbs. in *a*; e.g. קָטַלְתָּ, כָּבַדְתָּ. Vbs. in *ō*, which are very few, retain the *ō* in the accented shut syllable, e.g. קָטֹנְתָּ, *qāṭṓntā* (§ 4. 4a), but naturally change it to *o* in the 2nd plur. where the second syllable is unaccented (§ 11. 3), e.g. קְטָנְתֶּם *qᵉṭontem.*

[1] Cf. § 18. 2 (a) iv.

(c) The perfect of verbs of this type usually corresponds to the English present; e.g. זָקַנְתִּי *I am old,* יָכֹלְתִּי *I am able,* יָדַעְתִּי *I know* (cf. Lat. *novi*). This use of the perf. is found with other verbs denoting affections or states of the mind: בָּטַחְתִּי *I trust* (have set my confidence), זָכַרְתִּי *I remember, memini,* μέμνημαι. The condition or state is regarded as the abiding result of a past experience.

3. *The Imperfect.* The Perf. in *á* (Active verb) gives the Impf. in *ṓ*, קָטַל, יִקְטֹל (originally יַקְטֹל, cf. § 17. 4a); the Perf. in *ḗ* or *ṓ* (Intransitive verb) gives the Impf. in *á* כָּבֵד, יִכְבַּד (*yi* in first syllable, not *ya,* is the *orig.* form in intrans. vbs.), קָטֹן, יִקְטַן. Very rarely the impf. of an intrans. vb. may be in *ō*; נָבֵל *to wither,* יִבֹּל (§ 34. 1a); שָׁכַן (in pause שָׁכֵן) *to dwell,* יִשְׁכֹּן.

4. *The Imper. and Infin. Cstr.* As is the case with *á* class verbs, the imper. of *ē* and *ō* class verbs is identical in form with the 2nd pers. Imperf. forms with the preformative dropped; e.g. Imperf. תִּכְבַּד, Imper. כְּבַד; so תִּכְבְּדוּ, כִּבְדוּ (cf. § 18. 1). The infin. cstr. is generally in *ō* (not *a*) e.g. שְׂנֹא, קְרֹב. Sometimes the inf. cstr. has a fem. ending of the type יִרְאָה from יָרֵא; e.g. לְיִרְאָה אֶת־יהוה *to fear Yahweh.* Other rarer forms occur.

5. *The Participle.* The Participle is of the same form as the 3rd sing. masc. Perf.; the *qāmeṣ* being tone-long, יָרֵא *fearing* has fem. יְרֵאָה, plur. יְרֵאִים. These participles frequently retain their ֵ in the cstr. plur.; e.g. שְׂמֵחֵי (as well as שִׂמְחֵי) from שָׂמֵחַ *rejoicing.* The cstr. plur. of יָרֵא *fearing* is always יִרְאֵי; e.g. יִרְאֵי יהוה *those fearing* (who fear) *Yahweh.* Their use may be truly participial; e.g. יָרֵא *fearing,* קָרֵב *drawing near;* but more often it is adjectival; e.g. מָתוֹק *sweet,* עָמֹק *deep,* קָטֹן *little,* זָקֵן *old,* רָעֵב *hungry.* Note that the part. of שָׂנֵא *to hate* is שֹׂנֵא, and of אָהֵב *to love* is אֹהֵב.

קָדֵשׁ	to be holy	יָרֵא	to fear	קָטֹן	to be little
קָדוֹשׁ	holy	„	fearing	„	little
גָּדַל	to be great, become great	יָכֹל	to be able	קָרֵב	to draw near
		מָתֹק	to be sweet	לָמַד	to learn
זָקֵן	to be old	חָפֵץ	to delight in	רָעֵב	to be hungry
צָדַק	to be just	שָׁפֵל	to be low, abased	מָלֵא	to be full (*acc.*)
לֶחֶם	bread				
רָקֵב	to rot	רִנָּה	*f.* ringing cry	זֵכֶר	remembrance, memorial
חַיִּים	*pl.* life	שׁוֹפָר	horn, trumpet		
מַר	bitter	חָכְמָה	wisdom	לְמַעַן	in order that

EXERCISE

Parse

תִּשְׁפַּלְנָה, קָטֹנְתִּי, תִּקְטַן, יֶהֶדָלָה, יְכָלְתֶּם, לִבְשִׁי, נִכְבַּד, תִּכְבְּדִי,
אֶגְדַּל, רָעֵבוּ:

Translate

קוֹל שׁוֹפָר לֹא נִשְׁמַע וְלַלֶּחֶם לֹא נִרְעָב: 2 לֹא יָכֹלְתָּ לִסְפֹּר
הַכּוֹכָבִים: 3 יִגְדַּל שֵׁם יהוה עַד עוֹלָם: 4 עַתָּה יָדַעְתִּי כִּי יְרֵא
אֱלֹהִים אָתָּה: 5 יהוה אֱלֹהַי גָּדַלְתָּ מְאֹד: 6 זֵכֶר צַדִּיק לִבְרָכָה
וְשֵׁם רְשָׁעִים יִרְקָב: 7 קָרוֹב אַתָּה יהוה וְכָל־מִצְוֹתֶיךָ אֱמֶת
תִּקְרַב רִנָּתִי לְפָנֶיךָ: 8 יִקְרָא הַמֶּלֶךְ בְּסֵפֶר הַתּוֹרָה כָּל־יְמֵי חַיָּיו
לְמַעַן יִלְמַד לְיִרְאָה אֶת־יהוה אֱלֹהָיו: 9 לֹא יִצְדַּק לְפָנֶיךָ כָּל־
בָּשָׂר: 10 צַדִּיק אַתָּה יהוה הַנּוֹתֵן לֶחֶם לָרָעֵב וְטוֹבֹת לִירֵאֶיךָ:
11 לֹא־יָכֹלְתִּי לִשְׁפֹּט אֶת־הָעָם הַזֶּה: 12 קְרַב אֵלַי לְמַעַן תִּלְמַד
אֶת־הַחָכְמָה אֲשֶׁר לֹא יָדְעוּ זִקְנֵי הַגּוֹיִם: 13 כָּל־מַר מָתֹק לָרָעֵב:
14 הָרְשָׁעִים חָפְצוּ בְּמַיִם גְּנוּבִים: 15 קדוש אתה יהוה מלאה
כל־הארץ כבודך:

I cannot draw near. 2 I will be great. 3 Draw near. 4 The God who made the heavens and the earth I (am) fearing.

5 Ye cannot keep my statutes with (בְּ) all your heart. 6 Thou art little. 7 Hear[1] in order that thou mayest learn to fear Yahweh thy God. 8 They are not able to pursue after me. 9 I know that thou shalt assuredly reign. 10 Cease to draw near before me, for your hands are full of blood (*pl.*). 11 How great art thou (O) my God; thy glory is great in the heavens and in the earth men know thy righteousness and thine honour. 12 Before your eyes the righteous are rejoicing in the blessing of Yahweh and the wicked are hungering for bread. 13 Thou canst delight in the kindness of Yahweh but thou canst not number the stars.

§ 20. THE JUSSIVE, COHORTATIVE AND *WĀW* CONSECUTIVE

1. *The Jussive.* In § 18. 1a it is noted that the imperatival forms correspond closely to the impf. forms related to them in number and gender, with the preformatives elided or modified (e.g. 2 s.m. impf. Qal תִּקְטֹל, imper. קְטֹל; 2 s.m. impf. Niph. תִּקָּטֵל; imper. הִקָּטֵל). The Jussive forms also show a close correspondence to the related impf. forms; and the view has often been held that they arose through a contraction, where possible, of the final syllable of the impf. But the Jussive should be understood as an extension of the imper. rather than a derivative of the impf. (cf. § 18. 1a). It is formed by prefixing the appropriate preformative (or pronominal element, § 17. 3) to the imper.; e.g. יִקְטֹל (קְטֹל+י), יִקְטְלוּ (קִטְלוּ+י). *The Jussive coincides in form with the impf.* in all parts of the regular verb except the *Hiph'il* (cf. § 24. 1a: impf. יַקְטִיל; juss. יַקְטֵל; imper. הַקְטֵל); and in all forms with inflectional endings the jussive and the ordinary impf. forms coincide. *The Jussive is found only in the 2nd and 3rd persons.*

The Jussive (as the name implies) expresses a *command*,

[1] שְׁמַע (not שְׁמֹע; cf. § 7. 4).

as יִקְטֹל *let him kill* (thus taking the place of the non-existent 3rd pers. Imperative); or, less strongly, an *entreaty*, *request*, etc.—*may he kill*; or, with a negative, *a prohibition*, *a dissuasion* as אַל־תִּקְטְלוּ *do not* (ye) *kill*.

Note i. that the imperative is used only for commands, *not for prohibitions*—these require the jussive; e.g. *kill*, קִטְלוּ, but *do not kill*, אַל־תִּקְטְלוּ (not אַל־קִטְלוּ).

ii. the regular negative with prohibitions is אַל; e.g. אַל־תִּקְטְלוּ, not לֹא תִקְטְלוּ. But לֹא can be used of a very emphatic, and especially of a divine, prohibition, exactly like our *thou shalt not*; e.g. לֹא תִגְנֹב *thou shalt not steal*.

2. *The Cohortative*. The Cohortative, like the Jussive, is an extension of the imper., and *is found* (with rare exceptions) *in 1st pers. only*—sing. and plur.; but instead of אֶקְטֹל (א+קְטֹל) and נִקְטֹל (נ+קְטֹל), the forms in use have final ָה and the vowel of the second syllable becomes vocal shᵉwa; i.e. אֶקְטְלָה and נִקְטְלָה.

The Cohort. is used to express *desire*, *intention*, *self-encouragement*, or (in 1st plur.) *exhortation*; אֶשְׁמְרָה *let me keep*, *I would keep*, *I will keep* (but more emotional than the simple אֶשְׁמֹר), נִשְׁמְרָה *let us keep*, etc.

3. *The Emphatic Imperative*. The same termination ָה *ā* is added to the imper. 2 sing. masc. to give it emphasis, as קָטְלָה *Oh kill*! *qoṭᵉlā* (ָה + קְטֹל > קְטְלָה > קָטְלָה); [1] a form of the type קִטְלָה *qiṭᵉlā* also occurs, but chiefly in verbs whose impf. and imperative end in *a*; e.g. impf. יִשְׁמַע, imper. שְׁמַע *hear*, and שִׁמְעָה. This Emph. Imper. appears chiefly in certain classes of verbs; e.g. קוּמָה *arise* (from קוּם)—frequently with no appreciable emphasis.

4. *Wāw Consecutive*. What the *Wāw* Consecutive is may best be indicated by means of an illustration: לָקַח אֶת־הַסֵּפֶר

[1] This form cannot be fully understood till §§ 25, 27 are reached.

וַיִּכְתֹּב he took the book and wrote .... It is at once noticed that the second verb in the Hebrew is not the expected וְכָתַב but וַיִּכְתֹּב. The fact that the *wāw* in וַיִּכְתֹּב seems to convert an imperf. into a perf. in meaning persuaded grammarians of a former generation to speak of it as the *Wāw* Conversive; the fact that the usage is found in narrative passages has induced more recently the use of the term *Wāw* Consecutive. But both these terms are descriptive, not explanatory, and the first contains an unjustifiable assumption. The usage is an illustration of the fact that ancient Palestine stood at the confluence of several cultural streams which affected her language as well as her customs and ideas. The uses of the perf. קָטַל and the imperf. יִקְטֹל are in accordance with those found in west-Semitic languages like *Aramaic* and *Arabic*; but the east-Semitic group, as illustrated by Accadian, had different uses which happen to be preserved in Hebrew in the *Wāw* Consecutive forms. Thus the Accadian permansive *qátil,* which at first had no restriction of use with regard to time, but later came to be used for future reference, is preserved in use in Hebrew in וְקָטַל *and he will kill.* Similarly, the Accadian preterite *íqtul he killed* is preserved in use in Hebrew in the imperf. consec. וַיִּקְטֹל *and he killed.* The fact that such Accadian form usages were thus preserved has induced some modern scholars to use the term *Wāw* Conservative.

The usage in Hebrew is this:

After a simple *perfect* events conceived as following upon this perf. are expressed by *wāw* with the *imperfect*; and conversely, after a simple *imperfect* the events conceived as following on it are expressed by *wāw* with the *perfect.*

(a) *The Wāw Consecutive Imperfect.* i. All the verbs following a perfect are put in the impf. *if they are immediately preceded by wāw*; but if any word, however small (e.g. a pronoun, הוּא, or a negative, לֹא) intervene, then the construction reverts to the proper and natural tense: e.g. Noah opened (perf. or consec. imperf.) the window of the ark and sent out (consec. imperf.) a raven and it went (consec. imperf.) to and fro. Then he sent (consec. imperf.) a dove but it did not find (Heb. *but not it found*; hence the verb is a perf. because the negative intervenes between the *wāw* and the verb).

ii. *Wāw consecutive* with the imperf. is pointed *exactly like the Article* (§ 8); e.g. וַיִּקְטֹל *and he killed,* וָאֶקְטֹל *and I killed,* וַנִּקְטֹל *and we killed*. Examples of usage:

he found the place and lay down	מָצָא אֶת־הַמָּקוֹם וַיִּשְׁכַּב
he found the place and did not lie down	,, וְלֹא שָׁכַב
and the man lay down	וַיִּשְׁכַּב הָאִישׁ or וְהָאִישׁ שָׁכַב

(b) *The Wāw Consecutive Perfect.* i. Similarly all the verbs following an impf. are put in the pf. *if they are immediately preceded by wāw*, cf. 1 Sam. 19. 3, אֵצֵא וְעָמַדְתִּי *I will go out and stand*; but if the connection is in any way broken, the imperfect reappears. E.g. In that day *I will raise up* (impf.) the tabernacle of David, and *close up* (ו with pf.) the breaches thereof, and-its-ruins *I will raise up* (impf.) and *I will build it* (ו with pf.) as in the days of old. (Am. 9. 11). Cf. Ezek. 11. 20.

ii. *Wāw consecutive* with the perf. is pointed exactly like *wāw* copulative (§ 11); וְקָטַל *and he will kill,* וּקְטַלְתֶּם *and ye will kill,* וּמָשַׁל *and he will rule*. Examples of usage:

he will find the place and lie down	יִמְצָא אֶת־הַמָּקוֹם וְשָׁכַב
he will find the place and will not lie down	,, וְלֹא יִשְׁכַּב

So completely does this construction with *wāw consecutive* pervade the language that it may be employed even when no simple tense actually precedes: a book may even begin with it (cf. Ruth, Esther, Jonah).

(c) To summarize: *and* with English *past* tenses in continuous narrative is usually *wāw* consec. *impf.* following an initial (expressed or implied) perfect: *and* with English *future* tenses is usually *wāw* consec. *perf.* following an initial (expressed or implied) impf. E.g. (a) God was (הָיָה) with me and kept (וַיִּשְׁמְרֵ֫) me, and gave (וַיִּתֵּן) me bread; (b) God will be (יִהְיֶה) with me and keep (וְשָׁמַר) me and give (וְנָתַן) me bread. In translating into Hebrew, the choice of the first verb as pf. or impf. is scrupulously determined by the nature of the idea to be expressed.

(d) The accentuation of verbal forms with consecutive *wāw*, like the forms themselves (see above) follows the Accadian usage. In *wāw* consec. Imperf. forms the accent is on the first syllable of the verb (cf. Accad. *íqtul*) and this is the reason for the differences in vocalization between simple Imperf. and *wāw* consec. Imperf. forms in cases in which the final syllable is closed and the penultimate is open (cf. §4. 1b); e.g. Imperf. יֵשֵׁב, but וַיֵּ֫שֶׁב *and he dwelt*. In *wāw* consec. Perf. forms the situation is not so clear; it affects 1st and 2nd sing. forms in Hebrew, in which the accent is on the final syllable; e.g. קָטַ֫לְתָּ, but וְקָֽטַלְתָּ֫; קָטַ֫לְתִּי, but וְקָֽטַלְתִּ֫י (note the *methegh* in the consec. forms in the syllable which is two places from the tone; cf. note to Ex. 9). This use of *methegh* also is probably related to Accadian usage (cf. *qátil*), but in such forms as וְקָֽטַלְתָּ֫ and וְקָֽטַלְתִּ֫י the accent on the קָ is now subsidiary and the main accent is on the final syllable.

(e) i. *Wāw* consec. with impf. may follow not only an actual perf. but an expression equivalent to a perf.: e.g. in the year of king Uzziah's death *I saw* וָאֶרְאֶה (= *and-I-saw*, after an implied pf.—Uzziah *died*).

ii. Similarly *wāw* consec. with pf. may follow not only an actual impf. but its equivalent, e.g. *a participle*, thus: Behold, I am about to raise up (*ptc.* מֵקִים) a nation, *and they shall oppress* you (וְלָחֲצוּ)—or an *imperative*, לֵךְ וְאָמַרְתָּ֫ *go and say*.

5. (a) Final clauses, i.e. those indicating the purpose or design of a preceding act, may be expressed by *simple wāw*

(*not wāw* consec.) and impf.—or to be more correct, jussive or cohortative, e.g. *Draw near that I may judge* קְרַב וְאֶשְׁפְּטָה. *Serve him that he may keep you* עִבְדוּ אֹתוֹ וְיִשְׁמֹר אֶתְכֶם. That is, Hebrew simply places the facts side by side, *Draw near and I will judge*. It may, of course, also use (with the impf.) the final particle לְמַעַן *in order that*—which may or may not be followed by אֲשֶׁר; e.g. I will do marvellous things, *in order that thou mayst learn* that there is none like me לְמַעַן (אֲשֶׁר) תִּלְמַד.

(b) Two verbs of which the meaning is synonymous or the action contemporaneous are sometimes joined by *simple wāw* rather than by *wāw* consec.; e.g. אֲנִי זָקַנְתִּי וָשַׂבְתִּי *as for me I am old and* (וָ pretonic, § 11 II e) *greyheaded*, כָּשְׁלוּ וְנָפָלוּ *they have stumbled and fallen.*

יָרַשׁ	to possess, inherit	שָׂרַף	to burn	תְּבוּאָה	increase, revenue
שָׂבַע	to be satisfied	אָמַר בִּלְבָבוֹ	to say within oneself, to think, consider	שָׂרָה	Sarah
קָצַף	to be angry	לָכַד	to take (capture)	חֵת	Heth
חַיִל	wealth, strength, army	הֲלֹם	hither	בְּנֵי־חֵת	the Hittites
בְּכֹרָה	birth-right	זֶרַע	seed	מוֹאָב	Moab
זָרַע	to sow	קֹדֶשׁ	holiness	חָיָה	to live
שָׁלַח	to send, stretch out (the hand)	הֲ	interrogative particle	עֹצֶם / גְּבוּרָה	(abs. and cstr.) strength
עֵד	witness	בֵּין	between (cf. Voc. *in loc.*)	בּוֹר	pit, cistern
אִם	if			פֶּן־	(§ 9, note 1 to Ex.) lest

מַעֲלָל deed, practice (only in *plur.*, and usually in bad sense).

כְּ . . . כְּ (also כְּ . . . כֵּן) *as . . . so.* Usually with כְּ . . . כְּ the first term is the subject and the second the standard with which it is compared; e.g. וְהָיָה כַצַּדִּיק כָּרָשָׁע and the righteous shall be as the wicked; כַּגֵּר כָּאֶזְרָח the sojourner as the home-born; כָּמוֹךָ כְּפַרְעֹה thou art as Pharaoh (cf. § 12. 2. b. ii).

EXERCISE

Translate

אֶשְׁמְרָה תּוֹרָתְךָ תָמִיד׃ נִכְרְתָה בְרִית אֲנִי וְאַתָּה וְהָיָה לְעֵד
בֵּינִי וּבֵינֶךָ׃ 2 אָמַר אַבְרָהָם אֶל־בְּנֵי חֵת מִכְרוּ לִי קֶבֶר וְאֶקְבְּרָה
מֵתִי מִלְּפָנָי׃ 3 אַל־תִּקְצֹף יהוה עַד־מְאֹד׃ 4 אַל־תִּקְרַב הֲלֹם
כִּי הַמָּקוֹם [1]אֲשֶׁר אַתָּה עוֹמֵד עָלָיו אַדְמַת קֹדֶשׁ הוּא׃ 5 וַיִּמְכֹּר
לוֹ אֶת־בְּכֹרָתוֹ׃ 6 אָמַר יהוה הֵן הָאָדָם הָיָה כֵּאלֹהִים יֹדֵעַ טוֹב
וָרָע וְעַתָּה פֶּן־[2]יִשְׁלַח אֶת־יָדוֹ וְלָקַח מֵעֵץ הַחַיִּים וְאָכַל [3]וָחַי
לְעוֹלָם׃ 7 וְהָיָה כָעָם כַּכֹּהֵן וּפָקַדְתִּי עָלָיו מַעֲלָלָיו׃ וְאָכְלוּ וְלֹא
יִשְׂבָּעוּ כִּי אֶת־יהוה עָזָבוּ׃ 8 אָמַר אֲלֵיהֶם הָאִישׁ אַל־תִּשְׁפְּכוּ־
דָם עִזְבוּ אֹתוֹ בַּבּוֹר הַזֶּה אֲשֶׁר בַּמִּדְבָּר וְיָד אַל־תִּשְׁלְחוּ־בוֹ׃
9 קְרַב אַתָּה וְלָמַדְתָּ אֶת־כָּל־אֲשֶׁר אֱלֹהֵינוּ אֹמֵר לָנוּ וְלָמַדְנוּ
מִמְּךָ וְשָׁמָעְנוּ׃ 10 תִּשְׁמְרוּ אֶת־כָּל־הַמִּצְוָה אֲשֶׁר אָנֹכִי נוֹתֵן לָכֶם
הַיּוֹם לְמַעַן־תִּקְדְּשׁוּ לַיהוה [4]וִירִשְׁתֶּם אֶת־הָאָרֶץ׃ 11 נקרבה
אל־יהוה וישפט ביני ובינך׃ 12 וישכחו בני־ישראל את־יהוה
אלהיהם וימכר אותם ביד מלך מוֹאָב׃

Thou shalt not lie down in that place. 2 Let me lie down. 3 Do not (ye) draw near. 4 May Yahweh judge between me and (between) this people. 5 Hear my prayer (O) our God. 6 The man ate of the tree which (was) in the garden and God was very angry. 7 Thus saith (*perf.*) Yahweh: Behold I will give (*ptc.*) this city into the hand of the king of Moab, and he will burn it [5] with fire. 8 And God called the light (*dat.*) day and the darkness he called night. 9 And thou shalt keep

---

[1] עליו ... אשר = *on which* (cf. § 10. 4). [2] Impf. of שלח.

[3] חַי pf. Qal of חָיַי, the ultimate form of חָיָה *to live* (cf. סַב, סָבַב, § 39); and for change of ultimate ־ַי into ־ָה, see § 32. The word cannot be completely understood till these later paragraphs are reached. The *wāw* has ָ, because it is in pretone, § 11. II e.

[4] Note refinement of *paṯaḥ* to *ḥîreq* (ִר) and for וִי cf. § 11. II. d.

[5] אֵת with suffix, § 11. I. 6.

his law continually. 10 And I remembered his words. 11 And it shall be, like prophet, like priest. 12 Is there here a prophet of the Lord that we may inquire of the Lord and keep his law? 13 Joseph said to the people: 'You have sold this land to me this day; here is seed for you and you shall sow the seed and eat the increase of your land. 14 If you say within yourself: The strength of my own hand has gathered for me this wealth; then you shall remember (Perf. Consec.) the Lord, for it is he who gives you this wealth.

§ 21. SCHEME OF THE REGULAR VERB

1. *Modifications of the stem idea.* The stem idea or meaning of the verb is presented in a variety of modified forms,[1] of which the commonest are:

	simple	*intens.*	*caus.*	*simple*	*intens.*	*caus.*
act.	qal	piʿēl	hiphʿîl	פָּעַל	פִּעֵל	הִפְעִיל
pass.	—	puʿal	hophʿal	—	פֻּעַל	הָפְעַל
refl.	niphʿal	hithpaʿēl	—	נִפְעַל	הִתְפַּעֵל	—
				קָטַל	קִטֵּל	הִקְטִיל
				—	קֻטַּל	הָקְטַל
				נִקְטַל	הִתְקַטֵּל	—

2. The Intensives express an accentuation or other development of the stem idea (e.g. simple שָׁבַר *to break*; Intens. שִׁבֵּר *to break in pieces*) and the Causatives extend the verbal action over a second agent (e.g. simple נָחַל *to inherit*; Caus. הִנְחִיל *to cause* (someone) *to inherit*. Originally a Simple Pass. and a Causative Reflex. were in use, but these are now mostly lost. The various modifications or forms, as they may be called, are contrived by means of inner inflections, consonantal or vocalic, of the Simple form or by the addition of preformatives. (The nearest analogies in other languages which can be

[1] The names of these forms have been adopted into the English vocabulary for the purposes of the Grammar (see note on sheʷwa in § 3. 1). Hence hiphʿîl, not hiphʿîl, etc.

suggested are such as these: fall, fell; fallen, fällen; cadere, caedere; to be calm, to becalm; to moan, to bemoan.)

3. *Conjugations.* What are called in other languages conjugations, do not exist. The various classes of irregular or weak verbs most nearly correspond to conjugations; but if the regular verbs be thoroughly learned, it will be found that the so-called irregular verbs follow naturally from them by the application of the fundamental rules of the language (§§ 3-7).

4. The word פָּעַל *to do,* formed the paradigm of the original grammarians. Now the language, possessing no general terms like *reflexive, intensive act.*, and such like, made use of the parts of *this* verb that were *simple reflex., intens. act.* and the like, as names for the same parts in all verbs. Thus the *intens. act.* of פָּעַל *Pāʿal* is פִּעֵל *Piʿēl*; hence instead of speaking of the *intens. act.* of a verb we speak of its *Piʿēl*: the *caus. act.* of פָּעַל is הִפְעִיל *Hiphʿîl*; hence instead of speaking of the *caus. act.* of a vb. we speak of its *Hiphʿîl,* &c.;—much as if, taking *amare* as the paradigm Latin verb, we should describe *monebo* as the *amabo* of *monere,* or *rexi* as the *amavi* of *regere.*

The *simple* form of the vb., however, is always called the *Qal,* not the *Pāʿal.*

The use of פָּעַל as a Paradigm is unfortunate, because, its second radical being a guttural, the characteristics of several of the parts, such as the intensive, which duplicates the middle radical, are obscured; פִּעֵל necessarily fails to indicate this duplication, which is obvious, e.g., in such a word as קִטֵּל. Hence the word קָטַל (though poetical and defective) is generally used in modern grammars. [1]

5. In the passives the vowel of the penultimate syllable is *u* (cf. Puʿal) or *o* (cf. Hophʿal) and of the final *a*. There are residual remains of the pass. of the Qal, e.g. יֻקַּח, יֻתַּן (cf.

[1] The learner must not use קָטַל in Prose composition for "kill". The word is rare in Heb., and in use only in Poetry. A prose equivalent is הָרַג.

§ 34. 3d). The use of the dagh. forte in the Intensives probably had the effect in speech of conveying the effect of the intensification of the verbal idea.

6. Very few verbs are used in all these parts—only six, it is said, out of about fourteen hundred; but they must all be equally familiar to the student, because, with many verbs, the intensive or the causative forms are as frequent as, or more frequent than, the *Qal*, and are sometimes even the only form in use: e.g. נִסָּה, intensive, *to try, test*; הִשְׁלִיךְ, causative, *to cast*. But these forms are modelled exactly on the *Qal*; so that when the *Qal*, in its pf., impf., imper., inf., and ptc., is thoroughly understood, the other forms put no additional strain on the memory. Hence the importance of knowing the *Qal*.

It should be noted that in verbs like בִּקֵּשׁ *to seek*, דִּבֶּר *to speak*, נִסָּה *to test*, which are very little or not at all used in the Qal, the commonly used Pi'el forms have lost their intensive value, e.g. דִּבֶּר does not mean *to chatter*.

WORDS FOR PRACTICE ON THE ABOVE SCHEME

כתב to write	גדל to be great	כבד to be heavy
גנב to steal	משל to rule	למד to learn
מלך to govern	פקד to visit	מכר to sell
לכד to capture	דבר to speak	קדש be holy

§ 22. THE SIMPLE REFLEXIVE OR NIPH'AL

(See Paradigm, p. 264)

1. The characteristic letter of the Niph'al is *n*. In the Perf. *ni* (probably originally *na*) is prefixed to the stem and is united with the first root letter to form a closed syllable, e.g. נִקְטַל *niq-ṭal*, נִשְׁבַּר. In the Imperf. the prefixed syllable is *yin*, the *n* of which naturally becomes assimilated to the following consonant thus: יִנְקָטֵל > יִקָּטֵל. The imperative, as we have seen (§ 18. 1a)), is like the corresponding imperf.

in form with the preformative dropped; but, as such a form as קְטֵל *qqāṭēl* is impossible, a secondary ה was prefixed (perhaps on the analogy of the Hiph'îl, § 24), yielding the form הִקָּטֵל, which is also, as we should expect (§ 18. 2a, i), infinitive construct. With the perf. (נִקְטַל) the inf. abs. is נִקְטֹל; with the impf. it is הִקָּטֹל (also הִקָּטֵל). The participle is like the pf., only with long *ā*: נִקְטָל *m.*, נִקְטָלָה *f.*

2. Niph. Perf. is inflected exactly like the Qal: נִקְטַל, נִקְטְלָה, נִקְטַלְתָּ, &c.; in the 2nd plur., of course, there is no vocalic modification made in the first syllable *niq* (נִקְטַלְתֶּם) because it is closed. The Imperf. is יִקָּטֵל (in pause often יִקָּטַל), תִּקָּטֵל, &c., אֶקָּטֵל (or אִקָּטֵל), but cohortative always אִקָּטְלָה. In the *wāw* consec. Imperf., since the final syllable is closed and the penult is open, the accent is usually on the penult (§ 20. 4d) and the vowel of the final syllable is short; thus יִקָּטֵל, but וַיִּקָּטֶל.

3. In meaning the Niph'al is: i. Properly the reflexive of the simple form or Qal, as שָׁמַר *to keep*, נִשְׁמַר *to keep oneself, to beware*, נִסְתַּר *to hide oneself*. ii. It is also used of reciprocal action: נִלְחַם *to fight* (i.e. with *one another*; cf. Greek middles and Latin deponents, μάχεσθαι, *luctari*); נִדְבְּרוּ they spoke to *one another*. iii. It has a use which is designated *Niph'al Tolerativum*; e.g. נִמְצָא *he let himself be found*, נֶעְתַּר [1] *he let himself be entreated*. iv. But the common use of the Niph'al is as *passive* to the Qal, as שָׁבַר *to break*, נִשְׁבַּר *to be broken*, קָבַר *to bury*, נִקְבַּר *to be buried*.

4. The Niph. part. has sometimes the force of the Latin gerundive; e.g. נֶחְמָד *to be desired, desirable* (ֶ for ִ before guttural, § 7. 2).

5. The agent after the Niph. is usually expressed by לְ; e.g. *And death shall be chosen by all the remnant*, וְנִבְחַר מָוֶת לְכֹל הַשְּׁאֵרִית; *And Yahweh let himself be entreated by him*, וַיֵּעָתֶר לוֹ יהוה.

[1] For the ֶ cf. § 7. 2.

מָלֵא	to be full, *Niph.* to be filled	בָּרַח	to flee	סָתַר	*N.* to hide oneself, to be hidden
		גֵּרֵשׁ	*Pi.* to drive out		
		לָחַם	*N.* to fight		
מָלַט	*N.* to escape	נָחַם	*N.* (נִחַם) to repent	שָׁחַת	*N.* (נִשְׁחַת) to be corrupted
מֵת	dead	יָצָא	to go out		
שָׁעַן	*N.* to lean	מָצָא	to find	שָׁקַל	to weigh
חָמָס	violence	זְרוֹעַ	*f.* arm	רִשְׁעָה	wickedness
בָּבֶל	Babylon	פַּח	bird-trap, snare	בִּינָה	*f.* understanding (*noun*)

EXERCISE

Translate

נִשְׁמַר, הִשָּׁפֵט, נִפְקַדְתֶּם, אֶשָּׁבֵר, נִכְתְּבוּ, נִשְׁפְּטָה, לְהִמָּלֵט,
יִשָּׁקֵל, תִּלָּחֵם, נִלְחַמְתִּי, תִּזָּכַרְנָה׃
הָֽרְשָׁעִים לֹא יִכָּֽתְבוּ בְּסֵפֶר חַיִּים׃ 2 הַפַּח נִשְׁבָּר וַאֲנַחְנוּ נִמְלָֽטְנוּ׃
3 [1]וַתִּשָּׁחֵת הָאָרֶץ לִפְנֵי אֱלֹהִים וַתִּמָּלֵא הָאָרֶץ חָמָס׃ 4 שֹׁפֵךְ
דַּם הָֽאָדָם בָּֽאָדָם דָּמוֹ יִשָּׁפֵךְ׃ 5 נִגְרַשְׁתִּי הַיּוֹם מֵעַל פְּנֵי הָֽאֲדָמָה
וּמִפָּנֶיךָ אֶסָּתֵר׃ 6 וַיִּנָּחֶם יהוה כִּי עָשָׂה אֶת־הָֽאָדָם בָּאָֽרֶץ׃ 7 בָּא
הָֽאֹיֵב אֶל־הָעִיר וְלֹא יָכֹל לְהִלָּחֵם עָלֶיהָ׃ 8 בַּיּוֹם הַהוּא לֹא
יִשָּׁעֵן עוֹד יִשְׂרָאֵל עַל־גְּבוּרָתוֹ וְעַל־זְהָבוֹ וְנִשְׁעַן עַל־יהוה קְדוֹשׁ
יִשְׂרָאֵל בֶּֽאֱמֶת׃ 9 תִּשָּׁקֵל רִשְׁעַתְכֶם וּמַֽעַלְלֵיכֶם יִסָּפְרוּ וְשָׁפַט
יהוה אֶת־כָּל־הָֽאָדָם בִּצְדָקָה׃ 10 בַּיּוֹם הַהוּא יִזָּכֵר יהוה אֶת־
יְרֵאָיו וּבָֽרְחוּ אֶל־הַמִּדְבָּר הָֽרְשָׁעִים אֲשֶׁר נִסְתְּרוּ מִפָּנָיו׃ 11
ותשרף העיר באש׃ 12 השמר לך פן־תכרת ברית ליושב
הארץ ולקחת מבנותיו לבניך׃

Yahweh is near to the broken of heart. 2 I am hidden from the face of my God. 3 Hide thyself from his face. 4 Ye shall hide yourselves on that day. 5 And the earth was corrupted, and all flesh was cut off by the waters. 6 The arms

[1] The vocalization of this form in Gen. 6. 11 is וַתִּשָּׁחֵת.

of the wicked shall be broken. 7 Let me escape in the day of fighting (*inf. cons.*). 8 And the earth was filled with blood (*acc.*). 9 His dead was buried out of his sight.[1] 10 Thus saith (*perf.*) Yahweh the God of Israel: Behold I give (*ptc.*) this city into the hand of the king of Babylon and he shall burn it with fire, and thou shalt not escape from his hand, but thou shalt be captured and given[2] into his hand. 11 Trust in Yahweh with all thy heart, and lean not unto (אֶל־) thine own understanding.

§ 23. THE INTENSIVE, ACTIVE, PASSIVE, AND REFLEXIVE, PI'ĒL, PU'AL, HITHPA'ĒL

(See Paradigm, p. 265)

The characteristic of the Intensive, both in verbs (קִטֵּל) and nouns (גַּנָּב *a thief*) is the duplication of the middle root letter.

1. *The Pi'ēl.* (a) *Form.* i. The original form of the perf. of the Pi'ēl or Intensive active was *qaṭṭal(a)*. The *a* of the penult has in Hebrew been refined to *i*; the *a* of the final syllable is found in many cases (e.g. לִמַּד *to teach,* אִבַּד *to destroy,* קִדַּשׁ *to sanctify*), but frequently *ē* (e.g. בִּקֵּשׁ *to seek,* שִׁבֵּר *to break in pieces*) and three times *e* (דִּבֶּר *to speak,* כִּבֶּס *to wash,* כִּפֶּר *to atone,* in which the *e* is found in the 3rd sing. masc. perf. only). The original form of the imperf. was *y^eqaṭṭil(u)*; in Hebrew the *a* of the penult is regularly found but the *i* has been lengthened to tone-long *ē,* i.e. יְקַטֵּל. Characteristic of imperf. Pi'ēl and Pu'al is the ְ at the beginning; the 1st sing. masc. begins, of course, with אֲ (cf. § 7. 1); note that the י is without dagh. forte in *wāw* consec. forms, e.g. וַיְקַטֵּל, not וַיְּקַטֵּל (§ 6. 5). The imper. and the infin. cstr. (usually also the infin. absol., which rarely is קַטֹּל) are of the type קַטֵּל (§ 18. 2a, i).

ii. Pi'ēl is inflected exactly like Qal: קִטֵּל, קִטְּלָה, &c., except

[1] *From before him.* [2] Niph. of נָתַן is נִתַּן (< נִנְתַּן).

that in pf. (apart from 3rd sing. masc.) the second syllable, when closed, has the original vowel *a*; e.g. קִטַּלְתָּ. The impf. is also regular יְקַטֵּל, תְּקַטֵּל (the *ē* is retained in the 2nd and 3rd pl. fem. תְּקַטֵּלְנָה). See Paradigm, p. 265.

iii. The dagh. f. is omitted from certain letters when they are followed by vocal shᵉwa (cf. §. 6. 5); e.g. בִּקְשׁוּ (not בקשו) *they sought*, הַלְלוּ (§ 6. 5) *praise ye* (not הללו).

(b) *Meaning*. i. The Piʿel often serves as an intensive of the Qal: שָׁבַר *to break*, שִׁבֵּר *to break in pieces*: שָׁאַל *to ask*, שִׁאֵל *to beg*; possibly רָנַן *to cry out*, רִנֵּן *to raise a clamour* (in joy or sorrow). But see § 21. 6 (final para.) for Piʿel forms which are used *without* any intensive value.

ii. It can, like the Hiph., have a causative sense: לָמַד *to learn*, לִמַּד *to teach*; חָיָה *to live*, חִיָּה (§ 32. 2) *to revive*; אָבַד *to perish*, אִבַּד *to destroy*.

iii. It can have a factitive force: שָׁלֵם *to be whole*, שִׁלֵּם *to make whole*; אָמֵץ *to be strong, courageous*, אִמֵּץ *to make strong, courageous*. Note a combination of ii and iii in גָּדַל *to become great* and *to grow up* and גִּדֵּל *to make great* and *to rear, to bring up* (children).

iv. It has sometimes a notable double usage: שֵׁרֵשׁ *to cause to take root* and *to uproot*, סִקֵּל *to pelt with stones* and *to remove stones*.

2. *Puʿal*. Puʿal is the proper *passive* of Piʿēl in its various senses; e.g. בִּקֵּשׁ *to seek*. Pu. בֻּקַּשׁ *to be sought*.

It is inflected exactly like Qal: pf. קֻטַּל, קֻטְּלָה, קֻטַּלְתָּ, &c.; impf. יְקֻטַּל, תְּקֻטַּל, תְּקֻטְּלִי, &c.

3. *Hithpaʿēl*. (a) i. The Hithpaʿēl is formed by prefixing the syllable *hith*, having reflexive force, to the root-form of the Piʿēl, as קִטֵּל, הִתְקַטֵּל.

ii. When the syllable *hith* precedes the sibilants ס, צ, שׂ, שׁ, the ת changes places with the sibilant, as הִשְׁתַּמֵּר for הִתְשַׁמֵּר *to take heed to oneself*; but in association with צ the ת is modified to ט, as הִצְטַדֵּק *to justify oneself*, from צָדֵק.

iii. With unsibilant dentals (ד, ט, ת) the ת is assimilated, as הִטַּהֵר for 'הִתְטַ *to purify oneself*, from טָהֵר *to be clean, pure*; מִדַּבֵּר (ptc.) *conversing*.

(b) *Meaning*. The Hithpa'ēl is: i. Properly reflexive of Pi'ēl, as קִדֵּשׁ *to sanctify*, הִתְקַדֵּשׁ *to sanctify oneself*. ii. But it very often implies that one *shows himself as*, or *gives himself out as*, performing the action of the simple verb; e.g. הִתְנַקֵּם *to show oneself revengeful*, הִתְעַשֵּׁר *to give oneself out to be rich*, הִתְנַבֵּא *to act like an ecstatic prophet, rave*. iii. It may express reciprocal action תִּתְרָאוּ (fr. רָאָה *to see*, cf. § 36. 1c, § 32) *ye look upon one another*. iv. It may express action *upon* or *for oneself*; cf. הִתְהַלֵּךְ (fr. הָלַךְ *to go*) *to go to and fro for oneself*, i.e. *to walk about*.

(c) As in Pi. pf. the final vowel is frequently (the original) *a*; cf. הִתְאַנַּף *he was angry* (so also in impf. and imper.) and always in pause (as *ā*); e.g. הִתְאַזָּר *he has girded himself*.

4. The participles of Pi., Pu., and Hithp. are related in form to the imperfect, with preformative מ taking the place of י: מְקַטֵּל, מְקֻטָּל, מִתְקַטֵּל. The מְ of Pi. and Pu. is written without a dagh. f. after the article (cf. § 6. 5), but *methegh* is used to indicate that the first syllable is not closed: הַֽמְהַלֵּךְ *he who walks* (not הַמְּ), לַֽמְנַצֵּחַ *for the musical director* (not לַמְּ).

5. Some rare intensives are formed by doubling the final root letter, e.g. רוֹמֵם *to exalt, to set on high*; כּוֹנֵן *to prepare* (Pô'lēl of רום and כון respectively); or the first and the last (omitting the middle weak letter), e.g. Pilpēl כִּלְכֵּל *to sustain*, pass. כָּלְכַּל (kolkal) from כול (§ 30. 4).

6. Nouns of the class גַּנָּב *a thief* frequently indicate one who practises a trade or profession—one who performs a certain act *often, habitually*; e.g. גַּנָּב *a thief*, טַבָּח *a cook*, חָרָשׁ *an artificer* (primarily חַרָּשׁ; therefore the cstr. is not חֲרַשׁ but חָרַשׁ, § 7. 7b).

שָׁבַר	to break	שִׁבֵּר	to break in pieces	דִּבֶּר	to speak (pausal דִּבֵּר)
סָפַר	to count	סִפֵּר	to recount, tell	בִּקֵּשׁ	to seek
קָדַשׁ	to be holy	*Pi.*	to sanctify	*Hithp.*	to sanctify oneself
כָּבֵד	to be heavy	*Pi.*	to honour, harden	*Hithp.*	to get honour
גָּדַל	to be great, grow	*Pi.*	to bring up, magnify	*Hithp.*	to magnify oneself
הָלַךְ	to go, *Hithp.* to walk about, to range through	סתר	*Hithp.* to hide oneself	נֹחַ	Noah
				מִלֵּט	to save (act.)
		רוֹמֵם	to exalt	אַיִן	(cstr. אֵין) nothing, none; there is not, cf. אֵין לֶחֶם there is no food
		כִּי אִם	except, but		
פַּרְעֹה	Pharaoh	עַל־כֵּן	therefore		
רָחוֹק	far, distant	יַחְדָּו	together	פָּשַׁע	to rebel (against בְּ)
		נְעוּרִים	youth (נַעַר a young man)	אֲנָשִׁים	(pl. of אִישׁ) men; cstr. אַנְשֵׁי

EXERCISE

Translate

שִׁמְעוּ שָׁמַיִם כִּי יהוה דִּבֵּר בָּנִים גִּדַּלְתִּי וְהֵם פָּשְׁעוּ בִי׃ 2 וְלָמָּה
תְּכַבְּדוּ אֶת־לְבַבְכֶם כַּאֲשֶׁר כִּבְּדוּ מִצְרַיִם וּפַרְעֹה אֶת־לְבָבָם׃
3 הַשָּׁמַיִם מְסַפְּרִים כְּבוֹד אֱלֹהִים׃ 4 זִכְרוּ אֶת־יוֹם הַשַּׁבָּת לְקַדְּשׁוֹ׃
אֹתוֹ׃ 5 וְלָאָרֶץ לֹא יְכֻפַּר לַדָּם אֲשֶׁר שֻׁפַּךְ בָּהּ כִּי אִם בְּדַם [1]שֹׁפְכוֹ׃
6 מַה־נְּדַבֵּר וּמַה־נִּצְטַדָּק׃ 7 הָאֶבְיוֹנִים מְבַקְשִׁים מַיִם וָאָיִן׃
8 עִיר [2]קְטַנָּה וַאֲנָשִׁים בָּהּ מְעָט בָּא שָׁם מֶלֶךְ גָּדוֹל וַיִּשְׂרֹף אֹתָהּ׃
9 וַיִּמָּצֵא בָהּ אִישׁ חָכָם וַיְמַלֵּט הוּא אֶת־הָעִיר בְּחָכְמָתוֹ וְאַנְשֵׁי
הָעִיר לֹא־יִזְכְּרוּ אֶת־הֶחָכָם וְלֹא־יְכַבְּדוּ אֹתוֹ׃ 10 את־פניך
יהוה אבקש׃ 11 נמצאו החמורים אשר הלכת לבקש׃ 12 ויקרא
פרעה את־כל־חכמי מצרים ויספר להם את־חלמו׃

[1] שֹׁפֵךְ with 3 s.m. pron. suff. (cf. § 18. 3). [2] Fem. of קָטָן.

These are the words which I have spoken. 2 Harden not your heart, lest Yahweh your God be angry. 3 Seek ye his face. 4 Walk before me and sanctify yourselves. 5 I cannot speak to this people, for they have hardened their heart. 6 We heard the voice of Yahweh walking in the garden and we hid ourselves from his face. 7 He said unto the woman, Speak, and the woman spoke. 8 I will honour them that honour me. 9 And now, behold, the king walketh (*ptc.*) before you, and I am old, and I have walked before you from my youth until this day. 10 Magnify Yahweh with me[1] and let us exalt[2] his name[2] together. 11 I sought Yahweh and he hid himself from me; I cried unto him and he visited me with his salvation. 12 They honour me with their lips but their heart is far from me; they keep the commandments of men which they have been taught and forget my law which my prophets gave them; therefore, the wisdom of the wise shall be hidden from them and I will hide myself from their presence.

§ 24. THE CAUSATIVE, HIPH'ÎL, HOPH'AL. THE ACCUSATIVE

(See Paradigm, p. 265)

I. 1. *Hiph'îl.* (a) i. The perfect of the Hiph. or causative is formed by prefixing the preformative הַ, refined in the perfect to הִ, to the stem in such a way that the הַ (or הִ) unites with the first root letter to form a closed syllable, whilst the original *a* of the final syllable, refined likewise to *i*, is lengthened to *î*; so הִקְטִיל, *hiq-ṭîl.* In the imperf. the *a* of the penult is retained, the ה in יְהַקְ' being elided to give יַקְ', whilst the final syllable, as in the perf., has *î*; so יַקְטִיל (< יְהַקְטִיל) *yaq-ṭîl.* The jussive (which in the regular verb differs from the imperf. only in the Hiph'il) is יַקְטֵל, *yaq-ṭēl* (cf. § 20. 1); so *wāw consec.* וַיַּקְטֵל, but 1st s.c. וָאַקְטִיל. The imper. is of the type הַקְטֵל (cf. § 18. 1), but the *î* is found in the open syllable in forms

[1] אִתִּי or עִמִּי cf. Voc. § 16. [2] . . . [2] שְׁמוֹ.

with vocalic afformatives; e.g. הַקְטִילוּ, הַקְטִילִי. Infin. absol. also is הַקְטֵל, *haq-ṭēl*; the infin. constr. is הַקְטִיל *haq-ṭîl*.

ii. The Hiph. is inflected regularly. We have only to remember that the distinctive vowel *î* is maintained, as is natural, in open syllables, i.e. with vocalic afformatives (*ā î û*) and has the accent; e.g. הִקְטִ֫ילָה f., הִקְטִ֫ילוּ pl., הַקְטִ֫ילִי imper. s. f., הַקְטִ֫ילָה emph. imper. (§ 20. 3); in shut syllables it becomes the original *a* in the perf. (e.g. הִקְטַלְתָּ) and generally *ē* in other parts (e.g. imperf. תַּקְטֵלְנָה). In both these respects it resembles the Pi'el.

iii. Pf. הִקְטִיל, הִקְטִ֫ילָה, הִקְטַ֫לְתָּ, &c.; impf. יַקְטִיל, תַּקְטִיל, &c. See Paradigm.

Note:	יַסְתִּיר פָּנָיו	*he will hide his face*
	יַסְתֵּר ,,	*may he hide his face*
	וַיַּסְתֵּר ,,	*and he hid his face*
	הַסְתֵּר, הַסְתִּ֫ירָה פָּנֶיךָ	*hide thy face*
	אַל־תַּסְתֵּר ,,	*hide not thy face*
	אַסְתִּ֫ירָה פָּנַי	*let me hide my face*
	הַסְתֵּר יַסְתִּיר פָּנָיו	*he will assuredly hide his face*

(b) In meaning the Hiph. is: i. Causative; e.g. פָּקַד *to oversee,* הִפְקִיד *to appoint* (*someone*) *an overseer, to put in charge of*; קָדַשׁ *to be holy,* הִקְדִּישׁ *to sanctify*. Probably the most useful analogy which can be suggested is the use of the ending -ζω in Greek, as in σωφρονίζω *to cause to practise self-control, to correct*; ὀργίζω *to enrage*; μακαρίζω *to account happy*.

ii. Permissive; e.g. the Hiph. of יָרַד can mean *to let down* as well as *to bring down,* and of כָּשַׁל *to let stumble* (or *fall*) as well as *to cause to stumble* (or *fall*).

iii. Declaratory; e.g. הִצְדִּיק *to declare* (*someone*) *to be* צַדִּיק i.e. *in the right, to acquit*; הִרְשִׁיעַ *to declare* (*someone*)*to be* רָשָׁע i.e. *in the wrong, to condemn*.

iv. Expressive of the development of a state or quality, sometimes with the effect of an inceptive like *lucescere* or *crescere*; e.g. הֶחֱזִיק *to develop strength,* הֶחֱרִישׁ *to become silent,* הֶעֱשִׁיר *to become rich,* הֶחֱשִׁיךְ *to become dark,* הִלְבִּין *to become white.*

(c) Since the Pi'ēl, as we have seen (§ 23. 1b) frequently has causative force, it happens that in some vbs. *both* forms are used causatively; e.g. אִבַּד (Pi.) and הֶאֱבִיד (Hiph.) *to destroy*; but generally if both forms are in use, they differ in meaning; e.g. כָּבֵד *to be heavy,* Pi. כִּבֵּד *to honour,* Hiph. הִכְבִּיד *to make heavy* (also *to bring to honour*).

(d) If the Qal is transitive, the Hiph. takes two accusatives: לָבֵשׁ *to put on* (clothes, acc.); וַיַּלְבֵּשׁ אֹתוֹ בִּגְדֵי־שֵׁשׁ *and he clothed him with garments of fine linen*; נָחַל *to inherit* (property), הִנְחִיל אֶת־הָאֲנָשִׁים אֶת־הָאָרֶץ *he caused the men to inherit the land.*

2. *Hoph'al.* The Hoph. is *passive* of the Hiph. in its various senses; e.g. הִשְׁלִיךְ *to cast,* הָשְׁלַךְ (*hošlakh*) *to be cast.* It is inflected exactly like Qal in pf.: impf. יָקְטַל (fr. יְהָקְטַל, *h* dropped). See Paradigm, p. 265. In the first syllable, especially in the participle under the influence of the מ, the vowel is sometimes *u*; cf. מֻשְׁלָךְ.

3. The participles have preformative מ and follow the imperfect (except that Hoph., like Niph., has ָ in the second syllable); יַקְטִיל, מַקְטִיל; יָקְטַל, מָקְטָל.

II. *The Accusative.* In addition to the use of the Accus. for a direct object governed by a verb, the following uses of it may now be noted:

1. Accus. of 'motion to'; e.g. יָצָא הַשָּׂדֶה *he went out to the field*; יֵרְדוּ כָל־יִשְׂרָאֵל הַפְּלִשְׁתִּים *all Israel went down to the Philistines.*

2. Accus. of time; e.g. תִּזְכֹּר מִצְרַיִם כָּל־יְמֵי חַיֶּיךָ *you must remember Egypt all the days of your life*; יהוה בֹּקֶר תִּשְׁמַע קוֹלִי *in the morning, O Yahweh, Thou hearest my voice.*

3. Accus. of respect; e.g. often used in the case of verbs expressing the idea of *fulness* or *want*; וַיִּמָּלֵא הַבַּיִת עָשָׁן *and the house became filled with smoke*; [1]מִלְאוּ אֶת־הַמָּקוֹם הַזֶּה דַּם נְקִיִּם *they filled this place with the blood of innocent men*; הִיא אֶרֶץ אֲשֶׁר אָכַלְתָּ־בָּהּ לֶחֶם וַתִּשְׂבַּע וְלֹא חָסַרְתָּ כֹּל בָּהּ *it is a land in which you ate bread and were satisfied and suffered no lack*; לָמָּה אֶשְׁכַּל גַּם־שְׁנֵיכֶם יוֹם אֶחָד *why should I be bereaved of both of you in the one day*? Cf. also נָגַף אֶת־הַזָּקֵן נֶפֶשׁ *he beat the old man in respect of his life*, i.e. *to death.*

מָלַךְ	to be king, rule		*Hiph.* to make king	שָׁלַךְ	*Hiph.* to cast
צָדַק	to be just		*Hiph.* to justify, to acquit	שָׁמַד	*Hiph.* to destroy
שָׁכַן	to dwell		*Hiph.* to place	בָּדַל	*Hiph.* to divide
זָכַר	to remember		*Hiph.* to commemorate	שָׁחַת	*Hiph.* to corrupt, deal corruptly
נָטַשׁ	to leave, forsake	בָּגַד	to deal treacherously	בָּחַר	to choose
בָּחִיר	chosen (one)	עֶזְרָה	help	כָּרַע	to bow down
מטר	*Hiph.* to send rain, rain	בּוֹר	pit, cistern	כְּרוּב	cherub
		רְאוּבֵן	Reuben	יֵשׁ (יֶשׁ־)	there is
בֶּגֶד	garment, covering (constr. pl. בִּגְדֵי)			עֵדֶן	Eden
		בַּעֲבוּר	on account of, for the sake of		

EXERCISE

Translate

אַתָּה הִמְלַכְתָּ אֹתִי תַּחַת דָּוִד אָבִי: 2 הִנֵּה פָנַי בָּעָם הַזֶּה וְהִשְׁמַדְתִּי אֹתָם מֵעַל־פְּנֵי הָאֲדָמָה: 3 וַיַּשְׁכֵּן אֱלֹהִים לִפְנֵי גַן עֵדֶן אֶת־הַכְּרֻבִים לִשְׁמֹר דֶּרֶךְ עֵץ הַחַיִּים: 4 נָתַן אֱלֹהִים מְאֹרוֹת בִּרְקִיעַ הַשָּׁמַיִם לְהַבְדִּיל בֵּין הַיּוֹם וּבֵין הַלָּיְלָה: 5 אַל־תַּסְתֵּר

[1] Cf. § 6. 5. Jer. xix, 4, in which this clause appears, has מָֽלְאוּ.

אֶת־פָּנֶיךָ מִמֶּנִּי כִּי עֶזְרָתִי אָתָּה אַל־[1]תִּטֹּשׁ אֹתִי אֱלֹהֵי יִשְׁעָתִי:
6 אַתֶּם בְּגַדְתֶּם בִּי תָמִיד וְאָנֹכִי לֹא־אַסְתִּיר אֶת־פָּנַי מִכֶּם
וְהִזְכַּרְתִּי אֶת־בְּרִיתִי אֲשֶׁר [2]כָּרַתִּי עִם־אֲבֹתֵיכֶם וְהִבְדַּלְתִּי אֶתְכֶם
מִן־הַגּוֹיִם אֲשֶׁר גֵּרַשְׁתִּי שָׁמָּה: וְקִבַּצְתִּי אֶתְכֶם אֶל־הָאָרֶץ הַזֹּאת
וְהִמְלַכְתִּי עֲלֵיכֶם אֶת־בְּחִירִי דָוִד וְהוּא יְבַקֵּשׁ אֶת־הַטּוֹב וְהִשְׁמִיד
מִן־הָאָרֶץ כָּל־רָע: 7 הִפְקִיד אֶת־יוֹסֵף עַל־הָאָרֶץ וְעַל־כָּל־
אֲשֶׁר־לוֹ וְלֹא יָדַע מְאוּמָה אֲשֶׁר בְּיַד יוֹסֵף כִּי־אִם הַלֶּחֶם אֲשֶׁר
הוּא אוֹכֵל: 8 כִּי לְהַשְׁמִיד בִּלְבָבוֹ וּלְהַכְרִית גּוֹיִם לֹא מְעָט:
9 אל־תסתר את־פניך מהעם הזה: 10 וימטר יהוה על־העיר
אש מן־השמים וישמד אותה מעל־פני האדמה:

There is a time to keep and a time to cast away. 2 Justify not the wicked. 3 Let me hide my face from this evil people, for they have done-corruptly (*Hiph.*) before me upon the earth. 4 For he will surely (*inf. abs.*) rain fire from heaven upon that evil city and will destroy it, and it shall not be remembered any more for ever. 5 The prophet found the child laid (*Hoph. ptc.* of שָׁכַב) upon his bed. 6 We went down unto the city to fight against it, but we could not destroy it. 7 Reuben said, Spill not blood, cast him into this pit which (is) in the wilderness; destroy not an innocent man and do not acquit the wicked. 8 God saw the light which he had made and it was good and he separated [between the] light and [between the] darkness. 9 Hide not thy face from me, O God, but let me dwell in thy temple and cause me to remember all thy goodness to me and clothe me in the garments of righteousness that I may no more do corruptly but honour thee all the days of my life.

§ 25. SECOND DECLENSION

1. This declension is composed of nouns originally monosyllabic. In מַלְכִּי *my king* (first syllable closed) it is clear that the inflectional stem is מַלְךְ; in סִפְרִי *my book* it is סִפְר; in

[1] < תִּנְטֹשׁ.   [2] < כָּרַתְתִּי.

קָדְשִׁי *my holiness* it is קָדְשׁ. These inflectional stems are the original monosyllabic forms of the nouns. But Hebrew dislikes the collocation of two consonants at the end, as at the beginning of a word (§ 4. 2), doubtless from constitutional inability to pronounce them easily together; consequently it separated them by means of an intrusive, helping vowel, normally *s^eghôl* [1] (cf. alarm and alarum). Corresponding to the original stem forms מַלְךְ, סִפְרְ, and קָדְשְׁ, we have, therefore, the absolute forms מֶ֫לֶךְ, סֵ֫פֶר, and קֹ֫דֶשׁ. Since the nouns were originally monosyllabic, the tone in the absolute forms falls on the open, penultimate syllable which, in the case of the second and third types, leads to the tone-long *ṣērê* and *ḥôlem* respectively. In the case of the first type, tone-long *qāmeṣ* would have been expected; in actual fact that vocalization is found only *in pause*, and not always even there (e.g. מֶלֶךְ and צֶדֶק are always written thus, never as מָלֶךְ and צָדֶק). In the case of מֶ֫לֶךְ, the first ֶ, which is under the tone, should be considered a short vowel under the tone rather than a long vowel (§ 3. 3d); the original vowel *a* may have become a *s^eghôl* by attraction—the more so as the two vowels have a certain affinity.

Thus there are three types:

a type	*i* type	*u* type	
מַלְךְ *qaṭl*	סִפְרְ *qiṭl*	קָדְשְׁ *qoṭl, quṭl*	original form
מַלֶךְ *qaṭel*	סִפֶר *qiṭel*	קָדֶשׁ *qoṭel,* (*quṭel*)	with helping *s^eghôl*
מֶ֫לֶךְ *qéṭel*	סֵ֫פֶר *qḗṭel*	קֹ֫דֶשׁ *qṓṭel*	regular form

Forms without a helping vowel are rare; e.g. גַּיְא *gay, valley,* נֵרְדְּ *nērd, nard,* חֵטְא *ḥēṭ, sin,* קֹשְׁטְ *qōšṭ, truth.*

[1] Hence they are often named segholates, not an altogether happy name, because (i) it calls attention to a feature that is of secondary rather than of primary importance, and (ii) *s^eghôl* is sometimes replaced by other vowels, e.g. by *pathaḥ,* if the 2nd or the 3rd radical be a guttural, e.g. רֹחַב *breadth,* זֶרַע *seed* (§ 36); while if the 2nd radical be י, it either becomes *ḥîreq,* cf. זַיִת *an olive-tree,* or contracts (*ay* > *ê,* § 2. 2a) into monosyllabic form, cf. חֵיק *bosom* (§ 31).

2. *Rules for declension.* (a) The constr. form of the sing. is the same as that of the absolute, with few exceptions (e.g. זֶ֫רַע *seed* has as its constr. form both זֶ֫רַע and זְרַע).

(b) With inflectional additions or pronominal suffixes in the sing. and the dual, the inflectional stem which is used is the original monosyllabic form of the noun; *my king,* מַלְכִּי (from מֶ֫לֶךְ; therefore, not מֶלֶכִי); *my book* סִפְרִי (from סֵ֫פֶר; not סֵפֶרִי); *my ear* אָזְנִי (from אֹ֫זֶן; not אֹזֶנִי).

Similarly feminine types are of the forms מַלְכָּה *malkā, queen* (constr. מַלְכַּת), כִּבְשָׂה *kibhśā, ewe-lamb* (constr. כִּבְשַׂת), and אָכְלָה *'okhlā, food* (constr. אָכְלַת); so *my queen* is מַלְכָּתִי, *my ewe-lamb* כִּבְשָׂתִי, and *my food* אָכְלָתִי.

(c) The plural, *both mas. and fem.,* assumes the form *qᵉṭālîm, qᵉṭālôth,* with pretonic *ā*. The presence of this *ā* (cf. מְלָכִים) is difficult to explain in a word whose original form (*malk*) has no vowel between the 2nd and 3rd radicals; it has possibly followed the analogy of nouns of the first declension, cf. דְּבָרִים.

(d) In the constr. pl. the vowel characteristic of each type is resumed: e.g. מְלָכִים, constr. מַלְכֵי *malᵉkhê* (not מִלְכֵי); סְפָרִים, סִפְרֵי *siphᵉrê;* בְּקָרִים, בָּקְרֵי *boqᵉrê;* מְלָכוֹת, מַלְכוֹת *malᵉkhôth;* כְּבָשׂוֹת, כִּבְשׂוֹת *kibhᵉśôth;* (אֲכָלוֹת), (אָכְלוֹת)[1] *'okhᵉlôth.*

3. (a)

	Masc.				Fem.		
s.abs.	מֶ֫לֶךְ	סֵ֫פֶר	בֹּ֫קֶר	s.abs.	מַלְכָּה	כִּבְשָׂה	אָכְלָה
cstr.	מֶ֫לֶךְ	סֵ֫פֶר	בֹּ֫קֶר	cstr.	מַלְכַּת	כִּבְשַׂת	אָכְלַת
1. s.suf.	מַלְכִּי	סִפְרִי	בָּקְרִי	1. s.suf.	מַלְכָּתִי	כִּבְשָׂתִי	אָכְלָתִי
2. s.m.s.	מַלְכְּךָ	סִפְרְךָ	בָּקְרְךָ	2. s.m.s.	מַלְכָּתְךָ	כִּבְשָׂתְךָ	אָכְלָתְךָ
2. s.f.s.	מַלְכֵּךְ	סִפְרֵךְ	בָּקְרֵךְ	2. s.f.s.	מַלְכָּתֵךְ	כִּבְשָׂתֵךְ	אָכְלָתֵךְ
3. s.m.s.	מַלְכּוֹ	סִפְרוֹ	בָּקְרוֹ	3. s.m.s.	מַלְכָּתוֹ	כִּבְשָׂתוֹ	אָכְלָתוֹ
3. s.f.s.	מַלְכָּהּ	סִפְרָהּ	בָּקְרָהּ	3. s.f.s.	מַלְכָּתָהּ	כִּבְשָׂתָהּ	אָכְלָתָהּ

[1] The brackets mean that אָכְלָה is not actually found in the plural.

1. pl.s.	מַלְכֵּנוּ	סִפְרֵנוּ	בָּקְרֵנוּ	1. pl. s.	מַלְכָּתֵנוּ	כִּבְשָׂתֵנוּ	אָכְלָתֵנוּ
2. pl.m.s.	מַלְכְּכֶם	סִפְרְכֶם	בָּקְרְכֶם	2. pl.m.s.	מַלְכַּתְכֶם	כִּבְשַׂתְכֶם	אָכְלַתְכֶם
2. pl.f.s.	מַלְכְּכֶן	סִפְרְכֶן	בָּקְרְכֶן	2. pl.f.s.	מַלְכַּתְכֶן	כִּבְשַׂתְכֶן	אָכְלַתְכֶן
3. pl.m.s.	מַלְכָּם	סִפְרָם	בָּקְרָם	3. pl.m.s.	מַלְכָּתָם	כִּבְשָׂתָם	אָכְלָתָם
3. pl. f. s.	מַלְכָּן	סִפְרָן	בָּקְרָן	3. pl.f.s.	מַלְכָּתָן	כִּבְשָׂתָן	אָכְלָתָן
pl.abs.	מְלָכִים	סְפָרִים	בְּקָרִים	pl.abs.	מְלָכוֹת	כְּבָשׂוֹת	אֲכָלוֹת
cstr.	מַלְכֵי	סִפְרֵי	בָּקְרֵי	cstr.	מַלְכוֹת	כִּבְשׂוֹת	אָכְלוֹת
1. s.suf.	מְלָכַי	סְפָרַי	בְּקָרַי	1. s.suf.	מַלְכוֹתַי	כִּבְשׂוֹתַי	אָכְלוֹתַי
2. s.m.s.	מְלָכֶיךָ	סְפָרֶיךָ	בְּקָרֶיךָ	2. s.m.s.	מַלְכוֹתֶיךָ	כִּבְשׂוֹתֶיךָ	אָכְלוֹתֶיךָ
2. s.f.s.	מְלָכַיִךְ	סְפָרַיִךְ	בְּקָרַיִךְ	2. s.f.s.	מַלְכוֹתַיִךְ	כִּבְשׂוֹתַיִךְ	אָכְלוֹתַיִךְ
3. s.m.s.	מְלָכָיו	סְפָרָיו	בְּקָרָיו	3. s.m.s.	מַלְכוֹתָיו	כִּבְשׂוֹתָיו	אָכְלוֹתָיו
3. s.f.s.	מְלָכֶיהָ	סְפָרֶיהָ	בְּקָרֶיהָ	3. s.f.s.	מַלְכוֹתֶיהָ	כִּבְשׂוֹתֶיהָ	אָכְלוֹתֶיהָ
1. pl.s.	מְלָכֵינוּ	סְפָרֵינוּ	בְּקָרֵינוּ	1. pl.s.	מַלְכוֹתֵינוּ	כִּבְשׂוֹתֵינוּ	אָכְלוֹתֵינוּ
2. pl.m.s.	מַלְכֵיכֶם	סִפְרֵיכֶם	בָּקְרֵיכֶם	2. pl.m.s.	מַלְכוֹתֵיכֶם	כִּבְשׂוֹתֵיכֶם	אָכְלוֹתֵיכֶם
2. pl.f.s.	מַלְכֵיכֶן	סִפְרֵיכֶן	בָּקְרֵיכֶן	2. pl.f.s.	מַלְכוֹתֵיכֶן	כִּבְשׂוֹתֵיכֶן	אָכְלוֹתֵיכֶן
3. pl.m.s.	מַלְכֵיהֶם	סִפְרֵיהֶם	בָּקְרֵיהֶם	3. pl.m.s.	מַלְכוֹתֵיהֶם	כִּבְשׂוֹתֵיהֶם	אָכְלוֹתֵיהֶם
3. pl.f.s.	מַלְכֵיהֶן	סִפְרֵיהֶן	בָּקְרֵיהֶן	3. pl.f.s.	מַלְכוֹתֵיהֶן	כִּבְשׂוֹתֵיהֶן	אָכְלוֹתֵיהֶן

Dual

abs.	רַגְלַיִם [1]	בִּרְכַּיִם [2]	אָזְנַיִם [3]
cstr.	רַגְלֵי	בִּרְכֵּי	אָזְנֵי
1. s.suf.	רַגְלַי	בִּרְכַּי	אָזְנַי
2. s.m.s.	רַגְלֶיךָ	בִּרְכֶּיךָ	אָזְנֶיךָ
2. pl.m.s.	רַגְלֵיכֶם	בִּרְכֵּיכֶם	אָזְנֵיכֶם

(b) In many nouns of the *a* class the *a* has been thinned before suffixes to *i* (cf. §§ 5. 2d, i; 17. 4a); e.g. שֶׁמֶשׁ *sun*, שִׁמְשֵׁךְ (not שַׁמְשֵׁךְ) *thy* (f.) *sun*; צֶדֶק *righteousness*. צִדְקֵנוּ *our*

---

[1] *Feet* (רֶגֶל). The dual termination ַ‍יִם is usually attached to the ground form; consequently the first syllable is closed. This differentiates the cstr. dual from the cstr. plur.

[2] *Knees* (בֶּרֶךְ).

[3] *Ears* (אֹזֶן).

righteousness. Conversely a noun of the *i* class (בִּרְכַּיִם) may have an absolute form of the *a* type בֶּרֶךְ (not בֵּרֶךְ). Some nouns have both forms in the absolute; e.g. נִדְרִי *my vow*; abs. נֵדֶר or נֶדֶר *vow*.

(c) There are certain nouns which may suitably be attributed to the Second Declension because of the form which they take with pronominal suffixes, although in the absol. they appear to show no resemblance to מֶ֫לֶךְ, סֵ֫פֶר, בֹּ֫קֶר. Such nouns, which may be illustrated by דְּבַשׁ *honey* (*a* class), בְּאֵר *well* (*i* class, but *i* lengthened to *ē*) and בְּאשׁ *stench* (*o* class, but *o* lengthened to *ō*), have the characteristic vowel in the *final* syllable (unlike מֶ֫לֶךְ, &c.) and vocal shᵉwa under the first radical. But with pronominal suffixes they commonly have forms which are parallel with those of ordinary Second Declension types; e.g. דִּבְשִׁי *dibh-šî* (מַלְכִּי, שִׁמְשִׁי; cf. b above) and בָּאְשִׁי *boʾ-šî* (בָּקְרִי); it must, however, be inferred from the only form of בְּאֵר with suff. in OT (בְּאֵרֶךָ) that it did not take the expected form בִּאְרִי *biʾ-rî* (סִפְרִי), but בְּאֵרִי.

4. *Feminines with segholate ending.*

fem.	[1]מַמְלָכָה	קְטָלָה	[2]גְּבִירָה	(מֵינִיקָה)	נְחוּשָׁה	קְטוֹרָה
abs., cstr.	מַמְלֶכֶת	קֹטֶלֶת	גְּבֶרֶת	[3]מֵינֶקֶת	[4]נְחֹשֶׁת	[5]קְטֹרֶת
	(מַמְלַכְתְּ)	(קֹטַלְתְּ)	(גְּבִרְתְּ)	(מֵינִקְתְּ)	(נְחֻשְׁתְּ)	(קְטָרְתְּ)
suff.	מַמְלַכְתִּי	קֹטַלְתִּי	גְּבִרְתִּי	מֵינִקְתִּי	נְחֻשְׁתִּי	קְטָרְתִּי
plur.	מַמְלָכוֹת	קְטָלוֹת	גְּבִירוֹת	מֵינִיקוֹת	נְחוּשׁוֹת	קְטוֹרוֹת
cstr.	מַמְלְכוֹת	,,	,,	,,	,,	,,

[1] *Kingdom.*
[2] *Lady, mistress.*
[3] *One who gives suck, a nurse,* Hiph. ptc. of יָנַק *to suck* (§ 29. I. 2).
[4] *Copper, bronze* (נְחוּשָׁה is only poetical).
[5] *Smoke of sacrifice, incense.*

(a) מַמְלַכְתּוֹ *his kingdom*, points back to מַמְלַכְתְּ *kingdom*, which becomes מַמְלֶכֶת exactly as מַלְךְ becomes מֶלֶךְ. In point of fact, however, while the segholate form (e.g. מַמְלֶכֶת) is invariably used for the construct, and sometimes for the absolute (e.g. מִשְׁמֶרֶת *guard, charge*), the absolute frequently assumes the form in ָה; e.g. the abs. of *kingdom* is always מַמְלָכָה. Some nouns have both forms in the absolute; e.g. עֲצֶרֶת and עֲצָרָה *an assembly*. Similarly ptc. *m.* קֹטֵל, *f.* קֹטְלָה or קֹטֶלֶת, cstr. קֹטֶלֶת, suff. קֹטַלְתִּי, &c.

(b) So with nouns in *o* or *u*. E.g. נְחֻשְׁתִּי comes from נְחֻשְׁתְּ (bronze) which becomes נְחֹשֶׁת (cf. בֹּקֶר), which is abs. as well as cstr. Similarly from גְּבִירָה *mistress*, גְּבִרְתּוֹ *his mistress*; we should expect the abs./cstr. to be גְּבֶרֶת (cf. סֵפֶר, סִפְרוֹ). In point of fact, however, it is גְּבֶרֶת, and so almost always with fem. nouns whose origin would lead us to expect ֶ ֵ; e.g. מֵינִקְתּוֹ *his nurse*, מֵינֶקֶת *nurse* (not נֵ).

(c) In general the plurals are formed regularly from the *ordinary* fem., or from what would be the ordinary fem. if it were found; e.g. גְּבִירָה, *pl.* גְּבִירוֹת (i.e. the plur. is *not* formed from segholate form גְּבֶרֶת).

(d) A suffix defining a compound expression in the construct relationship is appended to the last word of the expression, as the connection between construct and absolute must not be interrupted (§ 14. 4, Rule 2); e.g.

הַר קֹדֶשׁ	(*a hill of holiness* =) *a holy hill*
הַר קָדְשִׁי	*my holy hill* (*the hill of my holiness*; or, more strictly, *my* הַר קֹדֶשׁ *my hill-of-holiness*)
אֱלִיל כֶּסֶף	*an idol of silver* אֱלִיל כַּסְפִּי *my idol of silver*
כְּלֵי מִלְחַמְתּוֹ	*his weapons* [1] *of warfare* (the weapons of his w.)

[1] Weapon (article, instrument, vessel) כְּלִי, pl. כֵּלִים.

דֶּרֶךְ	way [1]	קֶרֶן	*f.* horn	שִׁפְחָה	*f.* maid
יֶלֶד	boy	רֶגֶל	*f.* foot	בֶּרֶךְ [2]	*f.* knee *i*
יַלְדָּה	*f.* girl	עֵשֶׂב	grass	צֶדֶק [2]	righteousness *i*
נֶפֶשׁ	*f.* soul	אֹזֶן	*f.* ear	קֶרֶב [2]	midst *i*
אָכְלָה	*f.* food	גֹּדֶל	greatness	מֵינֶקֶת [2]	*f.* nurse *i*
צֶלֶם	image	נֵדֶר	vow	יְרוּשָׁלַםִ	*f.* Jerusalem [3]
גֹּרֶן	threshing floor	חָכְמָה	*f.* wisdom	צִיּוֹן	*f.* Zion
		שֵׁבֶט	tribe	שלם	Piel to fulfil, pay, recompense
כֶּרֶם	vineyard	אַדֶּרֶת	*f.* mantle		
זֵכֶר	memory	מָוֶת	death		
בִּקְעָה	*f.* valley	נָפַל	to fall	רָחַץ	to wash
בְּהֵמָה	cattle; *suf.* בְּהֶמְתִּי	בַּחוּץ	outside	כִּסֵּא	throne; *pl.* כִּסְאוֹת
		קַל	light, swift		
נָגַף	(Impf. יִגֹּף) to strike, defeat	אַחַר	afterwards (adv.); after (prep.)		
		אַחֲרֵי	after (prep.)	תָּוֶךְ	(cstr. תּוֹךְ) midst
נָא	enclitic particle of entreaty				

EXERCISE

Translate

וְעַתָּה יוֹשֵׁב יְרוּשָׁלַםִ וְאִישׁ יְהוּדָה שִׁפְטוּ־נָא בֵּינִי וּבֵין כַּרְמִי׃
2 וַיְסַתְּרוּ אֶת־הַיֶּלֶד וְאֶת־מֵינִקְתּוֹ מִפְּנֵי הַמַּלְכָּה׃ 3 לֹא דְרָכַי
דַּרְכֵיכֶם׃ 4 לָקַח הַנָּבִיא הַזָּקֵן אֶת־אַדַּרְתּוֹ וַיַּגֹּף אֶת־מֵי־הַיַּרְדֵּן
וַיִּבָּדֵל אֹתָם וּשְׁנֵי הָאֲנָשִׁים עָבְרוּ בַּיַּבָּשָׁה בְּתוֹךְ־הַמַּיִם וְאַחַר
הָלְכוּ לְדַרְכָּם׃ 5 אִם־תִּשְׁמְעוּ אֶל־מִצְוֹתַי לְבַקֵּשׁ אֶת־יהוה
אֱלֹהֵיכֶם בְּכָל־לְבַבְכֶם וּבְכָל־נַפְשְׁכֶם אֲנִי גַּם אֲנִי אַמְטִיר אֶת־
הַמָּטָר בְּיוֹמוֹ וְנָתַתִּי[4] אֶת־הָעֵשֶׂב לְאָכְלָה לִבְהֶמְתְּכֶם וַאֲכַלְתֶּם

---

[1] Usually *masc.*, sometimes *fem.*

[2] These four words take *i* instead of *a* with suffixes, &c.; e.g. צִדְקוֹ, בִּרְכַּיִם &c.

[3] The older pronunciation was undoubtedly יְרוּשָׁלֵם. The later form, however, יְרוּשָׁלַםִ (*jerûšāláyim*) is (like יְהוָה, § 15, Note to Ex.) a so-called *Qerê perpetuum*.

[4] נָתַתִּי < נָתַנְתִּי.

וּשְׁבַעְתֶּם׃ 6 אָמְרָה לוֹ הַיַּלְדָּה לָמָּה תִשְׁכֹּן בַּחוּץ׃ יֶשׁ־לְךָ מָקוֹם
בַּבַּיִת וְנָתַתִּי מַיִם לָכֶם לִרְחֹץ אֶת־רַגְלֵיכֶם וְאֶת־רַגְלֵי הָאֲנָשִׁים
אֲשֶׁר [1]אִתָּךְ׃ 7 וְהַנַּעַר קַל בְּרַגְלָיו וַיִּרְדֹּף אַחֲרֵי הַשַּׂר עַד־גֹּרֶן
הַמֶּלֶךְ וַיַּגֵּף אֹתוֹ שָׁם׃ 8 הִנֵּה עַבְדִּי אֲשֶׁר בָּטַחְתִּי־בוֹ בְּחִירִי אֲשֶׁר
חָפַצְתִּי׃ 9 נָתַתִּי אֹתוֹ לְמֶלֶךְ עַל־כִּסֵּא דָוִד וּלְאוֹר לַגּוֹיִם לְמַעַן
יִבְטְחוּ־בִי גַּם־הֵם׃ 10 פני יהוה ברשעים להכרית מהארץ
זכרם׃ 11 כספך וזהבך לא חפצתי׃

My way is hid (*perf. fem.*) from my God. 2 For all flesh had corrupted his way upon the earth. 3 Their ways are not our ways. 4 And all the people bowed-down upon their knees before the king. 5 Let thine hand-maid speak in the ears of the king. 6 My God and my king reigns upon Zion his holy hill. 7 My mantle. Her mistress. 8 His kingdom is an everlasting kingdom (k. of eternity). 9 I will cut off their bow and all their weapons of warfare. 10 I have trusted in thy kindness; let my heart be satisfied with thy salvation. 11 Thy silver and thy gold are mine; thy boys and thy girls too are mine. 12 I will perform my vows unto thee, for thou art my king and my God and I will teach my boys and my girls to keep thy commandments and to cast away all the images which they have gathered. 13 I said to my servant, My mantle has fallen upon you and you shall walk in my way and teach my servants to remember my words, in order that the nations may call upon the name of the Lord because of his greatness and because of the kindness of those who seek him (lit. his seekers). 14 Hear my prayer for thy mercy's sake, for there is no remembrance of thee in death.

§ 26. THIRD DECLENSION—FURTHER USES OF PREPOSITIONS

1. The third declension is composed of nouns and participles which have *ṣērê* in the final syllable and an unchangeable vowel (unchangeable by nature, e.g. קוֹטֵל, or unchangeable by

[1] Pausal form of אִתָּךְ; cf. לָךְ, pausal form of לְךָ.

position in a closed syllable, e.g. מִסְפֵּד) in the penult. Therefore, it does not include nouns like זָקֵן, whose pretonic vowel is changeable (§ 15).

2. *Rules for Inflection.*

abs. sing.	קֹטֵל	מְקַטֵּל	מַקֵּל	מִסְפֵּד	שֵׁם
cstr.s.	קֹטֵל	מְקַטֵּל	מַקֵּל	מִסְפַּד	שֵׁם
1 s.suf.	קֹטְלִי	מְקַטְּלִי	[1]מַקְלִי	מִסְפְּדִי	שְׁמִי
2 s.m.s.	קֹטֶלְךָ	מְקַטֶּלְךָ	מַקֶּלְךָ		שִׁמְךָ
abs. pl.	קֹטְלִים	מְקַטְּלִים	[1] מַקְלוֹת		שֵׁמוֹת
cstr. pl.	קֹטְלֵי	מְקַטְּלֵי	[1] מַקְלוֹת		שְׁמוֹת
1 s.suf.	קֹטְלַי	מְקַטְּלַי	[1] מַקְלוֹתַי		שְׁמוֹתַי
2 s.m.s.	קֹטְלֶיךָ	מְקַטְּלֶיךָ	[1] מַקְלוֹתֶיךָ		שְׁמוֹתֶיךָ

(a) Words of this declension are said to follow the verbal law of inflection (§ 5. 2f); with vocalic afformatives (inflectional additions such as ִים., ִי., וֹת, or pronominal suffixes such as ִי., וֹ, ֵנוּ, ָם, ַי, ֶיךָ, &c.) the *ē* vowel becomes vocal shᵉwa; e.g. קֹטֵל, קֹטְלִים, קֹטְלִי, קֹטְלֵנוּ, קֹטְלֶיךָ, &c.

(b) With consonantal afformatives, e.g. ךָ, כֶם, the *ē* vowel cannot become vocal shᵉwa because that would mean two vocal shᵉwas in collocation (e.g. קֹטְלְךָ). It, therefore, becomes a short vowel, *e* or *i*, the latter particularly with labials; e.g. קֹטֶלְךָ (<קֹטְלְךָ), קֹטֶלְכֶם (<קֹטְלְכֶם), but שִׁמְךָ *thy name.*

(c) As קוֹטֵל (often קֹטֵל) and similar forms come from an ultimate qâṭil (the short *i* in the last syllable becoming in Hebrew, where it is accented, the tone-long *ē*, § 5. 2a), the proper vowel is strictly *i*, but this has been modified in the majority of words into *e* before the consonantal addition.

(d) Words of the participial form (קֹטֵל, מְקַטֵּל) retain *ē* in cstr., and other words commonly do likewise, though some take *a*; e.g. מִסְפֵּד *mourning.* cstr. מִסְפַּד.

---

[1] For the omission of the dagh. forte, cf. § 6. 5.

(e) A few monosyllabic words in *ē* attach themselves to this declension, the chief being בֵּן *son*, and שֵׁם *name*, which are irregular in the plural—בָּנִים, שֵׁמוֹת. Note the vocalization with a pronominal suffix; בְּנִי, בִּנְךָ, שְׁמִי, שִׁמְךָ.

(f) Many nouns are formed by prefixing מַ to the stem (cf. § 13. 2b (v)). Such words express *place* (מַרְבֵּץ *stall*, from רָבַץ *to lie*) or *instrument* (מַפְתֵּחַ *key*, from פָּתַח *to open*) or some more general idea (מַלְקוֹחַ *plunder*, from לָקַח *to take*).

3. *Further Uses of the Prepositions* בְּ, כְּ, לְ. The common uses of these prepositions are given in § 12. 1, but the following additional uses may be noted now:

(a) בְּ *essentiae*; e.g. בְּעֹכְרַי *as a troubler of me*; בְּחָזָק *as a strong man.*

(b) כְּ meaning *about, approximately*; כִּמְאַת אִישׁ *about a hundred men* (i.e. a group which looks like that number); כְּדֶרֶךְ יוֹם about a day's journey.

(c) i. לְ meaning *according to*; e.g. לְשִׁבְטֵיהֶם *according to their tribes*, לְמֵאוֹת *according to hundreds*, i.e. *by hundreds*, and לַעֲצָמֶיהָ *according to her bones*, i.e. *limb by limb.*

ii. לְ as distributive; e.g. לִבְקָרִים or לַבְּקָרִים *every morning.*

אֹיֵב	enemy	אִלֵּם	dumb	מַקֵּל	staff
כֹּהֵן	priest	עִוֵּר	blind	יָרֵחַ	moon
מִזְבֵּחַ	altar	מַפְתֵּחַ	key	מַזְלֵג	fork
מִשְׁפָּט	custom, judgment, justice	דּוֹר	generation	דֶּ֫לֶת	door
צִנָּה	shield	נַ֫עַר	youth, servant	נַ֫חַל	wadi, torrent, valley
חֲנִית	spear	חֻקָּה	statute	אֲדֹנִיָּהוּ	Adonijah
הִבִּיט	(<הִנְבִּיט Hiph. of נבט) to look, behold	קָטֹן	to be small	צָרַף	to smelt, test
		קָטֹן מִן	to be too small for, to be unworthy of	שׁבע	*Niph.* to swear

עִם with

קָלַל to be light, *Pi.* to make light of, to curse

קְלָלָה a curse

שָׁלַח to send

שִׁלַּח *Pi.* to send away, to let go

עָשָׂה חֶסֶד עִם to deal kindly with, to show kindness to

EXERCISE

Translate

[1]שֹׂנְאֵי טוֹב [1]וְאֹהֲבֵי רָע׃ 2 עָשָׂה מַלְכָּם חֶסֶד עִם־מַלְכֵּנוּ וְעִם
כֹּהֲנֵינוּ וְעִם־נְבִיאֵינוּ׃ 3 שִׁלַּחְתִּי אֶת־אֹיְבִי וַיְמַלֵּט׃ 4 מֵת אֹיְבֵךְ
הַמְבַקֵּשׁ אֶת־נַפְשֵׁךְ׃ 5 וְהָלְכוּ יוֹשְׁבֵי הָאָרֶץ כַּעִוְרִים וְשֻׁפַּךְ דָּמָם
כֶּעָפָר׃ 6 לָקַח דָּוִד אֶת־מַקְלוֹ בְּיָדוֹ וַיִּבְחַר־לוֹ אֲבָנִים מִן־
הַנַּחַל וַיִּקְרַב אֶל־הָאֹיֵב וְהָאֹיֵב נֹשֵׂא צִנָּה לְפָנָיו׃ וַיַּבֵּט אֶת־דָּוִד
כִּי נַעַר הוּא וַיְקַלֵּל אֹתוֹ׃ 7 הֲכֶלֶב אָנֹכִי כִּי אַתָּה קָרֵב אֵלַי
בְּמַקְלוֹת׃ 8 אָמַר לוֹ דָּוִד אַתָּה קָרֵב אֵלַי בְּחֶרֶב וּבַחֲנִית וְאָנֹכִי
קָרֵב אֵלֶיךָ בְּשֵׁם יהוה אֱלֹהֵי יִשְׂרָאֵל׃ 9 זֶה [2]מִשְׁפַּט הַכֹּהֵן עִם־
הָעָם כָּל־אִישׁ זֹבֵחַ זֶבַח וְקָרַב נַעַר הַכֹּהֵן וּמַזְלְגוֹ בְּיָדוֹ וְשָׁלַח
אֶת־מַזְלְגוֹ אֶל־הַכְּלִי וְלָקַח־לוֹ אֶת־כָּל־אֲשֶׁר יִמָּצֵא בְּתוֹךְ
הַכְּלִי בְּמַזְלְגוֹ׃ 10 מָצְאוּ הַיְלָדִים אֶת־הַמַּפְתֵּחַ וַיִּפְתְּחוּ אֶת־
דַּלְתוֹת הַהֵיכָל וְהִנֵּה הַמֶּלֶךְ שֹׁכֵב עַל־הָאָרֶץ מֵת׃ 11 בני אתה׃
12 אתם בני׃ 13 לא־אדבר עוד בשמו׃ 14 ולקחתם את־
מקלכם [3]בידכם׃

This (is) my son and these (are) my son's sons. 2 We took our staves in our hands. 3 Our enemy dealt kindly with our children. 4 These are the statutes and the judgments which ye shall keep in the land whither ye (are) crossing,

---

[1] Cf. § 19. 5.

[2] Custom.

[3] יֶדְכֶם (not יַדְכֶם).

thou and thy son and thy son's son. 5 Thou tester of the heart of men, preserve the souls of thy servants that those who love thy name may dwell in thy land in peace. 6 I am unworthy of all the kindness which Yahweh has shown me, for with my staff I crossed this Jordan and now I have become great and have destroyed all my enemies. 7 Didst thou not swear to me[1] that my son should reign after thee and should sit on thy throne[2] and judge the people? But now Adonijah has gone from the palace and has called the king's sons and they have made him king. 8 This is the generation of those who seek thee (lit. thy seekers), who seek the face of the God of Jacob.

§ 27. VERBAL SUFFIXES

(See Paradigm, p. 268 f.)

1. (a) The pronominal object after a verb may be expressed by the appropriate form of the objective particle את (*me*, אֹתִי, &c.; cf. § 11. 6). In point of fact, however, this construction, though relatively common in the later style, is, in the earlier style, usually reserved for cases of emphasis: אֹתְךָ רָאִיתִי צַדִּיק thee *have I seen righteous*, אֹתִי צִוָּה יהוה לְלַמֵּד אֶתְכֶם חֻקּוֹת וּמִשְׁפָּטִים me *Yahweh commanded to teach you statutes and regulations*, אֹתִי שָׁלַח יהוה לְהַמְלִיכְךָ עַל־יִשְׂרָאֵל me *Yahweh sent to make you king over Israel*. Note that in such cases the object frequently precedes the verb.

2. Ordinarily the pronom. obj. is expressed by a pronom. suffix to the verb, after the fashion of the suffixes appended to nouns; the following table illustrates the use of the verbal suffixes:

[1] Introduce direct speech at this point in Hebrew with לֵאמֹר.

[2] Form found in OT is כִּסְאֲךָ.

VERBAL SUFFIXES TO HIPH'IL

PERF.	הִקְטִיל		INFIN. CSTR.	הִקְטַלְתָּ
1 *s. c.*	הִקְטִילַנִי	הַקְטִילִי (subj.)	הַקְטִילֵנִי (obj.)	הִקְטַלְתַּנִי
2 *s. m.*	הִקְטִילְךָ	הַקְטִילְךָ (subj. and obj.)		–
2 *s. f.*	הִקְטִילֵךְ	,,		–
3 *s. m.*	הִקְטִילוֹ	,,	PARTIC.	הִקְטַלְתּוֹ
3 *s. f.*	הִקְטִילָהּ	,,	מַקְטִיל	הִקְטַלְתָּהּ
1 *pl. c.*	הִקְטִילָנוּ	הַקְטִילֵנוּ	מַקְטִילִי	הִקְטַלְתָּנוּ
2 *pl. m.*	הִקְטִילְכֶם	&c.	&c., mostly as	–
2 *pl. f.*	הִקְטִילְכֶן	as noun	the noun	–
3 *pl. m.*	הִקְטִילָם			הִקְטַלְתָּם
3 *pl. f.*	הִקְטִילָן			הִקְטַלְתָּן
IMPERF.	יַקְטִיל		IMPER. AS IMPF.	יַקְטִילוּ
1 *s. c.*	יַקְטִילֵנִי		הַקְטִילֵנִי	יַקְטִילוּנִי
2 *s. m.*.	יַקְטִילְךָ		–	יַקְטִילוּךָ
2 *s. f.*	יַקְטִילֵךְ		–	יַקְטִילוּךְ
3 *s. m.*	יַקְטִילֵהוּ		הַקְטִילֵהוּ	יַקְטִילֻהוּ
3 *s. f.*	יַקְטִילֶהָ		הַקְטִילֶהָ	יַקְטִילוּהָ
1 *pl c.*	יַקְטִילֵנוּ		הַקְטִילֵנוּ	
2 *pl. m.*	יַקְטִילְכֶם		–	
2 *pl. f.*	יַקְטִילְכֶן		–	
3 *pl. m.*	יַקְטִילֵם		הַקְטִילֵם	יַקְטִילוּם
3 *pl. f.*	יַקְטִילֵן		הַקְטִילֵן	יַקְטִילוּן

(a) The 3rd s.m. Hiph'îl is chosen for the paradigm rather than the Qal because, both its vowels being unchangeable (the first short in the closed syllable, the second naturally long), the suffixes cause no vocalic change in the verbal form, and their real nature and form can be most simply seen; thus הִקְטִיל with 3rd s.m. suffix gives הִקְטִילוֹ.

(b) The suffixes to the verb, alike in the perf. and the imperf. (which differ slightly), very closely resemble those of the noun (§ 16). The chief differences are:

i. The 1st sing. suffix is not *î*, but *nî*;

ii. The 3rd sing. m. and f. suffixes to the imperf. and imper. are *ḗhû* and *ḗhā* (cf. §§ 16. 1; 33. 3);

iii. The so-called connecting vowel between the verb and the suffix is *a* in the perf. (cf. הִקְטִילָם) and *ē* in the imperf. (cf. יַקְטִילֵם) and the imper. (cf. הַקְטִילֵם).

This vowel, however, is not really an arbitrary *connecting* vowel, but the *a* is, strictly speaking, the final vowel in the ultimate form of the *verb*, seen, e.g., in the Arabic *qatala* = Hebr. קָטַל. The origin of the *e* is not so obvious; probably it is due to the analogy of *Lāmedh Hē* vbs., § 32, where the *ē* is really part of the verb (*ay* > *ai* > *ê* > *ē*, cf. § 2. 2).

3. In cases where one or both of the syllables before the suffix is open, the laws of the tone apply (§ 5):

(a) Thus קָטַל with the 3rd s.m. suffix becomes קְטָלוֹ; the accent falls on the *ô*, in the open pretonic syllable the original ַ naturally becomes the tone-long ָ, and the original ָ being now two places from the tone is reduced to shᵉwa. It follows exactly the analogy of דְּבָרוֹ. Thus קָטַל with the verbal suffixes becomes קְטָלַנִי קְטָלְךָ קְטָלֵךְ קְטָלוֹ קְטָלָהּ קְטָלָנוּ קְטַלְכֶם קְטָלָם. This *first declension* analogy (§ 15) is followed by the pf. Qal in *all* its forms (e.g. שְׂנֵאָהּ *he hated her*) and by the impf. and imper. Qal in *a* (e.g. וַיִּשְׁכָּחֵהוּ not "וַיִּשְׁכְּ" *and he forgot him*, from יִשְׁכַּח; שְׁלָחֵנִי *send me*, from שְׁלַח).

Note that the vb., with 1st sing. suff. ends in ַנִי (*ánî*); with 1st pl. suff., in ָנוּ (*ánû*).

(b) Imperfs. and Impers. in *ē* (Pi'ēl, &c.) may be said to follow the analogy of the third declension (§ 26); e.g. יְקַבֵּץ *he will gather*, יְקַבְּצֵנִי *he will gather me*, יְקַבֶּצְךָ *he will gather thee*, אֲקַבְּצֵם *I will gather them*, קַבְּצֵנִי *gather me*, קַבְּצֵם *gather them*.

(c) Imperfs. and Impers. in *ō* are treated in the same way as those in *ē*; thus from יִשְׁמֹר *he will keep*, יִשְׁמְרֵנִי *he will keep me*, יִשְׁמְרֵהוּ *he will keep him*, יִשְׁמָרְךָ *he will keep thee*; and from the Imper. שְׁמֹר, שָׁמְרֵנִי *keep me* (< שְׁמְרֵנִי, the short vowel *qāmeṣ ḥaṭûph*, corresponding to the *ḥôlem* of שְׁמֹר, taking the place of the first vocal shᵉwa (§ 3. 6)), שָׁמְרֵהוּ *keep him*, שָׁמְרֵם *keep them*.

4. (a) When the verbal form ends in a vowel, the suffix is directly affixed; e.g. קְטַלְתִּי, קְטַלְתִּיךָ (note that the accent moves a place forward—hence קְ), קְטַלְתִּים; in the 3rd pers. it appears as הוּ or ו (masc.), and הָ (fem.), e.g. קְטַלְתִּיהוּ, קְטַלְתִּיו (*-tîw*), קְטַלְתִּיהָ; so יִקְטְלוּךָ (3 pl. impf.) יִקְטְלוּם, &c. With suffixes ending in ּוּ the *û* of the vb. is usually written ָ, e.g. יִקְטְלֻהוּ, יִקְטְלֻנוּ, cf. § 2. 7d (*they will kill him, us*).

In the case of קְטַלְוּ with suffixes, as illustrated in קְטָלוּנִי, the original *paṯhaḥ* in קְטַל, which is reduced to vocal shᵉwa in the form קְטְלוּ, becomes here pretonic *qāmeṣ*, and the preceding vowel, being removed two places from the tone, becomes vocal shᵉwa. So קְטָלוּךָ, קְטָלֻהוּ, &c.

(b) Similarly in the 2nd pers. (קְטַלְתָּ) the final ָ is maintained with all the suffixes except the *first sing., which always ends in* ַנִי (except in pause ָנִי), e.g. קְטַלְתַּנִי; with the 3 s. m. suffix, *ā-hû* by dropping the *h* (§ 12. 1e) contracts (through *au*) to *ô*, קְטַלְתּוֹ (§ 16. 1).

(c) The gaps which appear in the paradigms are explained by the fact that the reflexive idea which would be expressed by the absent forms is in Hebrew expressed in other ways, e.g. Niph. Hithp. &c. (§§ 22, 23). E.g. *I hid myself*, not הִסְתַּרְתִּינִי but נִסְתַּרְתִּי.

5. Before the suffixes, original verbal forms are restored.

(a) The 3rd sing. fem. pf. ָה becomes ַת or ָת, e.g. הִקְטִילָתַם, הִקְטִילַתְנִי. In the case of קָטְלָה, vocalic modifications take place when suffixes are added; e.g. קְטָלַתְנִי and קְטָלָתַם, in which pretonic *qāmeṣ* appears after the ט, and the preceding vowel, being removed two places from the tone, becomes vocal shᵉwa (cf. 4a above).

(b) The 2nd sing. fem. pf. ְתְּ becomes תִּי (or תִּ); e.g. הִקְטַלְתִּינִי (Hiph.), קְטַלְתִּיהוּ (Qal). Only the context enables us to distinguish this from the suff. to the 1st pers. sing.

(c) The 2nd pl. masc. pf. תֶּם becomes—but very rarely—תּוּ; e.g. הֶעֱלִיתֻנוּ *you have brought us up* (Hiph. of עלה, §§ 32, 35).

6. Singular suffixes to the impf. and imper. are occasionally strengthened by the addition of *nûn* (known as the *nûn energicum*) which is usually assimilated to the following consonant, or, if that be ה, the ה, it may be assumed, becomes regressively assimilated to the *nûn*. The following forms result: יִקְטְלֶנִּי יִקְטְלֶךָּ יִקְטְלֶנּוּ יִקְטְלֶנָּה. They occur chiefly in pause.

7. *Participle.* The suffixes to the participle are practically always those of the *noun*, not of the verb; e.g. מַצְדִּיקִי (not מַצְדִּיקֵנִי) *he who justifies me* (Hiph. ptc. of צדק), מְבַקְשָׁיו (not מְבַקְשֵׁיהוּ) *those who seek him* (Pi. of בקשׁ; cf. § 6. 5), רֹדְפַי *those who pursue me, my persecutors.*

8. *Infin. Constr.* (a) The vocalization of the infin. constr. in *ē* and *ō* with suffixes is generally similar to that of the imper. in *ē* or *ō* respectively (e.g. שָׁמְרִי < שְׁמֹרִי), but

i. The suffixes are those of the *noun*, except that the *first* pers. sing. suff., when nominal is ִי. and, when verbal, is ֵנִי, the nominal being used to denote the *subject*, and the verbal the *object*; e.g. יוֹם פָּקְדִי *the day of my visiting*, i.e. *when I visit* (*poq·dhî*); but לְפָקְדֵנִי *to visit me.* In the other persons the suffix may express either subject or object; e.g. עַל־שָׂרְפוֹ (*śor·phô*) *because he burned* (lit. *on account of his burning*), לְשָׂרְפוֹ *to burn it.*

ii. With 2nd pers. suffixes there are alternative forms קְטָלְךָ and קָטְלְךָ (*qoṭl·khā*), קְטָלְכֶם and קָטְלְכֶם (*qoṭl·khem*), of which the second in each case is the commoner.

(b) The *infin. cstr.*, partaking as it does of the character of both verb and noun, has (like a verb) the power of governing an object, besides (like a noun) being able to take suffixes and prefixes (cf. § 18. 2a). The usual order is infin., subject, object.

בִּשְׁמֹר הָאִישׁ *when the man kept* בְּשָׁמְרוֹ *when he kept*

לִפְנֵי שָׁמְרוֹ אֹתִי *before he kept me*

לִפְנֵי שְׁמֹר הָאִישׁ אֹתִי *before the man kept me*

בְּיוֹם פָּקְדִי אֹתָם *on the day when I visit them*

(c) Instead of the infin. cstr. with preposition the finite form may be used with a conjunctional expression formed of the prep. and relative.

כַּאֲשֶׁר שָׁמַרְתִּי אֶת־הָאִישׁ or כְּשָׁמְרִי אֶת־הָאִישׁ *when I kept the man*

עַד אֲשֶׁר אֶשְׁמֹר ,, or עַד שָׁמְרִי ,, *until I keep the man*

אַחֲרֵי אֲשֶׁר כָּרְתוּ בְּרִית or אַחֲרֵי כָּרְתָם בְּרִית *after they had made a covenant*

גָּמַל	to deal fully with, recompense, requite	טָמַן	to hide	דָּרַךְ	to tread
		קָבַץ	(*Qal*) *Pi'ēl*, to gather	כָּשַׁל	*Qal* and *Niph.* to stumble, fall
לוּחַ	tablet	בֵּיתְאֵל	Bethel	מִצְרִי	Egyptian
לוּחֹת	*pl.*	שִׂמְחָה	joy, gladness	קְבוּרָה	*f.* burying-place
חָצֵר	(pl. *îm* or *ô<u>th</u>*) court, village	נָתִיב	path, way	מוֹלֶדֶת	kindred

EXERCISE

Translate

שְׁמַרְתַּנִי, שְׁמַרְתִּיךָ, וּשְׁמָרוֹ, לִשְׁמָרְךָ, וּלְשָׁמְרָהּ, שָׁמְרֵנִי, וַיִּשְׁמְרֵנִי, וַיַּלְבִּשֵׁנִי, תִּשְׁמְרֵם, וְאֶשְׁמְרֶנָּה, יִשְׁמְרֵהוּ, תִּשְׁמְרֶךָּ, שְׁפָטוּנִי, שְׁפָטוּם, בְּשָׁפְטֶךָ, שָׁפְטֵנִי, זְכַרְתָּם, אֶזְכְּרֶנָּה, וַיִּזְכְּרֶהָ, יִזְכְּרוּנִי, כְּהַזְכִּירוֹ, הַזְכִּירֵנִי, גְּנָבוּךָ, וְקִבֶּצְךָ, קִבְּצָם, וְקִבַּצְתִּים, וּמְקַבְּצָיו, בְּקַבְּצִי, אֲקַבֶּצְךָ, יְקַבֶּצְךָ:

אַתָּה גְּמַלְתַּנִי הַטּוֹבָה וַאֲנִי גְּמַלְתִּיךָ הָרָעָה: 2 כִּבְּדוּנִי בְּשִׂפְתֵיהֶם:
3 שְׁמֹר אֶת־דִּבְרֵי יהוה כָּתְבֵם עַל־לוּחַ לְבָבֶךָ: 4 בַּקֵּשׁ שָׁלוֹם
וְרָדְפֵהוּ: 5 הַדְרִיכֵנִי בִּנְתִיב מִצְוֹתֶיךָ כִּי בוֹ חָפָצְתִּי: 6 דִּרְשׁוּ

יהוה בְּהִמָּֽצְאוֹ׃ 7 אָמַר לוֹ הַזָּקֵן עֲמֹד לְפָנַי לְמַעַן אַשְׁבִּֽיעֲךָ כִּי
תְבַקֵּשׁ אִשָּׁה לִבְנִי בְּאֶרֶץ מוֹלַדְתּוֹ׃ 8 יהוה אֱלֹהֵי יִשְׂרָאֵל אֲשֶׁר
לְקָחַנִי מֵאֶרֶץ מוֹלַדְתִּי הוּא יִשְׁלַח אֶת־מַלְאָכוֹ לִשְׁמָרְךָ בַּדָּֽרֶךְ׃
9 שְׁלָחֲךָ יהוה לְקַבֵּץ אֶת־נִשְׁבְּרֵי הַלֵּב וּשְׁמָרְךָ בְּכָל־הַמְּקֹמוֹת
אֲשֶׁר שְׁלָחֲךָ שָֽׁמָּה׃ 10 אַל־תִּשְׁכָּחֵנִי אֱלֹהֵי יְשׁוּעָתִי זָכְרֵנִי לְמַעַן־
חַסְדֶּֽךָ׃ 11 לַמְּדֵנִי אֶת־דֶּרֶךְ חֻקֹּתֶיךָ וְגַדְּלְתִּיךָ כָּל־יְמֵי חַיָּֽי׃
12 בָּרוּךְ הָאִישׁ אֲשֶׁר [1]בְּחַרְתּוֹ כִּי יִשְׁכֹּן הוּא בַּֽחֲצֵרֶיךָ וּבָטַח בְּךָ
וְכִבֶּדְךָ בְּכָל־לְבָבוֹ׃ 13 הרג משה את־המצרי ויטמנהו בחול׃
14 יהוה ישמרך מכל־רע ישמר את־נפשך׃

I have gathered thee. 2 I will gather her from the distant places of the earth. 3 And thou shalt keep me in thy way. 4 Keep thou him. 5 Before she kept the man. 6 In the day when I visit (of my visiting) Israel, I will destroy the altars of Bethel. 7 Judge me according-to my righteousness. 8 Bury me not in Egypt, but I will lie with my fathers and thou shalt bury me in their burying-place. 9 What is man that thou rememberest him, or (and) the son of man that thou visitest him? 10 He promised (said) to mention him before the priests of the temple. 11 Cause me to remember thy kindness and visit me with thy righteousness that I may magnify thee and recount thy goodness to my children. 12 Him who honours me I will honour and him who forgets me I will cast off. 13 Seek ye me with your whole heart and I will keep you from the power of your enemies; trust in me and I will send to you rain for your ground and gladness for your souls.

§ 28. VERBS WITH GUTTURALS OR WEAK LETTERS AS RADICALS

1. The verb **פעל** *to do* was used as a paradigm by the older Grammarians. Now the first letter of this verb being *Pē*, the first letter of any verb was called its *Pē*; and in like manner the second letter was called its *ʿAyin* and the third its *Lāmedh*.

[1] cf. § 27. 4 (b).

This mode of designation is used in the case of verbs with gutturals or weak letters as radicals.

2. The verbs which have gutturals as radicals have to be treated separately because gutturals have certain peculiarities of usage (§ 7); with them ר has to some extent to be associated, because it, like the gutturals, does not take dagh. forte. But, in addition, since א, when final, is quiescent and, when it occurs at the end of a syllable which is not final, tends to be quiescent, פ״א and ל״א verbs have to be dealt with separately; ל״ה verbs have to be similarly dealt with, since a final ה is not a guttural but is a vowel letter (§ 2. 2). Again, since ו and י can be vowel letters as well as consonants, commonly becoming vowel letters when they fall at the end of a syllable, we have classes of verbs פ״ו and פ״י, and ע״ו and ע״י. Finally, since נ is a weak letter and tends to be assimilated to the following consonant, פ״נ verbs have to be dealt with by themselves. If a verb has more than one of these letters which have been specified, it is named according to the classes whose peculiarities it shares; e.g. ידה is a פ״י and ל״ה. A verb like גלל, whose second and third radicals are the same, is named a *Double ʿAyin* verb.

3. The forms which these classes of verbs assume when they are inflected are neither arbitrary nor anomalous; most of them are quite regular, but the paradigm form of the regular verb may be modified owing to the presence of one of the letters specified. E.g. the Piʿēl which doubles the middle radical (קִטֵּל) may undergo modification when the middle radical is a guttural, since gutturals cannot be doubled, but that modification is according to the laws affecting gutturals (§ 7; e.g. מֵאֵן *to refuse,* בֵּרֵךְ *to bless,* in which the *ḥîreq* of the paradigm form of the regular verb is lengthened to *ṣērê*).

EXERCISE

Designate the classes of these verbs

קרא, אכל, שלח, שחט, שאף, בין, ילד, ישע, רום, ברך,

עבר, שאל, נחה, נחם, נגף, רעע, קלל, בוא, סבב, קרע, ירא, ירה:

§ 29. PĒ YÔDH AND PĒ WĀW VERBS

(See Paradigm, p. 270-273)

As Hebrew words hardly ever begin with *w*, and a primary *w* at the beginning of a word becomes in Hebrew *y* (cf. Arabic *walada*, Heb. יָלַד), it is impossible to distinguish in the Qal between *Pē Yô<u>dh</u>* and *Pē Wāw* verbs, i.e. between verbs whose first radical is basically י (e.g. יָנַק) and those in which it is basically ו (e.g. יָלַד), both being written in Hebrew with initial י. Nevertheless the two types must be carefully distinguished, and in Hebrew the distinction is most obvious in the Hiph. (and Niph.); e.g. הֵינִיק (from ינק), but הוֹלִיד (from ילד < ולד). Let us take the *Pē Yô<u>dh</u>* verbs first—i.e. those whose י in the Qal is basically a י.

1. *Pē Yô<u>dh</u> Verbs*. (1) The Imperf. Qal (יִינַק) is formed quite regularly: the final vowel is *a*. Thus יִיְנַק (cf. יִכְבַּד) becomes יִינַק, since the second י, falling at the end of a syllable, loses consonantal value (§ 2. 2).

(2) The Imperf. Hiph. (יֵינִיק) is also regular. Thus יַיְנִיק (cf. יַקְטִיל) becomes יֵינִיק (*ay* > *ai* > *ê*; cf. § 2. 2).

(3) The pf. Hiph., which we should expect to be הִינִיק (from הִקְטִיל, הִיְנִיק; cf. impf. Qal), is הֵינִיק, either < הַיְנִיק with the original vowel *pa<u>th</u>aḥ* of the penult (§ 24. 1) or on the analogy of the impf.

(4) The verbs of this class, which are very few, are chiefly יָנַק *to suck* (Hiph. *to suckle*), יָטַב *to be good* (Hiph. *to do good, to do well*), יָלַל in Hiph. הֵילִיל *to howl*.

2. *Pē Wāw Verbs*. (1) (a) In the Hiph., as we have seen (perf. הוֹלִיד, imperf. יוֹלִיד, from Qal יָלַד), the original *wāw* reappears. The Imperf. יַוְלִיד (יַקְטִיל) becomes יוֹלִיד (*aw* > *au* > *ô*; cf. § 2. 2). The Perf. is הוֹלִיד, either < הַוְלִיד with the original

pathaḥ of the penult (§ 24. 1), or on the analogy of the Imperf. The Imperf. with *wāw consec.* is וַיּ֫וֹלֶד (§ 20. 4d). The Hoph. is הוּלַד (*hûladh*, from הֻוְלַד, *huwladh*); cf. הָשְׁלַךְ (alternative form to הָשְׁלַךְ).

(b) In the Niph. also the *wāw* reappears; e.g. נוֹלַד. The Niph. prefix *na* (which ordinarily appears as *ni*, as in נִקְטַל, cf. § 22. 1) combined with *w* (נַוְלַד) yields *nô* (נוֹלַד). In the imperf. Niph. (and derived parts) the *wāw* is retained and quite properly treated as a consonant; e.g. יִוָּלֵד (cf. יִקָּטֵל). The 1st sing. imperf. has always the form אִוָּלֵד, not אֶוָּלֵד (§ 22. 2).

(c) *Wāw* is sometimes found in the Hithp.; e.g. הִתְוַדַּע *to make oneself known*.

(2) Of the imperf. Qal (and infin. and imper.) there are two types:

(a) In some vbs. it is formed exactly as in impf. Qal of *Pē Yôdh* vbs.; e.g. יָרַשׁ, יִירַשׁ *to possess*, יָרֵא, יִירָא *to fear*, יָבֵשׁ *to be dry*, יָעַץ *to counsel*, יָעֵף *to be weary*, יָגַע *to be exhausted*, יָשֵׁן *to sleep*, &c.

(b) i. In others the initial י falls out. In this case the vowel of the preformative is *ē* (pretonic, long), and the final vowel is also *ē* (e.g. יֵשֵׁב, יֵלֵד: with *wāw cons.* וַיֵּ֫שֶׁב, וַתֵּ֫לֶד, § 20. 4d) or *a* before gutturals (e.g. יֵדַע).

ii. The chief verbs which inflect thus are six in number, and as they are of very common occurrence, they should be carefully noted: יָרַד *to go down*, יָשַׁב *to sit, dwell*, יָלַד *to bear*, יָדַע *to know*, יָצָא (impf. יֵצֵא) *to go out*, and הָלַךְ *to go* (impf. יֵלֵךְ as if from יָלַךְ, i.e. ולך; cf. Hiph. הוֹלִיךְ).

iii. The imper. (רֵד, שֵׁב, לֵד, דַּע, צֵא, לֵךְ) and infin. constr. (רֶדֶת, שֶׁבֶת, לֶדֶת, דַּעַת, צֵאת, לֶכֶת) are related in form to the imperf. (§ 18. 1a); note the form צֵאת (< צֶאֶת) owing to the quiescent א. The infin. constr., by the addition of ת, assumes segholate form; with suffixes צֵאתִי, דַּעְתִּי [1], לִדְתִּי [1], שִׁבְתִּי [1], רִדְתִּי, but לֶכְתִּי (sᵉghôl, under the influence of the following velar כ).

ל before such (segholate or monosyllabic) infins. construct is pointed לָ; e.g. לָצֵאת, לָשֶׁבֶת (§ 12. 1d, cf. § 34. 2a).

(3) *Verbal forms with suffixes*. The forms which are found in the Perf. Qal are normal and do not require comment; e.g. יְלָדְךָ *he begat thee*, יְלִדְתִּיהוּ *I begat him*, יְדָעָנוּ *he knows us*, יְדַעְתִּיךָ *I know thee*. Note that there is sometimes found the attenuation of a *pathaḥ* to *ḥîreq* as in the second example above. In the imperf. Qal and in the Hiph perf., imperf. and imper. the first vowel, which is long and is commonly a diphthong in origin, is unchangeably long (cf. § 2. 2). Thus we find in imperf. Qal such forms as יֵדָעֵנִי *he knows me*, יֵדָעֵהוּ *he knows him*, יֵדָעֵם *he knows them*; in the perf. Hiph. הוֹדִיעַנִי *he caused me to know*, הוֹלִידוֹ *he begat him*, in the imperf. Hiph. וַיּוֹלִידֵהוּ *and he begat him*, יוֹדִיעֵנִי *he will cause me to know*, and in the imper. Hiph. הוֹדִיעֵנִי *cause me to know*. Since many of the verbs in this class are intransitive, the examples with suffixes to be found in the Old Testament are comparatively few.

3. *Verbs assimilating the first radical*. The initial *w y* are subject to still another mode of treatment; instead of coalescing with a preceding vowel (as *iy* > *î*, *uw* > *û*, *ay* > *ê*, *aw* > *ô*), they may be assimilated, like *n*, to the following consonant, which is then doubled, as יָצַק *to pour*, impf. יִצֹּק; יצג in Hiph. הִצִּיג *to set, place*; יָצַת *to burn*, in Niph. נִצַּת, Hiph. הִצִּית.

4. *to be able* יָכֹל, perf. Qal; impf. יוּכַל
to add יָסַף, perf. Qal; impf. Hiph. יוֹסִיף

English adverbs, e.g. *again*, *well*, are rendered idiomatically by Hebrew verbs: thus

---

[1] Note the vowel *ḥîreq* instead of *pathaḥ*; cf. § 25. 3b.

and she bore again (lit. "*added to bear*", or "*added and bore*") — וַתֹּ֫וסֶף לָ֫דֶת ,, לָלֶ֫דֶת ,, וַתֵּ֫לֶד

he played the instrument well (lit. *he did well as regards playing*) — הֵיטִיב נַגֵּן ,, לְנַגֵּן

thou hast found it quickly (lit. *thou hast hastened*—מהר, *Pi.*—*as regards finding*) — מִהַרְתָּ לִמְצֹא ,, מְצֹא

נֶ֫גַע stroke, plague
בַּעֲבוּר for the sake of
שֶׁבֶר grain, corn
אָח brother
בָּחוּר a young man
אָב father
נגד Hi. (הִגִּיד) to tell
שאר *Niph.* remain, be left
עַל פִּי according to the measure of, in accordance with

אַרְבָּעִים forty
אוּר Ur
כַּשְׂדִּים Chaldeans
לָקַח (impf. יִקַּח, Imper. קַח) to take, marry
שכל Hiph. to prosper, to act prudently
אִשָּׁה *cstr.* אֵשֶׁת wife, אִשְׁתּוֹ his wife (§ 42)
פֶּה mouth, *cstr.* פִּי
יָגַע to be exhausted

חַי alive
שָׁאוּל Saul
שֵׂיבָה *f.* grey hair
תֵּבָה *f.* ark [1]
חֵן grace, favour
יעץ to advise, counsel, *Niph* to take or exchange counsel with
הֲ, הַ particle of interrogation (§ 46. 1)
בַּמֶּה (בַּמָּה in pause and before א) by what?

EXERCISE

Parse

רֵד, רְדָה, לָ֫רֶדֶת, דַּע, דַּ֫עַת, נֵֽלְכָה, אִינַק, תִּירָא, הַנּוֹרָא, אוֹרֵשׁ, וַיִּ֫וֹרֶשׁ, וָאִישָׁ֫נָה, תּוּשַׁב, בְּהוֹרִידִי, תֵּ֫רַדְנָה, וַיֹּרְדֵהוּ, הוּרַד, מַצִּיג, וַיִּדָּעֵם, יִירָשׁוּם׃

---

[1] Never the ark of the covenant (which is always אֲרוֹן, הָאָרוֹן) but Noah's ark in Gen. 6-9 (and in Ex. 2. 3, 5 the papyrus vessel in which the infant Moses was laid).

Translate

וַיֵּ֫רֶד אַבְרָם מִצְרַ֫יְמָה עִם־אִשְׁתּוֹ וְלֹא יָדַע מֶ֫לֶךְ מִצְרַ֫יִם כִּי אִשְׁתּוֹ
הִיא׃ וַיִּקָּחֶהָ לְאִשָּׁה וּלְאַבְרָם הֵיטִיב בַּעֲבוּרָהּ׃ וַיְנַגַּע יהוה אֹתוֹ
נְגָעִים גְּדֹלִים וַיֵּדַע כִּי אִשְׁתּוֹ הִיא׃ 2 אָמַר יהוה אֶל־אַבְרָם אֲנִי
יהוה אֲשֶׁר הוֹצֵאתִ֫יךָ מֵאוּר כַּשְׂדִּים [1]לָ֫תֶת לְךָ אֶת־הָאָ֫רֶץ הַזֹּאת
לְרִשְׁתָּהּ׃ [2]וַיֹּאמַר אֲדֹנָי יהוה בַּמָּה אֵדַע כִּי אִירָשֶׁ֫נָּה׃ 3 [2]וַיֹּאמְרוּ
בְּנֵי יַעֲקֹב אֵלָיו שָׁאוֹל שָׁאַל הָאִישׁ לָ֫נוּ וּלְמוֹלַדְתֵּ֫נוּ [2]לֵאמֹר הַעוֹד
[3]אֲבִיכֶם חַי [4]הֲיֵשׁ לָכֶם אָח וַנַּגֶּד־לוֹ עַל־פִּי הַדְּבָרִים הָאֵ֫לֶּה
הֲיָדוֹעַ נֵדַע כִּי יֹאמַר הוֹרִידוּ אֶת־ [3]אֲחִיכֶם׃ 4 אֱלֹהֵי עוֹלָם יהוה
בֹּרֵא הַשָּׁמַיִם וְהָאָ֫רֶץ לֹא יִיעַף וְלֹא יִיגָע׃ יִיעֲפוּ נְעָרִים וְיִיגְעוּ
וּבַחוּרִים כָּשׁוֹל יִכָּשֵׁ֫לוּ וְהַבֹּטְחִים בַּיהוה יֵלְכוּ וְלֹא יִיעָ֫פוּ׃ 5
וְעַתָּה אִם־נָא [5]מָצָאתִי חֵן בְּעֵינֶ֫יךָ הוֹדִעֵ֫נִי־נָא אֶת־דְּרָכֶ֫יךָ וְאֵדָעֲךָ
לְמַעַן [5]אֶמְצָא חֵן בְּעֵינֶ֫יךָ׃ 6 וַיֵּצֵא דָוִד וַיַּשְׂכֵּל בְּכֹל אֲשֶׁר יִשְׁלָחֶ֫נּוּ
שָׁאוּל וַיִּיטַב בְּעֵינֵי כָל־הָעָם וְגַם בְּעֵינֵי עַבְדֵי שָׁאוּל׃ 7 וזכרת
את־כל־הדרך אשר הוליכך יהוה אלהיך זה ארבעים שנה
במדבר לדעת את־אשר בלבבך הֲתשמר מצותיו אם־לא׃

And the ark went upon the face of the waters. 2 Make me to know thy ways. 3 And they said unto her, Wilt thou go with this man? and she said, I will go. 4 And he said, Cause every man to go out of the house; and there stood no man with him, when he made himself known to his brethren.

---

[1] Cf. § 34. 3a.

[2] אָמַר, imperf. יֹאמַר, imperf. consec. וַיֹּאמֶר (in pause, וַיֹּאמַר); לֵאמֹר, *saying* (cf. § 37).

[3] אָב, constr. אֲבִי, *thy father* אָבִיךָ, *his father* אָבִיהוּ or אָבִיו, *your father* אֲבִיכֶם; so אָח (see § 42); pl. אַחִים; with suff. אַחַי, אַחֶיךָ but אֶחָיו.

[4] יֵשׁ *there is, there are* (opposite of אַיִן, § 31. 4, Note 1), a particle —with suffixes, יֶשְׁךָ *thou art*, יֶשְׁכֶם *you are* (הֲ is interrogative particle, § 46. 1).

[5] *qāmeṣ* with the צ owing to the quiescent א following it (cf. §7.6 b. ii).

5 And the man opened the doors of the house and went out to go on (*dat.*) his way. 6 And the daughter of Pharaoh said to her, Take this child and nurse (suckle) it for me, and she took the child and nursed it. 7 Behold I have heard that there is corn in Egypt, go down thither and buy us a little food. 8 And Yahweh said unto him, Go not down to Egypt, dwell in the land which I shall say unto thee. 9 And he was afraid and said, How terrible (ירא, *Niph. ptc.*) is this place! 10 That man cursed me with a heavy curse on the day when I went to the Jordan and I resolved[1] to kill him with the sword. 11 Now then do not forget him for you are a wise man and you will know (how) to requite him and you shall bring down his grey hairs in blood to Sheol.

§ 30. ʿAYIN WĀW AND ʿAYIN YÔDH VERBS

(See Paradigm, p. 274-277)

This class includes the verbs whose middle letter, ו or י, is a *vowel* letter (e.g. קוּם *to arise*, רִיב *to contend*), but not the vbs. in which that letter is a real consonant (e.g. גָּוַע *to expire*, חָיָה *to live*). Whether these vbs. were always monosyllabic, or whether they are contracted forms of verbs of the ordinary type, the middle letter being originally consonantal (e.g. pf. קָם from קָוַם, מֵת from מָוֵת *to die*? cf. the noun מָוֶת *māweth*, *death*), is a question difficult to decide, and need not be here discussed. In these verbs the inf. cstr. (קוּם, רִיב, &c.), not the pf. Qal, is treated as the ground-form, as the pf. Qal (קָם, רָב, &c.) does not exhibit the characteristic ו or י. The following vbs. illustrate the various types.

1. *The Qal.*

	to arise	to die	to come	to discern	to be ashamed
Infin. cstr.	קוּם	מוּת	בּוֹא	בִּין	בּוֹשׁ
Imperf.	יָקוּם	יָמוּת	יָבוֹא	יָבִין	יֵבוֹשׁ
Perf.	קָם	מֵת	בָּא	בָּן	בּוֹשׁ

[1] Heb.: said in my heart.

(a) The infins. constr. being monosyllabic, the pointing of לְ before them is with *qāmeṣ*; e.g. לָמוּת (§ 12. 1d; cf. § 29. 2, (2) b. iii).

(b) i. *Imperf.* The vowel of the ground-form (infin. constr.) is preserved, and the original form of the preformative, *ya*, of the strong verb (§ 17. 4a), lengthened in the open syllable before the tone to *yā* (cf. § 5. 2b): hence יָקוּם, יָמוּת, יָבוֹא, יָבִין; *pl.* יָקֽוּמוּ, &c. In יֵבוֹשׁ the preformative is the regular *yi* (proper and original to *stative* vbs.; § 19. 3), lengthened to *yē* (§ 5. 2b).

ii. Only in impf. Qal do ע״ו and ע״י vbs. differ (יָקוּם, יָבִין): there the characteristic י or ו appears. But in Hiph., e.g., they are alike: הֵקִים, הֵבִין; יָקִים, יָבִין.

iii. Jussive יָקֹם; impf. with *wāw cons.* וַיָּֽקָם (*way-yā́-qom*); with final guttural or *r* וַיָּֽסַר *and he turned aside* (§ 7. 3b), from סוּר. Cohortative: Qal אָקֽוּמָה, Hiph. אָקִימָה; etc.

(c) *Perf.* As in the regular verbs (קָטֵל, כָּבֵד, קָטֹן) the vowel may be *a ē* or *ō*; e.g. קָם, מֵת, בּוֹשׁ, בָּא, בָּן.

fem. קָֽמָה, מֵֽתָה, &c.; 1 *s.c.* קַֽמְתִּי, מַֽתִּי, בֹּֽשְׁתִּי, בָּֽאתִי[1], בַּֽנְתִּי, &c.

(d) *Participle.* The active part. s. m. is the same in form as the 3rd s.m. perf.: קָם, מֵת, &c.: *fem.* קָֽמָה, *pl.* קָֽמִים, *cstr.* קָמֵי (*â* unchangeable, § 31. 1a).

2. *Hiph.* (a) The Hiph. is of the regular form (הִקְטִיל, יַקְטִיל); only the vowel of the preformative (*hi*, *ya*), being now in the open syllable, becomes the corresponding tone-long vowel (*hē*, *yā*): הֵקִים (*f.* הֵקִֽימָה), impf. יָקִים; ptc. not מָקִים (cf. מַקְטִיל) but מֵקִים (formed from the perf.). Hoph. הוּקַם, יוּקַם, מוּקָם.

(b) Jussive יָקֵם: impf. with *wāw consec.* וַיָּֽקֶם; with final guttural or *r* וַיָּֽסַר (same as Qal) *and he removed* (§ 7. 3b).

3. *Niph.* נָקוֹם (נִקְטַל). The original preformative of the perf. Niph. being *na*, it may be presumed that the basic form was נַקְוַם, which became נָקוֹם when the *wāw* lost consonantal

[1] *qāmeṣ* with the בּ owing to the quiescent א following it (cf. §7. 6. b. ii).

value, and the vowel *a* became lengthened in the open penultimate syllable; fem. נָקֹ֫ומָה; imperf. יִקּוֹם (from יִנְקוֹם).

4. *Piʻēl*, &c. The regular intensive forms, duplicating the middle radical (e.g. עִוֵּד *to surround*, from עוד), are very rare and late. The intensive is usually formed by the reduplication of the last radical—*Pôʻlēl* (e.g. קוֹמֵם *to raise up, pass.* קוֹמַם ; רוֹמֵם *to exalt*), or the first and last—*Pilpēl* (e.g. כִּלְכֵּל *to sustain*). Cf. § 23. 5.

5. (a) The vowels *î û* being so characteristic of these verbs, a great effort is made to give them expression; but as they cannot stand in a shut syllable with two consonants following them (cf. § 4. 4b; e.g. תָּקוּמְנָה, 3 *f. pl. impf. Qal*, הֲקִימְתָּ, 2 *s. m. pf. Hiph.*, are impossible), a vowel is often inserted between the stem and the consonantal afformatives, and *î û* thus remain in the open syllable. The inserted vowel is *ô* in perf., and *ê* in impf.; e.g. תְּקוּמֶ֫ינָה, impf. Qal, הֲקִימ֫וֹתָ, pf. Hiph., נְקוּמ֫וֹתִי, pf. Niph. (for נְקוּמ֫וֹתִי).

(b) Sometimes the regular vb. is followed, and no vowel is inserted. In that case *î û* become *ē* (*a* in pf. Hiph.) *ō* in the shut syllable; e.g. תָּשֹׁ֫בְנָה (*they shall return*, fem. impf. Qal from שׁוּב; but also תְּשׁוּבֶ֫ינָה), תָּשֵׁבְנָה (impf. Hiph.), הֵנַפְתָּ (pf. Hiph. of נוף *to wave, swing*; but also הֲנִיפ֫וֹתָ). Sometimes, as we have just noted, both forms are found.

6. Some vbs. are both ע״ו and ע״י, though one form usually predominates; e.g. שׂוּם or שִׂים *to place* (impf. יָשִׂים, very rarely יָשׂוּם), שׂוּשׂ or שִׂישׂ *to rejoice*.

7. *Verbal forms with suffixes.* As may be inferred from the vocabulary, almost all the common verbs of this class are intransitive in the Qal. But forms with suffixes are found in the Hiph. and the important thing to notice is that the first vowel of Hiph. forms is tone-long and, therefore, subject to modification; e.g. הֱשִׁיבַ֫נִי *he restored me*, הֱשִׁיבְךָ *he restored thee*. וַהֲשִׁיבוֹתָם *and thou shalt restore them*; יְשִׁיבֵ֫נִי *he will restore me*, יְשִׁיבֶ֫הָ *he will restore it*; הֲשִׁיבֵ֫נוּ *restore us*.

- קוּם to arise; *Hiph.* to establish
- נוּחַ to rest; *Hiph.* הֵנִיחַ to cause to rest, give rest to; הִנִּיחַ to place, set down
- צוּד to hunt
- אֹהֶל tent
- מוּת to die
- רוּץ to run
- שָׁלֹשׁ three; שְׁלִישִׁי third
- מָנוֹחַ resting-place
- מֵרָחוֹק in the distance
- נֹחַ Noah
- שִׂים שׂוּם to set
- שׁוּב to return; *Hiph.* to restore
- רוּם to be high
- בּוֹשׁ to be ashamed
- בּוֹא to come
- נוּס to flee
- כּוּן to be firm(?) (not found in *Qal*); כּוֹנֵן, הֵכִין *Hiph. Pôʿlēl* to establish
- סוּר to turn aside; *Hiph.* to remove
- אֶחָד (constr. אַחַד) fem. אַחַת one
- חֵטְא, חַטָּאת sin
- עוֹלָה burnt-offering
- קרב *Hiph.* to bring near, to offer
- יוֹנָה *f.*, יוֹנִים *pl.* dove
- ישׁב *Hiph.* to settle, to place
- הָלַךְ to go; *Hiph.* הוֹלִיךְ to carry away, to lead away
- אוֹר to shine
- רִיב to contend
- עוּד[1] *Hiph.* to testify
- כַּף *f.* palm (of hand), sole (of foot)

Note the idiomatic usage illustrated in the sentence: אָנֹכִי נַעַר קָטֹן לֹא אֵדַע צֵאת וָבֹא׃ lit. *I am a young lad; I do not know how to go out and come in,* i.e. *I am young and inexperienced in human life and affairs.*

EXERCISE

Parse and translate

נָס, סָרָה, שָׁבָה, וּבָאָה, וְסָרוּ, אָרוּם, תָּשֹׁבִי, תְּשׁוּבֶינָה, יָרֹם, אָמוּתָה, וַיָּמָת, לָסוּר, תִּכּוֹן, הֲרִימוֹת, וַהֲשִׁבֹתִי, יָאִיר, וַיָּרֶם׃

הוּא מֵקִים מֵעָפָר אֶבְיוֹנִים וְכִסֵּא שָׂרִים יַנְחִלֵם׃ 2 יָדֹעַ תֵּדְעוּ כִּי אִם מְמִתִים אַתֶּם אֹתִי כִּי־דָם נָקִי אַתֶּם נֹתְנִים עֲלֵיכֶם׃ 3 וְלֹא מָצְאָה הַיּוֹנָה מָנוֹחַ לְכַף רַגְלָהּ וַתָּשָׁב אֶל־נֹחַ אֶל־הַתֵּבָה וַיִּשְׁלַח

[1] Note the uncommon verb עוּד, whose *Pi.* עִוֵּד means *to surround* (cf. 4 above) and the denominative verb עוּד, whose *Hiph.* הֵעִיד means *to testify* (עֵד *witness, testimony; witness* (a person)).

יָדוֹ וַיִּקָּחֶהָ וַיָּבֵא אֹתָהּ אֵלָיו אֶל־הַתֵּבָה׃ 4 יהוה אֱלֹהָי תָּשָׁב־נָא
נֶפֶשׁ הַיֶּלֶד הַזֶּה׃ 5 וַיִּקְרָא הַמֶּלֶךְ אֶל־דָּוִד וַיְדַבֵּר אֵלָיו לֵאמֹר׃
יָשָׁר אַתָּה וְטוֹב בְּעֵינַי צֵאתְךָ וּבוֹאֲךָ אִתִּי בַּמִּלְחָמָה לֹא־נִמְצְאָה
בְךָ רָעָה מִיּוֹם בּוֹאֲךָ אֵלַי עַד־הַיּוֹם הַזֶּה׃ 6 וַיֹּאמֶר לוֹ יהוה
[1]קַח־נָא אֶת־בִּנְךָ אֲשֶׁר אָהַבְתָּ וְלֶךְ אֶל־אֶרֶץ רְחוֹקָה וְהַקְרִיבֵהוּ
לְעֹלָה עַל־אַחַד הֶהָרִים שָׁם׃ וַיֵּלֶךְ לְדַרְכּוֹ בַּבֹּקֶר הוּא וּבְנוֹ
אֶל־הַמָּקוֹם אֲשֶׁר אָמַר לוֹ יהוה׃ בַּיּוֹם הַשְּׁלִישִׁי נָשָׂא אַבְרָהָם
אֶת־עֵינָיו [1a]וַיַּבֵּט אֶל־הַמָּקוֹם מֵרָחוֹק׃ וַיֹּאמֶר אֶל־נְעָרָיו שְׁבוּ
לָכֶם בַּמָּקוֹם הַזֶּה וַאֲנִי וּבְנִי נֵלְכָה לְדַרְכֵּנוּ וְנָשׁוּבָה אֲלֵיכֶם׃ וַיָּבֹאוּ
אַבְרָהָם וּבְנוֹ אֶל־הַמָּקוֹם וַיָּשֶׂם אֶת־בְּנוֹ עַל־הַמִּזְבֵּחַ וַיִּשְׁלַח
אַבְרָהָם אֶת־יָדוֹ לַהֲמִיתוֹ׃ וַיִּקְרָא אֵלָיו מַלְאַךְ יהוה מִן־הַשָּׁמַיִם
וַיֹּאמֶר אַבְרָהָם אַל־תִּשְׁלַח אֶת־יָדְךָ עַל־הַיֶּלֶד כִּי עַתָּה יָדַעְתִּי
כִּי יְרֵא אֱלֹהִים אָתָּה׃ 7 הנה אנכי מת והיה אלהים [2]עִמָּכֶם
והשיב אתכם אל־ארץ אבותיכם׃ 8 אם־שכח תשכח את־
יהוה אלהיך והלכת אחרי אלהים אחרים ועבדתם [3]העדתי
בך היום כי מות תמות׃

Suggested further reading: 1 Sam. ix, 6-14.

And they fled the way of the wilderness. 2 Depart not from-after Yahweh, but (and) ye shall serve him with all your heart. 3 Arise, shine, for thy (*f.*) light is come. 4 And he took not from his hand (that) which he had brought. 5 I will surely-return (*inf. abs.*) unto thee (*f.*). 6 And he arose in the morning and went with the princes of Moab. 7 And he called the man (*dat.*) and said unto him, Thou hast brought upon me and upon my kingdom a great sin. 8 And the woman went out and came to the captain of the king's host and said, Turn aside, my lord, turn aside unto me, fear not; and he

---

[1] Imper. s. m. of לָקַח. [1a] See Voc. § 26.

[2] *With you*, from עִם (see § 40. 6b).

[3] הַעִדֹתִי. The pf. Hiph. of עוד has ַ instead of ֲ.

turned aside unto her to-the-tent. 9 I know your sitting down, your going out and your coming in. 10 The people of Israel walked in all the sins which the king committed (עָשָׂה); they did not depart from them until Yahweh removed Israel out of his sight. 11 The nations which you have carried away (Hiph. of הָלַךְ) and settled in the cities[1] of the land do not know the law of the god of the land.

§ 31. NOUNS FROM ʻAYIN WĀW AND YÔDH

1. First declension. See § 15.

קָם	*rising* (part. of קוּם)	*plur.*	קָמִים	*cstr.*	קָמֵי	*fem.*	קָמָה
מֵת	*dead* (part. of מוּת)	*plur.*	מֵתִים	*cstr.*	מֵתֵי	*fem.*	מֵתָה
טוֹב	*good*	*plur.*	טוֹבִים	*cstr.*	טוֹבֵי	*fem.*	טוֹבָה
מָקוֹם	*place*	*plur.*	מְקוֹמוֹת	&c.			
(מָגוֹר)	*sojourning-place*	*plur.*	מְגוּרִים	(גּוּר *to sojourn*)			
מָנוֹחַ	*resting-place*	*fem.*	מְנוּחָה	(נוּחַ *to rest*)			
		fem.	מְדִינָה	*a province* (דִּין *to judge*)			

(a) Whether or not the first three words are to be regarded as contracted from קָוָם, מָוֵת, טָוֹב (and therefore ideally falling within the first declension (§ 15), it is important to note that words of this type, derived from roots whose middle letter is י or ו, have *unchangeable* vowels; e.g. *pl. cstr.* קָמֵי, not קְמֵי (unlike דָּם *blood*, which, not being from a root דּוּם, has pl. cstr. דְּמֵי), מֵתֵי, not מְתֵי.

(b) Note, too, that ע״ו nouns with מ preformative have often, with inflectional additions (e.g. *pl.* or *fem.*), וּ instead of וֹ; cf. pf. Niph. נָקוֹם נְקוּמֹתָ (§ 30. 5a; so מָתוֹק *sweet*, מְתוּקָה, &c.).

2. Second declension. See § 25.

ע״ו Nouns

	a class			*i* class	*u* class	
abs.	אוֹר	שׁוֹר	מָוֶת	none	סוּס	שׁוּק

1 עִיר *city*; pl. עָרִים, cstr. עָרֵי (cf. § 31. 5).

cstr.	אוֹר	שׁוֹר	מוֹת	סוּס	שׁוּק
suff.	אוֹרִי	שׁוֹרִי	מוֹתִי	סוּסִי	שׁוּקִי
plur.	אוֹרִים	שְׁוָרִים	מוֹתִים	סוּסִים	שְׁוָקִים
cstr.	אוֹרֵי	שׁוֹרֵי	מוֹתֵי	סוּסֵי	שׁוּקֵי
	(light)	(ox)	(death)	(horse)	(street)

ע״י Nouns

		a class		*i* class	*u* class
abs.	חֵיק	זַ֫יִת	חַ֫יִל	שִׁיר	none
cstr.	,,	זֵית	חֵיל	,,	
suff.	חֵיקִי	זֵיתִי	חֵילִי	שִׁירִי	
plur.	(חֵיקִים)	זֵיתִים	חֲיָלִים	שִׁירִים	
cstr.	(חֵיקֵי)	זֵיתֵי	חֵילֵי	שִׁירֵי	
	(bosom)	(olive)	(force)	(song)	

(a) Some of these words, in the absolute form, are manifestly segholates; e.g. מָוֶת, זַיִת (for *ḥîreq*, see § 25. I, footnote).

Others, the majority, are not; e.g. אוֹר, חֵיק, which are simply monosyllables with long, unchangeable vowels. Originally, however, these nouns were of the form *'awr* (or *'aur*) and *ḥayq* (or *ḥaiq*), corresponding to *malk*, and, therefore, not unfairly regarded as basically segholates.

(b) There is a distinct preference for the shorter (which is probable the later) form. Note that the shorter form appears in *all* the constructs (i.e. even where the abs. is dissyllabic, e.g. מָוֶת *c.* מוֹת, זַיִת *c.* זֵית, חַיִל *c.* חֵיל), and of course with suffixes (מוֹתִי, זֵיתִי, &c.); also, in most cases, even with the abs. plur.; e.g. מוֹתִים, זֵיתִים.

(c) In a few cases, however, the plur. has the longer form as in ordinary segholates (e.g. חֲיָלִים from חַיִל. cf. מְלָכִים), even (though rarely) when the sing. is monosyllabic (cf. שְׁוָרִים from שׁוֹר, שְׁוָקִים from שׁוּק).

(d) With the rare exception just mentioned, the inflection of monosyllabic nouns of this type proceeds with absolute regularity, because of the unchangeableness of the vowel (cf. סוּס, § 16).

3. (a) In *ʿAyin Wāw* nouns of the *a* class the primary vowel *a* is not assimilated to *e* (as, e.g., in *malk, mélekh,* מֶלֶךְ) but lengthened, probably under the influence of the *wāw*, to *ā* (the form reserved in ordinary segholates for pause; e.g. דֶּרֶךְ, p. דָּרֶךְ, § 25. 1): thus מָוֶת (not מֶוֶת), תָּוֶךְ. (With suffix, בְּתוֹכָם *in their midst*.)

(b) In *ʿAyin Yôdh* nouns of the *a* class the primary *a* was not lengthened to *ā*, probably because the word was pronounced practically as a monosyllable, and the helping vowel is not *sᵉghôl* but *ḥîreq*, which is homogeneous with the י; e.g. not זָיֶת but זַיִת.

4. There are no ע״ו nouns of the *i* class, nor ע״י nouns of the *u* class, because these consonants have no affinity for these vowels (§ 2. 2, § 2. 4g).

death מָוֶת and so: midst תָּוֶךְ, evil אָוֶן.
light אוֹר and so: voice קוֹל, *pl. ôth*, pit בּוֹר *ôth*, generation דּוֹר *îm* and *ôth*, fowl עוֹף.
horse סוּס and so: spirit רוּחַ *ôth*, street חוּץ *ôth*.
olive זַיִת and so: ram אַיִל, wine יַיִן, no אַיִן[1]
force חַיִל and so: eye עַיִן *ôth* (wells), colt עַיִר.
bosom חֵיק and so: calamity אֵיד, smell רֵיחַ.
song שִׁיר and so: vanity רִיק, judgment דִּין, joy גִּיל.

[1] אַ֫יִן, which often appears with a sort of verbal function, and is = *there is not* (cf. יֵשׁ *there is*, § 29. Exer., n. 4), not unnaturally takes verbal suffixes, occasionally strengthened by the *nun energicum* (§ 31. 6); they are אֵינֶנִּי, אֵינְךָ, אֵינֵךְ, אֵינֶנּוּ, אֵינֶנָּה, אֵינֶנּוּ, אֵינְכֶם, אֵינָם. E.g. Enoch walked with God וְאֵינֶנּוּ *and he was not*. A verb accompanying אין must be in the participle; e.g. *ye do not keep* my ways, אֵינְכֶם שֹׁמְרִים.

Somewhat similarly עוֹד *yet, still*: עוֹדֶנִּי (עוֹדִי), עוֹדְךָ, עוֹדֵךְ, עוֹדֶנּוּ, 3 *pl.* עוֹדָם.

5. Many words have some irregularity:

house בַּיִת, *pl.* בָּתִּים, probably *bāttîm* or *bâtîm* (see § 42).

eye עַיִן, *du.* עֵינַיִם eyes, *pl.* עֲיָנוֹת *wells.*

night לַיִל, more usually לַ֫יְלָה, where ָה is acc. termination; *cstr.* לֵיל, *pl.* לֵילוֹת.

day יוֹם, *pl.* יָמִים (< יְוָמִים). This word is very irregular in treating its *â* as merely tone-long: hence *pl. cstr.* יְמֵי.

city עִיר, *pl.* עָרִים (< עֲיָרִים), constr. pl. עָרֵי.

head רֹאשׁ, probably = רָאשׁ (§ 2. 6a) *râš* < *ra'š* (like *malk*), *plur.* רָאשִׁים (contracted from רְאָשִׁים), cstr. רָאשֵׁי.

The א, now silent, indicates by its presence in these forms that originally it had consonantal value.

שׁכם	*Hiph.* to rise early	עוז	*Hiph.* to bring into safety	דָּבַק	to cleave to
				פָּרַח	to flourish
בֶּגֶד	garment, coat	עֵת	time	הָדָר	glory
בָּרָד	hail	שָׂדֶה	field, country	רֵיחַ	smell

אִשָּׁה woman, wife; constr. אֵשֶׁת; with suf. אִשְׁתִּי, &c.

אֵצֶל beside; with suf. אֶצְלִי, &c. גֶּ֫פֶן 2 vine.

EXERCISE

Translate

עֵינַי עַל־כָּל־דַּרְכֵיהֶם לֹא נִסְתְּרוּ מִלְּפָנָי וְלֹא־נִצְפַּן עֲוֺנָם מִנֶּגֶד
עֵינָי׃ 2 חֵיל גּוֹיִם יָבֹאוּ לָךְ׃ 3 הִצַּלְתֶּם אֶת־נַפְשֹׁתֵינוּ מִמָּוֶת׃
4 לֹא אֶחְפֹּץ בְּמוֹת הַמֵּת׃ 5 וַיַּשְׁכִּימוּ בַבֹּקֶר וַיָּשׁוּבוּ וַיָּבֹאוּ אֶל־
בֵּיתָם וַיֵּדַע הָאִישׁ אֶת־אִשְׁתּוֹ וַיִּזְכְּרֶהָ יהוה׃ 6 וְעַתָּה שְׁלַח הָעֵז
אֶת־כָּל־אֲשֶׁר לְךָ בַּשָּׂדֶה וְלֹא יֵרֵד עֲלֵיהֶם הַבָּרָד וָמֵתוּ׃ 7 הִנֵּה־
נָא מָצָא עַבְדְּךָ חֵן בְּעֵינֶיךָ וַתַּגְדֵּל אֶת־חַסְדְּךָ עִמִּי וְאָנֹכִי לֹא
אוּכַל לְהִמָּלֵט הָהָרָה פֶּן־תִּדְבָּקַנִי הָרָעָה וָמַתִּי׃ 8 הַעַתָּה לָקַחַתְּ

אֶת־הַכֶּסֶף וְלָקַחַת בּוֹ גַּנִּים וְזֵיתִים וּכְרָמִים וְצֹאן וּבָקָר וַעֲבָדִים
וּשְׁפָחוֹת׃ 9 וישמעו את־קול יהוה מתהלך בתוך עץ הגן לרוח
היום ויסתר האדם ואשתו מפניו׃ 10 ולמדתם את־דברי את־
בניכם לדבר בם בשבתך בביתך ובלכתך בדרך ובשכבך
ובקומך׃

Behold I am old, I know not the day of my death. 2 In
those days there-was-not a king in Israel, (every) man did[1]
the (thing) upright in his (own) eyes. 3 And he offered the ram
of the burnt-offering. 4 And the men feared to return to their
houses. 5 Its glory shall be like an olive[2] and the smell of
it like Lebanon; they shall return and dwell in their land and
flourish like the vine of Lebanon. 6 She placed his coat
beside her until his master should return home. 7 In the days
of the old prophet the people planted vineyards but did not
gather the wine of them and they sowed in the field but
did not eat their food in peace.

§ 32. LĀMEDH HĒ (LĀMEDH WĀW AND LĀMEDH YÔDH) VERBS

(See Paradigm, p. 278-281)

1. The ה in this class of verbs (e.g. גָּלָה *to uncover, reveal*) is not a genuine letter of the root, but a mere vowel sign, indicating *ā* (When the ה is truly consonantal, it takes *mappîq*, § 6. 8, e.g. גָּבַהּ *to be high*, and the vb. is treated like a *Lamedh guttural*, § 36).

The last letter of the stem is properly either י (גלי *gālay*) or ו (e.g. שלו *shālaw*), though forms with *yôdh* have acquired such a preponderance that only a few traces of stems with *wāw* now appear. *Lāmedh Yôdh* (or *Lāmedh Wāw*) would therefore be a more appropriate term, as ה is not integral to the root.

1 יַעֲשֶׂה *impf.*, § 43. II 2.

2 § 12. 2b ii.

The original י of גלי (now גָּלָה) is still seen in the pass. ptc. Qal, גָּלוּי (gālûy, cf. קָטוּל), and in some pausal forms; e.g. חָסָיוּ *they sought refuge* (cf. קָטָלוּ). The original ו of שלו (שָׁלָה) is seen in the words שָׁלֵו (šālēw) *at ease*, שַׁלְוָה (šalwā) *ease* (שָׁלַוְתִּי *I was at ease*, 1 s. pf. Qal, in Job 3. 26).

2. The letter ה, appropriate as indicating the vowel *ā* in the 3rd s.m. perf. Qal, is used commonly in verbal forms of *Lāmedh Hē* verbs which have no afformative (the exceptions are the infins. constr. and the pass. part. Qal); but the vowel preceding the ה frequently differs, in a way difficult to account for, from that of the corresponding part of the regular verb. The endings in use are as follows:

(a) ָה in *all* perfects, e.g. גָּלָה, נִגְלָה, גִּלָּה, הִגְלָה, &c.

(b) ֶה in *all* imperfects, e.g. יִגְלֶה, יִגָּלֶה, יְגַלֶּה, יַגְלֶה, &c.

(c) ֶה in *all* participles (exc. pass. Qal) absolute; e.g. גֹּלֶה (*f.* גֹּלָה), נִגְלֶה, מְגַלֶּה, מַגְלֶה, &c.

Ptc. cstr. is in ֵה; e.g. גֹּלֵה, &c.

(d) ֵה in *all* imperatives; e.g. גְּלֵה, גַּלֵּה, הַגְלֵה, &c.

(e) Inf. abs. has the ordinary vowel of the regular vb.; Qal גָּלֹה, Hiph. הַגְלֵה.

(f) Inf. cstr. adds the fem. ending ת, making the termination וֹת; e.g. Qal גְּלוֹת, Pi. גַּלּוֹת, Hiph. הַגְלוֹת.

3. In parts of *Lāmedh Hē* verbs which have afformatives, the rule is as follows:

(a) Before vocalic afformatives, וּ, ִי, or ָה, the *yôdh*, coming between two vowels (cf. קָטְלוּ), loses consonantal value and disappears; e.g. not גָּלְיוּ, but גָּלוּ.

So 3 s.f. Qal would be גָּלְיָה > גָּלָה, which is the same in form as the 3 s.m. This is doubtless the reason for the form גָּלְתָה as 3 s.f.; in it the fem. is doubly represented, by the ת (cf. § 27. 5a) and the ָה.

The *yôdh* is also dropped before suffixes; e.g. עָנָנִי (not עֲנָהַנִי nor עֲנָיַנִי), *he answered me*, עָנָהוּ (not עֲנָיו; in עָנָהוּ the ה belongs to the suffix הוּ, and is not the ה of ענה) *he answered him*, עָנָם (not עֲנָיָם); likewise יַעֲנֵם *he will answer them*, וַיִּרְאֵהוּ *and he saw him* (רָאָה).

(b) When the *yôdh* occurs at the end of a syllable before a consonantal afformative (cf. נִגְלַיְתִּי, נִקְטַלְתִּי), the *yôdh*, preceded as it always is by *a*, creates in the first instance the combination *ay*, the *yôdh* being consonantal.

i. This *ay* most naturally becomes the diphthongal *ê*, § 2. 2a. Thus נִגְלַיְתִּי becomes נִגְלֵיתִי. This *ê*, prevails exclusively in perff. pass., i.e. Niph. Pu. (גֻּלֵּיתִי) and Hoph..

ii. But in the other parts it also appears as *î*, which in perf. Qal is found exclusively, and in other perff. alternatively with *ê*, as Qal גָּלִ֫יתָ; Pi. גִּלִּיתָ and גִּלֵּיתָ.

iii. Before נָה of imperf. and imper. it becomes *é* (*sᵉghôl* fairly regarded as pure long; cf. § 3. 3d), as גְּלֶ֫ינָה, תִּגְלֶ֫ינָה.

4. Of the few verbs ending in *waw*, שָׁחָה (שחו) is found very frequently, usually in the Hithpaʿlel (הִתְקַטְלֵל) *to bow down, to prostrate oneself*. The perf. would be strictly הִתְשַׁחְוֵו > הִתְשַׁחֲוָה (ח with a helping vowel (§ 7. 5) and the uninflected perf. form ending in *ā* (cf. section 1 above)) > הִשְׁתַּחֲוָה (§ 23. 3a, ii); imperf. יִשְׁתַּחֲוֶה, pl. יִשְׁתַּחֲווּ. Apoc. imperf. sing. (§ 33. 1) is יִשְׁתַּחַו > יִשְׁתַּחוּ, since it is characteristic of final consonantal *w* to pass into the unaccented, homogeneous (vocalic) *û*. תַּ, not תָּ, is found in יִשְׁתַּחוּ, because the following ח was felt to be virtually doubled.[1]

In pf. with *waw consec.* the accent is not usually on the final syllable: e.g. וְעָשִׂ֫יתָ, not וְעָשִׂיתָ֫ *and thou shalt make*.

[1] An alternative interpretation of הִשְׁתַּחֲוָה and related forms which is now available is that they are reflexives of Shaphʿel forms of the root *ḥwy to bow down*.

5. *Forms with suffixes* (cf. section 2a above).

	Perf.	Qal			Impf. Qal	Imper. Qal
	גָּלָה	גָּלִיתָ	גָּלִיתִי	גָּלוּ	יִגְלֶה	גְּלֵה
1st s.suffix	גָּלַנִי	גְּלִיתַנִי		גָּלוּנִי	יִגְלֵנִי	גְּלֵנִי
2nd s.m.	גָּלְךָ		גְּלִיתִיךָ	גָּלוּךָ	יִגְלְךָ	
2nd s.f.	גָּלֵךְ		גְּלִיתִיךְ	גָּלוּךְ	יִגְלֵךְ	
3rd s.m.	גָּלָהוּ	גְּלִיתָהוּ (or תוֹ)	גְּלִיתִיהוּ (or תִיו)	גָּלוּהוּ	יִגְלֵהוּ	גְּלֵהוּ
3rd s.f.	גָּלָהּ	גְּלִיתָהּ	גְּלִיתִיהָ	גָּלוּהָ	יִגְלֶהָ	גְּלֶהָ
1st pl.	גָּלָנוּ	גְּלִיתָנוּ		גָּלוּנוּ	יִגְלֵנוּ	גְּלֵנוּ
3rd pl.m.	גָּלָם	גְּלִיתָם	גְּלִיתִים	גָּלוּם	יִגְלֵם	גְּלֵם

6. *Idiomatic Usages.* (a) רְאֵה אֶת־שְׁלוֹם אַחֶיךָ וְאֶת־שְׁלוֹם הַצֹּאן *see how your brothers and the sheep are faring* (Gen. 37. 14)[1]; (b) נִקְרֵיתִי בְּהַר הַגִּלְבֹּעַ וְהִנֵּה שָׁאוּל נִשְׁעָן עַל־חֲנִיתוֹ *I happened to be on Mt. Gilboa when I caught sight of* (lit; and behold) *Saul leaning on his spear* (2 Sam. 1. 6).

היה to be
עשׂה to do
קנה to acquire
רֶכֶב chariot
אֲרוֹן (with article הָאָרוֹן) chest, ark
ראה to see
כסה *Pi.* to cover
רבה (intrans.) to increase
שִׁיר to sing
פוץ (*Qal or Niph.*) to be scattered

שׁתה to drink
שׁקה [2] *Hiph.* to give drink, water
מנה to count
בכה to weep
מחה to blot out
הַיַּרְדֵּן the Jordan
עָנָן cloud
פרה to be fruitful
צוה *Pi.* to command
סבב to surround
נָכְרִי foreign, strange
רְחַבְעָם Rehoboam
רַב much; pl. many

פקח to open (eyes)
נכה *Hiph.* (הִכָּה) to smite
פִּנָּה *f.* corner
פנה to turn
הרה to conceive
עלה to go up
גלה to reveal, open
בנה to build
שְׁכֶם Shechem
פלל *Hithpa'el* to pray
סָבִיב, סְבִיבֹת around (prep.)
מִסָּבִיב around (adv.)

[1] Cf. also 2 Sam. 11.7.

[2] Used instead of Hiph. of שׁתה.

EXERCISE

Translate

צַוֵּה אֶת־הַכֹּהֲנִים נֹשְׂאֵי אֲרוֹן יהוה וְיַעֲלוּ מִן־הַיַּרְדֵּן׃ 2 לֹא אֹסִף
עוֹד לְהַכּוֹת אֶת־כָּל־חַי כַּאֲשֶׁר עָשִׂיתִי׃ 3 אֶבֶן [1]מָאֲסוּ הַבּוֹנִים
הָיְתָה לְרֹאשׁ פִּנָּה׃ 4 [2]שָׂא נָא עֵינֶיךָ וּרְאֵה כִּי אֶת־כָּל־הָאָרֶץ
אֲשֶׁר אַתָּה רֹאֶה לְךָ [3]אֶתְּנֶנָּה׃ וְשַׂמְתִּי אֶת־זַרְעֲךָ כַּעֲפַר הָאָרֶץ אֲשֶׁר
אִם יוּכַל אִישׁ לִמְנוֹת עֲפַר הָאָרֶץ גַּם זַרְעֲךָ יִמָּנֶה׃ 5 וַיֹּאמֶר
פַּרְעֹה לְךָ מֵעָלָי הִשָּׁמֶר־לְךָ אַל־תֹּסֶף רְאוֹת פָּנַי כִּי בְּיוֹם רְאֹתְךָ
פָּנַי תָּמוּת׃ 6 מִי יַשְׁקֵנִי מָיִם׃ 7 כִּי יֵצֵא עַמְּךָ לַמִּלְחָמָה עַל־
אֹיְבָיו וְקָרְאוּ אֶל־הָעִיר אֲשֶׁר בָּחַרְתָּ בָּהּ וְהַבַּיִת אֲשֶׁר בָּנִיתִי
וְשָׁמַעְתָּ אֶת־תְּפִלָּתָם׃ 8 וְהָיָה כִּי תִרְבּוּ וּפְרִיתֶם בָּאָרֶץ בַּיָּמִים
הָהֵמָּה לֹא־תִזְכְּרוּ עוֹד אֲרוֹן בְּרִית יְהוָה׃ 9 וַיַּשְׁכֵּם עֶבֶד אִישׁ
הָאֱלֹהִים וַיֵּצֵא וְהִנֵּה חַיִל סוֹבֵב אֶת־הָעִיר וְסוּס וָרָכֶב וַיֹּאמֶר
הַנַּעַר לַנָּבִיא אֲדֹנִי מַה־נַּעֲשֶׂה[4]׃ וַיֹּאמֶר לוֹ [5]אֲדֹנָיו אַל־תִּירָא כִּי יֵשׁ
רַבִּים אִתָּנוּ׃ וַיִּתְפַּלֵּל הַנָּבִיא לֵאמֹר פְּקַח־נָא אֶת־עֵינָיו וְיִרְאֶה
וְהִנֵּה הָהָר מָלֵא סוּסִים וָרֶכֶב אֵשׁ סְבִיבֹת הַנָּבִיא׃ וַיִּתְפַּלֵּל עוֹד
הַנָּבִיא הַכֵּה אֶת־הַגּוֹי־הַזֶּה וַיַּכֵּם כִּדְבַר הַנָּבִיא׃ 10 ואני הנני
ממטיר על־הארץ ארבעים יום וארבעים לילה ומחיתי את־
כל אשר עשיתי מעל פני האדמה׃ 11 נער הייתי גם־זקנתי
ולא ראיתי צדיק נעזב וזרעו מבקש־לחם׃

Suggested further reading: Gen. 1, 6-19.

Behold, thy maid is in thy (*f.*) hand, do to her the (thing) good in thine eyes. 2 And they left off building the city. 3 I am not able to do anything until thou come thither. 4 And the waters increased very (much), and the heads of the mountains were covered. 5 I have commanded thee not to eat of the tree which is in the midst of the garden, lest thou die. 6 For thou, Yahweh of hosts, God of Israel, hast opened

---

[1] Relative unexpressed.

[2] Imper. s.m. of נָשָׂא to lift, carry.

[3] נָתַן, *to give*; impf. יִתֵּן.

[4] עָשָׂה; impf. יַעֲשֶׂה.

[5] See Eng.–Heb. Vocabulary under *lord*.

the ear of thy servant saying, A house will I build for thee. 7 Behold, I have shown kindness to him and have caused him to flourish and to increase greatly; he will beget sons and daughters and I will constitute (נָתַן) him a great nation. 8 There we sat down and wept when we remembered Zion; for our enemies asked of us (*Heb.*, Accus.) a song: 'Sing us a song of Zion'. How shall we sing Yahweh's song in a strange land? 9 And the men said: Let us build for ourselves a city whose top will be in the heavens, and let us make our name to be remembered lest we be scattered abroad upon the face of the earth. Then Yahweh went down to see the city which they had built. 10 The king built Shechem in the hill-country and lived in it. Then he reflected (*Heb.* said in his heart): The kingdom will return to the house of David; if this people go up to offer sacrifice in the house of Yahweh in Jerusalem, their heart will return to Rehoboam and they will slay me.

§ 33. APOCOPATED FORMS AND NOUNS FROM VERBS LĀMEDH HĒ

1. (a) Jussive and Imperf. Consec. forms ending in ֶה and Imper. forms ending in ֵה (with the exception of the imper. Qal) normally assume so-called apocopated forms by dropping the vocalic ending (ֶה or ֵה). This contraction occasions some vocalic modifications.

Let us take יִגְלֶה, the 3 s. m. Impf. Qal of גָּלָה, as type. The basic, apocopated form of יִגְלֶה is יִגְל.

i. This form is found in some verbs; e.g. וַיִּשְׁבְּ *and he took captive* (from שָׁבָה).

ii. Sometimes a helping vowel is inserted, יִגֶל; e.g. וַיִּבֶן *and he built* (with a gutt. וַיִּשַׁע *and he gazed*, from שָׁעָה). This is the common form with 3rd s.m. Juss. and Imperf. Consec.

iii. Sometimes the stem vowel is lengthened, as well as a helping vowel inserted, יֵגֶל (cf. סִפְר > סֵפֶר); e.g. וַתֵּפֶן *and she turned* (פָּנָה) or, with a gutt., וַתֵּתַע *and she wandered* (תָּעָה). This is the common form in 3rd s.f. and 2nd s.m. Juss. and Imperf. Consec.

iv. Occasionally the vowel is lengthened without a helping vowel being inserted, יֵגְל; e.g. וַיֵּבְךְּ *and he wept.*

(b) Similarly imperf. Hiph. יַגְלֶה has apocopated form יַגְל.

i. This form is found in a few verbs; e.g. וַיַּשְׁקְ *and he watered.*

ii. But the form commonly found is יֶגֶל with a helping vowel (cf. מַלְךְ > מֶלֶךְ); e.g. וַיֶּפֶר *and he made fruitful* (פָּרָה).

So imper. Hiph. הֶגֶל (< הַגְל < הַגְלֵה); e.g. הֶרֶב *make abundant* (< הַרְבְּ < הַרְבֵּה; imper. Hiph. of רָבָה).

(c) When the first radical is guttural, the helping vowel is *paṯhaḥ*; apoc. imperf. Qal and Hiph. of עָלָה is יַעַל (< יַעֲלֶה); apoc. imper. is הַעַל (< הַעֲלֵה) cf. §§ 7. 5a; 35. 2. b, d. In such verbs the imperfs. Qal and Hiph. are identical.

(d) While these apocopated forms are commonly used with *waw consec.*, the full forms without apocopation are frequently found. The cohort. forms are the same as the imperf.

The following list summarizes the apoc. forms in use:

impf. Qal	יִגְלֶה	*apoc.*	יִגְל, יִגֶל, יֶגֶל or יֵגֶל
impf. Hiph.	יַגְלֶה	*apoc.*	יַגְל, יֶגֶל
imper. Hiph.	הַגְלֵה	*apoc.*	הַגְל, הֶגֶל
impf. Niph.	יִגָּלֶה	*apoc.*	יִגָּל
impf. Pi.	יְגַלֶּה	*apoc.*	יְגַל
imper. Pi.	גַּלֵּה	*apoc.*	גַּל
imperf. Hithp.	יִתְגַּלֶּה	*apoc.*	יִתְגַּל
imper. Hithp.	הִתְגַּלֵּה	*apoc.*	הִתְגַּל
impf. Qal, Hiph.	יַעֲלֶה	*apoc.*	יַעַל
imper. Hiph.	הַעֲלֵה	*apoc.*	הַעַל
impf. Qal	יִרְאֶה	*apoc.*	יֵרֶא, &c.

With *waw cons.* 3 *s.m.* alone וַיַּרְא (*and he saw*; also Hiph. *and he showed*), 3 *s.f.* וַתֵּרֶא, 1 *s.* וָאֵרֶא, *impf. Niph.* יֵרָאֶה, *apoc.* יֵרָא

2. There are some notable features in the inflection of הָיָה *to become, to be,* and חָיָה *to live*:

(a) The gutt., when initial and followed by vocal shᵉwa, takes *ḥat. seghôl*; e.g. הֱיֵה, הֱיוֹת, הֱיִיתֶם.

(b) When the conjunction וְ or one of the inseparable prepositions בְּ, כְּ, לְ, is prefixed to such forms, it takes the vowel *ḥîreq* and forms a closed syllable with the initial radical of the verbal form; e.g. וִֽהְיִיתֶם, לִֽהְיוֹת, but וֶֽהְיֵה. Notice the *methegh* in these cases and in (c) below.[1]

(c) Likewise in forms of the imperf. Qal with a preformative, the preformative forms a closed syllable with the following gutt. and the vowel is *ḥîreq*; e.g. יִֽהְיֶה, נִֽחְיֶה.[1]

(d) Apocopated impf. is primarily יִהְיְ *yihy*. But, as it is characteristic of final (consonantal) *y* to pass into the accented homogeneous (vocalic) *î*, this becomes, יְהִי *y·hî*, with simple *wāw* וִיהִי, with *wāw consec.* וַיְהִי *and it came to pass.*

(e) As the original form of the vb. for *to live* is חָיַי, which appears in the form of חַי (§ 40) as well as of חָיָה (§ 32, § 20, Exer., n. 3), the plur. of חַי *living* is חַיִּים (which also means *life*).

3. *Nouns from Verbs* ל״ה.

First and third declensions

abs.	מִקְנֶה	קָנֶה	עָלֶה	שָׂדֶה	יָפֶה	*fem.* יָפָה
cstr.	מִקְנֵה	קְנֵה	עֲלֵה	שְׂדֵה	יְפֵה	יְפַת
1 *s.c. suff.*	מִקְנִי	קְנִי	עָלִי	שָׂדִי		
3 *m.*	מִקְנֵהוּ	קָנֵהוּ	עָלֵהוּ	שָׂדֵהוּ		
3 *f.*	מִקְנָהָ	קָנָהָ	עָלָהָ	שָׂדָהּ		
pl.	מִקְנִים	קָנִים	עָלִים	שָׂדוֹת	יָפִים	יָפוֹת
cstr.	מִקְנֵי	קְנֵי	עֲלֵי	שְׂדוֹת	יְפֵי	יְפוֹת
	(possession)	(possessor)	(leaf)	(field)	(fair)	(fair)

---

[1] Cf. § 9, Note 2 to the Ex.

Second declension

		a class				*i* class	*u* class	
abs. sing.	אֲרִי	(קָ֫צוּ)	גְּדִי	פְּרִי	פְּתִי	חֲצִי	חֳלִי	תֹּהוּ
pause			גְּ֫דִי	פֶּ֫רִי	פֶּ֫תִי	חֵ֫צִי	חֹ֫לִי	
suff. 3 *m.*	”		(גְּדִיוֹ)	פִּרְיוֹ		חֶצְיוֹ	חָלְיוֹ	
plur.	אֲרָיִים		גְּדָיִים		פְּתָאִים and		חֳלָיִים	
cstr.		קַצְוֵי	גְּדָיֵי		פְּתָיִים		חֳלָיֵנוּ	1 *pl. suff*
	(lion)	(end)	(kid)	(fruit)	(simple)	(half)	(sickness)	(waste)

(a) *First and third declensions*. i. The vocalic sound at the end of these words is, in the absolute (cf. מִקְנֶה), the broad *s•ghôl*, which becomes the closer *ṣērê* in the construct (מִקְנֵה). Comp. the relation of the impf. יִגְלֶה and imper. גְּלֵה in the verb.

ii. The vocalic ending is absorbed in the vowel of the afformative: e.g. מִקְנֶה with suffix מִקְנִי, &c. So רֹעֶה *shepherd*, רֹעִי *my shepherd*; יָפֶה, *beautiful*, pl. יָפִים; &c.

iii. The final *e* sound naturally admits the suffixes *hû*, *hā*, &c. of 3rd pers. (cf. §§ 16. 1; 27. 2b). In 3 m.s. ־ֵהוּ is found exclusively (e.g. מִקְנֵהוּ, not מִקְנוֹ); in 3 f. usually ֶ‍הָ (cf. suffix to impf. of vbs.), e.g. עָלֶהָ; rarely ָ‍הּ (e.g. שָׂדָהּ).

(b) *Second Declension*. i. α. Nouns of the regular formation, e.g. בֶּכֶה *weeping*, הֶגֶה *murmuring* (like מֶלֶךְ) are rare. As a rule the basic י or ו reappears. Thus an original פַּרְיְ (from פָּרָה *to be fruitful*) becomes פְּרִי (cf. 2d above) and in pause פֶּ֫רִי, with the accent on the original syllable; an original חִצְיְ (from חָצָה *to divide*) becomes חֲצִי, and in pause חֵ֫צִי, with tone-long *ē* in the original syllable; an original חָלְיְ or חֻלְיְ (from חָלָה *to be sick*) becomes חֳלִי, and in pause חֹ֫לִי.

β. Nouns ending in ו are few. An original קַצְוְ would become קָ֫צוּ (1st syll. open and accented, therefore *ā*; not found, but cf. שָׂחוּ *swimming*), cstr. pl. קַצְוֵי (like מַלְכֵי) in which the *wāw* resumes its primary consonantal power. So an orig. *tohw* or *tuhw* becomes *tōhû*, תֹּהוּ, cf. § 32. 4.

ii. As in the case of other segholates, a pron. suffix is added to the original monosyllabic stem; e.g. חָלְיוֹ *his sickness* (cf. קָדְשׁוֹ), *ḥolyô*. In many nouns of the *a* class the *a* has been thinned to *i* (cf. פִּרְיוֹ, גִּדְיוֹ) so that with suffixes they have all the appearance of *i* class nouns (cf. שֶׁמֶשׁ, שִׁמְשֵׁךְ, § 25. 3. b).

iii. In the plur. *yôdh* is sometimes softened into *'aleph* before another *yôdh*; e.g. פְּתָאִים oftener than פְּתָיִים; and in the *cstr*. the pretonic *ā* many times remains; e.g. גְּדָיֵי.

(c) The final *î* in the cstr. form of such nouns as אָב *father* (cstr. אֲבִי), אָח *brother* (cstr. אֲחִי) and חָם *father-in-law* (cstr. חֲמִי) is either a residual termination (cf. § 14. 5) or is evidence that these nouns are derived from ל״ה stems. See § 42.

4. Our reciprocal pronouns are expressed in Hebrew more concretely by nouns, *man, woman, brother, sister, friend*, &c.; e.g.

and they spake to one another	וַיְדַבְּרוּ אִישׁ אֶל־רֵעֵהוּ
	,, ,, אֶל־אָחִיו
and they smote one another	וַיַּכּוּ אִישׁ אֶת־אָחִיו
and they (f.) *clave to one another*	וַתִּדְבַּקְנָה אִשָּׁה בַּאֲחוֹתָהּ
	,, ,, בִּרְעוּתָהּ

5. Our reflexive pronouns are rendered chiefly in two ways i. by the Niph. or Hithp. of the verb; e.g. *they hid themselves* נִסְתְּרוּ, *they girded themselves* הִתְאַזְּרוּ; ii. by nouns, such as לֵב *heart*, קֶרֶב *inward part*, נֶפֶשׁ *soul*; e.g. וַיֹּאמֶר אֶל־לִבּוֹ *and he said to himself* (lit. in his heart), *he considered, he thought*; וַתִּצְחַק בְּקִרְבָּהּ *and she laughed within herself, and she ridiculed* (the idea); נִשְׁבַּע בְּנַפְשׁוֹ *he swore by himself*.

מַעֲשֶׂה work
יֳפִי beauty
רֵעֶה friend
בְּאֵר *f.* well
יָקָר precious
אֲרָם Aram, Syria, the Syrians
מַכָּה *f.* blow, plague
תָּמִים whole, sound, innocent
נטה to bend, incline; Hi. הִטָּה trans. to bend, bow

עֳנִי affliction
רֹעֶה shepherd
מַרְאֶה appearance
שְׁבִי *i* captivity
מַשְׁקֶה butler (butlership)
מִקְנֶה cattle
רָפָא to heal; *Hithp.* to be healed, to recover
נָטַע to plant (Impf. יִטַּע)

רִיב (מְרִיבָה *f.*) strife
פָּנִים face, presence
לוּז Luz
חָלָה to be sick
גָּמָל (*pl.* גְּמַלִּים) camel
מָבוֹא entrance
שָׁכַר to be drunken
תֵּבָה ark, basket
מְבֹרָךְ blessed

EXERCISE

Translate

הִתְהַלֵּךְ לְפָנַי וֶהְיֵה תָמִים וַהֲקִמֹתִי אֶת־בְּרִיתִי לִהְיוֹת לְךָ
לֵאלֹהִים׃ 2 [1]וַיִּטַּע נֹחַ כֶּרֶם וַיֵּשְׁתְּ מִן־הַיַּיִן וַיִּשְׁכָּר וַיִּתְגַּל בְּתוֹךְ
אָהֳלוֹ׃ 3 וַיֶּחַל הַמֶּלֶךְ בְּרַגְלָיו וְגַם־בְּחָלְיוֹ לֹא דָרַשׁ אֶת־יְהוָה׃
4 וַיְהִי רִיב בֵּין רֹעֵי מִקְנֵה אַבְרָם וּבֵין רֹעֵי מִקְנֵה לוֹט וַיֹּאמְרוּ
אִישׁ אֶל־רֵעֵהוּ אַל־נָא תְהִי מְרִיבָה בֵּינִי וּבֵינֶךָ׃ 5 וַיֵּרָא יהוה
אֶל־אַבְרָם וַיִּבֶן שָׁם אַבְרָם מִזְבֵּחַ לַיהוה הַנִּרְאֶה אֵלָיו׃ 6 יְהִי
שֵׁם יהוה מְבֹרָךְ׃ 7 וַיֹּאמֶר לוֹ הַרְאֵנִי אֶת־כְּבוֹדֶךָ׃ וַיֹּאמֶר לָאִישׁ
לֹא־תוּכַל לִרְאוֹת אֶת־פָּנָי כִּי לֹא יִרְאַנִי הָאָדָם [2]וָחָי׃ 8 וְעַתָּה
אִם־מָצָא עַבְדְּךָ חֵן בְּעֵינֶיךָ הוֹדִעֵנִי אֶת־דְּרָכֶיךָ וְאֵדָעֲךָ לְמַעַן
אֶמְצָא[3]־חֵן עוֹד בְּעֵינֶיךָ וְהַרְאֵנִי אֶת־כְּבוֹדְךָ וְאֶרְאֶה כִּי יָקָר
לְךָ הָעָם הַזֶּה׃ וַיֹּאמֶר פָּנַי יֵלְכוּ עִמָּכֶם וַהֲנִחֹתִי־לָךְ׃ וַיֹּאמֶר אֵלָיו
אִם־אֵין פָּנֶיךָ הֹלְכִים עִמָּנוּ אַל־תַּעֲלֵנוּ מִזֶּה׃ 9 וַיִּצְעֲקוּ הָעָם
אֶל־יְהוָה וַיִּשְׁמַע אֶת־קוֹלָם וַיַּרְא אֶת־עָנְיָם וַיִּרְפָּאֵם׃ 10 וְקָרְאוּ

---

[1] 3 s.m. Impf. consec. Qal of נָטַע.

[2] Cf. § 20, Exer., n. 3.

[3] For the final *qāmeṣ*, cf. § 7. 6 ii.

אִישׁ אֶל־רֵעֵהוּ קָדוֹשׁ אֱלֹהֵי יִשְׂרָאֵל צַדִּיק וְיָשָׁר הוּא בְּכָל־
מַעֲשָׂיו׃ 11 ויראו השמרים איש יוצא מן־העיר ויאמרו לו
הראנו נא את־מבוא העיר ועשינו עמך חסד׃ ויראם את־מבוא
העיר ויכו את־העיר לפי־חרב ואת־האיש שלחו׃

Suggested further reading: Num. xiv, 10-24.

And Noah did according to all that Yahweh commanded him. 2 And he commanded the priests, saying, Come up out of the Jordan; and they went up. 3 And the captain of the host said, Who (ever) shall smite this city and take it, then (*wāw cons.*) I will give him my daughter to wife. 4 Bow (**נטה**, *Hiph.*) thy heavens and come down. 5 She said to me: Drink, and I will water your camels also. So I drank and she watered my camels and to me she showed much kindness. 6 The woman conceived and bore a son; and when she saw that he was a fine (*Heb.* good) child, she took for him a basket and hid him. The king's daughter saw the basket and sent a servant to get it. When she opened it, she saw the child, and, behold, he was crying. She sent for a nurse and commanded her to keep the child. 7 The king returned to the city to recover from his illness and from the wounds which the enemy had inflicted on him when he fought against the army of Syria.

§ 34. PĒ NÛN VERBS

(See Paradigm, p. 282 f.)

1. The consonant *n* in Hebrew shows the same kind of weakness which it shows in other languages. When it occurs at the end of a syllable and is not sustained by an immediately following vowel, it tends to be assimilated to the following consonant (cf. in-licio > illicio; ἐν-γράφω > ἐγγράφω; **יִנְגַּשׁ** > **יִגַּשׁ** *yin-gaš* > *yig-gaš*).

(a) In the imperf. Qal, perf. and part. Niph., Hiph. and Hoph. such assimilation occurs in most cases; e.g. **יִנְפֹּל** > **יִפֹּל**.

(*yippōl*), יִנְפִּיל > יַפִּיל (*yappîl*). נִנְגַּף > נִגַּף (*niggaph*, Perf. Niph. of נָגַף *to smite*).

(b) In certain cases (e.g. ל״ה verbs) the Niph. and Piʿēl would be indistinguishable, except for the context; cf. נִקָּה, Niph. *to be clean, innocent*; Pi. *to declare innocent, acquit*.

(c) In the Hoph. *u* naturally appears instead of *o* before the doubled consonant (§ 6. 7); e.g. נָגַד, הֻגַּד (pf.) יֻגַּד (impf.).

(d) The *n* is not usually assimilated in verbs whose middle radical is a guttural; e.g. נָחַל *to inherit*, impf. Qal יִנְחַל, Hiph. יַנְחִיל. But the Niph. of נָחַם is נִחַם *to repent* (cf. § 36. 1c).

2. Verbs whose impfs. are in *ō* and *a* should be carefully distinguished.

(a) In vbs. with impf. in *a* (e.g. נָגַשׁ, יִגַּשׁ) the נ is almost always dropped in the imperat. Qal; e.g. גַּשׁ (for נְגַשׁ), *f.* גְּשִׁי, *pl.* גְּשׁוּ.

It is also usually dropped in the inf. cstr., which adds the fem. termination ת, and assumes the form of a segholate noun גֶּשֶׁת; the steps are גַּשׁ, גַּשְׁתְּ, גֶּשֶׁת (exactly like מַלְךְ ,מֶלֶךְ, § 25). Note, however, that the vowel is regularly *i* (not *a*) when inflected (cf. צֶדֶק, § 25. 3b); e.g. גִּשְׁתּוֹ *his approaching*.

ל before such (segholate) inf. constructs is pointed לָ; e.g. לָגֶשֶׁת (§ 12. 1d).

(b) In verbs whose imperf. is in *ō*, the נ is retained in the imper. and the infin. constr., and the forms in use are the normal ones; e.g. נָפַל, imperf. יִפֹּל, imper. and infin. constr. נְפֹל.

3. (a) The verb נָתַן *to give* assimilates its *final n* also in perf. נָתַתִּי, &c. (for נָתַנְתִּי), and infin. cstr. is תֵּת (< תֶּנֶת), and with suff. תִּתִּי (< תִּנְתִּי). It has *ē* in imperf. יִתֵּן and imper. תֵּן, emph. תְּנָה (§ 20. 3), *f.* תְּנִי, *pl.* תְּנוּ.

(b) In the verb לָקַח *to take* the ל is treated like the *nun* of *Pē Nûn* vbs.; e.g. impf. Qal יִקַּח (< יִלְקַח), *pl.* יִקְחוּ (§ 6. 5);

imper. קַח, קְחוּ, inf. cstr. קַ֫חַת, קַחְתִּי, &c. (§ 7. 3, *a* under influence of the guttural).

(c) לְ before these (monosyllabic or segholate) inf. constructs is pointed לָ; e.g. לָתֵת, לָקַחַת (§ 12. 1d).

(d) The form יֻקַּח is probably not impf. Hoph. but impf. of the old passive Qal, of which now few traces exist except the participle. לֻקַּח, which also exists, is to be regarded as the (old) pf. pass. Qal rather than as pf. Puʿal. So יֻתַּן pass. Qal rather than Hoph. of נתן. The Hoph. is unlikely, as no causative idea is present in these words, and the Hiph. of these verbs is not found.

4. *Nouns from Verbs* פ״ן. Nouns with *m* preformative are of the form מַתָּן *gifts* (coll. from נָתַן), as מַפָּל *offal* (from נָפַל *to fall*), מַכָּה *stroke* (from נָכָה, Hiph. *to strike*).

נצל	*Hi.* to deliver	נגע	to touch (*Hi.*	נשק	to kiss
נגש	to approach		to reach)	נשא	*Hi.* to deceive
נפל	to fall	נגף	to smite	נדר	to vow
נבט	*Hi.* to look	נגד	*Hi.* to tell	נצב	*Hi.* to set
נחל	to inherit	נסע	to strike camp,	כֹּחַ	strength
ברח	to flee		to journey	רדף	to pursue,
אֹרֶךְ	length	רֹחַב	breadth		to persecute
שבע	*Niph.* to	רְכוּשׁ	possessions	חזק	*Pi.* to streng-
	swear; *Hiph.*	אֶחָד	*m.* אַחַת *f.* one		then, to harden
	to cause to	אַיִל	ram	סֻלָּם	ladder
	swear	גַּת	Gath	גֵּר	sojourner

Note the idiomatic use of מִי יִתֵּן to express an optative; e.g. מִי יִתֵּן עֶרֶב *would that it were evening* (lit. *who will give evening*?), מִי יִתֵּן מוּתֵנוּ *would that we might die, would that we had died.*

EXERCISE

Translate

תֵּן, קְחוּ, נְפֹל, הִנָּגֵף, אַפִּיל, הִצַּלְתָּ, מַצִּיל, וַיִּנָּצְלוּ, תְּנָה, תַּצִּילֵם,

תִּגְּעוּ, נְגֹף, הֻגַּד, הַגִּידוּ, תַּבֵּט, לִנְפֹּל, לָגֶשֶׁת׃
הַצִּילֵנִי מִדָּמִים אֱלֹהֵי תְּשׁוּעָתִי וּלְשׁוֹנִי תַּגִּיד צִדְקָתֶךָ׃ 2 כִּי תִדּוֹר
נֶדֶר [1]לַיהוה אַל־תְּשַׁכַּח לְשַׁלְּמוֹ׃ 3 יֵרְאוּ אֹיְבָיו מִגֶּשֶׁת אֵלָיו׃
4 הַבֶּט־נָא הַשָּׁמַיְמָה וּסְפֹר הַכּוֹכָבִים׃ 5 אָמַר יהוה אֶל־אַבְרָם
הִתְהַלֵּךְ בָּאָרֶץ לְאָרְכָּהּ וּלְרָחְבָּהּ כִּי לְךָ אֶתְּנֶנָּה וַיִּפֹּל אַבְרָם עַל
פָּנָיו׃ 6 חָלַם יַעֲקֹב וְהִנֵּה סֻלָּם מֻצָּב אַ֫רְצָה וְרֹאשׁוֹ מַגִּיעַ הַשָּׁמָיְמָה׃
7 נִתְּנוּ בְּיַד מַלְכֵי הָאֲרָצוֹת׃ 8 וַיּוֹלֶךְ מֹשֶׁה אֶת־יִשְׂרָאֵל מִשָּׁם
וַיֵּצְאוּ אֶל־הַמִּדְבָּר׃ וַיָּרִיבוּ בְנֵי־יִשְׂרָאֵל עַל־מֹשֶׁה וַיֹּאמְרוּ אֵלָיו
מִי־יִתֵּן מוּתֵנוּ בְּיַד יהוה בְּאֶרֶץ מִצְרַיִם כִּי הוֹצֵאתָ אֹתָנוּ אֶל־
הַמִּדְבָּר הַזֶּה לְהָמִית אֶת־כָּל־יִשְׂרָאֵל בָּרָעָב׃ 9 אֲנִי בָּטַחְתִּי
בְךָ יְהוָה אָמַרְתִּי אֱלֹהַי אָתָּה׃ הַצִּילֵנִי מִיַּד אֹיְבַי וְהוֹשִׁיעֵנִי מִכֹּחַ
רֹדְפָי׃ הָאִירָה פָנֶיךָ עַל־עַבְדֶּךָ וְשַׂמְּחֵנִי בְּחַסְדֶּךָ׃ 10 וַיּוֹצֵא
אֹתוֹ וַיֹּאמֶר הַבֶּט־נָא הַשָּׁמַיְמָה וּסְפֹר אֶת־הַכּוֹכָבִים אִם־תּוּכַל
לִסְפֹּר אֹתָם וַיֹּאמֶר לוֹ כֹּה יִהְיֶה עַמֶּךָ׃ אֲנִי יהוה אֲשֶׁר הוֹצֵאתִיךָ
מֵאֶרֶץ רְחוֹקָה לָתֶת־לְךָ אֶת־הָאָרֶץ הַזֹּאת לְרִשְׁתָּהּ׃ וַיֹּאמֶר לוֹ
הָאִישׁ בַּמָּה אֵדַע כִּי אִירָשֶׁנָּה׃ וַיֹּאמֶר יהוה יָדֹעַ תֵּדַע כִּי גֵרִים
יִהְיוּ עַמְּךָ בְּאֶרֶץ לֹא לָהֶם וַעֲבָדוּם וְאֶת־הַגּוֹי אֲשֶׁר יַעֲבֹדוּ אָנֹכִי
אֶשְׁפֹּט וְאַחֲרֵי־כֵן יֵצְאוּ בִּרְכוּשׁ גָּדוֹל׃ 11 וַיֻּגַּד לְמֶלֶךְ מִצְרַיִם
כִּי בָרַח הָעָם וַיֵּהָפֵךְ לְבַב פַּרְעֹה וַעֲבָדָיו עַל־הָעָם וַיֹּאמְרוּ מַה־
זֹּאת עָשִׂינוּ כִּי־שִׁלַּחְנוּ אֶת־יִשְׂרָאֵל מֵעָבְדֵנוּ׃ וַיְחַזֵּק יהוה אֶת־לֵב
פַּרְעֹה מֶלֶךְ מִצְרַיִם וַיִּרְדֹּף אַחֲרֵי בְּנֵי יִשְׂרָאֵל וּבְנֵי יִשְׂרָאֵל יֹצְאִים
בְּיָד רָמָה׃ 12 ויאמר לו המלך תנה־לי את־כרמך בכסף
ויאמר לא־אתן לך את־כרמי׃

Give ye. 2 I will not give my silver and my gold. 3 Tell it not in Gath. 4 Look not (*f.*) after thee, lest God smite thee. 5 Deliver me, for thou art my salvation. 6 Let them

[1] לַ is pointed with *pathah* as before אֲדֹנָי which was read in place of the divine name יהוה (cf. § 15 in the note to the Exer.).

give glory to Yahweh because of his loving-kindness. 7 When I gave the woman to the man for wife. 8 I will deliver thee, and thy tongue shall tell-of my righteousness. 9 The serpent deceived her and she took of the tree and gave to her husband. 10 They feared to draw near, lest they should be smitten before their enemies. 11 And Joseph fell upon his father's face and wept over (*Heb.* upon) him. Then he said to Pharaoh: If I[1] have found favour in thy sight, listen to my prayer. My father made me swear that I would bury him in the grave he acquired in the land of Canaan. Now, pray, let me go up from Egypt that I may bury my father and return again. 12 No man shall stand before you all the days of your life; I shall be with you and shall not forget you, and you shall cause this people to inherit this land which I swear to your fathers to give them.

§ 35. PĒ GUTTURAL VERBS

(See Paradigm, p. 284-287)

See the rules for the gutturals and *rêš* in § 7.

1. (a) A guttural requires a *ḥaṭeph* in place of a simple vocal shᵉwa (§ 7. 1a); the commonest *ḥaṭeph* used for this purpose is *ḥaṭeph paṯhaḥ*, but א commonly takes *ḥaṭeph sᵉghôl*; e.g. קְטַלְתֶּם, עֲמַדְתֶּם, אֲכַלְתֶּם; קְטֹל, עֲמֹד, but אֱכֹל.

(b) A simple vocal shᵉwa before a *ḥaṭeph* becomes the full (short) vowel corresponding to the *ḥaṭeph* (§ 7. 1c); e.g. infin. constr. with ל, לְעֲמֹד > לַעֲמֹד.

2. (a) The vowel *i*, falling before a guttural not final, usually is modified to *e* (§ 7. 2); e.g. 3rd s.m. perf. Hiph. הֶחְבִּיא *he hid away*, 3rd s.m. perf. Niph. נֶחְשַׁב, *he was accounted*, part. Niph. נֶחְתָּם *sealed*, and נֶחְמָד *desired, desirable*.

(b) When a guttural falls at the end of a syllable not final, if it be א or ה, it commonly takes a helping vowel which is the *ḥaṭeph* corresponding to the preceding short vowel (§ 7. 5a); e.g. 3rd s.m. perf. Hiph. הִאְמִין > הֶאְמִין > הֶאֱמִין *he trusted*,

[1] *Heb.* thy servant.

so הִאְרִיךְ > הֶאְרִיךְ > הֶאֱרִיךְ *he prolonged,* 3rd s.m. perf. Niph. נִעְזַב > נֶעְזַב > נֶעֱזַב *he was forsaken.* ע commonly takes such a *ḥaṭeph* (e.g. Hiph. הֶעֱמִיד, יַעֲמִיד, Hoph. הָעֳמַד, יָעֳמַד) but not universally (e.g. נֶעְדָּר *lacking,* הֶעְלִים *he concealed*). ח seldom takes it (§ 7. 5b); e.g. יֶחְכַּם *he will be wise,* יֶחְדַּל *he will cease,* יֶחְסַר *he will lack,* יַחְמֹד *he will desire* (cf. § 7. 2), but note, e.g., יַחֲלֹם *he will dream,* יַחֲרִישׁ *he will be silent.* A few verbs use both forms, חָשַׁב *to devise,* יַחְשֹׁב and יַחֲשֹׁב.

(c) In the Hiph. pf. with *wāw cons.*, in which the accent falls on the final syllable (§ 20. 4d), the ֱ becomes ֲ thus הֶעֱמַ֫דְתָּ *thou hast stationed,* but וְהַעֲמַדְתָּ֫ *and thou wilt station.* This change occurs elsewhere at a distance from the tone; e.g. אֱלֵי (poetic form of אֶל־), but אֲלֵיכֶם, cf. § 7. 2b.

(d) In the imperf. Qal the original *pathaḥ* of the preformative syllable appears in the case of transitive verbs (§ 17. 4a); e.g. יַעֲמֹד *he will stand,* יַהֲפֹךְ *he will overturn.* With intransitive verbs the *ḥîreq* of the preformative syllable is original (e.g. יִכְבַּד; § 19. 3); hence יִחְזַק > יֶחֱזַק *he is strong,* יִחְכַּם > יֶחְכַּם *he is wise.* Thus the combinations are ־ַ־ֲ and ־ֶ־ֱ, except that before א even imperfs. in *ō* have *e*; e.g. יֶאֱסֹף *he will gather.*

(e) Note the cases in which the *ḥaṭeph* following a guttural is necessarily changed into the corresponding short vowel when a second vocal shᵉwa comes next; e.g. *sing.* יַעֲמֹד, *pl.* (cf. יִקְטְלוּ) יַעֲמְדוּ which, as two vocal shᵉwas cannot come together, becomes יַעַמְדוּ *ya'amᵉdhû* (§ 5. 2d, ii); 3 *s.m.* Niph. נֶאֱסַף, *f.* (cf. נִקְטְלָה) נֶאֱסְפָה which becomes נֶאֶסְפָה *she has been gathered* or *taken away.*

3. The vowel preceding a guttural which is in a position where it is subject to doubling falls in an open syllable (§ 7. 7a) and may undergo compensatory lengthening; this lengthening takes place commonly with א and very often with ע; e.g. imperf. Niph. יֵעָמֵד *he will be set,* יֵאָמֵר *it will be said* (so with ר; e.g.

יֵרָפֵא *he will be healed*). And it is to be noted that, whereas ה and ח very often take implicit doubling and keep the preceding vowel short (§ 7. 7), that is not the case with *Pē* Guttural verbs; compensatory lengthening of the vowel commonly takes place; e.g. יֵהָפֵךְ *it will be overturned*, יֵהָרֵס *it will be destroyed*, יֵחָלֵק *it will be apportioned*, יֵחָרֵשׁ *it will be ploughed*, יֵחָשֵׁב *it will be reckoned*.

4. *Nouns from Pē Gutt. verbs.*

	First declension			Second declension		
sing. abs.	חָכָם	אֲדָמָה	מַאֲכָל	עֶבֶד	עֵגֶל	חֹדֶשׁ
cstr.	חֲכַם	אַדְמַת	מַאֲכַל	"	"	"
plur. abs.	חֲכָמִים	אֲדָמוֹת		עֲבָדִים	עֲגָלִים	חֳדָשִׁים
cstr.	חַכְמֵי	אַדְמוֹת		עַבְדֵי	עֶגְלֵי	חָדְשֵׁי
	(wise)	(ground)	(food)	(servant)	(calf)	(month)

(a) *First Declension*. For חֲכַם, חֲכָמִים, &c. see 1a above, and for אַדְמוֹת, אַדְמַת, חַכְמֵי, &c. see 2e.

(b) *Second Declension*. In nouns of the second class the guttural often modifies the following *i* to *e* (§ 7. 2); e.g. עֶגְלֵי, not עִגְלֵי. In those of the first and second classes the *ḥaṭeph* which is found is *ḥaṭeph paṯaḥ* (e.g. עֲגָלִים, עֲבָדִים; § 5. 2c, ii); in those of the third class it is naturally *ḥaṭeph qāmeṣ* (e.g. חֳדָשִׁים; §§ 5. 2c, ii: 25).

(c) *Third Declension*. No effects follow, because the vowel accompanying the guttural is unchangeable; e.g. חֹמֵד, חֹמְדִים *desiring*, מְאַסֵּף, מְאַסְּפִים (Pi. ptc. *gathering*; for ס, cf. § 6. 5).

Verbs with *ō* in imperf.		with *a* in imperf.
אחז to grasp, to seize	עבד to serve, till	אמץ to be strong
אסף to gather	עבר to pass, cross, transgress	חדל to cease
הפך to turn, overturn		חזק to be strong
	עזב to forsake, leave	חכם to be wise

הרג to slay	עזר to help	רחק to be distant
חלם to dream	עמד to stand, endure	
חשב to count, think	ערך to arrange, to set in battle-order	
צבר to heap up, store	שׁבר to buy (corn) אֵיךְ how?	אמן *Hiph.* to believe, trust
שֶׁבֶר corn, grain	ארך *Hiph.* to prolong	נָהָר (pl. נְהָרִים, oftener נְהָרוֹת) river
אֶלֶף thousand		
חֲנִית spear	אַרְבָּעִים forty	אֲרָם Aram, Syria
לָבָן Laban		

EXERCISE

Translate

וַיַּעֲזֹב כָּל־אֲשֶׁר לוֹ בְּיַד יוֹסֵף׃ 2 הִנֵּה שְׁנֵי הַמְּלָכִים לֹא עָמְדוּ
לְפָנָיו וְאֵיךְ נַעֲמֹד אֲנָֽחְנוּ׃ 3 וַיִּזְכֹּר אֱלֹהִים אֶת־נֹחַ וַיַּעֲבֵר רוּחַ
גְּדוֹלָה עַל־הָאָֽרֶץ׃ 4 וַנַּֽחֲלֹם חֲלוֹם בְּלַיְלָה אֶחָד אֲנִי וָהוּא׃
5 חֲזַק וֶֽאֱמָץ כִּי אַתָּה תַּנְחִיל אֶת־הָעָם הַזֶּה אֶת־הָאָרֶץ אֲשֶׁר
נִשְׁבַּעְתִּי לַֽאֲבוֹתָם לָתֵת לָהֶם׃ 6 וְאַבְרָם הֶֽאֱמִין בַּיהוה וַיַּחְשְׁבֶהָ
לּוֹ צְדָקָה׃ 7 תְּנָה־לָּנוּ אֶת־הָאָרֶץ הַזֹּאת וְאַל־תַּֽעֲבִרֵנוּ אֶת־
הַנָּהָר׃ 8 שְׁלָחַנִי יהוה לַֽחֲבֹשׁ לְנִשְׁבְּרֵי לֵב׃ 9 אִם־רָעֵב שֹׂנַאֲךָ
הַֽאֲכִילֵהוּ לָחֶם׃ 10 מִי נְתָנְךָ לִשְׁפֹּט עָלֵינוּ הַלְהָרְגֵנִי אַתָּה אֹמֵר
כַּֽאֲשֶׁר הָרַגְתָּ אֶת־הַמִּצְרִי׃ 11 וַיַּרְא אֲרָם כִּי נִגַּף לִפְנֵי־יִשְׂרָאֵל
וַיֵּאָֽסְפוּ יָחַד׃ וַיִּשְׁלַח מֶלֶךְ אֲרָם וַיּוֹצֵא אֶת־אַנְשֵׁי הַמִּלְחָמָה מִכָּל־
הָאָֽרֶץ׃ וַיֻּגַּד לְדָוִד וַיֶּֽאֱסֹף אֶת־כָּל־יִשְׂרָאֵל וַיַּֽעֲבֹר אֶת־הַיַּרְדֵּן
וַיַּֽעַרְכוּ אֲרָם לְהִלָּחֵם עִם־דָּוִד׃ וַיָּנָס אֲרָם מִפְּנֵי יִשְׂרָאֵל וַיַּֽהֲרֹג
דָּוִד מֵֽאֲרָם אַרְבָּעִים אֶלֶף אֲנָשִׁים וַיַּֽעַבְדוּם אֲרָם יָמִים רַבִּים׃
12 שְׁמַע [1]תְּפִלָּתִי יהוה כִּי בְךָ בָטָחְתִּי אֶת־פָּנֶיךָ אֱלֹהַי אֲבַקֵּשׁ׃
אַל־תַּסְתֵּר [1]פָּנֶיךָ מִמֶּנִּי כִּי אַתָּה אֱלֹהָי אַל־תִּטְּשֵׁנִי וְאַל־תַּֽעַזְבֵנִי
אֱלֹהֵי יְשׁוּעָתִי׃ 13 וַיִּצְעֲקוּ הָעָם אֶל־פַּרְעֹה עַל־הָרָעָב וַיִּפְתַּח

[1] This illustrates the fact that the אֶת־ before a definite accus. is sometimes omitted in Hebrew, especially in rhythmic passages.

יוֹסֵף אֶת־כָּל־הָאָכְלָה אֲשֶׁר אָסַף בֶּעָרִים כִּי צָבַר יוֹסֵף שֶׁבֶר
כְּחוֹל הַיָּם וַיֶּחְדַּל לִסְפֹּר׃ וְכָל־הָאֲרָצוֹת בָּאוּ מִצְרַיְמָה לִשְׁבָּר־
שֶׁבֶר וַיַּשְׁבֵּר יוֹסֵף לָהֶם וַיֶּחֱזַק הָרָעָב בְּכָל־הָאֲרָצוֹת׃ 14 ואתם
אל־תעמדו רדפו אחרי איביכם כי נתנם יהוה אלהיכם בידכם׃

Abraham saw a ram taken by (בְּ) his horns. 2 Pass not the river, lest ye be smitten before your enemies. 3 Our land shall not be tilled, for our enemies shall stand in the midst-of-her. 4 Let me cross the river, that I may make this people inherit the land which Yahweh sware unto their fathers to give them. 5 Love wisdom, forsake her not. 6 You shall not forsake the tents of Israel to serve other gods and to dwell among a people who have never known me. 7 Abram trusted in God and God did not leave him to his enemies. 8 Jacob fled from Aram and set his face to cross the river and to go to his own land. And it was told Laban that he had fled and he gathered his servants and pursued after Jacob. 9 And the Israelites forsook Yahweh their God who brought them out from the land of Egypt and went after other gods to serve them. And Yahweh was angry against Israel and sold them into the power of their enemies and they could no longer stand before them; and he said: This people have transgressed my covenant and I will no more remember them. 10 And the people served (*pl.*) their God all the days of Joshua, and all the days of the elders who prolonged days after Joshua. 11 And he made his children pass through the fire.

§ 36. ʻAYIN GUTTURAL VERBS AND LĀMEDH GUTTURAL VERBS

(See Paradigms, p. 288-295)

1. *ʻAyin Guttural Verbs* (and *ʻAyin Reš* Verbs).

(a) i. The guttural tends to have the *a* sound associated with it (§ 7. 3a); hence e.g. יִשְׁחַט, שְׁחַט, not יִשְׁחֹט, שְׁחֹט. (But inf. cstr. *ō*; e.g. שְׁחֹט, § 19. 4).

ii. Impf. with suff. יִשְׁחָטֵנִי not "יִשְׁחֲ", cf. § 27. 3a.

iii. Often, too, the pf. Piʿēl has *a*; e.g. נִחַם (not נִחֵם) *to comfort*; but שִׁחֵת *to destroy*.

(b) The guttural takes a *ḥaṭeph* instead of simple shᵉwa vocal (§ 7. 1a); *ḥaṭeph pathaḥ* is commonly used (§ 7. 3a); שַׁחֲטָה, שַׁחֲטוּ. The first vowel of the imper. s.f. and pl.m. is naturally *a*; e.g. שַׁחֲטִי, שַׁחֲטוּ, &c. According to one tradition of Hebrew vocalization *ḥaṭeph pathaḥ* is also found with *rêš* when it is preceded by a vowel which has been lengthened by compensation and when the tone syllable immediately follows; e.g. בָּרֲכָה, יְבָרֲכוּ, &c.

(c) The gutturals and *rêš* cannot be doubled (§ 7. 7a, b). In Piʿēl, Puʿal and Hithpaʿel forms the vowel preceding the ʿ*Ayin rêš* is lengthened by compensation; e.g. Piʿel perf. בֵּרֵךְ, 2nd pl. בֵּרַכְתֶּם (§ 8. 7c), imperf. יְבָרֵךְ, imper. בָּרֵךְ; Puʿal perf. בֹּרַךְ, imperf. יְבֹרַךְ. A similar use is commonly found with ʿ*Ayin* ʾ*aleph* verbs; e.g. מֵאֵן *he refused*, imperf. יְמָאֵן. When the ʿ*Ayin* radical is ה, ח or ע, the preceding vowel remains short and the guttural is said to have dagh. forte implicitum: e.g. מִהַר *he hastened*, imperf. יְמַהֵר; נִחַם *he repented*, imperf, יְנַחֵם, Puʿal perf. נֻחַם; בִּעֵר *he burned, he consumed*.

2. *Lāmedh Guttural Verbs*.

(a) A final guttural (final ה without *mappîq* is not a guttural (§§ 2. 2a, b; 7. 6b, i; 32) and final א is quiescent (§ 7. 6b, ii)) must be preceded by *pathaḥ* or *qāmeṣ* (§ 7. 4).

i. Unchangeably long vowels before a final guttural are retained and *pathaḥ furtive* is used; e.g. infin. absol. שָׁלוֹחַ, pass. part. שָׁלוּחַ, Hiph. perf. הִשְׁלִיחַ, imperf. יַשְׁלִיחַ.

ii. The *tone*-long vowels *ē* and *ō* are displaced by *pathaḥ*; e.g. impf. and imper. Qal יִשְׁלַח (cf. יִקְטֹל), שְׁלַח (with suff. יִשְׁלָחֵנִי, שְׁלָחֵנִי, § 27. 3a); impf. Niph. יִשָּׁלַח (cf. יִקָּטֵל), impf.

Pi. יְשַׁלַּח, also pf. Pi. שִׁלַּח; Hiph. juss. יַשְׁלַח (*wāw* consec. וַיַּשְׁלַח), imper. הַשְׁלַח, &c.

Note 1. Exceptions: ō remains in the infin. cstr. Qal. שְׁלֹחַ. ē remains—(a) in pause, e.g. יִשָּׁלֵחַ (Niph.), יְשַׁלֵּחַ (Pi.); (b) in participles abs., e.g. שֹׁלֵחַ (*f.* שֹׁלַחַת), מְשַׁלֵּחַ; (c) in infins. abs., e.g. שַׁלֵּחַ, Pi. (but constr. שַׁלַּח).

Note 2. Final ר usually has ō in impf. (e.g. יִסְפֹּר *to count*, יַעֲבֹר *to cross*) except in intrans. verbs חָסֵר *to lack*, יֶחְסַר.

(b) Occurring at the end of a syllable under the tone, as in שָׁלַחְתִּי, the guttural does not require a helping vowel (§ 7. 5a), except before the following vowel-less consonant in the 2nd s.f. perf., in which a helping vowel does enter after the guttural; but, as it is in this case the vowel of a closed syllable, it has to be full *pathaḥ* and not *ḥaṭeph pathaḥ*; e.g. שָׁלַחַתְּ. Note that the dagh. lene is retained (probably an attempt to combine two traditions, שָׁלַחְתְּ and שָׁלַחַת).

3. *Idiomatic Usage*: מִהַרְתָּ לָבוֹא הַיּוֹם lit. *you have hastened to come today*, i.e. *you have come quickly today*; וַתְּאַחֵר לָבוֹא אֶל־בֵּיתָהּ lit. *and she delayed to come to her house*, i.e. *and she came home late*. These examples illustrate the Hebrew practice of expressing an English adverb by means of a verb.

4. *Nouns*.

(a) *From 'Ayin Guttural Verbs*.

	First Declension	Second Declension				Third Declension
sing. abs.	נָהָר	נַעַר	פַּחַד	פֹּעַל	רֹחַב	כֹּהֵן
cstr.	נְהַר	„	„	„	„	„
voc. suff.	נַהֲרִי	נַעֲרִי	פַּחְדִּי	פָּעֳלִי	רָחְבִּי	כֹּהֲנִי
cons. suff.	נַהַרְךָ	נַעַרְךָ	פַּחְדְּךָ	פָּעָלְךָ	רָחְבְּךָ	(כֹּהַנְךָ)
plur. abs.	נְהָרִים	נְעָרִים	פְּחָדִים	פְּעָלִים	(רְחָבִים)	כֹּהֲנִים
cstr.	נַהֲרֵי	נַעֲרֵי	פַּחֲדֵי	פָּעֳלֵי	(רָחֳבֵי)	כֹּהֲנֵי
	(river)	(lad)	(fear)	(work)	(breadth)	(priest)

i. Like פַּחַד is the preposition תַּחַת *under, instead of*, which, like אֶל־, עַל, takes *plur.* suffixes, תַּחְתַּי, תַּחְתֶּיךָ, תַּחְתָּיו, &c.

ii. In *second declens.* words primarily of the form נַעְרְ, פָּעְלְ, &c. (§ 25), naturally take, as their helping vowel, not ֶ (as in מֶלֶךְ, בֹּקֶר), but ַ, under the influence of the guttural. Words of the 1st class or *a*-type (מַלְךְ) preserve the original *pathaḥ* (cf. נַעְרְ), thus yielding the form נַעַר; words of the 2nd class, with the vowels ֵ ֶ (cf. סֵפֶר), do not exist; words of the 3rd class are formed as we should expect (cf. בֹּקֶר), e.g. פֹּעַל.

iii. Note the forms with suffixes which are according to the rules (§ 7. 5b, a; 7. 1a, c); e.g. נַעְרִי > נְעָרִי, the guttural taking a helping vowel; נַעְרְךָ > נַעֲרְךָ > נְעַרְךָ, because two vocal shᵉwas cannot come together. Likewise פָּעְלִי > פָּעֳלִי; פָּעְלְךָ > פָּעֳלְךָ > פָּעָלְךָ. ח does not require a helping vowel; e.g. פַּחְדִּי, רָחְבִּי (§ 7. 5b).

iv. *Seghôl* appears instead of *pathaḥ* in the words לֶחֶם *bread,* רֶחֶם *womb,* אֹהֶל *tent,* בֹּהֶן *thumb.*

(b) *From Lāmedh Guttural Verbs.*

	First declension		Second declension			Third declension
sing. abs.	רָשָׁע	שָׂמֵחַ	זֶרַע	שֵׁמַע	רֹמַח	מִזְבֵּחַ
cstr.	רְשַׁע	שְׂמַח	,,	,,	,,	מִזְבַּח
cons. suff.	רְשָׁעֲךָ	שְׂמֵחֲךָ	זַרְעֲךָ	שִׁמְעֲךָ	רָמְחֲךָ	מִזְבַּחֲךָ
plur. abs.	רְשָׁעִים	שְׂמֵחִים	זְרָעִים	(שְׁמָעִים)	רְמָחִים	מִזְבְּחוֹת
cstr.	רִשְׁעֵי	שִׂמְחֵי	זַרְעֵי	(שִׁמְעֵי)	רָמְחֵי	,,
		and שְׂמֵחֵי, § 19. 5				
	(wicked)	(rejoicing)	(seed)	(report)	(lance)	(altar)

In *second declension* the final short vowel is naturally *a* before the guttural (§ 7. 1), and in all the declensions the vocal shᵉwa before the consonantal suffixes *kha*, &c., becomes a *ḥateph* (therefore רְשָׁעֲךָ, not רְשָׁעְךָ; זַרְעֲךָ, not זַרְעְךָ; &c.).

טהר	to be clean; *Pi.* cleanse	שׁלח	to send	מִשְׁפָּחָה	family, clan
		שׁמע	to hear	שַׁעַר	gate
צעק / זעק	to cry, to cry out	שׂבע	to be satisfied	רַחֲמִים	mercy compassion
טעם	to taste	זרח	to rise, shine	פֶּשַׁע	transgression
לחם	*Niph.* to fight	זרע	to sow	שַׁחַר	dawn
ברך	*Piʿel* to bless	נטע	to plant	יֵשַׁע	salvation
שׁען	*Niph.* to lean	שׁכח	to forget	מַעֲבָר	crossing, ford
בחר	to choose	משׁח	to anoint	כְּנַעֲנִי	Canaanite
רחץ	to wash	צמח	to sprout	שׁוֹפָר	trumpet
סעד	to sustain, refresh	תקע	to blow (trumpet)	מִרְמָה	deceit
				לָבֶטַח	securely
גרשׁ	*Piʿel* to drive (out)	עָוֹן	iniquity, guilt, punishment	צֹפֶה	watchman
				אֵל	God

EXERCISE

Translate

טַהֲרֵנִי, טַעֲמוּ, בָּרֲכוּ, יְשָׁרֵת, זַעֲקִי, וַיִּלָּחֲמוּ, יְטַהֵר, אֶרְחַץ,
אֶרְחָצֵךְ, מְצַעֵק:

אֶשְׁמַע, אֶשְׁמְעָה, בְּהִשָּׁמַע, תַּשְׁמַע, שְׁלַח, שֹׁלֵחַ, יִשְׁכָּחֵהוּ,
שָׁכַחַתְּ:

[1]יֻקַּח־נָא מְעַט מַיִם וְרַחֲצוּ רַגְלֵיכֶם וְהִשָּׁעֲנוּ תַּחַת הָעֵץ: וְאֶקְחָה
פַת־לֶחֶם וְסַעֲדוּ לִבְּכֶם אַחַר תַּעֲבֹרוּ: 2 וַיְגָרֶשׁ יהוה אֶת־
הָאָדָם וַיְשַׁלְּחֵהוּ מִן־הַגָּן לַעֲבֹד אֶת־הָאֲדָמָה אֲשֶׁר [1]לֻקַּח [2]מִשָּׁם:
3 וַיִּזְעֲקוּ בְּנֵי יִשְׂרָאֵל אֶל־יהוה לֵאמֹר עָזַבְנוּ אֶת־אֱלֹהֵינוּ וַנַּעֲבֹד
אֶת־הַבְּעָלִים: 4 וַאֲבָרֶכְךָ וַאֲגַדְּלָה שְׁמֶךָ וַאֲבָרְכָה מְבָרְכֶיךָ
וְנִבְרְכוּ בְךָ כֹּל מִשְׁפְּחֹת הָאֲדָמָה: 5 טַעֲמוּ וּרְאוּ כִּי־טוֹב יְהוָה
בָּרוּךְ הָאִישׁ אֲשֶׁר יִבְטַח־בּוֹ: 6 זָכְרֵנִי יהוה כְּחַסְדְּךָ כְּרֹב רַחֲמֶיךָ
מְחֵה פְשָׁעָי: כַּבְּסֵנִי מִכָּל־עֲוֺנִי וּמֵחַטָּאתִי טַהֲרֵנִי: 7 בִּשְׁמֹעַ הָאִישׁ

---

[1] § 34. 3d. [2] § 10. 4.

אֶת־דִּבְרֵי אָבִיהוּ וַיִּצְעַק צְעָקָה גְּדוֹלָה וַיֹּאמֶר לְאָבִיהוּ בָּרֲכֵנִי
[1]גַם־אָנִי אָבִי׃ וַיֹּאמֶר בָּא אָחִיךָ בְּמִרְמָה וַיִּקַּח בִּרְכָתֶךָ׃ וַיַּעַן הָאִישׁ
אֶל־אָבִיהוּ הַבְרָכָה אַחַת־הִיא־לְךָ אָבִי בָּרֲכֵנִי גַם אָנִי׃ 8 הִנֵּה
אָנֹכִי שֹׁלֵחַ מַלְאָךְ לְפָנֶיךָ לִשְׁמָרְךָ בַּדָּרֶךְ הִשָּׁמֶר־מִפָּנָיו וּשְׁמַע
בְּקוֹלוֹ׃ 9 וַיִּטַּע יהוה גַּן וַיַּצְמַח מִן־הָאֲדָמָה כָּל־עֵץ נֶחְמָד
לְמַרְאֶה וְטוֹב לְמַאֲכָל׃ 10 וַיִּקַּח יַעֲקֹב אֶת־נָשָׁיו וְאֶת־יְלָדָיו
וַיַּעֲבֹר אֶת־הַמַּעֲבָר׃ וַיִּקָּחֵם וַיַּעֲבִרֵם אֶת־הַמַּעֲבָר וַיַּעֲבֵר אֶת־
אֲשֶׁר לוֹ׃ וַיִּלָּחֶם אִישׁ עִם יַעֲקֹב וַיֹּאמֶר הָאִישׁ שַׁלְּחֵנִי כִּי עָלָה
הַשָּׁחַר וַיֹּאמֶר לֹא אֲשַׁלֵּחֲךָ כִּי אִם בֵּרַכְתָּנִי׃ וַיֹּאמֶר לוֹ הַמַּלְאָךְ
לֹא יֵאָמֵר עוֹד יַעֲקֹב שִׁמְךָ כִּי אִם יִשְׂרָאֵל וַיְבָרֶךְ אֹתוֹ שָׁם׃ 11
וישביעני לאמר לא־תקח אשה לבני מבנות הכנעני אשר אנכי
ישֵׁב בארצו׃ 12 השמיעני בבקר חסדך כי־בך בטחתי׃ 13
ברכי נפשי את־יהוה ואל־תשכחי כל־חסדיו׃

Suggested further reading: Genesis xxviii, 10-19.

This song shall never be forgotten. 2 In the day of his being anointed (*Niph.*). 3 Thou shalt love Yahweh thy God and him thou shalt serve. 4 And your fathers cried unto me and said, We shall perish from the violence of our enemies. 5 Yahweh will give you in the evening flesh to eat, and bread in the morning to be satisfied (*inf. Qal*). 6 He caused thee to hear his words out of the fire. 7 Let those-loving (*ptc.* cstr.) thy salvation say: Let God be great! 8 Ye shall surely hearken to the voice of my messenger, when I send him to you. 9 And Samuel said, Speak, Yahweh, for thy servant is listening (*ptc.*). 10 And they forgot Yahweh, and he sold them into the hand of their enemies and they fought against[2] them. 11 And they took wives[3] from all whom they chose. 12 If I bring the sword upon a land, and the people of the land take a man and make him their watchman, and if he

---

[1] Cf. § 40. 8. [2] בְּ. [3] נָשִׁים, pl. of אִשָּׁה.

sees the sword coming upon the land and blows the trumpet to tell the people, then, if anyone hears the sound of the trumpet and does not listen and the sword comes and takes him away, his blood shall be upon his own head.

§ 37. PĒ ʾĀLEPH VERBS

(See Paradigm, p. 285)

1. (a) *Pē ʾĀleph* Verbs are a sub-class of *Pē Guttural* Verbs (§ 35). There are five verbs in the sub-class: אָבַד *to perish,* אָכַל *to eat,* אָמַר *to say,* אָבָה *to be willing,* אָפָה *to bake.* Their peculiarity is that in the Qal imperf. the א is quiescent. All other parts of these verbs are constructed on the model of the *Pē Gutturals.*

(b) The Qal imperf. of אָמַר is יֹאמַר; likewise יֹאבַד and יֹאכַל. Probably the development of the vocalization of this form was יַאֲמֹר (cf. יַעֲמֹד; § 35. 2d) > יָאמֹר (i.e. *ʾĀleph* quiescent) > יֹאמֹר (cf. שָׁלוֹם, Arab. *salâm*; קֹטֵל, Arab. *qâtil*; § 2. 6) > יֹאמַר, by a process of *dissimilation,* the object of which is to prevent two similar vowels (here *ō*) from falling in successive syllables (cf. רִאשׁוֹן *first,* from רֹאשׁ *head*).

(c) אָבָה and אָפָה likewise have יֹא– as the first syllable in the Qal imperf., but have the ending ֶה according to the regular form of *Lāmedh Hē* Verbs (§ 32. 2); so יֹאבֶה, יֹאפֶה.

2. (a) In the 1st sing. imperf. the radical א falls out in writing after the preformative א; i.e. אֹמַר (not אֹאמַר); so אֹבַד, אֹכַל. Occasionally the א falls out in other parts; e.g. תֹּמְרוּ for תֹּאמְרוּ, *ye shall say.*

(b) In pause ֵ is found in place of ַ; e.g. יֹאכֵל. In the *wāw* consec. imperf. the forms which are found are וַיֹּאכַל, וַיֹּאבַד, and וַיֹּאמֶר (§ 20. 4d), but in the 1st sing. וָאֹמַר; in pause we find וַיֹּאכֵל and וַיֹּאמַר.

3. The infin. constr. אֱמֹר, construed with ל, becomes לֶאֱמֹר > לֵאמֹר, dicendo, *saying* (§ 12. 1c). Not so when it is construed with ב or כ; בֶּאֱמֹר, כֶּאֱמֹר; nor is it so with other *Pē 'Āleph* verbs; e.g. לֶאֱכֹל (not לֵאכֹל) *to eat.*

4. A few verbs have both this quiescent form and the regular *Pē Gutt.* form; e.g. אָחַז *grasp, seize,* impf. יֹאחֵז and (rarely) יֶאֱחֹז; אָסַף *to gather,* impf. יֶאֱסֹף and (rarely) יֹסֵף (for יֹאסֵף).

קשב	*Hiph.* pay heed	רֹגֶז	turmoil, raging	אָדוֹן	master, lord
מָחָר	tomorrow	שָׁלָל	spoil, plunder	אֲדוֹנִי	my master
נָקִיא, נָקִי	innocent	נחם	*Niph.* נִחַם to repent	or אֲדֹנִי	my master
אַחֵר	another (next)			אֲדֹנָי	the Lord
				הֵנָּה	here, hither
				חֹרֵב	Horeb

חָלִילָה God forbid; חָלִילָה לִּי, followed by מִן and an infin. constr., God forbid that I should . . . .

EXERCISE

Translate

וַיֹּאמֶר יהוה אֶל־הָֽאָדָם מִכָּל־עֵץ הַגָּן אָכֹל תֹּאכֵל׃ 2 אִם־
תֹּאבוּ וּשְׁמַעְתֶּם טוּב הָאָרֶץ תֹּאכֵלוּ׃ 3 קַח־לְךָ מִכָּל־מַאֲכָל
אֲשֶׁר יֵאָכֵל וְהָיָה לְךָ וְלָהֶם לְאָכְלָה׃ 4 יהוה אַל־נָא נֹאבְדָה
בְּנֶפֶשׁ הָאִישׁ הַזֶּה וְאַל־תִּתֵּן עָלֵינוּ דָּם נָקִיא׃ 5 מַהֲרוּ וַעֲלוּ אֶל־
אָבִי וַאֲמַרְתֶּם אֵלָיו כֹּה אָמַר בִּנְךָ יוֹסֵף שָׂמַנִי אֱלֹהִים לְאָדוֹן
בְּמִצְרָיִם רְדָה אֵלַי אַל־תַּעֲמֹד׃ וְיָשַׁבְתָּ בְּאֶרֶץ הַזֹּאת וְהָיִיתָ קָרוֹב
אֵלָי׃ וְהִגַּדְתֶּם לְאָבִי אֶת־כָּל־אֲשֶׁר רְאִיתֶם וְאֶת־כָּל־כְּבוֹדִי
בְּמִצְרָיִם וּמִהַרְתֶּם וְהוֹרַדְתֶּם אֶת־אָבִי הֵנָּה׃ 6 וַיֹּאמֶר יְהוּדָה
מַה־נֹּאמַר לַֽאדֹנִי מַה־נְּדַבֵּר וּמַה־נִּצְטַדָּק הִנֶּנּוּ עֲבָדִים לַֽאדֹנִי׃
וַיֹּאמֶר חָלִילָה־לִּי מֵעֲשׂוֹת זֹאת הָאִישׁ אֲשֶׁר נִמְצָא הַשָּׁלָל בְּיָדוֹ
הוּא יִֽהְיֶה־לִּי עָבֶד וְאַתֶּם תָּשׁוּבוּ לְשָׁלוֹם אֶל־אַרְצְכֶם׃ 7 וַיִּקְרְאוּ

אֶל־אֱלֹהִים וַיֹּאמְרוּ מִי יוֹדֵעַ אִם יָשׁוּב וְנִחַם [1] הָאֱלֹהִים וְלֹא
נֹאבֵד׃ 8 הִשָּׁמֶר־לְךָ פֶּן־תִּשְׁכַּח אֶת־הַיּוֹם אֲשֶׁר עָמַדְתָּ לִפְנֵי
אֲדֹנָי אֱלֹהֶיךָ בְּחֹרֵב בֶּאֱמֹר יהוה אֵלַי אֱסָף־לִי אֶת־הָעָם׃ 9
ותקח האשה מפרי העץ ותאכל ותתן גם לאישה ויאכל׃ 10
האכלתם לחם במדבר׃

Suggested further reading: Genesis xxvii, 18-27.

Ye shall eat of the fruit of your ways. 2 Let us not perish for his life. 3 And he called the people to eat and they ate. 4 And the children of Israel said, Who will let-us-eat (*Hiph.*) flesh? 5 Ye shall not eat any carcase; to the stranger ye shall give it and he shall eat it. 6 It shall not be eaten, it shall be burned in the fire. And the dogs ate the flesh of my calf. 7 And the man rose-early in the morning and he told all these words in the ears of his servants. 8 Do not let us pay heed to his words, for a ruling [2] will not fail us from the priest, nor counsel from the wise, nor a word from the prophet. 9 Then they called upon Yahweh and said: Pray, let us not perish for this man's life. Let us take him up and cast him into the sea, that the sea may cease from its raging.

§ 38. LĀMEDH ʼĀLEPH VERBS

(See Paradigm, p. 296-299)

1. ʼ*Āleph* is a weak letter; when it occurs at the end of a syllable, it commonly loses all consonantal value; when it occurs at the end of a final syllable, it always does so.

(a) In *Lāmedh* ʼ*Āleph* verbs **א** at the end of a syllable is quiescent; therefore,

i. There cannot be a *pathah furtive* before a final **א**; e.g. Hiph. perf. **הִמְצִיא**, not **הִמְצִיאַ**; imperf. **יַמְצִיא**, not **יַמְצִיאַ**.

ii. A short vowel before such an **א** is lengthened; e.g. Qal perf. **מָצָא** (cf. **קָטַל**, **שָׁלַח**), Niph. perf. **נִמְצָא**, Hoph. perf. **הָמְצָא**.

---

1 *will return and have mercy*, i.e. *will have mercy again*.
2 מִשְׁפָּט.

The Qal imperf. is יִמְצָא (on the basis of יִשְׁלַח), imper. מְצָא; but note the retention of *ṣērê* in the final syllable before the א in the Niph. imperf. יִמָּצֵא, Pi'el perf. מִצֵּא, Pi'el imperf. יְמַצֵּא, Hithpa'el perf. הִתְמַצֵּא, imperf. יִתְמַצֵּא, Hiph. juss. יַמְצֵא, and in the imperatives., infins. cstr. and parts. of these forms.

(b) i. In the Qal perf. of transitive verbs (those in *a*) the vowel *ā* remains throughout the conjugated forms; e.g. מָצָאתָ (cf. קָטַלְתָּ, שָׁלַחְתָּ). In the other perfs. the vowel is *ē*; e.g. 2nd s.m. Niph. perf. נִמְצֵאתָ, Pi'el מִצֵּאתָ, Hiph. הִמְצֵאתָ, &c.

This *ē* is difficult to account for. In the Niph., e.g., we should have expected נִמְצָאתִי (cf. נִקְטַלְתִּי), and in the Pi., מִצָּאתִי (cf. קִטַּלְתִּי). It probably follows the analogy of *Lāmedh Hē* vbs. (§ 32).

ii. In the Qal perf. of intransitive verbs (those in *ē*; e.g. מָלֵא *to be full*), as well as in perfs. of the other forms, the vowel *ē* is found in the conjugated forms; e.g. 2nd s.m. Qal perf. מָלֵאתָ, Niph. נִמְלֵאתָ, Pi'el מִלֵּאתָ, &c.

(c) All imperfects and imperatives take ֶ (*é*) before נָה, again probably on the analogy of *Lāmedh Hē* vbs.; e.g. תִּמְצֶ֫אנָה, מְצֶ֫אנָה.

(d) א at the end of a syllable, being silent, may fall out in writing; e.g. מָצָתִי for מָצָאתִי (cf. נָקִי and נָקִיא, and § 37. 2a).

2. Note that in such forms with verbal suffixes as מְצָאַנִי, יִמְצָאֻנִי, &c., the א occurs *at the beginning of a syllable* and has consonantal value.

3. This class of verbs has a considerable tendency to adopt the vocalization and even the consonantal spelling of *Lāmedh Hē* verbs (§ 32); e.g. רְפָה *heal* (imperative) for רְפָא. There is frequent confusion between the roots קָרָא *to call*, and קָרָה *to meet*.

4. In pf. with *waw consec.* the accent is not usually on the final syllable; e.g. וְקָרָ֫אתָ, not וְקָרָאתָ֫ *and thou shalt call.*

5. *Nouns from verbs* ל״א.

	First declension		Second declension		Third declension	
abs.	צָבָא	מִקְרָא	כֶּלֶא	חֵטְא	יֹצֵא	
cstr.	צְבָא	מִקְרָא	„	„	יֹצֵאת	*fem.*
suff.	צְבָאֲךָ	מִקְרָאֲכֶם	כִּלְאוֹ	חֶטְאוֹ		
pl.	צְבָאוֹת	מִקְרָאִים	כְּלָאִים	חֲטָאִים	יֹצְאִים	
cstr.	צִבְאוֹת	מִקְרָאֵי	(כְּלָאֵי)	חֲטָאֵי	יֹצְאוֹת	*fem.*
	(army)	(assembly)	(prison)	(sin)	(going out, *ptc.*)	

(a) The quiescent א retains the long vowel *ā* before it even in the *cstr. sing.*, though the heavy suffix כֶם admits the short vowel.

(b) The long vowel often remains before the quiescent א even in the *cstr. plur.*; e.g. חֲטָאֵי. For the ֶ in חֶטְאוֹ, cf. §§ 7. 2; 35. 4b.

(c) In a fem. form like יֹצֵאת, the א, although it is at the beginning of the final syllable, is apt to become quiescent, so that the form commonly is found יֹצֵאת (§ 18. 3).

6. Intransitive verbs, such as those expressing the idea of *fulness* (מָלֵא *to be full*, שָׂבַע *to be satisfied*, שָׁרַץ *to swarm*, לָבֵשׁ or לָבַשׁ *to be clothed with, to wear*, &c.) and *want* (חָסֵר *to suffer lack*, שָׁכֹל *to be bereaved*, &c.) subordinate to themselves, as an accus. of respect, the noun which fulfils their meaning. When they become transitive (in Pi'el or Hiph'il, §§ 23, 24), they take two accusatives, the accus. of respect and a direct accus.

מָלֵא הַבַּיִת עָשָׁן	*The house was full of smoke*
נִמְלָא „ „	*The house was filled with smoke*
מִלֵּא הַבַּיִת עָשָׁן	*He filled the house with smoke*

מצא	to find	שָׂנֵא	to hate	גְּבוּרָה	*f.* strength, might, power
קרא	to call, read	מַחֲשָׁבָה	(constr. pl. מַחְ׳) thought, plan	כֹּחַ	
קָרָה / קרא	to befall, meet	נשׂא	to lift up, to carry	שׂחק	to laugh, to sport
חטא	to sin	נבא	*Ni., Hith.* to prophesy	פָּרַץ	to break through, to break down
מָלֵא	to be full	רפא	to heal	חבק	*Qal, Pi.* to embrace
פֶּלֶא	*i* a wonder	חֵפֶץ	pleasure, business	ברא	to create
צָמֵא	to be thirsty	אַחֲרִית	*f.* after-part, issue, end	בְּאַחֲרִית הַיָּמִים	in days to come
רחם	*Qal* to love; *Pi.* to show mercy	רעשׁ	to quake	אות	token, sign
כְּלִי	(pl. כֵּלִים) vessel				

EXERCISE

Translate

נִבְרָא, מַלְאָכֶיךָ, קְרָאַן, וַיִּמְצָאֵהוּ, יִמְצָאֻנּוּ, יְרָאוּנוּ, אֲמַלְּאֶה, יְשַׂנְאֵנִי, תַּחֲטִיא, וַחֲטָאתֶם, תֶּחֶטְאוּ׃

וַיֹּאמֶר יַעֲקֹב אֶל־בָּנָיו הֵאָסְפוּ וְאַגִּידָה לָכֶם אֵת אֲשֶׁר יִקְרָא
אֶתְכֶם בְּאַחֲרִית הַיָּמִים׃ 2 וַיֹּאמֶר מֶלֶךְ יִשְׂרָאֵל שְׂנֵאתִיו כִּי לֹא
יִתְנַבֵּא עָלַי טוֹב כִּי אִם רָע׃ 3 כֹּה אָמַר יהוה אֲנִי מַרְעִישׁ אֶת־
כָּל־הַגּוֹיִם וּמִלֵּאתִי אֶת־הַבַּיִת הַזֶּה כָּבוֹד׃ 4 כִּי יְבִיאֲךָ יהוה
אֱלֹהֶיךָ אֶל־הָאָרֶץ אֲשֶׁר נִשְׁבַּע לָתֶת־לָךְ עָרִים גְּדֹלֹת וְטֹבֹת
אֲשֶׁר לֹא־בָנִיתָ׃ בָּתִּים[1] מְלֵאִים כָּל־טוּב אֲשֶׁר לֹא־מִלֵּאתָ
כְּרָמִים וְזֵיתִים אֲשֶׁר לֹא־נָטָעְתָּ וְאָכַלְתָּ וְשָׂבָעְתָּ׃ הִשָּׁמֶר־לְךָ
פֶּן־תִּשְׁכַּח אֶת־יהוה אֱלֹהֶיךָ אֲשֶׁר הוֹצִיאֲךָ מֵאֶרֶץ מִצְרַיִם מִבֵּית
עֲבָדִים׃ 5 יֶשׁ־עֵת לְכָל־חֵפֶץ תַּחַת־הַשָּׁמָיִם׃ [2]עֵת לָלֶדֶת וְעֵת
לָמוּת עֵת לִנְטֹעַ וְעֵת לִקְצֹר׃ עֵת לַהֲרֹג וְעֵת לִרְפּוֹא עֵת לִפְרֹץ

[1] pl. of בַּיִת *house*.

[2] cf. § 18. 2a, i.

וְעֵת לִבְנוֹת׃ עֵת לִבְכּוֹת וְעֵת לִשְׂחֹק עֵת לַחֲבֹק וְעֵת לִרְחֹק
מֵחַבֵּק׃ עֵת לְבַקֵּשׁ וְעֵת לְאַבֵּד עֵת לִשְׁמֹר וְעֵת לְהַשְׁלִיךְ׃ עֵת
לֶאֱהֹב וְעֵת לִשְׂנֹא עֵת מִלְחָמָה וְעֵת שָׁלוֹם׃ 6 דִּרְשׁוּ יהוה בְּהִמָּצְאוֹ
קְרָאֻהוּ [1]בִּהְיוֹתוֹ קָרוֹב׃ יַעֲזֹב רָשָׁע דַּרְכּוֹ וְאִישׁ פֶּשַׁע מַחְשְׁבֹתָיו
וְיָשֹׁב אֶל־יהוה וִירַחֲמֵהוּ וְאֶל־אֱלֹהֵינוּ כִּי יִרְפָּא מְאֹד׃ 7 אמר
הכהן הגדול ספר התורה מצאתי ויתן את־הספר אל־הסֹּפֵר
ויקראהו׃ 8 וימצאהו איש וישאלהו לאמר מה־תבקש׃

Suggested further reading: Genesis xxii, 9-19.

Yahweh will hear when thou criest to him. 2 I am full (*perf.*) of the spirit of judgment and of power, to tell to Jacob his transgression and to Israel his sin. 3 And the earth was filled with violence. 4 Hast thou found-me, mine enemy? and he said, I have found-thee. 5 Thou hast filled this house with thy glory. 6 Thou hatest (*perf.*) all workers of iniquity. 7 And the spirit of Yahweh lifted-him up and cast him to-(the)-earth. 8 Thou shalt love thine enemy, thou shalt not hate him in thy heart. 9 And he said to her; Pray give me a little water to drink for I am thirsty; for it is said: If thine enemy hunger, feed him, and if he thirst, give him drink. 10 Joseph commanded his servants and they filled their vessels with corn and gave them food for the journey, and they lifted up their corn upon their asses and departed.

§ 39. DOUBLE ʿAYIN VERBS

(See Paradigm, p. 300-303)

1. According to § 6. 3b, when the same consonant occurs in a word at the end of a syllable and at the beginning of the syllable immediately following, it is written once with daghesh forte; e.g. נָתַנְנוּ > נָתַנּוּ; when a vowel intervenes between the two consonants in such a case, normally daghesh forte cannot be used; e.g. קְלָלָה. The main problem in connection with

[1] cf. § 33. 2b.

Double *'Ayin* Verbs is to define when the *'Ayin* radical is written twice and when daghesh forte is used. It is an open question whether the root is to be regarded as monosyllabic and biliteral (סַב), expanded in certain parts to סָבַב, or dissyllabic and triliteral (סָבַב), contracted in certain parts to סַב. The duplication which is so common a feature of these verbs (e.g. סַבֹּותִי, 1 *s.pf. Qal*; קַלּוּ, 3 *pl.pf.* &c.) might seem to point conclusively to the presence of a repeated letter in the stem (סָבַב, קָלַל); it may equally well be due, however, simply to the desire to strengthen the second consonant of the short biliteral stem (סַב, קַל), § 6. 3a.

2. The form with the *'Ayin* radical written twice is used when the verbal form requires it, owing to the presence of an unchangeably long vowel which must be preserved or because the verbal form is an intensive which itself is characterized by the strengthening of the *'Ayin* radical; e.g. act. and pass. ptc. Qal סוֹבֵב, סָבוּב; inf. abs. Qal סָבוֹב; Pi. סִבֵּב.

It is also usual in the 3rd pers. pf. Qal: סָבַב, סָבְבָה, סָבְבוּ.

3. In all other cases the simple form of the verbal stem is used, with the *'Ayin* radical written once:

(a) When there is no afformative, the *'Ayin* radical, standing vowelless at the end of the word, does not have dagh. forte written to it (§ 6. 3c); e.g. infin. constr. and imper. Qal סֹב (< סְבֹב), imperf. יָסֹב (< יִסְבֹּב), perf. Niph. נָסַב (< נִסְבַּב), imperf. Niph. יִסַּב (< יִסֵּב < יִסָּבֵב) (§ 22. 1; *pathaḥ* probably under the influence of the perf. נָסַב).

α. ל before such (monosyllabic) infins. construct is pointed לָ; e.g. לָבֹז *to plunder*, לָרֹב *to become many* (§ 12. 1d); cf. § 29. 2. 2b, iii.

β. With suffixes to the inf. cstr., *u* naturally appears in the sharpened syllable (§ 6. 7); e.g. בְּחֻקּוֹ *when he inscribed* (from חָקַק). Cf. § 40. 2a.

(b) Exceptions i. In the Hiph. *ē* (sometimes *a*, especially with gutt. and *reš*) is found in place of the pure long *î*; e.g.

הֵסֵב *to surround,* הֵחֵל *to begin,* הֵרַע *to do harm, to treat evilly;* imperf. יָסֵב, יָחֵל, יָרַע; imper. הָסֵב, הָחֵל, הָרַע; part. מֵסֵב, מֵחֵל, מֵרַע (pl. מְרֵעִים).

ii. The Niph. impf. follows the pf.: יִסַּב (cf. נָקוֹם, יִקּוֹם, § 30. 3).

iii. Intransitive vbs. have the vowel *a*, not *ē*; e.g. קַל, מַר, רַךְ.

(c) A few verbs have both forms; e.g. צָרַר *to bind;* צַר *to be narrow, to be confined.*

4. (a) As is illustrated in the imperf. Qal form given in 3a above, the vowel of a preformative, standing in the open pre-tonic syllable, is tone-long; e.g. imperf. Qal יָסֹב, the original *ya* lengthened to *yā* (§ 17. 4a; cf. § 30. 1b); with *wāw* consec. וַיָּסָב; pf. Niph. נָסַב—the primary *na* lengthened to *nā* (cf. נָקוֹם, § 30. 3); pf. Hiph. הֵסֵב—*hi* lengthened to *hē* (§ 5. 2b), ptc. follows the pf. מֵסֵב (cf. מֵקִים, § 30. 2), impf. יָסֵב, with *wāw cons.* וַיָּסֶב, Hoph. הוּסַב, יוּסַב.

(b) In intrans. verbs—impf. in *a*—the *yi* of the preformative (§ 19. 3) is naturally lengthened to *yē*; cf. יֵמַר, יֵרַךְ.

5. (a) When there is an afformative or a verbal suffix added to the verbal stem, the ʿ*Ayin* radical takes dagh. forte, so that the nature of the stem as Double ʿ*Ayin* is made explicit; the tone is, as a rule, on the penultimate syllable; e.g. Niph. perf. נָסַב, f. נָסַבָּה (נָ pretonic; therefore not נְ), 2nd s.m. נְסַבּוֹתָ (נְ now removed two places from the tone), but part. נָסָב, f. נְסַבָּה, pl. נְסַבִּים; with verbal suffix, יָסֹב, יְסֻבֵּנִי; יָחֹן, יְחֻנֵּנִי or יְחָנֵּנִי; imper. Qal סֹב, סֻבֵּנִי; חֹן, חָנֵּנִי; perf. Hiph. הֵסֵב, הֲסִבַּנִי; imperf. Hiph. יָסֵב, יְסִבֵּנִי.

(b) When the afformative begins with a consonant, a vowel is inserted, viz. in the perfects, *ô* and in the impff. and related parts, *é*; as pf. Qal סַבּוֹתָ, impf. Niph. תִּסַּבֶּינָה; cf. § 30. 5a.

(c) The tone long *ē ō*, which under the tone maintained themselves before the double letter, cf. § 4. 4a (2 f. s. impf.

Qal תָּסֹבִּי, impf. Hiph. תָּסֵבִּי), when they lose the tone become the sharp *i u* (§ 6. 7); as 2 pl. fem. imper. Qal סֻבֶּינָה, impf. תְּסֻבֶּינָה; impf. Hiph. תְּסִבֶּינָה.

6. The regular Intensive is quite common; e.g. הִלֵּל *to praise.* Another form of Intensive, also much in use, is the so-called *Pôʿēl*; e.g. סוֹבֵב (cf. קוֹמֵם, § 30. 4) *to encompass,* עוֹלֵל *to act severely,* pass. עוֹלַל, reflexive הִתְעוֹלֵל. More rare is the *Pilpēl*; e.g. גִּלְגֵּל *to roll* (§ 23. 5).

7. In the impf. some vbs. duplicate the *first* radical, as in Aramaic; e.g. קָבַב, impf. יִקֹּב *to curse,* קָדַד יִקֹּד *to bow down,* דָּמַם יִדֹּם *to be silent,* תָּמַם יִתֹּם *to be finished.* Some vbs. have both forms; e.g. סָבַב, Qal יָסֹב and יִסֹּב, Hiph. יָסֵב and יַסֵּב; שָׁמֵם *to be desolate* or *astonished,* יָשֹׁם and יִשֹּׁם.

בז to plunder
חן to be gracious to
חל *Hiph.* to begin
נָעֳמִי Naomi (No^{o}mi)
גּוּר to sojourn
הִתְגּוֹרֵר to seek hospitality with
אָמָה maidservant
יֶתֶר remainder
בַּד separation (always preceded by לְ)
לְבַד apart

מד to measure
מר [1] to be bitter
רע [1] to be evil
אר to curse
חג to hold a feast
קל [1] to be light (*Pi.* to curse)
פָּסַח to pass over
עָנָה to answer
עָנָה בְּ to testify against
מִדָּה measure
תְּחִנָּה / תַּחֲנוּנִים supplication(s)

שָׁלֹשׁ three
שָׁחַט to slay (ritually)
רב to be *or* become many, to multiply
רחם *Pi.* to have compassion
שַׁדַּי Shaddai [2]
אֶרֶךְ (*cstr.*) long, slow
רֵיק *adj.* empty, vain
רֵיקָם *adv.* with empty hands, in vain

[1] *stative* or *intransitive*; imperf. in *a*.
[2] Probable meaning: mountain god; used as an epithet of God in parts of the O.T.

בְּכֹר	firstborn	רַחוּם	merciful	חֶבֶל	cord
אָנָה	whither?	חַנּוּן	gracious	כַּמָּה	how much?

EXERCISE

Parse these Words

בַּזּוּנוּ, קַלּוּ, וְחַגֹּתֶם, אָאֹר, וַיָּחָן, גֹּל, תֵּרַע, בֹּזּוּ, לָסֹב, וְנָקַל,
וּנְסַבֹּתֶם, יִמַּד, הֲשִׁמּוֹתָ, הֵתַמּוּ, תִּדֹּם, אֶסֹּב, וַיִּתְּמוּ, תַּתֵּם׃

Translate

אֲנִי אַעֲבִיר כָּל־טוּבִי עַל־פָּנֶיךָ וְחַנֹּתִי אֶת־אֲשֶׁר אָחֹן וְרִחַמְתִּי
אֶת־אֲשֶׁר אֲרַחֵם׃ 2 הֵחֵל הָאָדָם לָרֹב בָּאָרֶץ וּבָנוֹת יֻלְּדוּ לָהֶם׃
3 עַל־הָאִשָּׁה אֲשֶׁר אֲנִי מִתְגּוֹרֵר עִמָּהּ הֲרֵעוֹתָ לְהָמִית אֶת־בְּנָהּ׃
4 וַתֹּאמֶר אֲלֵיהֶן אַל־תִּקְרֶאנָה לִי נָעֳמִי [1]קְרֶאןָ לִי מָרָא כִּי הֵמַר
שַׁדַּי לִי מְאֹד׃ אֲנִי מְלֵאָה הָלַכְתִּי וְרֵיקָם הֱשִׁבַנִי יְהוָה לָמָּה
תִקְרֶאנָה לִי נָעֳמִי [2]וַיהוָה עָנָה בִי וְשַׁדַּי הֵרַע לִי׃ 5 אָרוּר אַתָּה
בָּעִיר וְאָרוּר אַתָּה בַּשָּׂדֶה׃ אָרוּר אַתָּה בְּבֹאֶךָ וְאָרוּר אַתָּה
בְּצֵאתֶךָ׃ 6 וְאַתָּה אֲדֹנָי אֵל־רַחוּם וְחַנּוּן אֶרֶךְ אַפַּיִם וְרַב חֶסֶד
וֶאֱמֶת׃ פְּנֵה אֵלַי וְחָנֵּנִי עֲשֵׂה עִמִּי אוֹת לְטוֹבָה׃ תְּנָה־עֻזְּךָ לְעַבְדֶּךָ
וְהוֹשִׁיעָה בֶּן־אֲמָתֶךָ׃ 7 וְעָבַרְתִּי בְאֶרֶץ־מִצְרַיִם בַּלַּיְלָה הַזֶּה
וְהִכֵּיתִי כָל־בְּכוֹר בְּאֶרֶץ מֵאָדָם וְעַד־בְּהֵמָה׃ וְהָיָה הַדָּם לָכֶם
לְאוֹת עַל־הַבָּתִּים אֲשֶׁר אַתֶּם שָׁם וְרָאִיתִי אֶת־הַדָּם וּפָסַחְתִּי
עֲלֵיכֶם׃ וְהָיָה הַיּוֹם הַזֶּה לָכֶם לְזִכָּרוֹן וְחַגֹּתֶם אֹתוֹ חַג לַיהוָה
לְדֹרֹתֵיכֶם חֻקַּת עוֹלָם תְּחָגֻּהוּ׃ 8 וָאֶשָּׂא עֵינַי וָאֵרֶא וְהִנֵּה־אִישׁ
וּבְיָדוֹ חֶבֶל מִדָּה׃ וָאֹמַר אֵלָיו אָנָה אַתָּה הֹלֵךְ וַיֹּאמֶר אֵלַי לָמֹד
אֶת־הָעִיר לִרְאוֹת כַּמָּה־רָחְבָּהּ וְכַמָּה־אָרְכָּהּ׃ 9 וַיָּשָׁב מֹשֶׁה
אֶל־יהוה ויאמַר אדני למה הרעת לעם הזה למה שלחתני אל־

[1] Defective spelling, § 2. 7e.

[2] *Circumstantial clause*,—in which the order is: *wāw*, then *subject*, and last *predicate*. *Wāw* should be translated here "when".

פרְעֹה: הרביתי לבוא אל־פרעה לדבר בשמך והוא הרע לעם הַזֶּה ולא־הצלת את־עַמֶּךָ:

Suggested further reading: Genesis xxxvii, 5-23.

I will curse (אר) them that curse (קל) thee. 2 May Yahweh cause his face to shine upon thee and be gracious to thee. 3. When I call, answer me, O God of my salvation; be gracious to me and hear my prayer. 4 Make the soul of thy servant to rejoice, for unto thee, O Lord, I lift up my soul. For thou art good and right, and gracious and merciful to those who call unto thee. For thy mercy's sake hear my prayer and give heed to the voice of my supplications. How many are thy works, O Lord! In wisdom hast thou made[1] them all[1]; the whole earth is full of thy wonders. 5 And Saul began to build an altar to the Lord and he said to his servants: Bring, each of you, your ox to me and slay it here and eat it; but do not sin against Yahweh by eating (*Heb.* to eat) it with (עַל) the blood.

§ 40. NOUNS FROM DOUBLE ʿ*AYIN* VERBS

1. There are biliteral nouns and adjectives, as there are verbs, which duplicate the second radical before afformatives; e.g. קַל *fem.* קַלָּה *light*; עַם *people, suff.* עַמִּי *my people, pl.* עַמִּים.

	a class		*i* class	*u* class
abs.	עַם	הַר	חֵץ	חֹק
cstr.	עַם	הַר	חֵץ	חָק־
suff.	עַמִּי	הָרִי	חִצִּי	חֻקִּי
plur.	עַמִּים	הָרִים	חִצִּים	חֻקִּים
	(people)	(mountain)	(arrow)	(statute)

2. (a) The tone-long *ē* and *ō* of the *i* and *u* classes (illustrated in the Table by חֵץ and חֹק) go back to the primary vowels *i* and *u*, which are evident in the forms with suffixes and in the plural, &c.; e.g. חִצִּי *my arrow*, חִצִּים *arrows*, חֻקִּי *my statute*, חֻקִּים *statutes* (notice *u*, not *o*, in חֻקִּי and חֻקִּים;

[1] . . . [1] Cf. § 40. 6a, footnote on כֹּל.

cf. §§ 6. 7; 39. 3a, β). The vowel *a* of the *a* class usually remains short in the absolute; e.g. עַם *people,* שַׂר *prince,* צַר *adversary,* פַּר *ox,* הַר *mountain,* רַע *evil,* מַר *bitter.* But it becomes *ā* in certain nouns in combination with the def. art.; e.g. הַפָּר, הָעָם, הָהָר, הָרָע, but הַשַּׂר, הַמַּר; both הַצַּר and הַצָּר are found. Sometimes the *a* is thinned to *i* in the plur. and before suffixes; e.g. פַּת *morsel,* plur. פִּתִּים (cf. § 5. 2d, i).

(b) The vowel under preformative מ is sometimes reduced to vocal shᵉwa (e.g. מֵסַב *circle,* plur. מְסִבִּים) and sometimes preserved (e.g. מָסָךְ *curtain,* constr. מָסַךְ; מָגֵן *shield, my shield* מָגִנִּי).

(c) Rarely a triliteral form has been developed in the plur.; e.g. עֲמָמִים *peoples,* צְלָלִים from צֵל *shadow* (צִלִּי *my shadow*), הֲרָרֵי, cstr. pl. of הַר (cf. 3 below).

3. As gutturals and ר cannot be doubled, the preceding vowel is usually lengthened; thus קַל, *f.* קַלָּה, *m. pl.* קַלִּים, *f.* קַלּוֹת; but רַע *evil,* רָעָה, רָעִים, רָעוֹת. So הַר 1 *s.* הָרִי, *pl.* הָרִים. Before an implicitly doubled ח the short vowel remains. פַּח *snare,* פַּחִים. In either case, of course, the vowel is unchangeable, hence pl. cstr. רָעֵי (not רְ), הָרֵי, &c. § 7. 7b.

4. This type of noun can best be distinguished from other types by a knowledge of derivation; but it may be observed that — i. Words of this type belonging to the *a* class have usually short *a,* while the words of other types which they resemble, as דָּם *blood,* § 15, קָם *standing,* § 31, have *ā* (notice the very different cstr. plurals דְּמֵי, קָמֵי, עַמֵּי). ii. Those of the *i* class are distinguished from segholates of *ʿAyin Yōḏh* like חֵיק, § 31, by wanting *yōḏh.* They quite agree in form with words like מֵת, § 31, and שֵׁם, § 26, which, however, are not a numerous class (notice the difference before suffixes, מֵתִי, שְׁמִי, חִצִּי). iii. Those of the *u* class are distinguished from adj. and segholates of *ʿAyin Wāw* like טוֹב and קוֹל, § 31, by wanting *wāw.*

5. To this type may also be relegated i. a few words of the first declension type; e.g. גָּמָל *camel,* pl. גְּמַלִּים; עָצָב *idol,* pl. עֲצַבִּים; אוֹפָן *wheel* pl. אוֹפַנִּים, קָטָן *little,* קְטַנִּים, עָמֹק *deep,* fem. עֲמֻקָּה, &c.; ii. two or three monosyllables from roots with medial *n* (always assimilated);

e.g. אַף, *nostril, anger* (= *anp*, from root אנף), suff. אַפִּי, du. אַפַּיִם; עֵז (root ענז) *she-goat*, pl. עִזִּים; iii. words that repeat the last consonant; e.g. שַׁאֲנָן *at ease*, שַׁאֲנַנִּים.

6. (a) light קַל and so: weak דַּל, bitter מַר, living חַי.
people עַם and so: hill הַר, garden גַּן, prince שַׂר, ox פַּר, palm (hand) כַּף *f.*, separation בַּד.
shadow צֵל and so: heart לֵב, mother אֵם, end קֵץ, arrow חֵץ, time עֵת, with (prep.) אֵת, עִם.
statute חֹק and so: all כֹּל,[1] yoke עֹל, strength עֹז, heat חֹם, wholeness, moral integrity תֹּם, statute חֻקָּה.

(b) Note the use of preps. אֵת and עִם with suffixes: אִתִּי, אִתָּךְ, אִתְּךָ, אִתּוֹ, אִתָּהּ, אִתָּנוּ, אִתְּכֶם, אִתָּם. So עִמִּי, &c., except 2 *pl.* which is עִמָּכֶם. (Another form of 1 sing. is עִמָּדִי.) Like אֵת too is הִנֵּה *behold*, except in 1 pers. sing. and plur. It is as follows: הִנְנִי (or הִנֵּנִי, *pause* הִנָּנִי), הִנְּךָ, הִנָּךְ, הִנּוֹ, הִנָּהּ, הִנְנוּ (or הִנֵּנוּ, *pause* הִנָּנוּ), הִנְּכֶם, הִנָּם.

7. The indeterminate subject (Engl. *they*) may be expressed: (a) by the 3rd pers. plur.; or (b) by the 3rd sing.; or (c) by the passive voice, i.e. Niph. (Hoph. Pu.)—in the last case the Pass., used impersonally, still retains the Accus. after it in certain cases; e.g.

they called his name Sheth {
קָרְאוּ אֶת־שְׁמוֹ שֵׁת
קָרָא „
נִקְרָא „

8. When the Personal Pronoun is repeated for the sake of emphasis, it is repeated in the absolute or nominative form, e.g.

bless me, even me	בָּרֲכֵנִי גַם־אָנִי
thy blood, even thine	דָּמְךָ גַּם־אָתָּה
to Sheth, even him	לְשֵׁת גַּם־הוּא

[1] Note the use of כֹּל with pron. suff.: e.g. כֻּלָּם *their all*, i.e. all of them.

גָּבַר	to be strong	טָהוֹר	clean	מָאַס	to reject
תָּעָה	to wander	יֵצֶר	nature, form	פָּגַע	to meet, to encounter; *Hiph.* to cause to light upon, to interpose
יֶתֶר	remainder	נְעוּרִים	youth		
בְּתוּלָה	virgin	שְׁאֵלָה	request		
רָפָה	*Hiph.* to leave alone	נָשִׂיא	prince		
עֹל	(*suff.* עֻלִּי) yoke	אֲנִי לְבַדִּי	I alone		
עֲבוֹדָה	service, servitude	קָשָׁה	to be hard		
		קָשֶׁה	hard	אוֹ	or
		אֵם	mother		

EXERCISE

Translate

וּבְצִלּוֹ יֵשְׁבוּ גוֹיִם רַבִּים׃ 2 וְאֶתְּנֵם לַכֹּהֵן וּלְבָנָיו לְחָק־עוֹלָם׃
3 וַתָּבֹא הָאִשָּׁה אֵלָיו וַתֹּאמֶר הִנֵּה שָׁמְעָה שִׁפְחָתְךָ בְּקוֹלֶךָ וָאָשִׂים
נַפְשִׁי בְּכַפִּי׃ 4 קָרַב קִצֵּנוּ מָלְאוּ יָמֵינוּ׃ 5 אֱלֹהִים לֹא תְקַלֵּל
וְנָשִׂיא בְעַמְּךָ לֹא תָאֹר׃ 6 וַיֹּאמְרוּ לוֹ שִׂים יָדְךָ עַל־פִּיךָ וְלֵךְ
עִמָּנוּ וֶהְיֵה לָנוּ לְאָב וּלְכֹהֵן הֲטוֹב הֱיוֹתְךָ כֹהֵן לְבֵית אִישׁ אֶחָד
אוֹ הֱיוֹתְךָ כֹהֵן לְשֵׁבֶט וּלְמִשְׁפָּחָה בְּיִשְׂרָאֵל׃ 7 וַיִּבֶן נֹחַ מִזְבֵּחַ
לַיהוָה וַיִּקַּח מִכֹּל־הַבְּהֵמָה הַטְּהוֹרָה וּמִכֹּל־הָעוֹף הַטָּהוֹר וַיַּעַל
עֹלָה בַּמִּזְבֵּחַ׃ וַיֹּאמֶר יהוה בְּלִבּוֹ לֹא־אֹסִף לְקַלֵּל עוֹד אֶת־
הָאֲדָמָה בַּעֲבוּר הָאָדָם כִּי יֵצֶר לֵב הָאָדָם רַע מִנְּעֻרָיו וְלֹא אֹסִף
עוֹד לְהַכּוֹת אֶת־כָּל־חַי כַּאֲשֶׁר עָשִׂיתִי׃ וַיְבָרֶךְ יהוה אֶת־נֹחַ
וְאֶת־בָּנָיו וַיֹּאמֶר לָהֶם פְּרוּ וּרְבוּ וּמִלְאוּ אֶת־הָאָרֶץ׃ 8 כֻּלָּנוּ
כַּצֹּאן תָּעִינוּ אִישׁ לְדַרְכּוֹ פָּנִינוּ וַיהוה הִפְגִּיעַ בּוֹ אֵת עֲוֹן כֻּלָּנוּ׃
9 וַתֹּאמֶר שְׁאֵלָה אַחַת קְטַנָּה אָנֹכִי שֹׁאֶלֶת אַל־תָּשֶׁב אֶת־פָּנָי
וַיֹּאמֶר לָהּ הַמֶּלֶךְ שַׁאֲלִי אִמִּי כִּי לֹא אָשִׁיב אֶת־פָּנָיִךְ׃ וַתֹּאמֶר
יֻתַּן אֶת־הַנַּעֲרָה לְאָחִיךָ לְאִשָּׁה׃ וַיַּעַן הַמֶּלֶךְ לְאִמּוֹ וַיֹּאמֶר לָמָּה
אַתְּ שֹׁאֶלֶת אֶת־הַנַּעֲרָה לְאָחִי וְשַׁאֲלִי־לוֹ אֶת־הַמְּלוּכָה כִּי הוּא

אָחִי הַגָּדוֹל׃ 10 אָבִיךָ הִקְשָׁה אֶת־עֻלֵּנוּ וְאַתָּה הָקֵל מֵעֲבֹדַת
אָבִיךָ הַקָּשָׁה וּמֵעֻלּוֹ הַכָּבֵד אֲשֶׁר נָתַן עָלֵינוּ וְנַעַבְדֶךָּ׃ וַיַּעַן הַמֶּלֶךְ
אֶת־הָעָם קָשָׁה וַיַּעֲזֹב אֶת־עֲצַת הַזְּקֵנִים אֲשֶׁר יְעָצֻהוּ׃ וַיְדַבֵּר
אֲלֵיהֶם כַּעֲצַת הַיְלָדִים לֵאמֹר אָבִי הִכְבִּיד אֶת־עֻלְּכֶם וַאֲנִי
אֹסִיף עַל־עֻלְּכֶם׃ 11 אלה החקים והמשפטים אשר תשמרו
בארץ אשר נתתי לכם לרשתה כל הימים אשר־אתם חיים
על־האדמה כי עמי אתם׃

Suggested further reading: 1 Samuel xxxi.

Comfort ye my people, speak to (עַל־) their heart, and cry unto them that their warfare is fulfilled (full). 2 Plead with your mother, plead, for she is not my wife, and I am not her husband. 3 Thou shalt fall upon the mountains of Israel, thou and all the peoples that are with thee. 4 The prince lifted up his eyes and saw a man standing before him with his sword in his hand, and he said to him: Are you for us or for our adversaries? And he answered: No, but as the commander of the army of Yahweh have I come. 5 Let me know my end and the measure of my days, what it is, that I may know that I am a sojourner here. 6 The king sent the messengers to call the priests and they all came to the king. 7 The virgin said to the man: Let this thing be done to me; but leave me alone for a little that I may go by myself and weep upon the mountains of Israel. 8 Then Moses made the children of Israel journey into the wilderness and they travelled many days but found no water. They came to Marah (מָרָה) but were not able to drink the water there, for it was bitter; therefore, they called its name Marah. Then the people cried out against Moses, saying: What are we to do? And he cried out to Yahweh and he showed him a (piece of) wood and said: Throw it into the water. He threw it into the water and the water became sweet.

§ 41. DOUBLY WEAK AND DEFECTIVE VERBS

1. Many verbs have more than one weak letter. They are mostly ל״א or ל״ה with some other peculiarity. Some common verbs of this kind are these:

(1) ל״א and פ״ן.—נָשָׂא *to lift*, impf. יִשָּׂא, pl. יִשְׂאוּ (§ 6. 5); imp. שָׂא. suff. שָׂאֵהוּ, שָׂאוּנִי; inf. c. שְׂאֵת (rarely נְשׂא), בִּשְׂאֵת, &c., but לָשֵׂאת,

(2) ל״א and פ״ו.—יָצָא *go out*, impf. יֵצֵא, imp. צֵא, inf. c. צֵאת, לָצֵאת. Hiph. הוֹצִיא, הוֹצֵאתָ, &c. (cf. § 29. 2. (2) b).

(3) ל״א and ע״ו.—בּוֹא *to come*, perf. בָּא, בָּאתָ, &c., impf. יָבוֹא, inf., imp. בּוֹא, part. בָּא. Hiph. הֵבִיא, הֵבֵאתָ, &c., but usually הֲבִיאֹתָ, &c., before suff. (cf. § 30. 1-3, 6-7).

(4) ל״ה and פ״ן.—נָטָה *to stretch*, impf. יִטֶּה, apoc. וַיֵּט, יֵט. Hiph. הִטָּה, impf. יַטֶּה, apoc. וַיַּט, יַט. הִכָּה (Hiph. of נכה) *to smite*, impf. יַכֶּה, apoc. יַךְ, וַיַּךְ, imp. הַךְ, inf. הַכּוֹת, part. מַכֶּה.

(5) ל״ה and פ״א.—אָבָה *to be willing*, impf. יֹאבֶה, apoc. אַל־תֹּבֵא. Pr. 1.10 (cf. § 37. 1). אָתָה (*poet.*), *to come*, impf. יֶאֱתֶה, יֵאתֶה, apoc, וַיֵּאת, Is. 41. 25, cf. Deut. 33. 21. Piʿel אִוָּה, and Hithpaʿel הִתְאַוָּה *to desire*, imperfs. יְאַוֶּה (apoc. יְאַו) and יִתְאַוֶּה (apoc. יִתְאַו).

(6) ל״ה and פ״י.—יָרָה *to cast, shoot*, imp. יְרֵה, inf. יְרוֹת. Hiph. הוֹרָה *to direct, teach, instruct* (cf. תּוֹרָה *direction, instruction, law*), impf. יוֹרֶה, apoc. וַיּוֹר, 2 K. 13. 17. הוֹדָה (Hiph. of ידה) *to confess, to give thanks*, impf. יוֹדֶה; Hithpaʿel הִתְוַדָּה has the same meaning.

2. Stems composed of two strong radicals and any of the three weak letters י, ו, נ, are often allied in meaning. Thus: עוּץ, יָעַץ *to advise*, גּוּר, יָגֹר *to fear*, נָצַב, יָצַב *to place*, פּוּחַ, נָפַח *to blow*, עָטָה, יָעַט *to cover*. Hence one root supplements itself often from another. In many verbs also the forms in Qal have fallen into disuse, and the Qal supplements itself out of the other forms.

(1) בּוֹשׁ *to be ashamed*, see Parad. § 30. Hiph. הֵבִישׁ reg., and also הוֹבִישׁ from יבשׁ.

(2) טוֹב *to be good*, perf., part., inf. טוֹב; but impf. יִיטַב and Hiph. הֵיטִיב from יטב.

(3) הָלַךְ *to go*, perf., inf. abs. הָלוֹךְ, part. הֹלֵךְ; impf. יֵלֵךְ, inf. c. לֶכֶת, suff. לֶכְתִּי, imp. לֵךְ, Hiph. הוֹלִיךְ from ילך (ולך) (cf. § 29. 2. (2) b). Later style forms impf. and inf. cons. Qal from הָלַךְ (יְהַלֵּךְ, הֲלֹךְ).

(4) יָכֹל *to be able*, inf. abs. יָכוֹל, inf. cons. יְכֹלֶת, impf. יוּכַל (regarded by some, less probably, as impf. Hoph.).

(5) יָסַף *to add*, only perf., part., in Qal; Hiph. הוֹסִיף in perf., impf. (וַיּוֹסֶף, יוֹסִיף), and inf. cstr. הוֹסִיף. An imper. סְפוּ, Is. 29. 1, Jer. 7. 21.

(6) יָקַץ *to awake*, only impf. יִיקַץ in Qal; Hiph. הֵקִיץ, perf., impf., imp., infin., from קִיץ.

(7) כָּשַׁל *to fall*, perf., inf. abs., part., in Qal; impf., inf. cons. from Niph.

(8) נגשׁ *to draw near*, impf., imp., inf. cons. in Qal, but perf. and part. borrowed from Niph., which has only these two parts.

(9) נָחָה *to lead*, perf., imper. in Qal; impf. and inf. cons. in Hiph., which has also perf. twice in the OT.

(10) שָׁתָה (impf. יִשְׁתֶּה, apoc יֵשְׁתְּ) *to drink*, in Qal, but Hiph. הִשְׁקָה *to give to drink*, from שָׁקָה (the Qal of which is not used in Hebrew).

נָסַךְ	*Qal, Hiph.* to pour	חָמוֹת	mother-in-law	דַּל	poor, lowly, weak
שָׁאַב	to draw (water)	כָּנָף	wing, skirt border	עָשִׁיר	rich
עֲרֵמָה	heap (e.g. of grain)	אֵצֶל	beside (w.suff. אֶצְלִי &c.)	פָּרַשׂ	to spread
גָּאַל	to redeem	גֹּרֶן	threshing-floor	אוה	*Pi., Hithpa.* to desire, long for
בָּחוּר	young man	גֹּאֵל	redeemer	מַחֲנֶה	camp
אִם . . . וְאִם	either . . . or			אָמָה	maid

EXERCISE

Translate

וַיִּתְאַוֶּה דָוִד וַיֹּאמַר מִי יַשְׁקֵנִי מַיִם מִבְּאֵר בֵּית־לֶחֶם אֲשֶׁר בַּשָּׁעַר׃

וַיֵּצְאוּ שְׁלֹשֶׁת הַגִּבֹּרִים מִמַּחֲנֵה בְנֵי־יִשְׂרָאֵל וַיָּבֹאוּ אֶל־בְּאֵר
הָעִיר וַיִּשְׁאֲבוּ מַיִם מִשָּׁם וַיִּשְׂאוּ וַיָּבִאוּ אֶל־דָּוִד וְלֹא אָבָה לִשְׁתּוֹתָם
וַיַּסֵּךְ אֹתָם לַיהוָה׃ וַיֹּאמֶר חָלִילָה לִּי מֵעֲשֹׂתִי זֹאת הֲדַם הָאֲנָשִׁים
הַהֹלְכִים בְּנַפְשׁוֹתָם אֶשְׁתֶּה וְלֹא אָבָה לִשְׁתּוֹתָם׃ 2 וַתֹּאמֶר אֵלֶיהָ
כֹּל אֲשֶׁר־תֹּאמְרִי אֵלַי אֶעֱשֶׂה׃ וַתֵּרֶד הַגֹּרֶן וַתַּעַשׂ כְּכֹל אֲשֶׁר־צִוַּתָּה
חֲמוֹתָהּ׃ וַיֹּאכַל הָאִישׁ וַיֵּשְׁתְּ וַיִּיטַב לִבּוֹ וַיָּבֹא לִשְׁכַּב בִּקְצֵה
הָעֲרֵמָה וַתָּבוֹא גַם־הִיא וַתִּשְׁכַּב אֶצְלוֹ׃ וַיֹּאמֶר מִי־אָתְּ וַתֹּאמֶר
אָנֹכִי רוּת אֲמָתֶךָ וּפָרַשְׂתָּ כְנָפֶךָ עַל־אֲמָתְךָ כִּי גֹאֵל אָתָּה׃ וַיֹּאמֶר
בְּרוּכָה אַתְּ לַיהוָה כִּי הֵרְבִּית אֶת־חַסְדֵּךְ לְבִלְתִּי לֶכֶת אַחֲרֵי
הַבַּחוּרִים אִם־דַּל וְאִם־עָשִׁיר׃ 3 זְכֹר רַחֲמֶיךָ יְהוָה וַחֲסָדֶיךָ כִּי
מֵעוֹלָם הֵמָּה׃ חַטֹּאות נְעוּרַי וּפְשָׁעַי אַל־תִּזְכֹּר כְּחַסְדְּךָ זְכָר־
לִי־אַתָּה׃ טוֹב וְיָשָׁר יְהוָה יוֹרֶה חַטָּאִים בַּדָּרֶךְ׃ 4 אַל־תַּסְתֵּר פָּנֶיךָ
מִמֶּנִּי אַל־תַּט בְּאַף עַבְדֶּךָ עֶזְרָתִי הָיִיתָ אַל־תִּטְּשֵׁנִי וְאַל־תַּעַזְבֵנִי
אֱלֹהֵי יִשְׁעִי׃ כִּי [1]אָבִי וְאִמִּי יַעַזְבֻנִי וַיהוָה יַאַסְפֵנִי׃

Suggested further reading: Genesis xli, 25-45.

My lord asked his servants: Have you a father or a brother? And we said to my lord: We have a father, an old man, and a young brother, the child of his old age; he alone is left to his mother, and his father loves him. Then you said to us: Bring him down to me that I may set my eyes upon him. We said to my lord: The boy cannot leave his father [2], for if he should leave his father, his father would die. Then you said to your servants: Unless your young brother [2] comes down with you, you shall see my face no more. When we returned to our father's house, we told him all that you had said to us. And when he said to us: Go back to Egypt and buy us a little food, we said to him; We cannot go back. If our young brother [2] goes with us, then we will go back; for we cannot see

[1] my father; cf. אָבִיךָ, אָבִיהוּ, אָבִינוּ, &c.; so אָח with suffixes; cf. § 42.

[2] Cf. footnote above.

the man's face unless our young brother is with us. Now this evil has befallen us. How can I now return to my father, if the boy is not with me? Pray let me remain instead of him as a slave to my lord.

§ 42. SOME COMMON IRREGULAR NOUNS[1]

אָב *father, cstr.* אֲבִי, *my f.* אָבִי, *thy f.* אָבִ֫יךָ, *his f.* אָבִ֫יהוּ or אָבִיו *her f.* אָבִ֫יהָ, *your f.* אֲבִיכֶם, *their f.* אֲבִיהֶם, &c.; *plur.* אָבוֹת, *their f.* אֲבוֹתָם (rarer and late אֲבוֹתֵיהֶם).

אָח *brother*; in the sing. like אָב—*cstr.* אֲחִי, *my b.* אָחִי, *our b.* אָחִינוּ, *your b.* אֲחִיכֶם, &c. *Plur.* אַחִים[2], *cstr.* אֲחֵי, *my b.* אַחַי (pause אֶחָי), *his b.* אֶחָיו, *our b.* אַחֵינוּ, *your b.* אֲחֵיכֶם, &c.

אָחוֹת *sister, cstr.* אֲחוֹת, *suff.* אֲחוֹתִי, &c.; *pl.* (*abs.* אֲחָיוֹת not found), with *suff.* אַחְיֹתָיו, אַחְיֹתֵיהֶם, but also אֲחוֹתַיִךְ, אֲחוֹתֵיכֶם.

אִישׁ *man, pl.* אֲנָשִׁים, *cstr.* אַנְשֵׁי, *suff.* אֲנָשַׁי, אֲנָשֶׁיךָ, אַנְשֵׁיכֶם.

אִשָּׁה *woman, wife* (probably for אִנְשָׁה). The expected constr. of אִשָּׁה would be אִשַּׁת but the primary אִנְשְׁתְּ (fem. *t*) would give first אִשְׁתְּ, then אִשְׁתְּ. From אִשְׁתְּ comes the *cstr.* form אֵשֶׁת (cf סֵפֶר, § 25), and it is the form used with pronom. suffixes; *my w.* אִשְׁתִּי, &c.; *pl.* נָשִׁים 1, *cstr.* נְשֵׁי, *suff.* נָשַׁי, נָשֶׁיךָ, נְשֵׁיכֶם.

אָמָה 1 *maid, pl.* אֲמָהוֹת 1, *suff.* אַמְהֹתַי, אַמְהֹתֶיךָ, אַמְהֹתֵיכֶם.

---

[1] The numbers indicate the declensions.

[2] The *pathah* in the absol. pl. אַחִים is commonly explained as the *pathah* before the dagh. forte implic. in the *heth*. That is difficult in view of (a) אָחִי *my brother*, אָחִיךָ &c., which have *qāmeṣ*, and the constr. pl. אֲחֵי, and suffixed forms, such as אֲחֵיכֶם, which have *ḥaṭeph pathah*, and (b) the constr. sing. אֲחִי (cf. אֲבִי) and אָחוֹת *sister*, which suggest that the verbal root was not a double *'ayin* (אחח) but, possibly, אחו (cf. § 33. 3c).

בַּ֫יִת 2 *house, cstr.* בֵּית, *pl.* בָּתִּים (not *bottîm*, but probably *bāttîm*, or *bâtîm*; in latter case *dagh.* would be *lene* —irregularly, but the *methegh* with the *qāmeṣ*, in בָּֽתִּים, supports the reading *bâtîm*; on any view the ָ is unchangeable), *cstr.* בָּתֵּי, *suff.* בָּתַּי, בָּתֶּיךָ, בָּתֵּיכֶם.

בֵּן 3 *son, cstr.* בֶּן־, rarely בִּן־; *suff.* בְּנִי, בִּנְךָ, &c.; *pl.* בָּנִים 1, *cstr.* בְּנֵי, *suff.* בָּנַי, בָּנֶיךָ, בְּנֵיכֶם.

בַּת (contracted from בֶּנֶת basically בִּנְתְּ) 2 *daughter, my d.* בִּתִּי (for בִּנְתִּי, &c.); *pl.* בָּנוֹת 1; *suff.* בְּנֹתַי, בְּנֹתֶיךָ, בְּנֹתֵיכֶם.

יוֹם 2 *day* (contracted from *yawm* or *yaum*), *pl.* יָמִים (for יְוָ״); *cstr.* יְמֵי, cf. § 31. 5. (The plur. of יָם *sea* is יַמִּים).

כְּלִי *vessel, suff.* כֶּלְיְךָ; *pl.* כֵּלִים, *cstr.* כְּלֵי, *suff.* כֵּלַי, כֵּלֶיךָ, כְּלֵיכֶם.

מַ֫יִם *pl. water, cstr.* מֵי, מֵימֵי, *suff.* מֵימַי, מֵימֶיךָ, &c. (redupl. form always before suff.).

עִיר *f.* 2 *city, pl.* עָרִים, *cstr.* עָרֵי; *suff.* עָרַי, עָרֶיךָ, עָרֵיכֶם.

פֶּה *mouth, cstr.* פִּי, *my m.* פִּי; פִּ֫יךָ, פִּיו and פִּ֫יהוּ, פִּ֫יהָ, פִּיהֶם, &c., like אָב; *pl.* פִּיּוֹת.

רֹאשׁ 2 *head, pl.* רָאשִׁים, *cstr.* רָאשֵׁי; *suff.* רָאשַׁי, רָאשֶׁיךָ, רָאשֵׁיכֶם, (§ 31. 5).

שֵׁם *name, suff.* שְׁמִי, שִׁמְךָ, &c. *Pl.* שֵׁמוֹת, *cstr.* שְׁמוֹת.

בְּהֵמָה *f. cattle,* though hardly irregular, should be carefully noted: *cstr.* בֶּהֱמַת; *thy c.* בְּהֶמְתְּךָ, *his c.* בְּהֶמְתּוֹ (*pl.* בְּהֵמוֹת, *cstr.* בַּהֲמוֹת: rare and poetic).

שׁבה to take captive

מוֹשָׁב dwelling

אַשְׁרֵי only used in cstr. plu. (from אֶשֶׁר or אָשָׁר?), the happinesses of; used in practice as a kind of interjection: *happy* (*is, are,* &c.)!

חוד to propound a riddle;

חִידָה riddle

אָנָּא *part. of entreaty,* ah, now!, we beseech thee

לוּא, לוּ if; O that, would that

פתח to open

תִּפְאָרָה *f.* glory

עֲטָרָה *f.* (*cstr.* עֲטֶרֶת) crown
ישע *Hiph.* to deliver
מַדּוּעַ wherefore?
פתה *Pi.* to entice
שְׁנַיִם (*cstr.* שְׁנֵי) *f.* שְׁתַּיִם (*cstr.* שְׁתֵּי) two

כלה to be complete, ended; *Pi.* to finish
שִׁמְשׁוֹן Samson
ירשׁ *Hiph.* to cause to possess, or to dispossess.

EXERCISE

Translate

וַיָּבֹא דָוִד וַאֲנָשָׁיו אֶל־הָעִיר וְהִנֵּה שְׂרוּפָה בָּאֵשׁ וּנְשֵׁיהֶם וּבְנֵיהֶם
וּבְנֹתֵיהֶם נִשְׁבּוּ׃ 2 עֲטֶרֶת זְקֵנִים בְּנֵי בָנִים וְתִפְאֶרֶת בָּנִים אֲבוֹתָם׃
3 אַשְׁרֵי יוֹשְׁבֵי בֵיתֶךָ׃ 4 וַיִּקַּח אֶת־בַּת־פַּרְעֹה וַיְבִיאֶהָ אֶל־עִיר
דָּוִד עַד כַּלֹּתוֹ לִבְנוֹת אֶת־בֵּיתוֹ׃ 5 וַיִּשְׁכַּב עִם־אֲבֹתָיו וַיִּקָּבֵר
בְּעִיר אָבִיו׃ 6 וַיִּרְאוּ אֲחֵי יוֹסֵף כִּי מֵת אֲבִיהֶם וַיֹּאמְרוּ לוּ יִשְׂנָאֵנוּ
יוֹסֵף[1] וְהָשֵׁב יָשִׁיב לָנוּ אֵת כָּל־הָרָעָה אֲשֶׁר גָּמַלְנוּ אֹתוֹ׃ וַיִּגְּשׁוּ
אֶל־יוֹסֵף לֵאמֹר אָבִיךָ צִוָּה לִפְנֵי מוֹתוֹ לֵאמֹר׃ כֹּה־תֹאמְרוּ
לְיוֹסֵף אָנָּא שָׂא נָא פֶּשַׁע אַחֶיךָ וְחַטָּאתָם כִּי־רָעָה גְמָלוּךָ וְעַתָּה
שָׂא נָא לְפֶשַׁע עַבְדֵי אֱלֹהֵי אָבִיךָ וַיֵּבְךְּ יוֹסֵף בְּדַבְּרָם אֵלָיו׃ וַיֵּלְכוּ
גַּם־אֶחָיו וַיִּפְּלוּ לְפָנָיו וַיֹּאמְרוּ הִנֶּנּוּ לְךָ לַעֲבָדִים׃ 7 וַיֹּאמְרוּ
לְאֵשֶׁת־שִׁמְשׁוֹן פַּתִּי אֶת־אִישֵׁךְ וְיַגֶּד־לָנוּ אֶת־הַחִידָה פֶּן־נִשְׂרֹף
אֹתָךְ וְאֶת־בֵּית אָבִיךְ בָּאֵשׁ הַלְהוֹרִישֵׁנוּ קְרָאתֶם לָנוּ׃ וַתֵּבְךְּ אֵשֶׁת
שִׁמְשׁוֹן עָלָיו וַתֹּאמֶר שְׂנֵאתַנִי וְלֹא אֲהַבְתַּנִי הַחִידָה חַדְתָּ לִבְנֵי
עַמִּי וְלִי לֹא הִגַּדְתָּ וַיֹּאמֶר לָהּ הִנֵּה לְאָבִי וּלְאִמִּי לֹא הִגַּדְתִּי וְלָךְ
אַגִּיד׃ 8 וַיֹּאמֶר יהוה אֶל־מֹשֶׁה נְטֵה יָדְךָ עַל־הַשָּׁמַיִם וִיהִי חֹשֶׁךְ
עַל־אֶרֶץ מִצְרָיִם׃ וַיֵּט מֹשֶׁה אֶת־יָדוֹ עַל־הַשָּׁמָיִם וַיְהִי חֹשֶׁךְ
בְּכָל־אֶרֶץ מִצְרַיִם שְׁלֹשֶׁת יָמִים׃ לֹא רָאוּ אִישׁ אֶת־אָחִיו וְלֹא
קָמוּ אִישׁ מִמְּקוֹמוֹ שְׁלֹשֶׁת יָמִים וּלְכָל־בְּנֵי יִשְׂרָאֵל הָיָה אוֹר

---

[1] The apodosis is left to be understood.

בְּמוֹשְׁבֹתֵֽם׃ 9 ועתה לך ואנכי אהיה עם־פיך והוריתיך אשר תדבר׃ 10 והקימתי את־בריתי אתך ובאת אל־התבה אתה ובניך ואשתך ונשי־בניך אתך׃

Suggested further reading: II Chron. vi, 12, 14-21.

Honour thy father and thy mother, as thy God commanded thee. 2 And his daughters spoke to one another, saying: Let us make our father drink wine; and he drank and was drunken. 3 And again his wife bore a son; and, when he grew up, he loved his parents with all his heart, and did great good to his brothers and sisters. 4 They took captive their enemies' wives, and plundered their houses, and then went on their way; but they did not slay (מות, *Hiph.*) any one. 5 His daughter abode in her father's house two years. 6 For two days his father did not open his mouth. 7 My father and my mother have forsaken me. 8 His name shall continually be in my mouth. 9 I have found in thy house vessels of silver and gold. 10 Happy are thy men!

§ 43. PERFECT, IMPERFECT, AND PARTICIPLE

In § 17 it is stated that the Hebrew verb has no tenses in the proper sense of that word. The Perfect describes an action which is complete or is conceived to be complete, while the Imperfect expresses an action which is incomplete. Each has a wide range of meaning. It is right that some indication and illustration of that range of meaning should be given.

I. *The Perfect.* The Perfect expresses a completed action.

1. (a) In reference to *time* such an action may be: i. One just completed from the standpoint of the present (the classical perfect); e.g. *I have come* (בָּאתִי) to tell you the news; or, ii. One completed in the more or less distant past (the aorist or historic past); e.g. In the beginning God *created* (בָּרָא); so the complex example: נַעַר הָיִיתִי גַּם־זָקַנְתִּי וְלֹא רָאִיתִי צַדִּיק נֶעֱזָב *I was* (once) *young* and *I have* (now) *grown old* but *I have not seen* a righteous man forsaken; or, iii. One already completed

from the point of view of another past act (pluperfect); as, And God saw every thing that *he had made* עָשָׂה; or finally, on the opposite side, iv. One completed from the point of view of another action yet future (the future perfect); as, I will draw for thy camels also until *they have done* drinking כִּלּוּ לִשְׁתּוֹת (Pi. of כָּלָה).

(b) It will make no difference in the usage of the perf. if the completed actions, instead of being expressed absolutely, as in the above sentences, should be conceived and expressed conditionally, or if they should have no existence except in conception: as, i. O my God, *if I have done this* אִם עָשִׂיתִי זֹאת; ii. *If ye had not ploughed* with my heifer לוּלֵא חֲרַשְׁתֶּם (ל״ if not, unless); *Would that we had died* לוּ מַתְנוּ; iii. *If I bring him not* (i.e. *shall not have brought him*) *to thee* אִם־לֹא הֲבִיאֹתִיו אֵלֶיךָ.

2. The perfect is often used where the present is employed in English: (a) In the case of general truths or actions of frequent occurrence—truths or actions which *have been* often experienced or observed (perf. of experience, the Greek *gnomic aorist*); as, The grass *withereth* יָבֵשׁ חָצִיר; the sparrow *findeth* a house מָצְאָה. This usage is particularly common when general truths are expressed *negatively*; e.g. *He does no evil to his neighbour* לֹא־עָשָׂה לְרֵעֵהוּ רָעָה (i.e. that is his consistent attitude). (b) An action or attitude of the past may be continued into the present (the present perfect); e.g. *I stretch out* (פֵּרַשְׂתִּי) my hands to thee; *thou never forsakest* (לֹא־עָזַבְתָּ) those who seek thee, O Lord. (c) The perfect of intransitive (or Stative) verbs is used where English uses the present; the perfect in Hebrew in such a case emphasises a condition which has come into *complete existence* and realization (cf. § 17. 1d); e.g. *I know* יָדַעְתִּי that thou wilt be king; *I hate* שָׂנֵאתִי all workers of iniquity; so, *I remember*, זָכַרְתִּי; חָסִיתִי *I take refuge*, שָׂמַחְתִּי *I rejoice*, &c. (d) Sometimes in Hebrew future events are conceived so vividly and so realistically that they are regarded as having virtually taken place and are described

by the perfect. This happens often in making promises or threats, and in the language of contracts; as, The field *give I* thee נָתַתִּי; And if not, I *will take it* לָקַחְתִּי. This usage is very common in the elevated language of the prophets, whose faith and imagination so vividly project before them the event or scene which they predict that it appears already realized. It is part of the purpose of God, and therefore, to the clear eyes of the prophet, already as good as accomplished (*prophetic perfect*); e.g. גָּלָה עַמִּי my people *is gone into captivity* (i.e. *shall assuredly go*).

II. *The Imperfect.* The imperf. expresses an action, process or condition which is incomplete, and it has a wide range of meaning:

1. (a) If the imperfect is used to describe a single (as opposed to a *repeated*) action in the past, it differs from the perfect in being more vivid and pictorial. The pf. expresses the *fact*, the impf. adds colour and movement by suggesting the *process* preliminary to its completion. Often it may best be rendered by our graphic historical present; e.g. Jael יָדָהּ תִּשְׁלַחְ *puts forth her hand* to the pin—you see her in the act; יַעֲמֹד in Job 4. 16 should probably be rendered as *it came to a halt* (the imperf. describing the process which thus culminated) and דְּמָמָה וָקוֹל אֶשְׁמָע in the same verse as 'a faint whisper *I began to hear*'. The use of the imperf. which is common after אָז *then*, טֶרֶם *not yet*, בְּטֶרֶם *before*, as in, e.g., אָז יָשִׁיר *then he sang*, may illustrate this use of the imperf., but it is much more likely that in such cases the imperf. form represents the old preterite (cf. § 20. 4). (b) A phrase such as מַה־תְּבַקֵּשׁ *What seekest thou*?, refers not only to the present, but assumes that the search has been continued for some time. The words in 1 Sam. 1. 8 לָמָה תִבְכִּי וְלָמֶה לֹא תֹאכְלִי וְלָמֶה יֵרַע לְבָבֵךְ *Why do you weep? Why refuse to eat? Why are you distressed?* relate, not so much to one occasion, as to a continued condition.

So in 1 Sam. 11. 5; מַה־לָּעָם כִּי יִבְכּוּ *What is the matter with the people that they are weeping?*

2. The kind of progression or imperfection and unfinished condition of the action may consist in its frequent *repetition*: (a) Either in the present; as, It *is said* to this day, יֵאָמֵר (*Niph.*), Take of all food which *is* (regularly, customarily) *eaten*, יֵאָכֵל. In association with this, we may take מַעֲשִׂים אֲשֶׁר לֹא־יֵעָשׂוּ עָשִׂיתָ עִמָּדִי *you have done to me things which are not* (i.e. ought not to be) *done*. This usage is very common in comparisons and in the statements of general truths founded in the nature of things; as, A wise son *maketh a glad* father יְשַׂמַּח; As a (Heb. *the*) dog (habitually) *laps* כַּאֲשֶׁר יָלֹק הַכֶּלֶב (ילק, impf. of לקק, § 39; cf. also Exod. 23. 8). Or (b) In the past; as, And so *he did* regularly, year by year וְכֵן יַעֲשֶׂה שָׁנָה בְשָׁנָה. This usage is of very frequent occurrence, A mist *used to go up* אֵד יַעֲלֶה; We remember (note the *pf.*) the fish (collective, *fem.*) which *we used to eat* זָכַרְנוּ אֶת־הַדָּגָה אֲשֶׁר־נֹאכַל; The manna *came down* regularly יֵרֵד הַמָּן; *Moses spoke* repeatedly (kept speaking) *and God* repeatedly *answered* him יְדַבֵּר מֹשֶׁה וְהָאֱלֹהִים יַעֲנֶנּוּ (the tenses imply a colloquy); cf. also Exod. 1. 12, Deut. 32. 16 f. This is known as the *frequentative imperfect*.

3. The imperf. is used to express the *future*, referring not only to an action which is about to be accomplished but even to one which has not yet begun: (a) This may be a future from the point of view of the real present; as, Now *shalt thou see what I will do* עַתָּה תִרְאֶה אֲשֶׁר אֶעֱשֶׂה; *We will burn* thy house בֵּיתְךָ נִשְׂרֹף. Or (b) It may be a future from any other point of view assumed; as, He took his son that *was to reign* יִמְלֹךְ in his stead; or, She stood at a distance to see what *should be done* (יֵעָשֶׂה) to him.

4. The usage in 3b may be taken as the transition to a common use of the imperf. in which it serves for the expression of those shades of relation among acts and thoughts for which

English prefers the conditional moods (esp. the potential). Such actions are strictly *future* in reference to the assumed point of relation, and the simple imperf. sufficiently expresses them; e.g., Of every tree of the garden thou *mayest eat* תֹּאכֵל; *Could we* (*Were we to*) *know* הֲנֵדַע, that he *would say* יֹאמַר; How *shall* (How *can*) we *sing Yahweh's* song in a foreign land? אֵיךְ נָשִׁיר; Tomorrow is the full moon and *I should be in my place* (יָשֹׁב־אֵשֵׁב) at the king's table; Whom *am I to send*? (אֶשְׁלַח).

5. (a) The impf. follows particles expressing *transition, purpose, result,* and the like, as, לְמַעַן *in order that* פֶּן *lest,* &c.; e.g. Say thou art my sister, *that it may be well with me* לְמַעַן יִיטַב לִי; Let us deal wisely with the nation, *lest it multiplies* פֶּן־יִרְבֶּה. The actions introduced by such particles are strictly consequent upon, and future to, something just stated.

(b) When, however, there is a strong feeling of *purpose,* or when it is meant to be strongly marked, then, of course, the moods are employed, § 20. 5; e.g. Raise me up *that I may requite them* הֲקִימֵנִי וַאֲשַׁלְּמָה לָהֶם (cohort.); Who will entice Ahab *that he may go up*? מִי יְפַתֶּה אֶת־אַחְאָב וְיַעַל (juss.); What shall we do *that the sea may be calm*? מַה־נַּעֲשֶׂה וְיִשְׁתֹּק הַיָּם. The moods are also employed to express that class of future actions which we express in the *Optative,* &c.; *May I die* אָמוּתָה (coh.); *May* Yahweh *establish* his word יָקֵם יהוה אֶת־דְּבָרוֹ (juss.); *May* the soul of this child *return* תָּשָׁב־נָא נֶפֶשׁ הַיֶּלֶד הַזֶּה (*tāšobh,* shortened before נָא, § 9, Exer., n. 1, from תָּשֹׁב, juss.).

III. The *consecutive forms* have the same variety of use as the simple forms, the consec. impf. corresponding to the simple perf., and the consec. perf. to the simple impf. E.g., the perf. of general truths, like the ordinary historical pf., is followed by *wāw consec. impf.*; e.g. כָּלָה עָנָן וַיֵּלַךְ *the cloud comes to an end and is gone* (pausal impf. of הלך). Similarly the impf., in its frequentative as in its future sense, is followed by *wāw consec. pf.*; e.g. אֵד יַעֲלֶה וְהִשְׁקָה a mist used to go up *and water* (the ground).

IV. *The Participle.* 1. The participle represents an action or condition in its unbroken continuity, and corresponds to the English auxiliary *to be* with the pres. ptc.—*I am, was, shall be doing*; e.g. הוּא יֹשֵׁב *he was sitting* (not simply *he sat*). It may be used of present, past, or future time: (a) *pres.*, מָה אַתֶּם עֹשִׂים *what are you doing*? (b) *past*, עוֹד זֶה מְדַבֵּר וְזֶה בָּא he *was still speaking* when another came; (c) *fut.*, מַשְׁחִתִים אֲנַחְנוּ אֶת־הַמָּקוֹם הַזֶּה we *are destroying*, i.e. *are about to destroy*, this place (Hiph. שחת). The ptc. in this (fut.) sense is frequently introduced by הִנֵּה *behold*; e.g., הִנְנִי מֵקִים גּוֹי *Behold, I am about to raise up* a nation.

2. It must be carefully noted that the Hebrew participle cannot be used as the equivalent of the English past ptc. or the Greek aor. (or pf.) ptc. For ἀφέντες πάντα ἠκολούθησαν αὐτῷ *having left all they followed him*, Hebrew says, (*and*) *they left all and went after him*, וַיַּעַזְבוּ אֶת־הַכֹּל וַיֵּלְכוּ אַחֲרָיו

רעה to pasture, shepherd
אָתוֹן she-ass
שֶׂה a sheep (a goat)
פַּעַם step, time (*fois*)
עֵדֶר flock, herd
יֶקֶב wine-vat
רָשׁ (*ptc.*) poor
כִּבְשָׂה *f.* ewe-lamb
שְׁרִירוּת stubbornness
כּוֹס *f.* cup
יַחְדָּו together
נְאֻם utterance (always in *cstr.*)
קרע to tear, rend

פַּת *f.* morsel (1 suff. פִּתִּי)
בִּלְעָם Balaam
רבץ to lie (stretched out)
מֵאַיִן whence?
מִחוּץ (מִן, חוּץ) outside (§ 12. 3b)
שַׂק sackcloth
ידע to know, regard, care for
סכן *Hiph.* to be accustomed, show habit
דמה to destroy; *Niph.* to be undone
עלל *Po'el* to act severely, *Hithpa.* to deal severely

EXERCISE

Translate

יהוה רֹעִי לֹא אֶחְסָר׃ 2 אִישׁ הַיָּשָׁר בְּעֵינָיו יַעֲשֶׂה׃ 3 רֹעֶה הָיָה
עַבְדְּךָ לְאָבִיו בַּצֹּאן וּבָא הָאֲרִי וְנָשָׂא שֶׂה מֵהָעֵדֶר וְיָצָאתִי אַחֲרָיו
וְהִכִּתִיו וְהִצַּלְתִּי מִפִּיו׃ 4 וְלָרָשׁ אֵין־כֹּל כִּי אִם־כִּבְשָׂה אַחַת
קְטַנָּה אֲשֶׁר קָנָה וַיְחַיֶּהָ וַתִּגְדַּל עִמּוֹ וְעִם־בָּנָיו יַחְדָּו מִפִּתּוֹ תֹאכַל
וּמִכֹּסוֹ תִשְׁתֶּה וּבְחֵיקוֹ תִשְׁכָּב וַתְּהִי־לוֹ כְּבַת׃ 5 יוֹדֵעַ יהוה דֶּרֶךְ
צַדִּיקִים וְדֶרֶךְ רְשָׁעִים תֹּאבֵד׃ 6 וַיַּרְא וְהִנֵּה בְאֵר בַּשָּׂדֶה וְהִנֵּה־
שָׁם עֶדְרֵי־צֹאן רֹבְצִים עָלֶיהָ כִּי מִן־הַבְּאֵר הַהִיא יַשְׁקוּ הָעֲדָרִים׃
7 וַיִּפְתַּח יהוה אֶת־פִּי הָאָתוֹן וַתֹּאמֶר לְבִלְעָם מֶה עָשִׂיתִי לְךָ כִּי
הִכִּיתַנִי זֶה שָׁלֹשׁ פְּעָמִים׃ וַיֹּאמֶר בִּלְעָם לָאָתוֹן כִּי הִתְעַלַּלְתְּ בִּי
לוּ יֶשׁ־חֶרֶב בְּיָדִי כִּי עַתָּה הֲרַגְתִּיךְ׃ וַתֹּאמֶר הָאָתוֹן אֶל־בִּלְעָם
הֲלוֹא אָנֹכִי אֲתֹנְךָ אֲשֶׁר רָכַבְתָּ עָלַי מִנְּעוּרֶיךָ עַד־הַיּוֹם הַזֶּה
הַהַסְכֵּן הִסְכַּנְתִּי לַעֲשׂוֹת לְךָ כֹּה וַיֹּאמֶר לֹא׃ 8 וְלֹא שָׁמַע עַמִּי
לְקוֹלִי וְיִשְׂרָאֵל לֹא־אָבָה לִי׃ וָאֲשַׁלְּחֵם בִּשְׁרִירוּת לִבָּם יֵלְכוּ
בְּמַחְשְׁבֹתֵיהֶם׃ לוּ עַמִּי שֹׁמֵעַ לִי יִשְׂרָאֵל בִּדְרָכַי יְהַלֵּכוּ׃ 9 וַיְהִי
מֶלֶךְ יִשְׂרָאֵל עֹבֵר עַל־הַחוֹמָה וְאִשָּׁה צָעֲקָה אֵלָיו לֵאמֹר הוֹשִׁיעָה
אֲדֹנִי׃ וַיֹּאמֶר אִם־לֹא יוֹשִׁעֵךְ יהוה מֵאַיִן אוֹשִׁיעֵךְ הֲמִן־הַגֹּרֶן אוֹ
מִן־הַיָּקֶב׃ וַיֹּאמֶר־לָהּ הַמֶּלֶךְ מַה־לָּךְ וַתֹּאמֶר הָאִשָּׁה הַזֹּאת
אָמְרָה אֵלַי תְּנִי אֶת־בְּנֵךְ וְנֹאכְלֶנּוּ הַיּוֹם וְאֶת־בְּנִי נֹאכַל מָחָר׃
וַיְהִי כִשְׁמֹעַ הַמֶּלֶךְ אֶת־דִּבְרֵי הָאִשָּׁה וַיִּקְרַע אֶת־בְּגָדָיו וְהוּא
עֹבֵר עַל־הַחוֹמָה וַיַּרְא הָעָם וְהִנֵּה הַשַּׂק עַל־בְּשָׂרוֹ׃ 10 זֹאת
הברית אשר אכרת את־בית ישראל אחרי הימים ההם נאם־
יהוה נתתי את־תורתי בקרבם ועל־לבם אכתבנה והייתי להם
לאלהים והמה יהיו־לי לעם׃

Suggested further reading: 2 Samuel I. 1-16; Psalm 106. 1-15.

The more the enemy oppressed them, the more they increased. 2 He used to take the tent and pitch it outside the camp. 3 It is not wont to be done so in our land. 4 If I perish, I perish. 5 Then Moses and the children of Israel sang this song unto their God. 6 Whosoever shall harden his heart and transgress my law shall be put to death. 7 The earth standeth for ever. 8 They found maidens coming out to draw water. 9 All this I give thee, if thou wilt fall down and prostrate thyself before me. 10 A righteous man careth for the life of his beast. 11 Evermore Yahweh supports all who fall. 12 While he was yet speaking one of his servants came and said, We are undone—all of us. 13 Your sons and daughters were eating and drinking in the house of their eldest [1] brother, when a strong wind came from the desert and struck the house and it fell upon all who were sitting within it and they died.

§ 44. THE ADJECTIVE, COMPARATIVE AND SUPERLATIVE

1. *Comparative Degree.* (a) The adjective undergoes no change of termination or vocalization in comparison. The comparative degree is expressed by the positive followed by the prep. מִן, as, *Better than wine,* טוֹב מִיַּיִן, lit. *good away from,* or in distinction from, *wine*; *Sweeter than honey,* מָתוֹק מִדְּבַשׁ. So כָּבֵד מִמְּךָ הַדָּבָר *the matter is too hard for thee.* מִן is similarly used with verbs: אֶגְדַּל מִמְּךָ *I will be greater than thou,* קָטֹנְתִּי מִכֹּל הַחֲסָדִים *I am less than* (i.e. too insignificant for, unworthy of) *all the mercies*; כִּי יִרְבֶּה מִמְּךָ הַדֶּרֶךְ *should the journey be too much for thee,*...

(b) The correlative comparative (e.g. *the greater—the less*) is expressed by the simple adjective with the article; e.g. *the greater luminary* (of two), הַמָּאוֹר הַגָּדֹל; *her younger son,* בְּנָהּ הַקָּטָן.

2. *Superlative Degree.* (a) The superlative also is expressed by the positive, and typical examples of its use in this sense are these: *He is the greatest,* הוּא הַגָּדוֹל lit. *the great one* (among

[1] Cf. § 44. 2.

those referred to), קְטַן בָּנָיו *the youngest of his sons* (*his youngest son*), מִגְּדוֹלָם וְעַד־קְטַנָּם *from the greatest of them to the least of them*, i.e. *both small and great*.

(b) Absolute superlativeness is expressed variously, as by the word מְאֹד *very*, *exceedingly* (טוֹב מְאֹד *good exceedingly*), or בִּמְאֹד or עַד־מְאֹד or מְאֹד מְאֹד; or by the repetition of the word expressing the quality, קֹדֶשׁ קָדָשִׁים[1] *holy of holies* = most holy, עֶבֶד עֲבָדִים *a most abject slave*, שִׁיר הַשִּׁירִים *the best* or *most glorious of songs* (cf. *the Book of books*); or as הַרְרֵי אֵל (*lit.* mountains of God) *mighty mountains*, אַרְזֵי אֵל *mighty cedars*, כּוֹכְבֵי אֵל *lofty stars*.

3.	*I am taller than he*	גָּבֹהַּ אָנֹכִי מִמֶּנּוּ
	he is taller than his wife	„ הוּא מֵאִשְׁתּוֹ
	too little to be—	קָטֹן מִהְיוֹת
	his eldest son	בְּנוֹ הַגָּדוֹל
	his youngest daughter	בִּתּוֹ הַקְּטַנָּה

קָשַׁב	*Hiph.* to give attention	עַז	strong
עָמֹק	(*f.* עֲמֻקָּה) deep	מִשְׁכָּן	dwelling-place (*pl.* וֹת)
שְׁכֶם	shoulder (*suff.* שִׁכְמוֹ)	אָרֹךְ	(*f.* אֲרֻכָּה) long
עָרוּם	cunning (adj).	חַיָּה	*f.* beast, animal
שִׁית	to set, place	מַ֫עְלָה	(מַ֫עַל with ה ָ loc.) upwards
יָפֶה	(*f.* יָפָה), fair		
חָסֵר	to lack, be deficient	חֵלֶב	fat (noun)
דָּנִאֵל	Daniel	רָחָב	broad, wide
עטר	*Pi'el* to crown	קֶדֶם	east
גָּבוֹהַּ	high	אֶצְבַּע	finger, forefinger

[1] Unlike other 3rd class nouns of the 2nd declension, § 25, קֹדֶשׁ *holiness* and שֹׁרֶשׁ *a root*, form their plural not קְ and שְׁ but קֳדָשִׁים (*qodhāšîm*, not *qā*) and שָׁרָשִׁים (*šo*)—but the former also written ״קֳ (*q°*) like gutturals (חֳדָשִׁים).

אֶפְרַיִם Ephraim
יָרֵחַ moon
מְנַשֶּׁה Manasseh
אוּלָם but (a strong adversative)
תָּמַךְ to take hold of, to grasp

EXERCISE

Translate

קַח נַפְשִׁי כִּי לֹא־טוֹב אָנֹכִי מֵאֲבֹתָי׃ 2 מַה־מָּתוֹק מִדְּבַשׁ וּמֶה
עַז מֵאֲרִי׃ 3 אֹהֵב יהוה שַׁעֲרֵי צִיּוֹן מִכֹּל מִשְׁכְּנוֹת יַעֲקֹב׃ 4 טוֹב
יוֹם הַמָּוֶת מִיּוֹם הִוָּלְדוֹ׃ 5 וְאֵין אִישׁ מִבְּנֵי יִשְׂרָאֵל טוֹב מִמֶּנּוּ
מִשִּׁכְמוֹ וָמַעְלָה גָּבֹהַּ מִכָּל־הָעָם׃ 6 הַיָּפָה בַּנָּשִׁים׃ 7 הִנֵּה שְׁמֹעַ
מִזֶּבַח טוֹב [1]לְהַקְשִׁיב מֵחֵלֶב אֵילִים׃ 8 וְנִבְחַר מָוֶת מֵחַיִּים לְכֹל
הַנִּשְׁאָרִים מִן־הַמִּשְׁפָּחָה הָרָעָה הַזֹּאת׃ 9 וַיַּרְא יוֹסֵף כִּי־יָשִׁית
אָבִיו אֶת־יְמִינוֹ עַל־רֹאשׁ אֶפְרַיִם וַיֵּרַע בְּעֵינָיו וַיִּתְמֹךְ יַד־אָבִיו
לְהָסִיר אֹתָהּ מֵעַל־רֹאשׁ־אֶפְרַיִם עַל־רֹאשׁ מְנַשֶּׁה׃ וַיֹּאמֶר יוֹסֵף
אֶל־אָבִיו לֹא־כֵן אָבִי כִּי זֶה הַבְּכֹר שִׂים יְמִינְךָ עַל־רֹאשׁוֹ׃ וַיְמָאֵן
אָבִיו וַיֹּאמֶר יָדַעְתִּי בְנִי יָדַעְתִּי גַּם־הוּא יִהְיֶה־לְּעָם וְגַם־הוּא
יִגְדָּל וְאוּלָם אָחִיו הַקָּטֹן יִגְדַּל מִמֶּנּוּ וְזַרְעוֹ יִהְיֶה מְלֹא־הַגּוֹיִם׃
10 כִּי־אֶרְאֶה שָׁמֶיךָ מַעֲשֵׂי אֶצְבְּעֹתֶיךָ יָרֵחַ וְכוֹכָבִים אֲשֶׁר כּוֹנָנְתָּה׃
מָה אֱנוֹשׁ כִּי־תִזְכְּרֶנּוּ וּבֶן־אָדָם כִּי־תִפְקְדֶנּוּ׃ וַתְּחַסְּרֵהוּ מְּעַט
מֵאֱלֹהִים וְכָבוֹד וְהָדָר תְּעַטְּרֵהוּ׃ 11 ועתה יהוה קח־נא את־
נפשי ממני כי טוב מותי מחיי׃ 12 אעשה אותך לגוי־עצום
ורב ממנו׃

Suggested further reading: Proverbs 16. 8-19.

And the serpent was more cunning than all the beasts (*sing.*) of the field which God had made. 2 He has slain men more righteous than he. 3 Thou art wiser than Daniel. 4 A

---

[1] Inf. cstr. here practically = noun: *obedience*, *attention*. Usually, in this construction, without לְ (cf. here שְׁמֹעַ), sometimes with לְ (cf. לְהַקְשִׁיב).

living dog is better than a dead lion. 5 And that man was greater than all the children of (the) East. 6 And he loved Joseph more than all his sons, for a son of old age (was) he to him. 7 And he lifted up his eyes and saw his brother, the son of his mother, and he said, Is this your youngest brother, whom ye mentioned (said) to me? 8 And he had two daughters and the younger was fairer than the elder. 9 The greatest (men) of the city. 10 There was not left to him except the youngest of his sons. 11 The hand of Yahweh is not too short to save nor is his ear too dull to hear. 12 My master has put everything that he has in my hand; he is not greater in this house than I am. How, then, can I commit this great wickedness?

§ 45. THE NUMERALS

1. *The Cardinal Numbers.* (a) The numeral *one,* אֶחָד *m.,* אַחַת *f.,* is an adj. agreeing in gender with its noun and standing like other adjj. *after* it; as אִישׁ אֶחָד *one man,* אִשָּׁה אַחַת *one woman.*

(b) i. The numeral *two,* שְׁנַ֫יִם *m.,* שְׁתַּ֫יִם *f.* (cstr. שְׁנֵי, שְׁתֵּי), is a noun, and agrees in gender with the word which it enumerates, as שְׁנֵי אֲנָשִׁים *two men,* שְׁתֵּי הַנָּשִׁים *the two women.*

ii. The form שְׁתַּ֫יִם (*š*ᵉ*táyim*: *t,* not <u>th</u>) has a peculiar vocalization. Either it is derived from שְׁנָתַ֫יִם which, by an irregular assimilation of the *nûn* to the following *tāw* (cf. §§6. 3b; 39. 1) has become שְׁתַּ֫יִם, in which the daghesh is, therefore, a dagh. forte while the vocal shᵉwa of the *šîn* in שְׁנָתַ֫יִם has been retained; or, alternatively, the basic form is אֶשְׁתַּ֫יִם *eš-táyîm,* but in שְׁתַּ֫יִם the prosthetic א has been elided (cf. אַרְבַּע *four* (from the root רבע) and רְבִיעִי *fourth*), in which case the daghesh is dagh. lene and the shᵉwa is residual.

(c) i. The numerals 3 to 10 are nouns and stand commonly in the constr. state before the noun specifying that which is enumerated; but they may stand in the absol. in apposition to it, in front of it in most instances, but after it in late O.T. style. These numerals disagree in gender with their related nouns, the fem. form of the numeral being used with a related masc. noun, and vice versa; the related noun is expressed in the plural; e.g. *five sons*, חֲמֵשֶׁת בָּנִים or חֲמִשָּׁה בָנִים or בָּנִים חֲמִשָּׁה.

ii. This curious usage is to be explained by the fact that these numerals were originally abstract nouns in the feminine. *Three sons* = *a triad* (שְׁלֹשֶׁת, constr.) *of sons*. Then the absolute form of שְׁלֹשֶׁת, viz. שְׁלֹשָׁה, came to be used appositionally, *a triad, sons* or *sons, a triad* (שְׁלֹשָׁה בָנִים, בָּנִים שְׁלֹשָׁה). Later these fem. forms of the numeral were used only with related masc. nouns (the more numerous class) and a shortened form was used with related fem. nouns.

iii. Numerals which are nouns may be used with a pron. suffix; e.g. שְׁנֵינוּ *we two, the two of us*; שְׁלָשְׁתָּם *they three, the three of them* (*š*ᵉ*lošt̄ām*); &c.

	With the Masculine		*With the Feminine*	
	Absol.	Cstr.	Absol.	Cstr.
1	אֶחָד	אַחַד	אַחַת	אַחַת
2	שְׁנַיִם	שְׁנֵי	שְׁתַּיִם	שְׁתֵּי
3	שְׁלֹשָׁה	שְׁלֹשֶׁת	שָׁלֹשׁ	שְׁלֹשׁ
4	אַרְבָּעָה	אַרְבַּעַת	אַרְבַּע	אַרְבַּע
5	חֲמִשָּׁה	חֲמֵשֶׁת	חָמֵשׁ	חֲמֵשׁ
6	שִׁשָּׁה	שֵׁשֶׁת	שֵׁשׁ	שֵׁשׁ
7	שִׁבְעָה	שִׁבְעַת	שֶׁבַע	שְׁבַע
8	שְׁמֹנָה	שְׁמֹנַת	שְׁמֹנֶה	שְׁמֹנֶה
9	תִּשְׁעָה	תִּשְׁעַת	תֵּשַׁע	תְּשַׁע
10	עֲשָׂרָה	עֲשֶׂרֶת	עֶשֶׂר	עֶשֶׂר

(d) The numerals 13-19 are compounds, composed of, i. a unit, which is used in the fem. absol. with a masc. noun and in the masc. constr. with a fem. noun, and, ii. a by-form of the word for ten, viz. עָשָׂר with a masc. noun and עֶשְׂרֵה with a fem. one.

The numerals 11 and 12 require to be particularly noted. With these the unit is used in the constr., the masc. form (שְׁנֵי,אַחַד) with a masc. noun, and the fem. form (שְׁתֵּי, אַחַת) with a fem. noun; but, in addition, in the case of 11, עַשְׁתֵּי is used as an alternative for אַחַד and for אַחַת. and, in the case of 12, שְׁנֵים as an alternative for שְׁנֵי, and שְׁתֵּים for שְׁתֵּי (these forms שְׁנֵים and שְׁתֵּים seeming to be composite, agreeing consonantally with the absol. forms שְׁנַיִם and שְׁתַּיִם, and vocally with the constrs. שְׁנֵי and שְׁתֵּי).

The numerals 11-19 are used only in apposition with their related noun, and stand chiefly before, but occasionally after, it. The noun itself is usually in the plural, except with a few common nouns like יוֹם *day*, שָׁנָה *year*, אִישׁ *man*, נֶפֶשׁ *soul*, *person*, &c., and collectives; e.g. 19 *cities* (עִיר *f.*), עָרִים תְּשַׁע־עֶשְׂרֵה; *fifteen sons*, חֲמִשָּׁה עָשָׂר בָּנִים but 19 *men*, תִּשְׁעָה־עָשָׂר אִישׁ.

	With the Masculine	*With the Feminine*
11	אַחַד עָשָׂר	אַחַת עֶשְׂרֵה
	עַשְׁתֵּי עָשָׂר	עַשְׁתֵּי עֶשְׂרֵה
12	שְׁנֵים עָשָׂר	שְׁתֵּים עֶשְׂרֵה
	שְׁנֵי עָשָׂר	שְׁתֵּי עֶשְׂרֵה
13	שְׁלֹשָׁה עָשָׂר	שְׁלֹשׁ עֶשְׂרֵה
14	אַרְבָּעָה עָשָׂר	אַרְבַּע עֶשְׂרֵה
15	חֲמִשָּׁה עָשָׂר	חֲמֵשׁ עֶשְׂרֵה
16	שִׁשָּׁה עָשָׂר	שֵׁשׁ עֶשְׂרֵה
17	שִׁבְעָה עָשָׂר	שְׁבַע עֶשְׂרֵה
18	שְׁמֹנָה עָשָׂר	שְׁמֹנֶה עֶשְׂרֵה
19	תִּשְׁעָה עָשָׂר	תְּשַׁע עֶשְׂרֵה

(e) The *tens* are the plurals of the units (e.g. שָׁלֹשׁ 3, שְׁלֹשִׁים 30) except *twenty*, עֶשְׂרִים, which is the plur. of *ten*, עֶשֶׂר, there being a distinct word for *hundred*, מֵאָה. The *tens* end in *îm* alike with masc. and fem. nouns. Having no constr. forms, they are used only in apposition with their related nouns and commonly, but not invariably, precede them. The noun is often in the sing. when the numeral precedes it; it is always in the plur. when the numeral follows; e.g. חֲמִשִּׁים צַדִּיקִים *fifty righteous*; אַרְבָּעִים בָּנִים וּשְׁלֹשִׁים בְּנֵי בָנִים רֹכְבִים עַל־שִׁבְעִים עֲיָרִים *forty sons and thirty grandsons who rode on seventy asses*, אַרְבָּעִים שָׁנָה *forty years*, חֲמִשִּׁים אִישׁ *fifty men*; but אֵילִים עֶשְׂרִים וּגְמַלִּים שְׁלֹשִׁים וּפָרוֹת אַרְבָּעִים וּפָרִים עֲשָׂרָה *twenty rams, thirty camels, forty cows and ten oxen.*

(f) In numbers composed of tens and units such as 23, the order may be three and twenty, e.g. שְׁתַּיִם וְשִׁשִּׁים שָׁנָה *sixty-two years*, but also *twenty and three*, עֶשְׂרִים וְשָׁלֹשׁ שָׁנָה, and sometimes the noun is repeated with both, as *three years and twenty year*; e.g. חָמֵשׁ שָׁנִים וְשִׁבְעִים שָׁנָה *seventy-five years*; or again, עֶשְׂרִים שָׁנָה וְשֶׁבַע שָׁנִים *twenty-seven years.*

20	עֶשְׂרִים	60	שִׁשִּׁים
30	שְׁלֹשִׁים	70	שִׁבְעִים
40	אַרְבָּעִים	80	שְׁמֹנִים
50	חֲמִשִּׁים	90	תִּשְׁעִים

(g) 100 מֵאָה *fem., cstr.* מְאַת, *plur.* מֵאוֹת *hundreds.*

200 מָאתַיִם *dual* (for מְאָתַיִם).

300 שְׁלֹשׁ מֵאוֹת, 400 אַרְבַּע מֵאוֹת, &c.

1,000 אֶלֶף *masc,*

2,000 אַלְפַּיִם *dual.*

3,000 שְׁלֹשֶׁת אֲלָפִים, 4,000 אַרְבַּעַת אֲלָפִים, &c.

10,000 { רְבָבָה *pl.* regular, רְבָבוֹת.
{ רִבּוֹא רִבּוֹ *pl.* רִבֹּאוֹת and רִבּוֹת (later forms).

20,000 רִבּוֹתַיִם *dual.*

(h) The word מֵאָה *hundred* may be used either in the *cstr.* or *abs.* in the *sing.*—most often in *abs.*: *e.g.* בֶּן־מֵאָה שָׁנָה (*son of*, i.e.) *a hundred years old* (also מְאַת); in *du.* and *plur.* only in *absol.* The word אֶלֶף *thousand* is used in the *cstr.* also, though rarely, even in the *plur.* (אַלְפֵי).

(i) The numerical values of the letters of the Hebrew alphabet, used individually, are given in the Table of the alphabet at the beginning of the grammar. Compound use of letters fills up the gaps; e.g. 11 יא (i.e. י 10 + א 1 in the usual Hebrew order of writing), 12 יב (10+2), 21 כא, 31 לא, 101 קא, 121 קכא (100+20+1), 221 רכא; 500 תק (400+100), 600 תר (400+200), 700 תש (400+300), 800 תת (400+400), 900 תתק (400+400+100), 1,000 תתר (400+400+200).

Exception. By this system 15 and 16 should be denoted by יה and יו; but since these combinations of letters represent forms of the divine name יהוה, 15 is denoted by טו (9+6) and 16 by טז (9+7).

(j) Multiplicatives are expressed i. by the use of פַּעַם, *step, time*; e.g. פַּעֲמַיִם *twice*, שָׁלֹשׁ פְּעָמִים *three times*; or, ii. by the use of the fem. dual; e.g. שִׁבְעָתַיִם *seven times*.

2. *The Ordinal Numbers.* The Ordinal numbers from 1 to 10 are adjectives, and construed in the ordinary way. Beyond 10 the Cardinal numbers are used also as Ordinals. The Ordinals are these.

First	רִאשׁוֹן	*fem.*	רִאשׁוֹנָה	sixth	שִׁשִּׁי
second	שֵׁנִי	*fem.*	שֵׁנִית	seventh	שְׁבִיעִי
third	שְׁלִישִׁי	*fem.*	שְׁלִישִׁית, ־יָּה	eighth	שְׁמִינִי
fourth	רְבִיעִי	*fem.*	&c.	ninth	תְּשִׁיעִי
fifth	חֲמִישִׁי חֲמִשִׁי	or	&c.	tenth	עֲשִׂירִי

E.g. *on the seventh day*, בַּיּוֹם הַשְּׁבִיעִי; *in the eighteenth year of the king*, בִּשְׁמֹנֶה עֶשְׂרֵה שָׁנָה לַמֶּלֶךְ; or בִּשְׁנַת שְׁמֹנֶה עֶשְׂרֵה לַמֶּלֶךְ.

3. Fractions may be expressed by feminine forms of the ordinals; e.g. שְׁלִישִׁית *a third*; in a few cases also by segholate forms; e.g. רֶבַע and רֹבַע *a fourth*, חֹמֶשׁ *a fifth*; *a half* is חֲצִי, § 33. 3b, 1a.

עֵז	*f.* she-goat; *pl.* עִזִּים	גָּמָל	camel; *pl.* גְּמַלִּים (§ 40. 5)	עור	*Po'lel*, incite, wield
כֶּבֶשׂ	lamb	כֶּלֶא	imprisonment	בקע	to break through
חָלָל	wounded, slain	רֹמַח	spear	צִנָּה	*f.* shield
חָצֵר	court (*noun*)	שָׂכַר	to hire	כִּכָּר	talent
דּוֹר	generation (*pl.* ־ים. and oftener ־ות)	אַיִל	ram	תּוֹדָה	thanksgiving, thank-offering

EXERCISE

Translate

וַיֹּאמֶר אֶל־אָבִיו אֶת־שְׁנֵי בָנַי תָּמִית אִם־לֹא אֲבִיאֶנּוּ אֵלֶיךָ׃
2 וַיִּקַּח מִנְחָה לְאָחִיו עִזִּים מָאתַיִם וְאֵילִים עֶשְׂרִים וּגְמַלִּים
מֵינִיקוֹת וּבְנֵיהֶם שְׁלֹשִׁים׃ 3 וַיְהִי בְּאַחַת וְשֵׁשׁ־מֵאוֹת שָׁנָה לְחַיָּיו
בַּחֹדֶשׁ הַשֵּׁנִי בְּשִׁבְעָה וְעֶשְׂרִים יוֹם לַחֹדֶשׁ יָבְשָׁה הָאָרֶץ׃ 4
בִּשְׁלֹשִׁים וָשֶׁבַע שָׁנָה בִּשְׁנֵים עָשָׂר חֹדֶשׁ בְּעֶשְׂרִים וְשִׁבְעָה [1]לַחֹדֶשׁ
נָשָׂא מֶלֶךְ בָּבֶל אֶת־רֹאשׁ מֶלֶךְ יְהוּדָה מִבֵּית כֶּלֶא׃ 5 וַיִּבְקְעוּ
שְׁלֹשֶׁת הַגִּבֹּרִים בְּמַחֲנֵה הָאֹיֵב וַיִּשְׁאֲבוּ־מַיִם וַיָּבִאוּ אֵלָיו וְלֹא
אָבָה לִשְׁתּוֹתָם׃ 6 וְרָדְפוּ מִכֶּם חֲמִשָּׁה מֵאָה וּמֵאָה מִכֶּם רְבָבָה
יִרְדֹּפוּ׃ 7 וַיֹּאמֶר אֲלֵיהֶם צְאוּ שְׁלָשְׁתְּכֶם וַיֵּצְאוּ שְׁלָשְׁתָּם׃ 8
וְהָאִישׁ הַזֶּה הָיָה רֹאשׁ הַשְּׁלֹשִׁים וְהוּא עוֹרֵר אֶת־חֲנִיתוֹ עַל־שְׁלֹשׁ
מֵאוֹת חָלָל וְלוֹ שֵׁם בַּשְּׁלֹשִׁים׃ בַּשְּׁלֹשִׁים הוּא נִכְבָּד וַיְהִי לָהֶם
לְשָׂר וְעַד־הַשְּׁלוֹשָׁה לֹא־בָא׃ 9 וַיְקַבֵּץ הַמֶּלֶךְ אֶת־יְהוּדָה
וַיַּעֲמִידֵם לְשָׂרֵי הָאֲלָפִים וּלְשָׂרֵי הַמֵּאוֹת וַיִּפְקְדֵם [2]לְמִבֶּן־עֶשְׂרִים
שָׁנָה וָמָעְלָה וַיִּמְצָאֵם שְׁלֹשׁ־מֵאוֹת אֶלֶף בָּחוּר אֹחֵז רֹמַח וְצִנָּה׃
וַיִּשְׂכֹּר מִיִּשְׂרָאֵל מֵאָה אֶלֶף גִּבּוֹר חַיִל בְּמֵאָה כִּכַּר־כָּסֶף׃ 10
וַיַּעַן הַמֶּלֶךְ וַיֹּאמֶר הָבִיאוּ זְבָחִים וְתוֹדוֹת לְבֵית יְהוָה וַיָּבִיאוּ הָעָם
זְבָחִים וְתוֹדוֹת׃ וַיְהִי מִסְפַּר הַזְּבָחִים אֲשֶׁר הֵבִיאוּ בָּקָר שִׁבְעִים

[1] יוֹם unexpressed.

[2] לְמִן is used, as here, to express a *terminus a quo*.

אֵילִים מֵאָה כְּבָשִׂים מָאתָ֑יִם כָּל־אֵלֶּה הִקְרִיבוּ אֶל־יְהוָֹה: 11
ויחי אחרי־זאת מאה וארבעים שנה וירא את־בניו ואת־בני
בניו ארבעה דרות: 12 וימלך־שם שבע שנים וששה חדשים
ושלשים ושלוש שנה מלך בירושלם:

Suggested further reading: Numbers 11. 16-25; Genesis 18. 22-33.

His five brothers and three sisters went with him to the house of their father. 2 The queen reigned sixty-four years and died aged eighty-two: she had four sons and five daughters; her husband died in the forty-second year of her life and the twenty-fourth of her reign. 3 And there were born unto him three sons and seven daughters, and his substance was six thousand sheep, and four thousand camels, and seven hundred asses. 4 The days of the years of my life have been four and seventy years. 5 There were a hundred and twenty-seven cities in his land, and in one of those cities there were a hundred and twenty thousand people. 6 The half is better than the whole. 7 And one said to the other, Let the two of us swear in the name of our God; so they sware, the two of them.

§ 46. MISCELLANEA

1. *The Interrogative Particle.* The particles are mostly nouns in origin, but some are now so worn down and feeble that they cannot stand alone. Thus נָא, the precative particle, is enclitic (e.g. שְׁמַע־נָא pray hear), while the interrogative particle הֲ is preclitic.

Questions may have no interrogative word or particle at all introducing them, the interrogative effect being conveyed to a hearer by the tone of voice of a speaker, so that the reader of the written text may occasionally be in doubt as to whether, in a particular case, he has to do with a statement or a question; e.g. שָׁלוֹם לַנַּעַר, which can mean *all is well with the boy,* may have interrogative value, *is all well with the boy?* Usually the context will determine the choice of rendering. But commonly a question is introduced by the particle הֲ; disjunctive questions, *whether* ..... *or* are expressed by the use of הֲ ..... אִם; e.g. הֲלָנוּ אַתָּה אִם לְצָרֵינוּ (*whether*) *art thou for us or for our enemies?* The pointing of הֲ is as follows:

(a) Usually it is הֲ, as in הֲזֶה *is this?*

(b) Before simple shᵉwa it is הַ, as הַמְעַט *is it little?* occasionally followed by *Dagh. forte*; otherwise it is not infrequently marked by *Methegh*.

(c) Before Gutturals (except when they have ָ or ֳ) it is also pointed הַ, often marked by *Methegh*, as הַאֵלֵךְ *shall I go?*

(d) Before Gutt. with ָ or ֳ it is הֶ, as הֶחָזָק *whether it be strong?*

2. *Adverbs.* (a) In addition to the adverbs already met with in the course of the book may be mentioned the following: אֵי, אַיֵּה, אֵי־זֶה *where?* (with suff. אַיֶּכָּה *where art thou?* אַיּוֹ *where is he?* אַיָּם). מֵאַיִן, אֵי־מִזֶּה *whence?* אָנָה *whither?* אֵיךְ, אֵיכָה *how? how!*

(b) Some advbs. directly connected with nouns end in ָם, which may have been an old accus. ending; e.g. יוֹמָם *by day*, רֵיקָם *in vain* or (*with*) *empty* (*hands*), חִנָּם *for nothing* or *in vain* (from חֵן *grace*). In some words this *â* has passed into *ô* (§ 3. 2); e.g. פִּתְאֹם *suddenly*, שִׁלְשֹׁם *the day before yesterday* (*three days ago*, from שָׁלֹשׁ *three*).

(c) The noun סָבִיב *circuit* is mostly used as advb. and preposition, *round about* (e.g. יהוה סָבִיב לְעַמּוֹ *Yahweh is round about his people*). As a preposition it always takes the plur. form, sometimes masc., e.g. סְבִיבֶיךָ *round about thee*, more often fem. סְבִיבוֹתֶיךָ.

3. (a) *Conjunctions.* גַּם *also*, גַּם .... גַּם *both* .... *and* גַּם לֹא .... גַּם לֹא *neither* .... *nor*; אוֹ *or*; אִם *if*; אוֹ .... אוֹ or

אִם .... אִם *whether .... or.* לוּ (לוּא) also can mean *if*; but אִם is the ordinary conditional conjunction, e.g. הִפָּרֶד־נָא מֵעָלָי אִם הַשְּׂמֹאל וְאֵימִנָה *go your way apart from me; if you take to the left, I shall take to the right*; but לוּ (or לוּא) is used of unfulfilled conditions in the past, [1] לוּ חָפֵץ יהוה לַהֲמִיתֵנוּ לֹא לָקַח וגו *if Yahweh had desired to put us to death, he would not have accepted....* The negative of לוּ is לוּלֵא; e.g. לוּלֵא חֲרַשְׁתֶּם בְּעֶגְלָתִי לֹא מְצָאתֶם אֶת־חִידָתִי *if you had not ploughed with my heifer, you would not have discovered my riddle.*

(b) A simple wish may be expressed by מִי (cf. § 34, note to Voc.), מִי־יַשְׁקֵנִי מַיִם *O that I had water to drink,* or by מִי־יִתֵּן, מִי־יִתֵּן[2] תָּבוֹא שֶׁאֱלָתִי *O that my request might be granted*; a wish related to the past which may be expressed by מִי־יִתֵּן and the infin. cstr. e.g. מִי־יִתֵּן מוּתִי אֲנִי תַּחְתֶּיךָ *O that I had died instead of thee,* or by לוּ and the perf.; e.g. לוּ מַתְנוּ בְּאֶרֶץ מִצְרַיִם *would that we had died in the land of Egypt.*

(c) *But* is frequently expressed by *wāw*; e.g. וּמִן־הָעֵץ לֹא־תֹאכַל *but of the tree thou mayest not eat*; or by כִּי in its adversative sense; e.g. הוּא לֹא־כֵן יְדַמֶּה וּלְבָבוֹ לֹא־כֵן יַחְשֹׁב כִּי לְהַשְׁמִיד בִּלְבָבוֹ וּלְהַכְרִית גּוֹיִם לֹא מְעָט *he does not think in that way nor does his mind plan in that way, but his purpose is to destroy and to wipe out nations not a few*; or by the strong adversative particle אוּלָם; e.g. אוּלָם אֲנִי אֶדְרשׁ אֶל־אֵל *but I would seek unto God*; וַיִּקְרָא אֶת־שֵׁם הַמָּקוֹם הַהוּא בֵּית־אֵל וְאוּלָם לוּז שֵׁם הָעִיר לָרִאשֹׁנָה *so he called the name of that place Bethel, but the name of the city was Luz at the first.*

But after a negative is כִּי־אִם: e.g. אֲנִי שְׂנֵאתִיו כִּי לֹא־יִתְנַבֵּא עָלַי טוֹב כִּי־אִם רָע *I hate him because he does not prophesy good concerning me but evil*; or after a virtual negative; e.g. מִי־עִוֵּר כִּי אִם־עַבְדִּי *who is blind but my servant?*

(d) In oaths, אִם = *certainly not,* and אִם לֹא = *certainly*; e.g. אִם־אֶעֱשֶׂה אֶת־הַדָּבָר הַזֶּה *I shall assuredly not do this thing.*

[1] וגו is a contraction for וְגוֹמַר *and completion,* i.e. *etc.*

[2] *lit.* that what I asked for might come.

(The idiom is readily explained on the assumption of an ellipse; e.g. "*cursed be I*, if I do this thing.") אִם יִהְיֶה טַל *certainly there shall not be dew*. אִם־לֹא הָאָרֶץ לְךָ תִּהְיֶה לְנַחֲלָה *surely the land shall be to thee for an inheritance (cursed be I if the land does not become your inheritance)*. We may trace the origin of this usage in the fuller form of sentence which occasionally occurs; e.g. כֹּה יַעֲשֶׂה־לִּי אֱלֹהִים וְכֹה יוֹסִיף אִם־לֹא שַׂר־צָבָא תִּהְיֶה *so may God do to me and more also* (lit. *and so may he add*) *if thou do not become captain of the host* (i.e. I swear that thou shalt become). This imprecatory formula clearly implies that it was originally used as a sacrificial animal was slain; the later custom probably was that the person uttering the words made a symbolic act or gesture which gave meaning to the word *so*. The value of the formula was, more or less, *So may God destroy me and worse if*...

(e) Some prepositions become conjunctions by the addition of אֲשֶׁר; e.g. אַחֲרֵי אֲשֶׁר (cf. *après que*) *after*.

4. *Interjections* אָח, אֲהָהּ *ah*! אוֹי *woe*! הוֹי *ah, alas, ha*! הַס (even pl. הַסּוּ, as if הַס were imper.) *hush*! חָלִילָה[1] *far be it!*—lit. *ad profanum*! (as an exclamation; but also in construction, thus חָלִילָה לָּנוּ מֵעֲזֹב אֶת־יהוה *far be it from us that we should forsake Yahweh*).

ברח	to flee	מוּשׁ	to depart	אוֹת	*f*. sign, token
שָׁאוּל	Saul	הגה	to moan, muse, meditate	תְּשׁוּבָה	*f*. return, answer
עָוֺן	guilt, punishment	יָעֵף	to be weary, faint (§ 29. 2. 2*a*)	מְחִיר	price, hire
יָעֵף	weary, faint	יָגַע	to toil, grow weary (§ 29. 2. 2*a*)	מִישׁוֹר	plain, uprightness

EXERCISE

Translate

אָנָה אֵלֵךְ מֵרוּחֶךָ׃ 2 מֵאַיִן יָבֹא עֶזְרִי׃ 3 וַיֵּבְךְּ וְכֹה אָמַר בְּלֶכְתּוֹ
מִי יִתֵּן מוּתִי אֲנִי תַחְתֶּיךָ בְּנִי׃ 4 אִם־לֹא אֶל־בֵּית־אָבִי תֵּלֵךְ

[1] Cf. § 14. 5.

וְלָקַחְתָּ אִשָּׁה לִבְנִי׃ 5 אִם־אֶקַּח מִכָּל־אֲשֶׁר־לָךְ׃ 6 מַה־טּוֹב
לָכֶם הַמְשֹׁל בָּכֶם שִׁבְעִים אִישׁ אִם־מְשֹׁל בָּכֶם אִישׁ אֶחָד׃ 7 הָיָה
כֶרֶם לְאִישׁ אֵצֶל הֵיכַל הַמֶּלֶךְ בְּשֹׁמְרוֹן׃ וַיְדַבֵּר־לוֹ הַמֶּלֶךְ תְּנָה־
לִּי אֶת־כַּרְמְךָ וִיהִי לִי לְגַן כִּי הוּא קָרוֹב אֵצֶל בֵּיתִי וְאֶתְּנָה לְךָ
תַּחְתָּיו כֶּרֶם טוֹב מִמֶּנּוּ אוֹ אִם טוֹב בְּעֵינֶיךָ אֶתְּנָה־לְּךָ כֶסֶף
מְחִיר־כַּרְמֶךָ׃ וַיַּעַן הָאִישׁ חָלִילָה לִּי מִתִּתִּי אֶת־נַחֲלַת אֲבֹתַי
לָךְ׃ 8 וַיִּגַּשׁ הַנָּבִיא אֶל־מֶלֶךְ יִשְׂרָאֵל וַיֹּאמֶר לוֹ לֵךְ הִתְחַזֵּק וְדַע
וּרְאֵה אֶת־אֲשֶׁר־תַּעֲשֶׂה כִּי לִתְשׁוּבַת הַשָּׁנָה מֶלֶךְ אֲרָם עֹלֶה
עָלֶיךָ׃ וְעַבְדֵי מֶלֶךְ אֲרָם אָמְרוּ אֵלָיו אֱלֹהֵי הָרִים אֱלֹהֵיהֶם עַל־
כֵּן חָזְקוּ מִמֶּנּוּ וְאוּלָם נִלָּחֵם אִתָּם בַּמִּישׁוֹר אִם־לֹא נֶחֱזַק מֵהֶם׃
9 וְאוּלָם חַי אָנִי וְיִמָּלֵא כְבוֹד־יהוה אֶת־כָּל־הָאָרֶץ׃ כִּי כָל־
הָאֲנָשִׁים הָרֹאִים אֶת־כְּבֹדִי וְאֶת־אֹתֹתַי אֲשֶׁר עָשִׂיתִי בְמִצְרַיִם
וּבַמִּדְבָּר וְלֹא שָׁמְעוּ בְּקוֹלִי׃ אִם־יִרְאוּ אֶת־הָאָרֶץ אֲשֶׁר נִשְׁבַּעְתִּי
לַאֲבֹתָם וְכָל־מְקַלְלַי לֹא יִרְאוּהָ׃ 10 וישבע לה שאול ביהוה
לאמר חי־יהוה אם־[1]יקרך עון בדבר הזה ותאמר האשה את־
מי אעלה־לך ויאמר את־שמואל העלי־לי ותרא האשה את־
שמואל ותזעק בקול גדול ויאמר לה המלך אל־תיראי כי מה
ראית ותאמר האשה אלהים ראיתי עלים מן־הארץ׃

Suggested further reading: 2 Samuel 18. 24-33; Genesis 42. 8-17.

And he said to her, My daughter, wilt thou go with this man, or wilt thou stay with me? and she said, Alas, my father, I cannot stay with thee. 2 Whither shall I flee from thy presence? 3 Art thou my son or not? 4 O that we had died by the hand of our God in the land of Babylon, when we sat and wept by the waters thereof. 5 I have sworn in mine anger—ye shall not enter into my rest. 6 This book of the law shall not depart out of thy mouth, but thou

---

[1] קרה with suff.

shalt meditate therein day and night, in order that thou thyself mayest observe to do according to all that is written therein, and that thou mayest speak of it to thy children after thee, when thou sittest in thine house and when thou walkest by the way. 7 God never grows faint or weary: if ye believe in him, how can ye say, My way is hidden from my God?

§ 47. APPENDIX—THE ACCENTS

1. *Use of the Accents.* The accents have three uses: (1) they mark the tone-syllable; (2) they are punctuation marks, like our comma, &c.; and (3) they are musical expressions. In the first case they are guides to the pronunciation of the individual words; in the second they are guides to the syntax and logical sense of a sentence or verse; and in the third they are guides to the proper reading of the text as a whole, which is a kind of recitative or cantillation. The last use, of course, embraces the other two.

2. Of the accentual *signs* some stand above, and some below the word; when above, the sign usually stands upon the initial cons.of the accented syll., as מַ֔יִם; when below, it stands after the vowel of the syll., as מַ֖יִם, except in the case of *ḥôlem* and *šûreq*, when it is placed under the conson., as י֖וֹם, ר֖וּחַ. A few signs are restricted to particular positions, such as the initial or final letter of a word (e.g. הָֽרָקִ֒יעַ).

3. *The Accentual or Punctuational system.* [1] The Accentual or Punctuational system is very intricate and in some parts obscure. A brief outline of its uses as a means of interpunction will here suffice:

(a) The text is broken into verses, *P*ᵉ*sûqîm*, and the end of each *Pāsûq* is marked by the sign :, called *Sô<u>ph</u> pāsûq* (end of the verse). The accent on the final word is called *Sillûq*, its sign being like *Me<u>th</u>e<u>gh</u>*.

הָאָֽרֶץ׃ .... Gen. 1. 1.

(b) The greatest logical pause within the verse is indicated by a sign called ʾ*A<u>th</u>nāḥ* "breathing", or "rest".

הָאָֽרֶץ׃ .... אֱלֹהִ֑ים .... Gen. 1. 1.

(c) If there be two great pauses in the verse the greater or the one next the end of the verse is marked by ʾ*A<u>th</u>naḥ*, and the one nearer the beginning of the verse by sign ∴ called *S*ᵉ*gôltā*, as,

כֵֽן .... לָרָקִ֑יעַ .... הָֽרָקִ֒יעַ .... Gen. 1. 7.

---

[1] The accents described in (a)-(f) are known as disjunctives.

(d) If the clause of words lying between *Sillûq* and *ʾAṯhnaḥ*, or between *ʾAṯhnaḥ* and *Sᵉgôltā*, or between *ʾAṯhnaḥ* and the beginning of the verse, *Sᵉgôltā* being absent, requires to be divided by a pretty large pause, this is in all these cases marked by a sign ֔ called *Zāqēph qāṭôn*, resembling simple shᵉwa placed over the word,[1] as,

Gen. I. 6. ..... אֱלֹהִ֔ים ..... הַמָּ֑יִם ..... מַבְדִּ֔יל ..... לָמָֽיִם

(e) *Rᵉḇhîaʿ*, in appearance like *ḥôlem*, but standing higher, often indicates subdivisions within *zāqēph* sections, as,

Gen. I. 14. ..... וַיֹּ֣אמֶר אֱלֹהִ֗ים ..... הַשָּׁמַ֔יִם ..... הַלָּ֑יְלָה

(f) A disjunctive of less power than *Zāqēph* is *Ṭipḥḥā*, which marks a pause which the rhythm *requires* as a preliminary to the great pauses indicated by *Sillûq* and *ʾAthnaḥ*. Its sign ֖ is a line bent backward, as,

Gen. I. I. .... בְּרֵאשִׁ֖ית .... אֱלֹהִ֑ים .... הַשָּׁמַ֖יִם .... הָאָֽרֶץ׃

(g) These are the main disjunctive accents, and by stopping at them, as at the stops in modern languages, the reader will do justice to the sense. Very roughly (*a*) may be said to correspond to our full stop (.), (*b*) to our colon (:), (*c*), (*d*) and (*e*) to our semi-colon (;), and (*f*) to our comma(,).

There are several more disjunctives of lesser force. There is also a number of conjunctive accents or *Servants*, as they are called, to the disjunctives, accents which are placed on the words that stand immediately before and in close relation with those on which disjunctives are placed. It would seem to follow from the variety of the conjunctive signs that they had musical significance, otherwise one conjunctive might have served all disjunctives alike. The two most common *conjunctives* are *Mêrᵉḵhā* ֥, which serves *Sillûq* and *Ṭipḥḥā*, and *Mûnāḥ* ֣, which serves *ʾAṯhnaḥ* and *Zāqēpẖ*. See Gen. I. I. 2.

(h) The books *Job*, *Proverbs* and *Psalms* have an accentuation in some respects different from that of the other books, called the *Poetical*. The end of the verse is marked as in Prose by *Sillûq* and *Sôpẖ pāsûq*; also the great pause next the end by *ʾAṯhnaḥ*; but this is not the greatest pause in the verse, which is that next the beginning, marked by a sign ֥֫, *ʿÔlé wᵉyôrēḏh* (sometimes wrongly called *Mêrᵉḵhā Mahpāḵh* or *Mᵉhuppāḵh*), thus:

Ps. I. I. .... רְשָׁ֫עִ֥ים .... עָמָ֑ד .... יָשָֽׁב

---

[1] The sign ֕ called *z. gāḏhôl*, of the same disjunctive power, is used when its word is the only word in the accentual clause: as לְהַבְדִּ֕יל Gen. I. 14.

VOCABULARY

English and Hebrew

The figures 1, 2, 3 and 4 after nouns indicate the Declensions

A

Abigail, אֲבִיגַ֫יִל.

Abimelech, אֲבִימֶ֫לֶךְ.

able, be, יָכֹל; *impf.* יוּכַל, § 29.

Abraham, אַבְרָהָם.

Abram, אַבְרָם.

abundance, הָמוֹן 1.

according to, כְּ (prep.), עַל־פִּי.

accustomed, to be, סכן *Hiph.*

acquire, to, קָנָה.

acquit צדק *Hiph.*

add, to, יָסַף, *perf.* and *ptc.* in *Qal*; other parts in *Hiph.* See § 29.

adversary, צַר 4. § 40.

advise. See counsel.

afflict, to, ענה, *Pi.*; affliction, עֳנִי 2. § 33.

after, behind, אַחַר, אַחֲרֵי; אַחֲרַי after me, &c. See § 16. 5.

afterwards, אַחַר, אַחֲרֵי־כֵן.

again, עוֹד; and she *again* bore וַתֹּסֶף וַתֵּ֫לֶד, &c. See § 29. 4.

aged, vb. and adj. זָקֵן; old age, זְקֻנִים, זִקְנָה.

alas! אָח, אֲהָהּ.

alive, חַי.

all, כֹּל 4. § 40.

allow, to, נָתַן, *acc.* and *inf.*

alone, לְבַד 2. § 40. See בד in Lex. *I alone,* אֲנִי לְבַדִּי, &c.

also, גַּם; both . . . and also, גַּם . . . וְגַם.

altar, מִזְבֵּחַ. See sacrifice.

among, amongst (midst).

and, וְ, § 11; both...and, וְ...וְ (also).

angel, messenger, מַלְאָךְ 1.

anger, אַף (אנף); suff. אַפִּי. § 40. 4.

angry, be, קָצַף; חרה, used impers.: he was angry, חָרָה לוֹ.

anoint, to, מָשַׁח; Messiah, מָשִׁיחַ 1.

another, אַחֵר; one another...אִישׁ אָחִיו. See § 33. 4.

answer, to, עָנָה.

any (all); not any, none, ...לֹא כֹּל. § 10. 5.

anything (after a negative) מְאוּמָה.

appear, to, *Niph.* of *see.*

appearance, מַרְאֶה. § 33.

approach, to (draw near).

arise, to, קוּם. § 30.

ark, תֵּבָה (*e* firm).

ark (of covenant), אֲרוֹן, with art. הָאָרוֹן.

arm, זְרוֹעַ, *f.* (generally); pl. *îm*, *ôth*.

army, חַיִל, § 31 (force).

around (prep.), סָבִיב, סְבִיבוֹת; (adv.) מִסָּבִיב.

arrange, to עָרַךְ.

arrow, חֵץ 4. § 40.

as, like כְּ (see p. 55); as, when כַּאֲשֶׁר.

ascend, to (go up).

ashamed, be, בּוֹשׁ. § 30.

aside, to turn, סוּר. § 30.

ask, to, שָׁאַל. § 36.

ass, he-ass, חֲמוֹר; she-ass, אָתוֹן 1.

assemble, to קהל, *Hiph.* (gather).

assembly, עֵדָה 1, מִקְרָא, קָהָל.

atone, to, כִּפֶּר, *Pi.* § 23. 1a; pass. *Pu.*; *for* עַל.

attend to, to; attention to, to pay, קשׁב *Hiph.*

avenge, to, נָקַם; *Niph.* be avenged, avenge oneself.

awake, to, יקץ, *perf.* Qal not in use; *impf.* יִיקַץ; *perf.* הֵקִיץ, *Hiph.* of קִיץ.

B

Baal, בַּעַל 2.

bad, רַע 4. § 40.

Balaam, בִּלְעָם.

bank, שָׂפָה 1 (lip).

be, to, הָיָה. § 33.

bear, to, carry, נָשָׂא (lift up).

bear, to, bring forth, יָלַד, § 29; be born, *Niph.*; beget, *Hiph.*; a boy, יֶלֶד 2; girl, יַלְדָּה 2; kindred, מוֹלֶדֶת, § 25. 3.

beast, חַיָּה (cattle).

beauty, יְפִי 2, § 33 (fair).

because, כִּי.

bed, מִטָּה (stretch); מִשְׁכָּב 1 (lie).

befall, to, קָרָה; קָרָא, § 38. 1. 5.

before (face).

beget, to (bear)

begin, to, חלל, *Hiph.* (הֵחֵל); pass *Hoph.*; beginning תְּחִלָּה.

beguile, to, נשׁא, *Hiph.*

behind (after).

behold, הֵן הִנֵּה, § 40; *behold I* (*me*), הִנְנִי; *behold we* (*us*), הִנְנוּ. See § 40. 6b. Very often followed by the *participle*.

believe, to, אמן, *Hiph.*; לְ of pers.

belly, בֶּטֶן 2. *i.* (womb)

beneath, instead of, תַּחַת 2; plur. suff. תַּחְתַּי, &c., rarely sing except תַּחְתָּם, § 36. 3a, i.

bereaved, be, שָׁכֹל (intrans.).

beseech thee, I (we) *particle of entreaty* אָנָּא.

beside, אֵצֶל, — *me*, אֶצְלִי, § 35. 4b.

Bethel, בֵּיתְאֵל.

between, בֵּין 2, § 31; *between me and thee*, בֵּינִי וּבֵינְךָ; *between me and you* וּבֵינֵיכֶם —.

beware, to, *Niph.* of *keep.*

beyond (region b.), other side, עֵבֶר.

bind, to, saddle, חָבַשׁ; אָסַר.

bird, fowl, עוֹף 2; צִפּוֹר, pl. צִפֳּרִים.

bitter, to be, מַר (*intrans.*), *impf.* יֵמַר, § 39; bitter, מַר, § 40.

bless, to, ברך, *Pi.*; pass. *Pu.* § 36; blessed, בָּרוּךְ; אַשְׁרֵי (*cstr. pl.*) cf. p. 191; blessing, בְּרָכָה 1.

blind, עִוֵּר 3.

blood, דָּם 1; *pl.* bloodshed; with heavy suff. דִּמְכֶם.

blot out, to, destroy, מָחָה; pass. *Niph.*

blow, to (a trumpet), תָּקַע.

bone, עֶצֶם 2. *f.*; *pl. îm* and *ôth*.

book, סֵפֶר 2.

bosom, חֵיק 2. § 31.

both, שְׁנַיִם (two); with suff. *both of us, we both*, שְׁנֵינוּ, &c. § 45. 1a, c. iii.

bow, a, קֶשֶׁת 2. *f.*

bow down, to, כָּרַע; trans. *Hiph.*

boy (bear).

bread, לֶחֶם 2.

broad, be, רָחַב, *st.*; broad, רָחָב 1; breadth, רֹחַב 2. See § 36.

break, to, שָׁבַר; pass. *Niph.*; broken, נִשְׁבָּר; b. in pieces, *Pi.*

break down, to, פָּרַץ.

break through, to, פָּרַץ, בָּקַע.

break, to (of day), עָלָה; day-break, שַׁחַר 2.

breath, נְשָׁמָה 1.

bribe, כֹּפֶר 2.

brightness, נֹגַהּ 2.

bring, to, *Hiph.* of *come.*

bring down, to, *Hiph.* of *go down*, &c.

bring out, to, *Hiph.* of *go out.*

bring up, to, *Hiph.* of *go up.*

bring up, to = to rear, גִּדֵּל, *Pi.*

broad, wide, רָחָב 1.

brook, נַחַל 2.

brother, אָח. See § 42.

build, to, בָּנָה. § 32.

burn, to, שָׂרַף, pass. *Niph.*; *with fire*, בָּאֵשׁ.

burnt-offering, עוֹלָה.

bury, to, קָבַר; pass. *Niph.*; grave, קֶבֶר 2. *i.*; קְבוּרָה grave, burial.

but, אוּלָם, כִּי אִם; כִּי. § 46. 3c.

butler, butlership, מַשְׁקֶה. § 33.

buy, to, acquire, קָנָה (possess).

buy corn, to, שָׁבַר.

by (of cause), מִן. § 12. 3, 4.

by (beside), עַל. § 16. 5.

C

calamity, אֵיד 2. § 31.

calf, עֵגֶל 2; *f.* עֶגְלָה. § 35.

call, to, cry, קָרָא, *dat.*; *he called him Adam*, קרא לוֹ אָדָם; *he called his name Adam*, קרא אֶת־שְׁמוֹ אָדָם; *he was called Adam*, נִקְרָא לוֹ אָדָם. § 40. 6.

camel, גָּמָל, *pl.* גְּמַלִּים. § 40. 5.

camp, מַחֲנֶה.

Canaanite, כְּנַעֲנִי.

captain, שַׂר 4 (prince). § 40.

captive, to take, שָׁבָה.

capture, to (a city), לָכַד.

carcase (corpse).

care, to take, *Niph.* of *keep.*

cast, to, throw, שׁלך, *Hiph.*; pass. *Hoph.* § 24. 2. cast off נָטַשׁ

cast lots, to. See fall.

cattle, בְּהֵמָה 2; cstr. s. בֶּהֱ׳; cstr. pl. בַּהֲ׳. See § 42.

cease, to, חָדַל, (*intrans.*); *he ceased speaking*, חדל לְדַבֵּר.

Chaldees, כַּשְׂדִּים.

change, to, חלף, *Pi.*

chariot, רֶכֶב 2.

cherub, כְּרוּב.

child, יֶלֶד 2; עוֹלָל 1; עוֹלֵל 3; *children of* Israel, בְּנֵי יִשְׂרָאֵל (son).

choose, to, בָּחַר; בְּ.

chosen, בָּחִיר, בָּחוּר.

city, עִיר 2. *f.*; *pl.* עָרִים, § 42.

clan, מִשְׁפָּחָה 2. *f.*

clean, to be, טָהֵר, (*intrans.*); clean, טָהוֹר 1.

cleave, to, דָּבֵק, (*intrans.*); *to*, בְּ.

clothe oneself, to, put on, wear, לָבֵשׁ, (*intrans.*), *acc.*; *clothe* (another) *with* —, *Hiph.*, *two accus.* § 24. 1d.

cloud, עָנָן 1.

come, to, come in, enter, go in, בּוֹא; bring, *Hiph.*; pass. *Hoph*; entrance, מָבוֹא 1.

comfort, to, נחם, *Pi.*; pass. *Pu.*

command, to, צוה *Pi.*; pass. *Pu.*; a command, מִצְוָה 1.

commit, to, entrust (oversee).

compassion, to have, רחם *Pi.* (pity). § 36.

complete, to be, כָּלָה.

conceal, to (hide).

conceive, הָרָה; *impf.* 3 *s. f.* with *wāw* cons. וַתַּהַר. § 33. 1c.

confide, to, trust, בָּטַח; *in*, בְּ.

contend, to, רִיב. § 30.

continually, תָּמִיד.

cord, חֶבֶל 2.

corn, דָּגָן 1, שֶׁבֶר 2.

corner, פִּנָּה.

corpse, carcase, נְבֵלָה 1.

corrupt, to, שׁחת, *Hiph.* (*Pi.*); pass *Niph.*

counsel, to, advise, יָעַץ, *impf.* יִיעַץ; deliberate, *Niph.*, *Hithp.*; counsel, עֵצָה 1. § 29.

count, to, number, סָפַר; מָנָה. § 32.

count, to, impute, reckon, חָשַׁב.

country, the (field).

court, a, חָצֵר 1. *c.*, pl. *îm* and *ôth.*

covenant, a, בְּרִית, *f.*; *to make a covenant* — כָּרַת (cut); *establish, fulfil a* —, — הֵקִים (arise).

cover, to, כסה, *Pi.*; pass. *Pu.*; a covering, מִכְסֶה. § 33.

cow, פָּרָה 4 (ox).

create, to, בָּרָא; pass. *Niph.*

creep, to, רָמַשׂ, *impf.*in *o*; creeping things, רֶמֶשׂ 2, *coll.*

cross, to, pass over, by, עָבַר; *Hiph.*, bring over, make go through, &c.; a crossing, ford, מַעֲבָר 1.

crown, to, עטר *Pi'el.*

crown, עֲטָרָה (cstr. עֲטֶרֶת).

cry, to (call).

cry out, to, צָעַק, זָעַק; a cry, צְעָקָה 1.

cultivate, to (serve).

cunning, (adj.), עָרוּם 1.

cup, a, כּוֹס. § 31.

curse, a, ban, חֵרֶם 2.

curse, to, אָרַר; קלל, *Pi.*

cut down, to, cut, כָּרַת; pass. *Niph.*; to cut off, *Hiph.*

D

Daniel, דָּנִאֵל; later דָּנִיֵּאל.

darkness, חֹשֶׁךְ 2.

daughter, בַּת 2. *i.*; *my d.*, בִּתִּי, &c.; plur. בָּנוֹת 1. § 42.

David, דָּוִד, דָּוִיד.

dawn, daybreak, שַׁחַר 2.

day, יוֹם 2, § 31. 5; pl. יָמִים, יְמֵי. See § 42.

death, מָוֶת, § 31 (die).

Deborah, דְּבוֹרָה (= bee).

deceive, to, נשא *Hiph.*; רמה *Pi'ēl*

deceit, שֶׁקֶר 2, מִרְמָה.

declare, to (tell), (hear), (count).

deed, מַעֲלָל, מַעֲשֶׂה § 33.

deep, be, עָמֹק, (*intrans.*); deep, adj. עָמֹק 1, *fem.* עֲמֻקָּה. See § 40. 5.

deliberate, to (counsel).

delight in, to, חָפֵץ, (*intrans*); impf. יַחְפֹּץ.

delight, pleasure, חֵפֶץ 2. § 35; delighting in, adj. חָפֵץ 1.

deliver, to, נצל *Hiph.*, ישׁע *Hiph.*; pass. *Niph.*

depart, to, סוּר. § 30; מוּשׁ § 30.

descend, to, יָרַד. § 29.

desert, wilderness, pasture, מִדְבָּר 1.

desire, to, חָמַד; *impf.* יַחְמֹד, pass. *Niph.*; חָפֵץ, (*intrans.*); אוה *Pi.*, *Hithpa.*

desolation, חָרְבָּה 2.

despise, to, קִלֵּל; to be despised, קַל (*Qal*).

destroy, to, שׁחת, *Hiph.* (*Pi.*); pass. *Niph.*; שׁמד, *Hiph.* pass. *Hoph.*; דָּמָה.

die, to, מוּת; to kill, *Hiph.*, *Pôʿl.* (מוֹתֵת); pass. *Hoph.*; dead, מֵת *ptc.*; death, מָוֶת 2. § 31.

disease, sickness, חֳלִי 2. § 33.

dispossess, ירשׁ, *Hiph.*

distant, to be, רחק (*a*).; distant (*adj.*) רָחוֹק.

divide, to, בדל, *Hiph.*; pass. *Niph.*

do, to (make).

dog, כֶּלֶב 2.

door, דֶּלֶת 2. *f.*

draw near, to, approach, קָרֵב, (*intrans.*), *Hiph.* bring near, offer, present; נגשׁ, *perf.* used in *Niph.*, *impf.* in *Qal.* See § 34. *Hiph.* bring near; near, קָרוֹב 1.

draw (water) שָׁאַב.

dream, to, חָלַם; *impf.* יַחֲלֹם; a dream, חֲלוֹם, plur. *ôth*.

drink, to, שָׁתָה; to give to drink, water, שׁקה, *Hiph.*; feast, מִשְׁתֶּה, § 33; a butler, cupbearer, מַשְׁקֶה, § 33; cupbearer's office, *same*

drive out, to, גרשׁ, *Pi.*, pass. *Niph.*

drunk, be, שָׁכַר, (*intrans.*); strong drink, שֵׁכָר 1.

dry, be, יָבֵשׁ, (*intrans.*), § 39; חָרֵב; dry land, יַבָּשָׁה 1.

dust, עָפָר 1.

dwell, to, יָשַׁב, § 29; שָׁכַן, *impf.* in $\bar{o}$ (§ 19); *Hiph.*, to place; dwelling מוֹשָׁב; dwelling, tabernacle מִשְׁכָּן, pl. *ôth* (*îm*).

E

each, אִישׁ, אִשָּׁה; cf. § 10. 5.

ear, אֹזֶן 2. *f.*, *du.*; *give ear, hearken*, הֶאֱזִין, *Hiph.* denom. (hear).

earth, land, אֶרֶץ 2. *f.*

east, קֶדֶם; *on the east of* —, מִקֶּדֶם לְ.

eat, to, אָכַל, § 37; give to eat, *Hiph.*; meat, food (אֹכֶל 2), אָכְלָה 2, מַאֲכָל 1.

edge, פֶּה, *with the edge of the sword* לְפִי חֶרֶב. § 42.

Egypt, מִצְרַיִם *f.*; Egyptian, מִצְרִי fem. ־ִית. § 13. 5a.

elder, זָקֵן 1 (aged); elder, comp. = greater (great). § 44.

Elijah, אֵלִיָּהוּ (אֵלִיָּה).

Elisha, אֱלִישָׁע.

embrace, to, חבק, *Pi.*

empty, רֵק (רֵיק); with empty hands, רֵיקָם.

end, קֵץ 4, § 40; latter end, אַחֲרִית, *f.*

end, to, be ended, תַּם, (*intrans.*), § 39; כָּלָה, § 32; to finish, complete, *Hiph.* תם, *Pi.* כלה; perfect, תָּם 4, תָּמִים 1.

enemy, אֹיֵב 3; enmity אֵיבָה 2.

enter, to, בּוֹא. בְּ, אֶל־.

entice, *Pi.* of פָּתָה (to be simple).

entrance, מָבוֹא 1.

Ephraim, אֶפְרַיִם.

escape, to, מלט, *Niph.*; rescue, *Pi.*

establish, to, *Hiph.* of קום *arise.*

eternity (ever).

evening, עֶרֶב 2. *c.*

ever, eternity, עוֹלָם 1, עַד; *for ever,* לְעולם; *eternal hills,* הָרֵי ע׳; never, לע׳ . . . לֹא.

every, כֹּל; every day, כָּל־יוֹם (all); they went *every man to* his house, הָלְכוּ אִישׁ לְבֵיתוֹ (§ 10. 5).

evil, to be, רַע (*intrans.*); *Hiph.* to do evil to, to treat badly.

evil, adj. רַע 4, § 40; evil, *n.* רַע, רָעָה 4, § 40; אָוֶן 2, § 31.

ewe-lamb, כִּבְשָׂה 2.

except, כִּי אִם.

exhausted, to be, יָגַע.

eye, עַיִן 2. *f.*, § 31, du. עֵינַיִם; *pl.* עֲיָנוֹת, fountains (§ 31. 5).

F

face, faces, פָּנִים 1, *pl.*; before, formerly, לְפָנִים; *before me,* לְפָנַי, &c., § 16. 4a; used both of *time* and *place.*

fair, beautiful, יָפֶה 1, § 33; beauty, fairness, יֳפִי 2.

faithfulness אֱמֶת (with suf. אֲמִתִּי &c.).

fall, to, נָפַל, *impf.* in $\bar{o}$, § 34; let fall, drop, cast (lots), *Hiph.*

famine (hungry).

far, to be, רָחַק, (intrans.); far, adj. רָחוֹק 1.

fat, בָּרִיא 1; (noun) חֵלֶב 2.

father, אָב, irreg. § 42.

favour (n.), רָצוֹן 1; חֵן 4.

fear, to, יָרֵא, (*intrans.*), § 29, *impf.* יִירָא; *inf.* יִרְאָה; pass. *Niph.*; terrible, *ptc.* נוֹרָא; fear, יִרְאָה 2, מוֹרָא 1, § 38, פַּחַד 2.

feast (drink).

feast, to hold a (religious), חָגַג, § 39, a (religious) feast, חַג 4, § 40.

feed, to, pasture, רָעָה; shepherd, רֹעֶה.

field, שָׂדֶה 1, § 33, pl. *ôth* (*îm*).

fierceness (heat), חָרוֹן.

fight, to, לחם, *Niph.*; *with, against* בְּ; *for*, לְ; battle, war, מִלְחָמָה, *cstr.* מִלְחֶמֶת, § 25. 4.

fill, to (be full).

find, to, מָצָא; pass. *Niph.* § 38.

fine, thin, דַּק. § 40.

finger, אֶצְבַּע 3 (pl. ־וֹת).

finish, to, כלה, *Pi.*; pass. *Pu.* (be ended), also *Qal.*

fire, אֵשׁ 4. *f.* § 40.

firmament, expanse, רָקִיעַ 1.

first, former, רִאשׁוֹן (§ 37. 1b; § 45. 2); at first בָּרִאשֹׁנָה.

firstborn, בְּכוֹר; right of the firstborn, birthright בְּכוֹרָה.

fish, דָּגָה, דָּג 1. § 15. 3.

flee, to, בָּרַח; נוּס; to put to flight, הֵנִיס (*Hiph.*); a refuge, מָנוֹס 1. § 31.

flesh, בָּשָׂר 1.

fling, to (cast).

flock, צֹאן 2; עֵדֶר 2.

flood (of Noah), מַבּוּל.

flourish, to, פָּרַח.

foe, אֹיֵב (enemy) 3.

food, אָכְלָה (eat).

fool, נָבָל 1; אֱוִיל; folly, אִוֶּלֶת 2.

foot, רֶגֶל 2. *f.*

for, conj. כִּי.

forbid, God, חָלִילָה. Cf. § 46. 4.

force, forces, army, חַיִל 2, § 31; also wealth, valour.

ford, a, מַעֲבָר.

foreign, זָר, נָכְרִי.

ford, to (to cross)

forget, to, שָׁכַח; pass. *Niph.*

fork, מַזְלֵג 3; pl. in use מִזְלָגוֹת.

form, to, יָצַר, § 29; *impf.* with *wāw cons.* וַיִּיצֶר.

forsake, to, עָזַב (leave), נָטַשׁ.

forty, אַרְבָּעִים.

four, § 45; fourth, § 45. 2.

fowl (bird).

friend, רֵעֶה. § 33.

from, out of, prep. מִן, § 12. 3, 4.

fruit, to bear, be fruitful, פָּרָה; fruit, פְּרִי 2, § 33. 3b.

full, be, מָלֵא, (*intrans.*); *of*, acc.; be filled *with*, *Niph.*, *acc.*; to fill (a thing with), *Pi.*, *two acc.*, § 38. 3b; fulness, מְלֹא; full, adj. מָלֵא.

G

gain, to (property), רָכַשׁ; gain, property, רְכוּשׁ.

garden, גַּן § 40.

garment, בֶּגֶד 2. *i.*, suff. בִּגְדִי, &c. (not ד). שִׂמְלָה 2 and שַׂלְמָה 2 (by transposition).

gate, שַׁעַר 2.

gather, to, אָסַף, § 35; קבץ (*Qal*), *Pi.*; assemble, gather together, and pass., *Niph.* of both vbs.

genealogies, history, תּוֹלְדוֹת, pl. *f.* (bear).

generation, דּוֹר 2, § 31, pl. (*îm*) *ôth*.

Gentiles, גּוֹיִם. (גּוֹי nation).

Gideon, גִּדְעוֹן.

girl (bear), (lad).

give, to, נָתַן, § 34; gift(s), *coll.* מַתָּן 1.

glad, be (joyful).

glorify, to, כָּבֵד, *Pi.* (be heavy); glory, כָּבוֹד 1; הָדָר 1; תִּפְאֶרֶת 2.

go, to, הָלַךְ, § 29; walk, *Hithp.* § 23 3b.

go down, יָרַד, § 29, *Hiph.* bring down; pass. *Hoph.*

go in, בּוֹא, § 30; bring in, *Hiph.*, pass. *Hoph.*; followed by בְּ, אֶל־, acc.

go out, יָצָא, §§ 29, 38; bring out, *Hiph.*; pass. *Hoph.*; *of* מִן; outgoing, exit מוֹצָא 1. § 38.

go up, עָלָה; bring up, *Hiph.*; an ascent, מַעֲלֶה, § 33.

let go, to, שָׁלַח, *Pi.*

God, אֱלֹהִים, *pl.* (sing. in poetry אֱלוֹהַּ); with insep. prepp. לֵא׳, &c. (§ 12. 1c), but מֵאֱ׳.

gold, זָהָב 1.

good, be, pleasing, agreeable, טוֹב, *perf.*; *impf.* יִיטַב; do good to, do right, *Hiph.*; well, very, הֵיטֵיב, inf. abs. § 29.

good, adj. טוֹב; good things, goods, goodness, טוּב 2, the best (of), מֵיטָב (only in cstr.) 1.

govern, to, rule, *over*, מָשַׁל, בְּ (king).

gracious, to be, חָנַן; gracious (adj). חַנּוּן.

grain, בָּר, שֶׁבֶר.

grasp, to, אָחַז, § 35.

grass, דֶּשֶׁא 2; עֵשֶׂב 2.

grave (bury).

great, be, grow, גָּדַל, intrans.; bring up (a child), *Pi.*; magnify, *Hiph.* (*Pi.*);—oneself, *Hithp.*; great, גָּדוֹל 1; greatness, גֹּדֶל 2; great, רַב, § 40, pl. many.

grey hairs, שֵׂיבָה.

ground, אֲדָמָה 1.
grow up (be great).
guilty, be, אָשֵׁם, *(intrans.)*; suffer, to, be punished (as guilty), *Niph.*; guilt, אָשָׁם 1, עָוֹן 1.

H

habit, to show, סכן *Hiph.*
half, חֲצִי 2. § 33. 3.
hail, בָּרָד.
hand, יָד 1. *f.*, § 15; *your* —, יֶדְכֶם.
happen, to (befall).
happy, אַשְׁרֵי (*cstr. pl.*).
hard, be, קָשָׁה; harden, *Hiph.*; hard, severe, קָשֶׁה 1 (heavy).
hasten מהר Pi'el.
hate, to, שָׂנֵא, § 38; hatred, שִׂנְאָה 2.
head, רֹאשׁ, § 31. 5, pl. רָאשִׁים.
heal, רָפָא; pass. *Niph.*
hear, שָׁמַע; obey, אֶל־ or שָׁמַע בְּ; make be heard, declare, *Hiph.* (see *ear*); rumour, report, שֵׁמַע 2.
heart, לֵבָב 1, לֵב 4, § 40 (pl. *ôth* in both).
heaven, heavens, שָׁמַיִם 1, pl.
heavy, be, כָּבֵד, (intrans.); make heavy, harden (honour, glorify), *Pi.*; heavy, כָּבֵד 1.
heed, to pay, קשב *Hiph.*
heifer, עֶגְלָה 2.
help, to, עָזַר; help, עֵזֶר 2. § 35.
herd, עֵדֶר 2, מִקְנֶה. § 33.
here, hither הֵנָּה.
hero, mighty man, גִּבּוֹר.
hide, to, סתר, pass., reflex. *Niph.*; act. *Hiph.*; חבא, pass. reflex. *Niph.*, *Hithp.*; act. *Hiph.*; טָמַן (to bury out of sight).
high, be, רוּם; lift up, *Hiph.*, *Po'lel*; high, lofty (adj.) רָם 1 (*part.*), גָּבוֹהַּ.
hill, mountain, הַר § 40.
hire, to, שָׂכַר; hireling שָׂכִיר.
history (genealogies).
hither, here, adv. הֲלֹם.
ho! הוֹי.
holy, be, קָדַשׁ, (*intrans.*); sanctify, *Pi.*; — oneself, *Hithp.*; holy, saint, קָדוֹשׁ 1; holiness, קֹדֶשׁ 2; holy place, sanctuary, קֹדֶשׁ, מִקְדָּשׁ 1.
honour, to, כבד *Pi'el*; honour (noun.) כָּבוֹד.
Horeb חֹרֵב.
horn, קֶרֶן 2. *f.*
horse, סוּס 2; mare, סוּסָה, *f.*
host, army, time of service, צָבָא 1, pl. *ôth*. § 38. 2.
hot, be, חַם, (*intrans.*); hot, חַם, § 40; heat, חֹם.

house, בַּ֫יִת 2, § 31; home, (homewards) בַּ֫יְתָה; pl. בָּתִּים, § 42.
how! מָה, § 10. 3; how? אֵיךְ.
hundred, מֵאָה.
hungry, be, רָעֵב, (*intrans.*); hungry, רָעֵב; hunger, famine, רָעָב 1.
hunt, to, צוּד; venison, צַ֫יִד.
husband (man).

I

if, אִם, לוּ, לוּא, cf. § 46. 3.
ill (evil).
image, צֶלֶם 2.
imagination, יֵצֶר 2 (form).
imprisonment, כֶּלֶא 2.
impute, to, reckon, חָשַׁב.
in, prep. בְּ, § 12; into, בְּ, אֶל.
incite, עוּר *Poʿlel.*
increase, to (*intr.*), רָבָה.
inhabit, to, יָשַׁב, § 29. 2. 2b; inhabitant, יֹשֵׁב.
inherit, to, יָרַשׁ, § 29. 2. 2a, dispossess, *Hiph.*; נָחַל, give to inherit, *Hiph.*; inheritance, נַחֲלָה.
iniquity, אָוֶן 2, § 31 (evil, guilt).
innocent, נָקִי (very rarely נָקִיא).
inside, midst, heart, קֶרֶב, 2. *i.*; *within the city*, בְּקֶ׳ הָעִיר; *within me*, בְּקִרְבִּי (midst).
instead of, תַּ֫חַת (beneath), § 36. 4a, i.

interpose, פגע *Hiph.*
Israel, יִשְׂרָאֵל.

J

Jacob יַעֲקֹב.
Jeroboam, יָרָבְעָם.
Jerusalem, יְרוּשָׁלַםִ (יְרוּשָׁלַיִם), § 25, Voc., n. 4.
Jonathan, יְהוֹנָתָן, יוֹנָתָן.
Jordan (the), הַיַּרְדֵּן.
Joseph, יוֹסֵף.
Joshua, יְהוֹשׁוּעַ, יְהוֹשֻׁעַ.
journey, to, נָסַע; journey, מַסָּע 1.
joyful, be, rejoice, &c., שָׂמַח, (intrans.); glad, joyful, *ptc.*; gladness, joy, שִׂמְחָה 2, also גִּיל, verb and noun, §§ 30, 31.
Judah, יְהוּדָה.
judge, to, שָׁפַט; to litigate, to join issue, enter into judgment, *Niph.*; a judge, *ptc.* שֹׁפֵט; judgment, מִשְׁפָּט 1.
just, be, righteous, &c., צָדַק, (*intrans.*); justify, *Hiph.*; — oneself, *Hithp.*; just, righteous, צַדִּיק; righteousness, צֶדֶק 2. *i.*, צְדָקָה 1.

K

keep, to, watch, שָׁמַר; keep oneself, take care, beware, *Niph.*;

watchman, *ptc.* שֹׁמֵר, צֹפֶה; watch, מִשְׁמָר 1; watch, charge, מִשְׁמֶרֶת, § 25. 3a.

kill, to, הָרַג; *Hiph* of *die* (הֵמִית).

kindle, to, burn (*intr.*) יצת, יקד; (*trans.*) *Hiph.* of יצת (הִצִּית), § 29. 3.

kindness חֶסֶד 2.

kindred מוֹלֶדֶת 2. *f.*

king, be, rule, מָלַךְ, *over*, עַל, בְּ; make one king, *Hiph.*; pass. *Hoph.*; a king, מֶלֶךְ 2; queen, מַלְכָּה 2; kingdom, מַמְלָכָה, &c., § 25. 3a.

kiss, to, נָשַׁק, *impf.* in *a* (also *ō*); with לְ.

kneel, to, בָּרַךְ, (*intrans.*); to make (a beast) kneel, *Hiph.*; the other parts in sense of "bless"; knee, בֶּרֶךְ 2. *i.*, *f. du.* § 25. 3a.

know, to, יָדַע, § 29. 2; impf. יֵדַע, imp. דַּע, inf. cstr. דַּעַת; pass. *Niph.*; inform, make known, *Hiph.*; pass. *Hoph.*; knowledge, דַּעַת 2.

L

lad, נַעַר 2, girl, damsel, *f.* נַעֲרָה 2.

ladder, סֻלָּם.

lamb, כֶּבֶשׂ 2. (*f.* כִּבְשָׂה).

lamp, נֵר.

lance, רֹמַח 2. § 36. 4b.

land (earth).

last, אַחֲרוֹן (after).

laugh, שָׂחַק.

law, instruction, תּוֹרָה (teach).

leaf, leafage, עָלֶה 1. § 33. 3.

lean, to, rest, press, *act.* סָמַךְ; oneself, *Niph.*, and שָׁעַן, *Niph.*; upon, עַל.

learn, to, לָמַד, (*intrans.*); make learn, teach, *Pi.*, *two acc.*

leave, to. abandon, עָזַב, נָטַשׁ; pass. *Niph.*

leave off, to, stop (cease).

leave alone, to, let be, רָפָה *Hiph.*

left (over), be, remain, שָׁאַר *Qal* (rare) and *Niph.*; to leave over, let remain, *Hiph.*

left (hand), שְׂמֹאול.

length (long).

lest, conj. פֶּן־, joined with *impf.*

lie, to (speak falsely), כזב, *Pi.*; a lie, כָּזָב 1.

lie down, to, lie, שָׁכַב, (*intrans.*); a bed, מִשְׁכָּב 1; to lie down (of beasts), רָבַץ, (*intrans.*); a stall, resting-place, מַרְבֵּץ 3. § 26.

life (live).

lift up, to, bear, נָשָׂא.

light, be, shine, אוֹר, *perf.* in *ō*; give light, *Hiph.*, § 30; light,

אוֹר 2; luminary, light, מָאוֹר 1, pl. *ôth* (*îm*).

light, be, swift, קַל, *(intrans.)*, §39; to curse, *Pi.*; lighten, *Hiph.*; light, swift, קַל § 40.

like, prep. כְּ. § 12.

lion, אֲרִי 2, § 33; young lion, כְּפִיר.

lip, edge, shore, שָׂפָה 1, *du.* § 13.

listen, to, שָׁמַע בְּ, אֶל־.

little, be, קָטֹן, (*intrans.*); little, קָטֹן 1, קָטָן 1, — the first form is not inflected (found only in abs., and *once* in cstr.), the second is inflected קְטַנִּים קְטַנָּה. See § 40. 5.

little, a, some, a few, מְעַט; *a little water, food,* &c. מ׳ מַיִם, אֹכֶל; *a few people,* מְתֵי מ׳ (also מְתֵי מִסְפָּר).

live, to, חָיָה, § 33; living, חַי; life, חַיִּים; living creature, beast, חַיָּה.

lofty, be, גָּבַהּ, (*intrans.*); lofty, high, גָּבֹהַּ 1; loftiness, height, גֹּבַהּ 2.

long, be, אָרֵךְ, (*intrans.*); to prolong. *Hiph.*; long (אָרֵךְ) only in cstr. אֶרֶךְ (see § 15. 1), אָרֹךְ 1, fem. אֲרֻכָּה (see § 40. 5); length, אֹרֶךְ 2.

look, to, נבט, *Hiph.*

lord, אָדוֹן 1; takes pl. suff., except in 1st pers. s., where it admits sing. also (prob. a later device to distinguish a human lord אֲדֹנִי from the divine אֲדֹנָי = יהוה).

lot, גּוֹרָל 1, pl. *ôth.*

Lot, לוֹט.

loud, גָּדוֹל (great).

love, to, אָהֵב, (*intrans.*), רָחַם, § 34; love, אַהֲבָה (strictly *inf. cstr.*).

low, be, שָׁפֵל (*intrans.*); low, שָׁפָל to bring low, *Hiph.* of שפל or of כרע.

M

magnify, to (be great).

maid, שִׁפְחָה 2; אָמָה 1, pl. אֲמָהוֹת, see § 42.

make, to, do, עָשָׂה; pass. *Niph.*; to make one thing into another, *Qal* with *two accus.*; work, deed, מַעֲשֶׂה, § 33; פָּעַל *poet.*; a work, פֹּעַל, § 36. 4.

male, זָכָר 1.

man, husband, אִישׁ; man, mankind, אָדָם.

Manasseh, מְנַשֶּׁה.

manner, דֶּרֶךְ 2, מִשְׁפָּט 1.

mantle, מְעִיל; אַדֶּרֶת. § 25. 2.

many, be, increase, רָבָה; increase, to, (*act.*) *Hiph.*; many, *plur.* of רַב 4. § 40.

mare (horse).

master, אָדוֹן 1, בַּעַל 2.

matter (word).

measure, to, מָדַד. § 39; measure (noun) מִדָּה.

meat (eat).

meditate, muse, הָגָה.

meet, to, פָּגַע, קָרָה, קָרָא (infin. cstr. קְרָאָה); *to meet him*, לִקְרָאתוֹ, &c.

memory, זֵכֶר 2; memorial זֵכֶר, זִכָּרוֹן.

mention, to, *Hiph.* of *remember*.

merciful, to be, רחם, *Pi.*, *acc.*; חָנַן; mercy, loving-kindness, חֶסֶד, רַחֲמִים.

messenger (angel).

midst, תָּוֶךְ 1, § 31, קֶרֶב 2; within, in the midst of, בְּקֶרֶב, בְּתוֹךְ.

mighty man (hero).

minister, to, שׁרת, *Pi.* (serve).

Miriam, מִרְיָם.

missile (send).

Moab, מוֹאָב.

month, חֹדֶשׁ 2 (new).

moon, יָרֵחַ.

more (still), עוֹד (§ 31. 4. n. 1.

morning, בֹּקֶר 2.

morsel, fragment, פַּת *i. f.* § 40.

Moses, מֹשֶׁה.

mother, אֵם § 40.

mother-in-law, חָמוֹת.

mountain (hill).

mourn, to, אָבַל; סָפַד, (*intrans.*); mourning, מִסְפֵּד 3.

mouth, edge, פֶּה. See § 42.

much, רַב § 40 (many); how much כַּמָּה (§ 41).

N

name, שֵׁם 3, pl. שֵׁמוֹת (§ 42).

narrate, to, סָפַר, *Pi.*

nation, גּוֹי (people).

native land, מוֹלֶדֶת 2 (bear).

nature, form, יֵצֶר 2.

near, קָרוֹב 1 (draw near).

new, חָדָשׁ 1.

night, לַיִל 2, § 31, usually לַיְלָה 2.

no, not, לֹא, אַל, with prohibitions, § 20. 1, notes i, ii; no, none, אַיִן 2 (if with vb., vb. is in *ptc.*), § 31. 4, note 1.

north, צָפוֹן 1.

not to, לְבִלְתִּי, *inf.*, § 18. 2a, v.

now, עַתָּה.

number, to, מָנָה (count), סָפַר.

nurse, מֵינֶקֶת 2. *i.* § 25. 3.

O

offer, to, *Hiph.* of קרב, *draw near.*

offering, קָרְבָּן; cereal (i.e. bloodless) — מִנְחָה; drink — נֶסֶךְ 2. *i.*; burnt — עֹלָה.

ointment, oil שֶׁמֶן 2.

old, זָקֵן 1.

olive, זַיִת 2. § 31.

on, upon, בְּ, § 12. 1; עַל, § 16. 5.

one, § 48; one—another, § 33. 4 (friend), (brother).

only, אַךְ, רַק.

open, to, פָּתַח; pass. *Niph.*; entrance, doorway, פֶּתַח 2. *i.*; key, מַפְתֵּחַ 3; to open (of eyes), פָּקַח; pass. *Niph.*; open (of mouth), פָּצָה.

oppress, to, עָשַׁק, לָחַץ, עָנָה *Pi.*

or, אוֹ; אִם, וְאִם in interrogative or indirectly interr. sentences, —*shall we go or shall we forbear?* הֲנֵלֵךְ ... (וְאִם) אִם נֶחְדָּל; *or no, or not,* אִם לֹא, § 46. 1; *either ... or,* אִם ... וְאִם.

other, אַחֵר, pl. אֲחֵרִים.

out, out of, מִן. § 12. 3, 4.

out at, in at, בְּעַד (properly "interval", "distance").

outside, חוּץ; *to the outside,* הַחוּצָה; *on, at, the outside of the house,* מִחוּץ לַבַּיִת, § 12. 4.

over, upon, עַל, § 16. 5.

oversee, to, visit, פָּקַד; commit, entrust, *Hiph.*; an overseer, פָּקִיד 1.

ox, פַּר 4, § 40; שׁוֹר, § 31; cow, *fem.* פָּרָה.

P

pain, חֳלִי 2, § 33. 3; מַכְאֹב.

palace, temple הֵיכָל 1, pl. *ôth* (once); cstr. הֵיכְלֵי.

palm (hand), כַּף 4. § 40.

palm tree, תָּמָר 2.

pass by, עָבַר (cross).

pass over, to, פָּסַח.

passover, פֶּסַח 2.

pasture, to, רָעָה § 32; pasture (wilderness) מִדְבָּר 1.

pay, to, שׁלם, *Pi.*

people, עַם § 40.

perfect, תָּם 4, § 40; תָּמִים 1. *See* be ended.

perish, to, אָבַד, § 37; destroy, *Pi.*, *Hiph.*

permit, to, נָתַן, *acc.* and *inf.*

persecute, רָדַף.

Pharaoh, פַּרְעֹה.

Philistines, פְּלִשְׁתִּים.

pit, prison, בּוֹר 2, § 31; pl. *ôth*.

pity, to, רחם, *Pi.*, § 36; חָנַן, § 39.

place, to, שִׂים, שׂוּם, שִׁית, הִנִּיחַ

(*Hiph.* of נוּחַ); *Hiph.* of שׁכן. *See* set, dwell, rest.
place, a, מָקוֹם 1; pl. *ôth* (arise).
plague, נֶגַע 2; מַכָּה.
plant, to, נָטַע; a plant, נֶטַע 2. *i.*
play, to, sing, &c., זמר, *Pi.*
plead with, to, רִיב, בְּ, עִם, § 30.
plough, to, חָרַשׁ.
plunder, to, בָּזַז (spoil), (take). § 39.
poor, רָשׁ (*part.*) דַּל, אֶבְיוֹן § 40,
possess, to, קָנָה, יָרַשׁ; possessor, קֹנֶה; possession, מִקְנֶה, רְכוּשׁ, § 33.
pour out, שָׁפַךְ (spill), נסךְ *Qal, Hiph.*
powerful, עָצוּם 1.
pray, to, פלל, *Hithpaʿel.*
prayer, תְּפִלָּה.
presence, in p. of, לִפְנֵי (face), § 16. 4a.
priest, כֹּהֵן 3.
prince, שַׂר § 40, נָשִׂיא 1.
prison, כֶּלֶא 2
prolong, to, *Hiph.* of אָרֵךְ, *be long.*
promise, to, אָמַר, with *infin.*
prophesy, to, נבא, *Niph.* (*Hithp.*); *concerning,* ל, עַל; prophet, נָבִיא 1.
prosper, שׂכל *Hiph.*
prostrate oneself, to, שׁחה *Hithpaʿlel;* § 32. 4.
prove, to (try), צָרַף, בָּחַן, נסה *Pi.*
proverb, מָשָׁל 1.
punish, to, פָּקַד עַל; punished, to be (to be guilty), אָשֵׁם *Qal, Niph.*
pursue, to, רָדַף.
put on, wear, לָבֵשׁ, *acc.*; to clothe, dress with, *Hiph*, *two acc.*, § 24. 1d; § 38. 6.
put, to, place, set, נָתַן. See place.
put out, to (the hand), שָׁלַח.

Q

quake, to, רָעַשׁ.
queen, מַלְכָּה 2.
quiet, שַׁאֲנָן.

R

raging, רֹגֶז 2.
rain, מָטָר 1; rain, to, מָטַר, *Hiph.*
ram, אַיִל 2. § 31. 2.
ransom, כֹּפֶר 2 (atone).
read, to, קָרָא.
rebel, revolt, to, פָּשַׁע; *against,* בְּ.
receive, to, לָקַח. § 34. 3b.
recompense, to גָּמַל.
redeem, to, פָּדָה, גָּאַל; redemption, פְּדוּת, גְּאֻלָּה; redeemer, גֹּאֵל.
refresh, to, sustain, סָעַד.

refuge, מָעוֹז 1.
Rehoboam, רְחַבְעָם.
reign, to, מָלַךְ.
reject, to מָאַס.
rejoice, to (joyful, be).
remainder, יֶתֶר.
remember, to, זָכַר; pass. *Niph.*; call to remembrance, mention, *Hiph.*; memory, זֵכֶר 2.
remove, to, סוּר, *(intrans).*; *Hiph.* trans.
rend, to, קָרַע.
repent, to, נחם, *Niph.* (נִחַם), § 36.
report, שְׁמוּעָה (hear).
request, שְׁאֵלָה.
requite, to, גָּמַל.
rescue, to (escape), (deliver).
rest, to, שָׁבַת; make cease, *Hiph.*; נוּחַ; give rest, *Hiph.* הֵנִיחַ, *dat.*; place, set, *Hiph.* הִנִּיחַ; resting-place, מָנוֹחַ, מְנוּחָה, § 31; sabbath, שַׁבָּת 1.
restore, to (return).
return, to, שׁוּב; restore, *Hiph.*, *Pô'l.*; return, תְּשׁוּבָה.
reveal, to, גָּלָה.
review, to, פָּקַד (oversee).
riches, חַיִל 2 (force); עֹשֶׁר 2; rich, עָשִׁיר.
riddle, חִידָה.
ride, to, רָכַב (*intrans.*); to make ride, set on a horse, &c., *Hiph.*; chariot, רֶכֶב 2. *i.*, מֶרְכָּבָה.
righteous, be, צדק (*intrans.*); righteousness, צֶדֶק 2, צְדָקָה 1.
rise, to, קוּם.
rise, to (of star, &c.), זָרַח.
rise early, to, *Hiph.* שׁכם.
river, נָהָר 1, pl. *ôth* and *îm*; יְאֹר (mainly of *Nile* and its branches).
roll, to, גָּלַל, *Qal, Hiph.*; pass. *Niph.*
rot, to, רָקַב (*intrans.*).
rule over, to (govern).
ruling, law, תּוֹרָה.
rumour (report).
run, to, רוּץ; runner, post, *ptc.* רָץ 1; make run, bring hastily, *Hiph.*

S

sabbath (rest).
sackcloth, שַׂק.
sacrifice, to, זָבַח; sacrifice, זֶבַח 2 *i*; altar, מִזְבֵּחַ 3, pl. *ôth* (offer, offering).
saddle, to (bind).
safety, to bring to, עוּז *Hiph.*
saint (holy).
sake of, for, בַּעֲבוּר, — *of me*, בַּעֲבוּרִי, בִּגְלָלִי. See עבר, גלל in Lex.

salt, מֶלַח 2.

salvation (save).

Samson, שִׁמְשׁוֹן.

Samuel, שְׁמוּאֵל.

sanctify, to (holy).

sanctuary (holy).

sand, חוֹל 2. § 31.

satisfied, be, שָׂבַע, (*intrans.*), *with*, acc.; to satisfy with, *Hiph.*, *two acc.*, § 38. 6; satisfied, שָׂבֵעַ 1; fulness, שֹׂבַע 2, שָׂבָע 1.

Saul, שָׁאוּל.

save, to, מלט *Pi'el*, ישׁע, *Hiph.* (הוֹשִׁיעַ); pass. *Niph.*; salvation, safety, יֵשַׁע 2; יְשׁוּעָה.

say, to, promise, אָמַר. § 37.

scattered, be, פּוּץ (impf.); to scatter, *Hiph.*; pass. *Niph.*

sceptre, tribe, rod, שֵׁבֶט 2.

sea, יָם 4, § 40, *cstr.* יָם, יָם־, and יַם (only in יַם־סוּף).

securely, לָבֶטַח.

see, to, רָאָה, §§ 32, 33; pass. *Niph.*; show, let see, *Hiph.*, *two acc.*; seer, רֹאֶה; sight, aspect, face, מַרְאֶה.

seed, זֶרַע 2 (sow).

seek, to, inquire at, דָּרַשׁ; pass. *Niph.*

seek, to, בקשׁ, *Pi.*

seek hospitality, to, גּוּר *Hithpo'lel*

sell, to, מָכַר; pass. *Niph.*

send, to, שָׁלַח; send away, loose, *Pi.*; a missile, שֶׁלַח 2. *i.*

separation, בַּד, § 40. 6a; alone, לְבַד; with suff. לְבַדִּי, &c.

serpent, נָחָשׁ 1.

serve, to, till, עָבַד; pass. *Niph.*; enslave, *Hiph.*; servant, עֶבֶד 2; service, עֲבֹדָה; to serve = minister (mainly in sacred things), שׁרת, *Pi.*

set, to, נָתַן, שִׂים (שׂוּם), שִׁית; כּוּן, *Hiph.*, *Pô'l.* (§ 30. 4); pass. *Niph.* (place).

seven, seventh, § 45.

severe, to be, עלל *Pô'ēl* and *Hithpa'el.*

Shaddai, שַׁדַּי.

shadow, צֵל 4. § 40.

shake, to, רָעַשׁ; trans. *Hiph.*; an earthquake, רַעַשׁ 2.

she-ass, אָתוֹן 1. *f.*

Shechem, שְׁכֶם.

shed, to (spill).

sheep, צֹאן; a sheep שֶׂה.

she-goat, עֵז *f.* (pl. ־ִים), § 40. 5.

Sheol, the underworld שְׁאוֹל.

shepherd, herdsman, רֹעֶה (feed)

shield, צִנָּה.

shine, to, אוֹר. § 30.

shore (lip).
short, קָצֵר 1.
shoulder, שְׁכֶם 2. *i.*
shut, to, סָגַר; pass. *Niph.*
sick, be, חָלָה; sickness, חֳלִי 2.
silent, be, דָּם, (*intrans.*) (*impf.* יִדֹּם), חָרֵשׁ, *Hiph.*
silver, כֶּסֶף 2.
simple one, a, פְּתִי 2. § 33. 3b.
sin, to, חָטָא; sin, חֵטְא 2, חַטָּאת; sinner (sing.), חֹטֵא, *ptc.*, חַטָּא (used in plur.).
sing, to, שִׁיר; a song, שִׁיר, and *fem.*
sister, אָחוֹת 1. § 42.
sit, to, dwell, יָשַׁב, § 29. 2; make to sit, place, *Hiph.*; pass. *Hoph.*; a seat, assembly, dwelling-place מוֹשָׁב 1.
slay (ritually) to, שָׁחַט. § 36.
slay, kill, הרג, מות *Hiph.*; slain חָלָל.
sleep, to, יָשֵׁן, (*intrans.*); נוּם; sleep, שֵׁנָה 1, תְּנוּמָה.
slow (to anger), אֶרֶךְ (*constr.*).
smell, to, רוח, *Hiph.*; smell, רֵיחַ 2.
smite, to, נָגַף; pass. *Niph.*; נכה, *Hiph.* הִכָּה; pass. *Hoph.*; נָגַע; stroke, defeat, מַגֵּפָה, מַכָּה, נֶגַע 2. *i.* (The word מַכָּה is of general use, the other two very commonly of divine plagues.)
smoke, עָשָׁן 1.
snare, פַּח § 40.
sojourn, to, גּוּר.
sole (of foot), palm, כַּף *f.* § 40.
some (a little), מִן, partitive.
son, בֵּן 3. *See* § 42.
song, שִׁיר *m.* (שִׁירָה f.).
sore, רַע (bad).
soul, נֶפֶשׁ 2. *f.*
south, נֶגֶב 2.
sow, to, זָרַע; bear seed, *Hiph.*; seed, זֶרַע 2.
speak, to, דבר, *Pi.* (pf. דִּבֶּר)—in Qal used only in *act. ptc.*; a word, thing, דָּבָר 1; *everything*, כֹּל דָּבָר; *nothing*, לֹא—כֹּל ד׳ or לֹא—ד׳. § 10. 5.
spear, חֲנִית, רֹמַח 2.
spill, to, שָׁפַךְ; pass. *Niph.*
spirit, wind, רוּחַ 2. *usually f.*
spoil, to, plunder, שָׁלַל; spoil, שָׁלָל 1.
spread, to, spread out (hands), פָּרַשׂ; יצע *Hiph.* (*impf.* יַצִּיעַ), § 29. 3.
sprout, to, צָמַח; make to sprout, *Hiph.*; sprout, branch, צֶמַח 2. *i.*
staff, מַקֵּל 3, pl. *ôth*.
stand, to, עָמַד; set up, *Hiph.*, קוּם.

star, כּוֹכָב 1.

statute (command), חֹק 4, § 40, *fem.* חֻקָּה (precept).

steal, to, גָּנַב, *Qal* and *Pi.*; pass. *Pu.*, *Niph.*; thief, גַּנָּב.

still, yet, more, עוֹד; see § 31. 5, note 1; *still alive*, עוֹד חַי (again).

stone, אֶבֶן 2.

store, to, צָבַר.

stranger, sojourner, גֵּר 1, § 31.; strange, foreign, נָכְרִי (*nokhrî*).

street, חוּץ 2, pl. *ôth*; שׁוּק 2; רְחֹב, *f.*, pl. *ôth*.

strength (strong).

stretch, to, נָטָה, also *Hiph.* (put out); a bed, מִטָּה.

strong, be, חָזַק, (*intrans.*); אָמַץ, (*intrans.*); גָּבַר (*intrans.*); strengthen, *Pi.*; עָצַם, (*intrans.*); strong, חָזָק, עַז, עָצוּם; strength, חֹזֶק 2 and חֶזְקָה; עֹז 4, § 40; כֹּחַ.

strive, to, plead, רִיב, § 30; strife, plea, רִיב 2, מְרִיבָה.

suck, to, יָנַק, § 29. 1; suckle, give suck, *Hiph.*; nurse, *ptc. Hiph.*, מֵינֶקֶת, see § 25. 4.

suffer, to, punishment (be guilty); to suffer pain, כָּאַב, (*intrans.*) (pain).

sun, שֶׁמֶשׁ 2.

supplication תְּחִנָּה; תַּחֲנוּנִים.

surround, to, סָבַב.

sustain, to, סָמַךְ, סָעַד.

swear, to, שׁבע, *Niph.*; oath, שְׁבוּעָה.

sweet, be (מָתֹק), (*intrans.*); sweet, מָתוֹק 1, inflect. מְתוּקָה. § 31. 1b.

swift, light, קַל. § 40.

sword, חֶרֶב 2. *f.*

Syria, אֲרָם.

T

tabernacle, מִשְׁכָּן (dwell).

table, שֻׁלְחָן 1.

tablet, לוּחַ *m.*; pl. לוּחֹת.

take, to, לָקַח; pass. *Qal*, *Niph.*, § 34. 3b, c; prey, plunder, מַלְקוֹחַ; take (capture in war, &c.), לָכַד; pass. *Niph.*

talent (currency) כִּכָּר 1.

tall, גָּבֹהַּ (great). *Cstr.* גְּבַהּ.

taste, to, טָעַם; taste, sense, טַעַם 2.

teach, to, ירה, *Hiph.*, הוֹרָה; למד (learn) *Pi.*; law, instruction, תּוֹרָה.

tell, to, נגד, *Hiph.*; pass. *Hoph.* (count), (say), (speak).

temple, הֵיכָל (palace).

tent, אֹהֶל 2, pl. אֹהָלִים (but also, with *prep.* בָּאֳהָלִים).

terrible, נוֹרָא, *Niph. ptc.* of יָרֵא (fear).

testify, to, עוּד, *Hiph.*; witness, עֵד; testify against, הֵעִיד בְּ, עָנָה בְּ.

thanksgiving, thank-offering, תּוֹדָה.

that, conj. כִּי; in order that, לְמַעַן, with *infin. cstr.* § 18. 2a, iii, or *imperf.* (§ 20. 5a); *that* is very often expressed by *wāw consec.*, e.g. after וַיְהִי, *and it came to pass.* § 20. 4a.

then, of time, אָז; *then*, of transition in thought, וְ, simple and *consec.* § 20. 4.

thence (there).

there, שָׁם; thither, שָׁמָּה; thence, מִשָּׁם; where, whence, whither, § 10. 4a.

there is (was), יֵשׁ; — *water*, יֵשׁ מַיִם; *I have*, יֶשׁ־לִי, &c. (see § 29, Exer., note 4); *there is* (*was*) *not*, אַיִן; *there is no water*, אֵין מַיִם; *suff.*, see § 31.4, note 1.

therefore, עַל־כֵּן.

thief (steal).

thing (speak).

thirsty, to be, צָמֵא (*intrans.*).

thither (there).

thought, מַחֲשָׁבָה, § 29 3 (count); cstr. pl. מַחְ׳.

thousand, אֶלֶף 2.

threshing-floor, גֹּרֶן 2, pl. *ôth*.

throne, seat, כִּסֵּא 3, pl. כִּסְאוֹת.

thus, כֹּה.

tidings, to bring, preach, בשׂר, *Pi.*

till, cultivate (serve).

till, until, prep. עַד; conj. עַד אֲשֶׁר, with *perf.* or *impf.* according to sense. *Suff.*, § 16. 5.

time, עֵת, § 40; time (*fois*, *mal*), פַּעַם 2, gen. *fem.*, plur. *îm* (properly *step*); twice, פַּעֲמַיִם; three times, שָׁלֹשׁ פְּעָמִים.

together, יַחְדָּו, יַחַד.

to-morrow, מָחָר.

tongue, לָשׁוֹן 1, gen. *fem.*, pl. *ôth*.

touch, to, נָגַע, בְּ.

transgress, פָּשַׁע; *against*, בְּ; transgression, פֶּשַׁע 2. *i*.

treacherously, to deal, בָּגַד.

tread, to, רָמַס.

tree, עֵץ 1; wood, *pl.*

tribe (sceptre).

trust, to, בָּטַח, בְּ; seek refuge in, חָסָה, בְּ; a place of refuge, מָנוֹס, מָעוֹז, מַחֲסֶה or מַחְסֶה (flee).

truth, steadfastness, אֱמֶת; with suffix, אֲמִתִּי, &c.

to try (as silver), בָּחַן, צָרַף; to try, prove, tempt, נסה, *Pi.*

turn, to, overturn, turn into, הָפַךְ; pass. *Niph.* (return).

turn aside, to, סוּר.

two, § 45; they two, both of them, שְׁנֵיהֶם, &c. § 45. 1c, iii; the second time, שֵׁנִית.

U

under (beneath).

understanding, שֶׂכֶל, בִּינָה 2 *i. m.*

undone, to be, דמה, *Niph.*

unless, לוּלֵא, לוּלֵי (usually perf.).

until, עַד, עָדֵי, &c. (till), § 16. 5.

unto, אֶל־, אֱלֵי, &c. § 16. 5.

upon, עַל; *suff.*, § 16. 5.

upright, יָשָׁר 1.

upwards, מַ֫עְלָה. See על in Lex.

Ur, אוּר.

utterance (of), נְאֻם (*constr.*).

V

vain, empty, רֵק, רֵיק; vanity, שָׁוְא, רִיק.

valley, בִּקְעָה 2, נַחַל 2, גַּיְא 2.

valour, חַיִל 2 (force). § 31.

vengeance, נְקָמָה 1 (avenge).

very, מְאֹד (prop. a noun).

vessel, כְּלִי, *pl.* כֵּלִים.

vine, גֶּפֶן 2.

vineyard, כֶּרֶם 2; vinedresser, כֹּרֵם 3.

violence, wrong, חָמָס 1.

virgin, בְּתוּלָה.

vision, מַרְאָה, *f.* (see) חָזוֹן.

visit, to (review), (oversee).

voice, קוֹל 2.

vow, to, נָדַר; a vow, נֶדֶר and נֵדֶר 2.

W

walk, to, *Hithp.* of הָלַךְ. § 23. 3b.

wall, חוֹמָה.

wander, to, wave, tremble, תָּעָה, נוּעַ; a wanderer, נָע, *ptc.*

war (fight).

wash, to, רָחַץ;—clothes, כִּבֵּס, *Pi.* § 23. 1a.

watch, to (keep).

water, waters, מַיִם, pl.

water, to (שקה, *Hiph.*), הִשְׁקָה used as causative of שתה, § 41.

way, manner, דֶּרֶךְ 2. *c.*

weak, דַּל § 40.

wealth, חַיִל 2 (force). § 31. 2.

weapon, כְּלִי 2, *pl.* כֵּלִים, *c.* כְּלֵי.

wear, to (put on).

weary, be, יָעֵף, *intrans.* § 29, יָגַע, § 29; weary, יָעֵף 1.

weep, to, בָּכָה. § 32, § 33 1 (1).

weigh, to, שָׁקַל, pass. *Niph.*

well, בְּאֵר 2. *f.*

west, יָם. § 40.

what, מָה. § 10. 3.

when, בְּ, כְּ with inf. cstr.; כַּאֲשֶׁר, כִּי with finite forms (§ 27. 8c).

when? how long? מָתַי, עַד מ׳.
whence, where, whither, § 10. 4.
whence? מֵאַיִן.
wherefore? מַדּוּעַ.
whether?, הֲ, § 46. 1; אִם (or), § 46. 3a.
whither? אָנָה
who, which, אֲשֶׁר. § 10. 4.
who? מִי. § 10. 3.
whoever, whosoever, מִי, § 10. 3.
whole (all).
why? wherefore? לָמָּה (מַדּוּעַ).
wicked, רָשָׁע 1; wickedness, רִשְׁעָה 2.
wife (woman).
wilderness (desert).
willing, to be, אָבָה. § 37.
wind (spirit).
wine, יַיִן 2. § 31.
wing, border, extremity, כָּנָף 1. *f. du.* (pl. *ôth*).
wise, be, חָכַם, (*intrans.*), impf. יֶחְכַּם; wise, חָכָם 1; wisdom, חָכְמָה 2.
wish, to, חָפֵץ, (*intrans.*).
with, prep. עִם; אֵת. § 40. See *suff.*, § 40. 6b; with *of instrument*, בְּ, § 12. 1f.
within (inside), (midst).
witness, עֵד 1, § 31 (testify).
woman, אִשָּׁה. § 42.
womb, בֶּטֶן 2. *i. f.*; רֶחֶם 2. *c.*
wonder (n.), פֶּלֶא 2. i.m.; נִפְלָא.
wood, timber (tree).
word, thing, matter, דָּבָר 1.
work, to (make).
write, to, כָּתַב; pass. *Niph.* (count).

Y

Yahweh (Jehovah), יהוה; perhaps יַהְוֶה; usually read אֲדֹנָי, § 15, Exer., note 1.
year, שָׁנָה 1, pl. *im* (*ôth* poet.); a yearling בֶּן־ שׁ׳; 20 years old = son of 20 years.
yoke, עֹל 4. § 40.
young, younger (little). § 44. 1;
youth, young man, נַעַר 2, *f.* נַעֲרָה. time of youth, נְעוּרִים.

Z

Zion, צִיּוֹן.

VOCABULARY

Hebrew and English

א

אָב *a father*; cstr. אֲבִי. See § 42.

אָבַד *to perish* (§ 37).—Impf. יֹאבַד —Hiph. הֶאֱבִיד *to destroy*.

אָבָה *to be willing* (§ 37).—Impf. יֹאבֶה.

אֲבִיגַ֫יִל *Abigail*.

אֶבְיוֹן *m. poor*.

אֲבִימֶ֫לֶךְ *Abimelech*.

אֶ֫בֶן 2 *f., a stone*.

אַבְרָהָם *Abraham*.

אַבְרָם *Abram*.

אָדָם 1 *m., man*.

אֲדָמָה 1 *f., the ground*.

אָדוֹן 1 *m., lord*.—Takes suff. of plur. noun. See *lord* in Eng.-Hebr. With prefix לַאדֹנִי &c.

אַדֶּ֫רֶת 2 *f., a mantle*. § 25. 3.

אָהֵב *to love*.—Impf. יֶאֱהַב (1 pers. also אֹהַב). § 35, 37.

אֲהָהּ *alas!*

אֹהֶל 2 *m., a tent*; pl. אֹהָלִים (but בָּאֳהָלִים is found).

אוֹ *or*.

אוה Pi., *Hithp., to desire, long for*.

אוּלָם *but* (a strong adversative), § 46. 3c.

אָ֫וֶן 2 *m., vanity, wickedness*. § 31.

אוֹר *to be light, shine*, (ע״ו) Perf. אוֹר. Hiph. הֵאִיר *to give light*. § 30.

אוֹר 2 *m., light*. § 31.

מָאוֹר 1 *m., a light, luminary*; pl. *îm* and *ôth*.

אוּר *Ur*.

אוֹת *m., pl. ôth*, sign, token.

אָז adv. *then*; cf. § 43. II. 1a.

אֹ֫זֶן 2 *f., an ear*. § 25.

אָח *m., a brother*. See § 42.

אֶחָד *m.*, אַחַת *f., one*. § 45.

אָחַז *to grasp, seize*. § 35.

אַחַר adv. *afterward*; prep. *after, behind*; oftener אַחֲרֵי.—אַחֲרַי *after me* &c., § 16. 5.

אַחֵר adj., *another*; pl. אֲחֵרִים,

אַחֲרִית *f., end, latter end*.

אֹיֵב 3 *m., an enemy*. § 26.

אֵיד 2 *m., calamity*. § 31.

אֵיךְ adv. *how? how!*

אַיִן (*where?*, not used); מֵאַיִן *whence?*

אַ֫יִן 2 (*nothing*), *there is not*; cstr. **אֵין**. Cf. § 31. 4, note 1.

אִישׁ *m.*, *a man*. See § 42.

אִשָּׁה *f.*, *a woman*. See § 42.

אָכַל *to eat* (פ״א, § 37).—Hiph. **הֶאֱכִיל** *to give to eat*.

אֹ֫כֶל 2 *m.*, *food*; **אָכְלָה** 2 *f.*, *id.*

מַאֲכָל 1 *m.*, *id.*

אַל adv. *no*, *not*, with *Juss.* § 20. 1, notes i, ii.

אֶל prep. *unto*. Suff. § 16. 5.

אֱלֹהִים *pl. m.*, *God* (Sing. **אֱלוֹהַ** used in poetry.) With prefix, **לֵאלֹהִים** &c., § 12. 1c, but **מֵאֱ׳**.

אֵלִיָּהוּ, אֵלִיָּה *Elijah*.

אֱלִישָׁע *Elisha*.

אֱלִיל *m.*, *an idol*.

אִלֵּם 3 adj., *dumb*.

אֶ֫לֶף 2, *thousand*.

אִם adv. *if*; **וְאִם** . . . **אִם**, *either* . . . *or*; **כִּי אִם** *except*, § 46. 3c; **אִם** *in oaths*, § 46. 3d.

אֵם 4 *f.*, *mother*. § 40.

אָמָה *maidservant*. § 42.

אָמַן *to be firm*.—Hiph. **הֶאֱמִין** *to believe*, **בְּ**, **לְ**.

אֱמֶת 2 *i. f.*, *truth* (contr. fr. **אֱמֶנֶת**). Suff. **אֲמִתּוֹ**.

אָמֵץ *to be strong* (*intrans.* § 19).—Pi. *to make strong*.

אָמַר *to say*, *to promise*, *intend*. § 37.

אָנָּא (particle of entreaty) *we* (*I*) *beseech you* (*thee*).

אָנָה *whither?*

אֲנִי pron. *I*. § 10.

אָסַף *to gather*.—Impf. **יֶאֱסֹף**, § 35; § 37. 1b.—Niph. *to assemble*.

אַף *m.*, *nose*, *anger*. — Du. **אַפַּיִם** *nostrils*, *face* (**אנף** *to breathe*, *be angry*). § 40. 4.

אֶפְרַ֫יִם *Ephraim*.

אֶצְבַּע *f.*, *finger*, *forefinger*.

אֵ֫צֶל 2, used as prep. *beside*; *beside me*, **אֶצְלִי**. § 35. 4b.

אַרְבַּע *four*; **אַרְבָּעִים** *forty*; § 45

אֲרוֹן *chest*, *ark*.

אֲרִי *m.*, *a lion*. § 33. 3.

אָרֵךְ *to be long*; Hiph. *to be long*, *to prolong*; **אֹ֫רֶךְ** 2 *m.*, *length*; **אָרֹךְ** (*f.* **אֲרֻכָּה**) *long*; **אֶ֫רֶךְ** (constr.) *long*, *slow*.

אֲרָם *Syria*.

אֶ֫רֶץ 2 *f.*, *earth*, *land*; pl. *ôth*.

אָרַר *to curse*.—Impf. **יָאֹר**. § 39.

אֵשׁ 4 *f.*, *fire*. § 40.

אֲשֶׁר rel. pron. *who*, *which*. § 10. 4.

אַשְׁרֵי cstr. *the happinesses of* (= *happy*!). See § 42, voc.

אֵת a particle placed before the definite object, § 9. 4. Suff. § 11. 6.

אֵת prep. *with*. Suff. § 40. 6b.

אַתָּה pron. *thou*. § 10.

אָתוֹן 1 *f*, *a she-ass*.

ב

בְּ prep. *in*, *on*, *among*; *by* of instrument. § 12. 1.

בְּאֵר 2 *f*., *a well*; pl. *ôth*.

בָּגַד *to deal treacherously*.

בֶּגֶד 2 *i*. *m*., *a garment*, *covering*.—Suff. בִּגְדוֹ (without *dag*. *l*.).

בַּד 2 *m*. (*separation*), לְבַד *apart*, *alone*; *I alone* אֲנִי לְבַדִּי. § 40.

בדל Qal not in use.—Hiph. *to separate*, *divide*.—Niph. *pass*.

בְּהֵמָה 2 *f*., *cattle*, *tame beasts*; cstr. בֶּהֱמַת, cstr. pl. בַּהֲמוֹת. § 42.

בּוֹא *to come*, *go*, *go in* (ל״א, ע״ו).—Impf. יָבוֹא.—Hiph. הֵבִיא *to bring*. Hoph. *pass*. §§ 30, 38.

בּוֹר 2 *m*., *a pit*; pl. *ôth*. § 31.

בּוֹשׁ *to be ashamed* (ע״ו § 30).—Impf. יֵבוֹשׁ.

בָּזַז *to plunder*, *spoil* (§ 39).—Impf. יָבֹז.

בָּחַר *to choose* (§ 36); *with* בְּ.

בָּחוּר *young man*.

בָּחִיר 1, *chosen*.

בָּטַח *to trust* (§ 36); *in*, בְּ; לָבֶטַח *securely*, *with confidence*.

בֶּטֶן 2 *i*. *f*., *womb*.

בֵּין 2 (*interval*), prep. *between*, *among*. Repeated before the second word and usually takes the numb. of its suff.—*between me and you* בֵּינִי וּבֵינֵיכֶם.—For בֵּין ... בֵּין also בֵּין ... לְ.

בִּינָה *f*. *understanding*. § 31.

בַּיִת 2 *m*., *a house*. § 42.

בֵּיתְאֵל *Bethel*.

בְּכֹר *firstborn*; בְּכֹרָה *birthright*.

בִּלְעָם *Balaam*.

בֵּן 3 *m*., *a son*. See § 42.

בָּנָה *to build*, apoc. impf. וַיִּבֶן. § 42. 1.

בַּת 2 *f*., *a daughter*. See § 42.

בְּעַד 2 prep. *behind*, *in at*, *out at*, ב׳ הַחַלּוֹן *in at*, *out at the window*: ב׳ הַחוֹמָה *over the wall*.—Suff. בַּעֲדִי § 36. 4a, iii.

בָּעַל *to marry*; ptc. pass. *f*. בְּעֻלָה *married*.

בַּעַל 2 *m*., *lord*, *husband*, *Baal*. Suff. § 36. 4a, iii.

בָּקַע *to cleave*, *break through*.

בִּקְעָה *valley*.

בֹּקֶר 2 *m*., *morning*.

בקשׁ Qal not in use. Pi. בִּקֵּשׁ *to seek*.

בָּרָא *to cut*, *fashion*, *to create* (§ 38).—Niph. *pass*.

בָּרָד 1, *hail*.

בָּרַח *to flee.* § 36.

בָּרִיא 1 adj. *fat.*

בְּרִית *f., a covenant*; כָּרַת בְּ׳ *to make a covenant*; הֵקִים בְּ׳ *to establish a covenant.*

בָּרַךְ *to kneel.*—Pi. בֵּרַךְ *to bless*; Pu. *pass.* (§ 36);—*blessed* בָּרוּךְ 1 ptc. Qal.

בֶּרֶךְ 2 *i. f., a knee,* du. בִּרְכַּיִם.

בְּרָכָה 1 *f., a blessing,* cstr. בִּרְכַּת, suff. בִּרְכָתִי. § 15. 2.

בָּשָׂר 1 *m., flesh.*

בְּתוּלָה 1, *virgin.*

ג

גָּאַל *to redeem.* § 36.

גָּבוֹהַּ 1, *high.*

גָּבַר *to be strong, prevail* (*intrans.* § 19).

גִּבּוֹר *m., a hero, mighty man.*

גְּבוּרָה *strength.*

גְּבִירָה, גְּבֶרֶת 2 *i. f., lady, mistress.* § 25. 3b.

גָּדַל *to be great, to grow* (*intrans.* § 19).—Pi. *to magnify, bring up* (a child).—Hithp. *to magnify oneself.*

גֹּדֶל 2 *m., greatness.*

גָּדוֹל 1 adj., *great, elder.*

גִּדְעוֹן *Gideon.*

גּוֹי *m., a nation.* Pl. גּוֹיִם, cstr. גּוֹיֵי *the gentiles.*

גּוּר *to sojourn*; *Hithpoʿlel to seek hospitality.*

גּוֹרָל 1 *m., lot*; pl. *ôth.*

גִּיל 2 *m., joy.* § 31.

גָּלָה *to uncover, reveal* (ל״ה § 32).—Niph. *pass.*—Hithp. *to uncover oneself.*

גָּלַל *to roll* (§ 39).—Impf. יָגֹל.—Hiph. הֵגֵל *to roll.* Niph. נָגֹל *to be rolled, to roll up* (or *along*).

גַּם adv. *also*; גַּם . . . גַּם *both . . . and.* § 46. 3a.

גָּמַל *to wean*; *to deal fully, adequately with*; *recompense.* Niph. *to be weaned.*

גָּמָל (pl. גְּמַלִּים) *camel.* § 40. 5.

גַּן *c., garden.* § 40.

גָּנַב *to steal.*—Pi. *id.*—Pu. *pass.*

גֵּר 1 *m., a sojourner.* § 31.

גֹּרֶן 2 *m., threshing-floor.*

גָּרַשׁ *to drive out* (§ 36); oftener Pi. —Niph. *pass.*

גַּת *Gath.*

ד

דְּבוֹרָה *Deborah* (= bee).

דָּבֵק *to cleave* (*intrans.* § 19); *to* בְּ.

דבר Qal not in use except Act.

ptc. דֹּבֵר *speaking*.—Pi. דִּבֶּר *to speak*.—Pu. *pass*.

דָּבָר 1 *m., a word, thing.*

דְּבַשׁ *honey*, 2 *m.*, with suff. דִּבְשִׁי &c.

דָּג 1 *m., a fish*; coll. דָּגָה.

דָּוִד, דָּוִיד *David.*

דּוֹר 2 *m., generation*; pl. *îm.* and *ôth.* § 31.

דַּל *poor, lowly.* § 40.

דֶּלֶת 2 *f., a door* (door-leaf); du. דְּלָתַיִם.

דָּם 1 *m., blood, your blood* דִּמְכֶם. דָּמִים *blood* spilt, *acts of bloodshed.* § 15. 3.

דָּמָה *to destroy*; Niph. *to be undone.*

דָּמַם *to be silent.* Impf. יִדֹּם. § 39.

דָּנִאֵל (later) דָּנִיֵּאל Daniel.

דַּעַת see ידע.

דָּרַךְ *to tread.*

דֶּרֶךְ 2 *c., a way.*

דָּרַשׁ *to seek*; *unto* אֶל.

דֶּשֶׁא 2 *m.* (young) *grass.*

ה

הַ art., *the.* § 8.

הֲ particle of interrogation. § 46. 1.

הֲלֹא *not?*

הָדָר 1 *m., honour, majesty.*

הוּא pron. § 10.

הוֹד *m., glory, splendour.*

הָיָה *to be* (§ 33. 2).—Impf. יִהְיֶה, apoc. יְהִי.—Inf. *cstr.* הֱיוֹת, לִהְיוֹת &c.

הֵיכָל 1 *m, palace, temple.*

הַכּוֹת. See נכה.

הֲלֹם adv., *hither.*

הָלַךְ *to go.*—Impf. יֵלֵךְ.—Hiph. הוֹלִיךְ (see § 29. 2. 2b).—Hithp. הִתְהַלֵּךְ *to walk, go about.* § 23. 3b.

הֵן, הִנֵּה adv. *behold, lo*! Suff. § 40. 6b.—Followed chiefly by the ptc. הִנְנִי מֵבִיא *behold I* (do, will) *bring.*

הֵנָּה *here.*

הָפַךְ *to turn, to change into* (§ 35) —Niph. נֶהְפַּךְ *pass.*

הַר *m. hill, mountain.* § 40.

הָרַג *to kill, slay* (§ 35).—Niph. *pass.*

הָרָה *to conceive* (§ 32 f.) —Impf. 3 *s. f.* with waw cons. וַתַּהַר. § 33. 1a.

וְ conj., *and.* § 11.

ז

זָבַח *to sacrifice, slaughter.* § 36.

זֶבַח 2 *m., a sacrifice.*

מִזְבֵּחַ 3 *m., an altar*; pl. *ôth.* § 26.

זֶה *f.* זֹאת dem. pron. *this.* § 10.

זָהָב 1 *m., gold.*

זַ֫יִת 2 *m., an olive.* § 31.

זָכַר *to remember.*—Niph. *pass.*—Hiph. *to mention, commemorate.*

זֵ֫כֶר 2 *m., memory, memorial.*

זִכָּרוֹן *memorial.*

זָכָר 1 *m., a male.*

זָעַק *to cry out.* § 36.

זָקֵן *to be old* (*intrans.* § 19).

זָקֵן 1 adj. *old;* noun *elder.* § 15.

זְקֻנִים *m.,* זִקְנָה *f., old age.*

זְרוֹעַ *f., an arm;* pl. *îm, ôth.*

זָרַח *to shine, rise* (of star). § 36.

זָרַע *to sow* (§ 36).—Hiph. הִזְרִיעַ *to yield seed.*

זֶ֫רַע 2 *m., seed;* cstr. זֶרַע and זְרַע.

ח

חֶבֶל 2 *m., cord.*

חָבַק Qal, Piʿel, *to embrace.*

חָבַשׁ *to bind, bind up, saddle* (§ 35).

חָגַג *to keep a feast* (§ 39).—Impf. יָחֹג.

חַג 4 *m., a feast* (hajj), § 40. 2a.

חָדַל *to cease, leave off* (*intrans.* § 19).

חָדָשׁ 1 adj., *new.*

חֹדֶשׁ 2 *m., new moon, month.* § 35.

חוּד *to propound a riddle.* § 30.

חוֹל 2 *m., sand.* § 31.

חוֹמָה *f., a wall.*

חוּץ 2 *m., outside, street, field;* pl. *ôth.*—הַחוּצָה *to the outside.*—מִחוּץ לְ *on the outside of* —.

חָזַק *to be strong* (*intrans.* §§ 19, 35); Hiph. *to strengthen, to harden, to lay firm hold of.*

חָזָק 1 adj., *strong.*

חָטָא *to sin* (§ 35).—Hiph. הֶחֱטִיא *to condemn as sinful.*

חֹטֵא 3 (ptc.), *a sinner,* used in sing., but חַטָּא adj. used in pl.

חֵטְא 2 *m.,* חַטָּאת *sin.* § 38. 2.

חָיָה *to live* (§ 33. 2).

חַי *to live* (§ 39. § 20. Ex. n. 3).

חַי 1 adj., *living, f.* חַיָּה, § 40. In oaths חַי is used of God, and חֵי (cstr. or perhaps a contracted abs.) of men: e.g. חַי יהוה וְחֵי נַפְשְׁךָ *as J. liveth and as thy soul* (= thou) *liveth.*

חִידָה *f., a riddle.*

חַיָּה *f., a living creature, beast.*

חַיִּים *life.*

חַ֫יִל 2 *m., force, valour, power, army, wealth.* § 31.

חֵ֫יק 2 *m., bosom.* § 31.

חָכַם (*intrans.*) *to be wise.*

חָכָם 1 adj., *wise.* § 35.

חָכְמָה 2 *f., wisdom.* § 25.

חֵלֶב *m., fat.*

חָלָה *to be sick* (§§ 32 f, 35).—

Impf. with waw cons. וַיָּ֫חֶל.

חֳלִי 2 *m., sickness, disease.* § 33.

חָלִ֫ילָה *God forbid.* § 46. 4.

חלל—Hiph. הֵחֵל *to begin* (§ 39).

—Hoph. הוּחַל *pass.*

חָלָל 1, *slain.*

חָלַם *to dream* (§ 35).

חֲלוֹם *m., a dream*; pl. *ôth.*

חָמַד *to desire* (*intrans.* § 19).—

Impf. יַחְמֹד, (יֶחְמַד).—Niph.

נֶחְמַד *pass.*

חֲמוֹר *m., an ass.*

חָמוֹת *mother-in-law.*

חָמָס 1 *m., violence, injury.* § 35.

חֲנִית *spear.*

חָנַן *to pity* (§ 39).—Impf. יָחֹן.

חֵן 4, *grace, favour.*

חַנּוּן *gracious, compassionate.*

תְּחִנָּה, תַּחֲנוּנִים *supplication(s).*

חֶסֶד 2 *m., mercy, love, devotion.*

חָסָה *to seek refuge, to trust.*

חָסֵר (intrans) to *lack, to be deficient.*

חָפֵץ *to desire, wish* (*intrans.* §§ 19, 35).—Impf. יַחְפֹּץ, יֶחְפַּץ.

חָפֵץ 1 adj., *desiring,* § 35, cstr. pl. חֲפֵצֵי, see § 19. 5.

חֵפֶץ 2 *m., pleasure, business.*

חֵץ *arrow.* § 40.

חָצֵר 1 *c., enclosure, court, village*; pl. *îm, ôth.* § 35.

חֹק 4 *m., statute.* § 40.

חָרֵב *to dry up, be waste* (*intrans.* § 19).

חֶרֶב 2 *f., sword.*

חֹרֵב *Horeb.*

חָרָה *to be hot, angry.*—Impf. apoc. וַיִּ֫חַר. § 33. 1.

חֶרְפָּה 2 *f., a reproach.*

חָשַׁב *to think, reckon.*—Impf. יַחְשֹׁב and יַחֲ׳. § 35. 2b.

חֹ֫שֶׁךְ 2 *m., darkness.*

ט

טָהֵר *to be clean* (*intrans.* §§ 19, 36).—Pi. טִהַר *to cleanse.*

טָהוֹר 1 adj., *clean.*

טוֹב *to be good* (§ 30).—Perf. טוֹב. Other parts from יטב.—Impf. יִיטַב.—Hiph. הֵיטִיב. § 29. 1.

טוֹב 1 adj., *good.* § 31.

טוּב 2 *m., good things, goods, goodness.* § 31.

טַל *m., dew.*

טָמַן *to hide, to bury in the ground.*

טָעַם *to taste* (§ 36).

טַ֫עַם 2 *m., taste, sense.* § 36. 2.

טֶ֫רֶם *not yet,* בְּטֶ֫רֶם *before.* § 43. II. 1a.

י

יְאֹר *m., stream* (esp. Nile).

יָבֵשׁ *to be dry* (*intrans.* §§ 19, 29).

יַבָּשָׁה 1 *f., dry land.*

יָגַע *to be weary* (§ 29).

יָד 1 *f., hand. Your hand* יֶדְכֶם; du. יָדַיִם, pl. יָדוֹת *hands* fig. (handles). § 13. 6.

יָדַע *to know, to care for* (פ״ו § 29). —Impf. יֵדַע.—Inf. Cstr. דַּעַת. Niph. נוֹדַע *pass.*—Hiph. הוֹדִיעַ *to make known.*

יְהוָֹה *Jahweh.* The vowels are those of אֲדֹנָי *lord.* With prefix לַיהוָֹה (i.e. לַאדֹנָי). See § 15. Ex. note 1.

יְהוּדָה *Judah.*

יְהוֹנָתָן *Jonathan.*

יוֹם 2 *m., a day.* See § 42.

יוֹנָתָן *Jonathan.*

יוֹסֵף *Joseph.*

יַחַד, יַחְדָּו *together.*

יטב see טוב.

יַיִן 2 *m., wine.* § 31.

יָכֹל *to be able* (§ 29).—Impf. יוּכַל.

יָלַד *to bear* (פ״ו § 29).—Impf. יֵלֵד.—Hiph. *to beget.*—Pu. *to be born.*

יֶלֶד 2 *m., a boy.* § 25.

יַלְדָּה 2 *f., a girl.*

מוֹלֶדֶת 2 *f., kindred.* § 25. 2.

יָם 4 *m., sea;* cstr. יָם except in יַם־סוּף *Red sea.* § 40.

יָנַק *to suck* (פ״י § 29).—Hiph. הֵינִיק *to give suck;* hence מֵינֶקֶת 2 *f., a nurse.* § 25. 2.

יָסַף Qal, and Hiph. הוֹסִיף, *to add* (פ״ו § 29. 4).

יָעֵף *to be weary.*—Impf. יִיעַף. § 29. 2. 2a.

יָעֵף 1 adj., *weary.*

יַעֲקֹב *Jacob.*

יָעַץ *to advise, counsel* (§ 29).—Impf. יִיעַץ.—Niph. נוֹעַץ.

עֵצָה 1 *f., counsel.*

יָפֶה 1 adj., *fair.* § 33.

יָצָא *to go out* (פ״ו § 29).—Impf. יֵצֵא; inf. cstr. צֵאת (for צֶאֶת). —Hiph. *to bring out.*

מוֹצָא 1 *m., an outgoing.* § 29, 38.

יצג Hiph. הִצִּיג *to set, place.* (§ 29. 3).

יצע Hiph. הִצִּיעַ *to spread* (§ 29. 3).

יָצַר *to form* (§ 29).

יֵצֶר 2 *m., form, imagination.*

יֶקֶב 2 *m., wine-vat.*

יָקַד *to burn.*—Impf. יִיקַד, יֵקַד.—Hoph. *pass.* הוּקַד. § 29. 2.

יקץ Qal only in Impf. יִיקַץ *to awake* (§ 29).—Perf. &c. in Hiph. הֵקִיץ.

יָרֵא *to fear* (§ 29).—Impf. יִירָא. Inf. cstr. יִרְאָה.—Niph. נוֹרָא; ptc. *terrible.* Followed by מִן, מִפְּנֵי, and פֶּן־.

יָרֵא 1 adj. *fearing.*

יָרָבְעָם *Jeroboam.*

יָרַד *to go down* (§ 29. 2. 2b).—Impf. יֵרֵד &c.—Hiph. הוֹרִיד *to bring down.*—Hoph. *pass.*

הַיַּרְדֵּן *the Jordan.*

יְרוּשָׁלַםִ *Jerusalem.* See § 25. Voc., note 4.

יָרֵחַ 1 *m., a moon.*

יָרַשׁ *to inherit* (§ 29. 2).—Hiph. הוֹרִישׁ *to dispossess, destroy.* Niph. *pass.*

יִשְׂרָאֵל *Israel.*

יֵשׁ *there is—There is water* י״ מַיִם. See § 29. 4. Ex. note 4.

יָשַׁב *to sit, dwell, inhabit* (§ 29. 2).—Impf. יֵשֵׁב.

יֹשֵׁב 3 ptc., *inhabitant.*

מוֹשָׁב 1 *m., a seat, assembly, dwelling-place.*

יָשֵׁן *to sleep* (§ 29).—Impf. יִישַׁן.

ישׁע Qal not in use.—Hiph. הוֹשִׁיעַ *to save.*—Niph. *pass.* § 29. 2.

יֵשַׁע 2 *m., salvation.*

יְשׁוּעָה *f., id.*

תְּשׁוּעָה *f., id.*

יָשָׁר 1 adj., *upright, righteous.*

יֶ֫תֶר 2 *i., remnant, rest.*

כ

כְּ prep. *as, like.* § 12. Suff. § 12. 1f. With rel. כַּאֲשֶׁר *as, when. When he kept* כַּאֲשֶׁר שָׁמַר, *or* כְּשָׁמְרוֹ (inf. cstr. § 27. 8c).

כָּבֵד *to be heavy, severe* (*intrans.* § 19).—Pi. *to make heavy, harden, honour.*—Niph. *be honoured.*

כָּבֵד 1 adj., *heavy, severe, laden* (cstr. כְּבַד and כֶּבֶד; § 15. 1).

כָּבוֹד 1 *m., honour, glory.*

כֶּ֫בֶשׂ 2 *m., lamb.*

כִּבְשָׂה 2 *f., ewe-lamb.*

כֹּה adv. *thus.*

כֹּהֵן 3 *m., a priest.* § 37.

כּוֹכָב 1 *m., a star.*

כון Qal not in use.—Hiph. הֵכִין *to set, establish.*—Poʿlel כּוֹנֵן *id.*—Niph., Poʿlal, *pass.* § 30.

כּוֹס *f. cup, goblet.*

כֹּחַ *strength.*

כִּי conj., *that, for, because*; of time *when, whenever.* כִּי אִם *except.*

כִּכָּר 1, *talent* (currency).

כֶּ֫לֶא 2 *i. m., a prison.* § 38.

כֶּ֫לֶב 2 *m., a dog.*

כָּלָה *to be ended* (§ 32).—Pi. *to complete, finish.*—Pu. *pass.*

כֹּל 4 *m., all.* § 40. כָּל־דָּבָר *everything*; לֹא ... כָּל־דָּבָר *nothing.*

כַּמָּה *how much?*

כֵּן adv., *so, thus.* עַל־כֵּן *therefore.*

כְּנַעֲנִי *Canaanite.*

כָּנָף 1, *wing, skirt.*

כִּסֵּא (pl. כִּסְאוֹת) *throne.*

כָּסָה *to cover* (§ 32), Qal only in ptc. act. כֹּסֶה and pass. כָּסוּי. —Pi. כִּסָּה *to cover.*—Pu. *pass.*

מִכְסֶה 1 *m., a covering.* § 33.

כֶּסֶף 2 *m., silver, money.*

כַּף 4 *f., palm of hand, sole;* du. § 40. Pl. *ôth* (metaphorical) § 13. 6.

כָּפַר *to cover* (with pitch).—Pi. כִּפֶּר *to atone.*—Pu. *pass.*

כֹּ֫פֶר 2 *m., bribe, ransom.*

כְּפִיר *m., young lion.*

כְּרוּב *m., cherub.*

כֶּ֫רֶם 2 *m., vineyard.*

כַּרְמֶל *Carmel.*

כָּרַע *to bend the knee, bow down* (§ 36).

כָּרַת *to cut off, cut down.* — Niph. *pass.*; כ׳ בְּרִית *to make a covenant.*

כַּשְׂדִּים *Chaldeans.*

כָּתַב *to write.*—Niph. *pass.*

כָּתֵף 1 *f., shoulder;* cst. כֶּתֶף. § 15. 1.

ל

לְ prep., *to, for.* See §§ 12. 1; 22. 5; 26. 3.

לֹא adv., *not, no.* §§ 9. 3; 10. 1 n. ii.

לֵב *m., heart,* § 40. Pl. *ôth.*

לֵבָב 1 *m., id.* Pl. *ôth.*

לְבַד *alone.* See בַּד.

לָבַשׁ *to put on* (clothes), *wear* (*intrans.* § 19); *acc.*—Hiph. *to clothe, put on* (another); *two acc.* § 24. 1d, § 38. 6.

לוּ, לוּא *if, would that;* לוּלֵא *if not.* § 46. 3a.

לוּחַ *m., tablet;* pl. לוּחֹת.

לוֹט *Lot.*

לחם Niph. *to fight. With* עִם. *against* בְּ, עַל; *for* לְ. § 36.

לֶחֶם 2 *c., bread.* § 36. 2. 3.

מִלְחָמָה, cstr. מִלְחֶ֫מֶת *f., war.* § 25. 3.

לַ֫יִל usually לַ֫יְלָה with *He* of *acc.*, 2 *m., night.* Pl. לֵילוֹת § 31;

לָכַד *to take, capture.* — Niph. *pass.*

לָמַד *to learn* (*intrans.* § 19).— Pi. לִמַּד *to teach.*

לָ֫מָּה adv., *why*? (מָה, לְ).

לְמַ֫עַן conj., prep., *in order that, to; for the sake of,* with *infin.* and *impf.* (ענה). § 20. 5a.

לָקַח *to take* (§ 34. 3).—Impf. יִקַּח.—Inf. Cstr. קַחַת—Niph. נִלְקַח *pass.*—(Old) pass. Qal *pf.* לֻקַּח, *impf.* יֻקַּח. § 34. 3c.

לָשׁוֹן 1 *f., tongue.*

מ

מְאֹד adv., *very*; also עַד מ׳, בִּמְאֹד.

מֵאָה 1 *f., hundred*; du. מָאתַ֫יִם.

מְאוּמָה *anything* (perhaps = *a fleck*), used after a neg.

מֵאַיִן *whence?*

מָאוֹר. See אוֹר.

מַאֲכָל. See אָכַל.

מָאַס *to reject* (§ 37).

מַבּוּל *m., the flood (of Noah).*

מִדְבָּר 1 *m., pasture, desert.*

מָדַד *to measure* (§ 39).—Impf. יָמֹד—Niph. *pass.*

מִדָּה *f., measure*; § 40.

מַדּוּעַ *wherefore?*

מָה pron. *what? whatever*, § 10; interj. *how! how?*

מהר *Piʿel to hasten.*

מוֹלֶדֶת. See יָלַד.

מוֹצָא. See יָצָא.

מוֹשָׁב. See יָשַׁב.

מוּת *to die* (§ 30). Perf. מֵת.—Impf. יָמוּת.—Hiph. הֵמִית *to kill.*—Poʿlel מוֹתֵת *id.*—Hoph. *pass.*

מֵת 1 ptc., *dead, dying.*

מָתַי *when?*

מָ֫וֶת 2 *m., death* (§ 31).

מִזְבֵּחַ. See זָבַח.

מָחָה *to blot out, destroy* (§ 32).

מְחִיר *price, hire.*

מַחֲנֶה *camp.*

מָחָר 1, *to morrow.*

מַחֲשָׁבָה (cstr. מַחֲשֶׁבֶת) *thought, plan.* § 25. 4.

מִטָּה. See נָטָה.

מטר Qal not in use.—Hiph. *to rain.*

מָטָר 1 *m., rain.*

מִי, מָה pron. *who? whoever, whosoever; what? whatsoever.* § 10. With prep. בַּמֶּה *how? by what?* (בַּמָּה in *p.* and bef. א).—מִי יִתֵּן *Oh that!* with Impf. &c. § 46. 3b.

מַ֫יִם pl. *m., water.* See § 13. 6e.

מֵינֶ֫קֶת. See יָנַק.

מִישׁוֹר *a plain; uprightness.*

מִכְסֶה. See כסה.

מָכַר *to sell.*—Niph. *pass.*

מָלֵא *to be full* (*intrans.* § 19, 39); *of*, acc.—Niph. *to be filled.*—Pi. *to fill*; with *two acc.* § 38. 6.

מָלֵא 1 adj., *full.*

מַלְאָךְ 1 *m., angel, messenger.*

מְלָאכָה *f., work*; cstr. מְלֶאכֶת. § 25. 3.

מלט Qal not in use.—Niph. *to escape.*—Pi. *to rescue, deliver.*

מִלְחָמָה. See לָחַם.

מָלַךְ *to rule, be king; over,* בְּ, עַל.—Hiph. *to make one king.*—Hoph. *pass.*

מֶ֫לֶךְ 2 *m., a king.*

מַלְכָּה 2 *f., a queen.*

מְלוּכָה 1, *rule, kingship.*

מַמְלָכָה, מַמְלֶכֶת *a kingdom.* § 25. 3.

מִן prep. (§ 12. 3, 4), *out of, from, away from*; hence of cause *by, on account of*. Compar. degree § 44.

מָנָה *to count, number,* § 32.—Niph. *pass.*

מִנְחָה 2 *f., an offering, present.*

מְנַשֶּׁה *Manasseh.*

מַסָּע *a journeying* (from נָסַע). § 34. 4.

מִסְפֵּד 3 *m., mourning.* § 26.

מִסְפָּר. See סָפַר.

מַעֲבָר. See עָבַר.

מְעַט 2 *m., a little, some, a few.*

מַעְלָה *upwards.* See § 44, Voc.

מַעֲלָל 2 *m., deed, practice* (only in plur., and usually in bad sense).

מַעֲשֶׂה. See עָשָׂה.

מָצָא *to find* (§ 38).—Niph. *pass.*

מִצְוָה. See צִוָּה.

מִצְרַיִם *Egypt*; מִצְרִי *Egyptian.*

מָקוֹם. See קוּם.

מַרְאֶה. See רָאָה.

מִרְמָה *f., deceit, guile.*

מָרַר *to be bitter* (§ 39. 3).—Impf. יֵמַר.—Hiph. הֵמַר *to make bitter.*

מַר adj., *bitter*; מָרָא Aramaic form of *fem.* מָרָה.

מְרִיבָה. See רִיב.

מִרְיָם *Miriam.*

מֹשֶׁה *Moses.*

מִשְׁכָּן. See שָׁכַן.

מָשַׁל *to rule; over,* בְּ.

מָשָׁל 1 *m., a proverb.*

מִשְׁמָר. See שָׁמַר.

מִשְׁפָּט. See שָׁפַט.

מִשְׁפָּחָה 2 *f., clan,* § 25. 3.

מָתַי *when?*

מַתָּן 1, *gift* (see נָתַן).

מָתֹק *to be sweet* (*intrans.* § 19).

מָתוֹק 1 adj., *sweet*; *f.* מְתוּקָה. § 31. 1.

נ

נָא enclitic particle of entreaty; אַל־נָא dissuasive.

נְאֻם (cstr.) *utterance.*

נבא Qal not in use (§ 38).—Niph. *to prophesy.*—Hithp. *id.*; also *to act like an (ecstatic) prophet, to rave.*

נָבִיא 1 *m., a prophet.*

נבט Qal not in use (§ 34).—Hiph. הִבִּיט *to look.*

נְבֵלָה 1 *f., a corpse, carcase.*

נגד Qal not in use (§ 34).—Hiph. הִגִּיד *to tell, shew.*—Hoph. *pass.*

נֶגֶד 2 prep., *before, in presence of.* Suff. נֶגְדִּי.

נָגַע *to touch, smite* (§ 34, 36).—Pi. *id.*—Hiph. *make to touch, reach to,* בְּ.

נֶגַע 2 *i. m., a stroke, plague.*

נָגַף *to smite, defeat* (§ 34).—Impf. יִגֹּף.—Niph. *pass.*

נגשׁ Perf. Qal not in use.—Impf. יִגַּשׁ —Perf. in use Niph. נִגַּשׁ *to draw near.*—Hiph. *to bring near* (§ 34).

נָדַר *to vow* (§ 34).

נֶדֶר, נֵדֶר 2 *m., a vow.*

נָהָר 1 *m., a river* (§ 36). (pl. *îm* and *ôth*).

נוּחַ *to rest* (§ 30).—Hiph. הֵנִיחַ *to give rest to* (לְ of person); and הִנִּיחַ *to set down, deposit, place*; with *waw* וַתַּנַּח.

מָנוֹחַ 1 *m., resting-place.* § 31.

נוּס *to flee* (§ 30).

נוּעַ *to move about* (§ 30); ptc. נָע *a wanderer.*

נֹחַ *Noah.*

נָחַל *to inherit, possess.*—Hiph. *to give to inherit.* —Hoph. *pass.*

נַחֲלָה *f., inheritance.*

נַ֫חַל 2 *m., torrent, torrent-valley, wady.*

נחם Qal not in use.—Niph. נִחַם *to repent, to pity* (§ 34. 1d). —Pi. נִחַם *to comfort* (§ 36).

נָחָשׁ 1 *m., a serpent.*

נָטָה *to bend, incline, stretch* (§ 32, 34).—Impf. יִטֶּה, apoc. יֵט.—Hiph. *id.* הִטָּה, impf. יַטֶּה, apoc. יַט.

מִטָּה *f., a bed.*

נָטַע *to plant* (§ 34, 36).—Impf. יִטַּע.

נָטַשׁ *to leave, to forsake.* § 34.

נכה Qal not in use (§ 32, 34). —Hiph. הִכָּה, *to smite*; impf. apoc. יַךְ.—Hoph. *pass.*

מַכָּה *f., a stroke.*

נֶסֶךְ 2 *i. m., a drink-offering.*

נָסַע *to strike camp, to journey.*

נָע. See נוּעַ.

נַעַל 2 *f.*, sandal, shoe. § 36. 4.

נַ֫עַר 2 *m., a lad,* § 36. 4; *f.* נַעֲרָה *a girl.*

נָפַל *to fall* (§ 34). Impf. יִפֹּל.—Hiph. הִפִּיל *to make fall, cast.*

נֶפֶשׁ 2 *f., breath, soul.* Pl. *ôth.*

נצב Qal not in use. (§ 34).—Hiph. הִצִּיב *to set, place.*—Hoph. *pass.*—Niph. *reflex.* and *pass.*

נצל Qal not in use (§ 34).—Hiph. הִצִּיל *to deliver.*—Hoph. *pass.*

נָקִי, (very rarely נָקִיא) 1 adj., *innocent.*

נְקָמָה 1 *f., vengeance.*

נֵר *m., lamp.*

נשא Qal not in use (§§ 34, 38).

—Hiph. הִשִּׁיא *to deceive, beguile.*

נָשַׁק *to kiss* (§ 34).—Impf. יִשַּׁק (לְ of person).

נָשָׂא *to lift up, take up, raise* (§§ 34, 38). Impf. יִשָּׂא. Inf. cstr. שְׂאֵת (לָשֵׂאת). Niph. *pass.*

נָשִׂיא 1, *prince.*

נָתַן *to give, put, account* (34.3a). Perf. נָתַתָּ, נָתַ֫תִּי &c. Impf. יִתֵּן Inf. cstr. תֵּת, תִּתִּי, &c.

ס

סָבַב *to turn, turn away* (§ 39). —Hiph. *to turn* (act.).

סָגַר *to shut.*—Niph. *pass.*

סוּס 2 *m., a horse*; סוּסָה *f. mare.*

סוּר *to turn aside, remove, depart* (§ 30).—Hiph. *to remove, take away.*

סכן Hiph. *to be accustomed, to show a habit.*

סֻלָּם 1 *m., a ladder.*

סָמַךְ *to lean, press upon.*—Niph. *reflex. to lean.*

סָעַד *to sustain, refresh* (§ 36).

סָפַר *to count, write.*—Pi. סִפֵּר *to recount, declare.*

סֹפֵר 3 *m.*, ptc. *scribe.*

סֵ֫פֶר 2 *m., a book.*

מִסְפָּר 1 *m., number.*

סָתַר chiefly in Hiph. *to hide.*—Niph. *reflex.* and *pass.*, Hithp. *reflex.*

ע

עָבַד *to labour, till, serve* (§ 35). Niph. *pass.*

עֶבֶד 2 *m., a servant* (§ 35).

עֲבֹדָה *service.*

עָבַר *to pass, pass over, cross* (§ 35). —Hiph. *to bring over, make pass.*

עֵבֶר 2 *m., the other side*; בְּעֵבֶר *beyond.*

(מַעֲבָר) 1, *m., a ford* (only in cstr. מַעֲבַר).

עֲבוּר 1 *m.*, cstr., with בְּ as prep. *on account of*; בַּעֲבוּרִי *for my sake.*

עֵגֶל 2 *m.*, and עֶגְלָה 2 *f., calf, heifer* (§ 35).

עוד Hiph., הֵעִיד *to testify, bear witness, protest* (§ 30).

עֵד 1 *m., a witness.*

עַד prep. *until, till.* Suff. § 16. 5.

עֵדֶן *Eden.*

עֵדֶר 2 *m., flock, herd.*

עוֹד adv., *still, again* (encore). § 31. 5.

עוז Hiph. *to bring into safety.*

מָעוֹז *a refuge.*

עָוֹן 1 *m., guilt, sin, punishment.* Pl. *ôth.*

עוֹלָם 1 *m., age, eternity*; מֵעוֹלָם *from of old*; עַד ע׳, לְע׳ *for ever.*

עוּף *to fly* (§ 30).

עוֹף 2 *m., a bird, fowl.*

עור Po'lel *to incite, to wield.*

עִוֵּר 3 adj., *blind.*

עֵז *f., she-goat,* pl. עִזִּים. § 40. 4.

עֹז 4 *m., strength* (§ 40).

עַז *strong.* § 40.

עָזַב *to leave, forsake* (§ 35).—Niph. *pass.*

עָזַר *to help* (§ 35).

עֵזֶר 2 *m., help.* Suff. עֶזְרִי. § 35. 4b.

עֶזְרָה 2 *f., help.*

עטר Pi'el, *to crown.*

עֲטָרָה *f.,* cstr. עֲטֶרֶת *crown.*

עַיִן 2 *f., an eye,* du. עֵינַיִם. § 31. Pl. עֲיָנוֹת *wells.* [cf. § 42.

עִיר 2 *f., a city.* Pl. עָרִים, cstr. עָרֵי;

עָלָה *to go up, break* (of day) (§ 32, 35).—Impf. יַעֲלֶה, apoc. יַ֫עַל.—Hiph. *bring up, offer up.*

עֹלָה (עוֹלָה) *burnt-offering, whole-offering.*

עַל prep., *upon, over.* Suff. § 16. 5.

עֹל *yoke.* § 40.

עלל Po'el *to act severely or wantonly*; Hithpo'el, *to deal severely or wantonly.*

עִם prep., *with, along with.* Suff. §§ 40. 6b.

עַם 4 *m , people.* § 40.

עָמַד *to stand* (§ 35).—Hiph. *set, place.*

עָנָה *to be low, afflicted* (§ 32).—Pi. *to afflict.*

עֳנִי 2 *m., affliction.* § 33.

עָנָה *to answer, witness* (§ 32); *against* בְּ.

מַעֲנֶה *m., answer*; מַ֫עַן *purpose, intent*; used only with לְ in לְמַ֫עַן (i) as prep., *on account of, for the sake of*; (ii) as conj. followed by (a) inf. cstr., *to the intent that, in order to,* or (b) impf., with or without אֲשֶׁר, *to the intent that, in order that.* § 20. 5a.

עָפָר 1 *m., dust.* § 35.

עֵץ 1 *m., tree.* § 15. 3.

עֵצָה. See יָעַץ.

עָצַם *to become strong, numerous.*

עֶצֶם 2 *f., a bone.* Pl. *îm, ô<u>th</u>.*

עֶרֶב 2 *m., evening.*

עָרַךְ *to arrange, to set in order.*

עֲרֵמָה 1, *a heap* (as of grain).

עָרוּם *clever, cunning.*

עָשִׁיר *rich.*

עָשַׁן *to smoke* (§ 35).

עָשַׁק *to oppress, to injure* (§ 35).

עֵשֶׂב 2, *grass.*

עָשָׂה *to do, work, make* (§ 32, 35).—Impf. apoc. יַ֫עַשׂ—Niph.

נַעֲשָׂה *pass.*, but *fem.* נֶעֶשְׂתָה.

מַעֲשֶׂה *m., a work.* § 33.

עֵת *c., time.* Pl. *îm., ôth.* § 40. 4.

עַתָּה adv., *now.*

עָתַר Qal and Hiph. *to pray, entreat.*

פ

פָּגַע *to meet, to encounter*; Hiph. *to cause to light upon, to interpose.*

פֶּה *m., mouth.* See § 42.

עַל־פִּי *according to.* See § 29.

Voc. לְפִי חֶרֶב *with the edge of the sword, utterly.*

פֹּה *here.*

פַּח *m., snare.* § 40.

פֶּלֶא 2 *i. m., a wonder.*

פְּלִשְׁתִּים *Philistines.*

פָּנָה *to turn.*

פָּנִים 1 *m.,* pl. *face, faces.* לְפָנִים *formerly,* לִפְנֵי *before,* לְפָנַי *before me*; § 16. 4a.

פֶּן־ conj., *lest,* with *impf.*

פָּסַח *to pass over*; פֶּסַח 2, *Passover.*

פָּעַל *to do* (§ 36); ptc. פֹּעֵל *a worker.*

פֹּעַל 2 *m., a work.* § 36.

פַּעַם 2. *step, time* (*fois*).

פָּקַד *to visit, inspect, review.*—Niph. *pass.*—Hiph. *to commit to*; פָּקַד עַל *to punish.*

פָּקִיד 1 *m., an overseer.*

פַּר 4 *m., an ox; f.* פָּרָה *a cow,* § 13. Voc. note 1. § 40. 2a.

פָּרָה *to be fruitful, bear fruit* (§ 32).

פָּרַח *to flourish* (§ 36).

פְּרִי 2 *m*, *fruit.* § 33.

פַּרְעֹה *Pharaoh.*

פָּרַץ *to break through, to break down*

פָּרַשׂ *to spread.*

פָּשַׁע *to rebel*; *against,* בְּ.

פֶּשַׁע 2 *i. m., rebellion, transgression.*

פַּת *i.* 4 *m., a morsel, bit.* Suff. פִּתִּי. § 40. 1.

פָּתָה *to be open* (§ 32).—Pi. *to entice.*—Hiph. *to make open, to enlarge*; impf. apoc. יַפְתְּ.

פָּתַח *to open.* § 36.

פֶּתַח 2 *i. m., an opening, door.*

צ

צֹאן 2 *c., a flock* (small cattle); *sheep.*

צָבָא 1 *m., a host, time of service.* Pl. *ôth.* § 38. 2.

צָבַר *to heap up, to store.*

צָדַק *to be righteous, just* (*intrans.* § 19).—Hiph. (Pi.) *to justify.*—Hithp. *to justify oneself.*

צֶדֶק 2 *i. m., righteousness.* § 25. 1b.

צְדָקָה 1 *f., id.*

צַדִּיק *righteous, just*; only *mas.*

צוּד *to hunt* (§ 30).

צוה Qal not in use. Pi. צִוָּה *to command, charge*. Impf. apoc. יְצַו, *imper.* צַו—Pu. *pass.* § 32.

מִצְוָה *f., a command.*

צִיּוֹן *Zion.*

צֵל 4 *m., a shadow.* § 40.

צֶלֶם 2 *m., an image, likeness.*

צָמֵא (*intrans.*) *to be thirsty.*

צָמַח *to sprout* (§ 36).—Hiph. *to make sprout.*

צֶמַח 2 *i. m., a sprout, branch.*

צִנָּה 4 *f., shield.*

צָעַק *to cry out.* § 36.

צֹפֶה *watchman.* § 32.

צָפַן *to hide, lay up.*

צָפוֹן 1 *m., north.*

צַר 4 *adversary.* § 40.

ק

קָבַץ *to collect, gather.*—Pi. *id.*

קָבַר *to bury.*—Niph. *pass.*

קֶבֶר 2 *i. m., a grave.*

קְבוּרָה *burial-place.*

קֶדֶם *east.*

קָדַשׁ *to be holy, sacred* (*intrans.* § 19).—Pi. *to hallow, sanctify.* —Hiph. *id.*—Niph., Hithp. *reflexive.*

קָדוֹשׁ 1 adj., *holy.*

קֹדֶשׁ 2 *m., holiness, sanctuary.*

מִקְדָּשׁ 1 *m., sanctuary.*

קוֹל 2 *m., voice, sound.* § 31.

קוּם *to arise, stand* (§ 30, Parad.). —Hiph. *to set up, establish.*

קָם 1 ptc., *standing.* § 31.

מָקוֹם 1 *c., a place.* Pl. *ōth.*

קָטֹן *to be little* (intrans. § 19, Parad.).

קָטֹן 1 adj., *little* (not inflected but very common).

קָטָן 4 adj., *little, f.* קְטַנָּה (inflected form). See § 40. 5.

קָלַל *to be light, despised* (§ 39, Parad.).—Pi. *to make light of, to curse.*—Hiph. *to lighten of.*

קַל adj., *light, swift.* § 40.

קָנָה *to acquire, buy, possess.*, § 32.

מִקְנֶה *m., possession, property cattle.* § 33.

קֵץ 4 *m., end.* § 40.

קָצַף *to be angry.*

קָצֵר 1 adj., *short.*

קָרָא *to call, cry, read.* — Pu. *pass.*, קָרָא לוֹ קָיִן *he called him Cain;* נִקְרָא לוֹ *he was called.* § 40. 6.

מִקְרָא 1 *m., convocation, an assembly.* § 38.

קָרָה and קָרָא *to befall, acc.* § 38. 3. Inf. cstr. *f.* קְרָאָה, with prep. לִקְרָאתִי *to meet me;* לִקְרַאת הָאִישׁ *to meet the man.*

קָרַב *to draw near, come near* (*intrans.* § 19).—Hiph. *to bring near, to offer.*

קָרוֹב 1 adj., *near, neighbour, relative.*

קֶרֶב 2 *i. m., inside, heart.* בְּקִרְבִּי *within me*; בְּקֶרֶב הָעִיר *within, in the midst of, the city.* § 25. 3b.

קֶרֶן 2 *f., horn.*

קָרַע *to tear, rend* (§ 36).

קָשַׁב Hiph. *to attend, give attention.*

קָשָׁה *to be hard.*

קָשֶׁה *hard, severe.* (§ 33).

קֶשֶׁת 2 *f., a bow.*

ר

רָאָה *to see* (§ 32).—Impf. יִרְאֶה, apoc. יֵרֶא, תֵּרֶא &c., but וַיַּרְא 3 *m.*, 3 *f.*, וַתֵּרֶא.—Niph. *pass.*, *to appear.*—Hiph. *to shew, (two acc.)*

מַרְאֶה *m., a sight, appearance, face.* § 33.

רֹאשׁ 2 *m., head*; pl. רָאשִׁים. § 31. 5.

רִאשׁוֹן adj., *first, former.* § 37. 1b; 45. 2.

רָבַב *to be many* (§ 39), used only in Perf. and Inf. cstr.

רַב 1 adj., *great, much*; pl. *many.* § 40.

רָבָה *to increase, multiply* (§ 32); impf. apoc. יֶרֶב and יִרֶב.—Hiph. *to multiply, cause to increase.*—Inf. abs. הַרְבָּה and הַרְבֵּה used as adv., *much.*

רְבִיעִי adj., *fourth.* § 45.

רָבַץ *to lie down* (of beasts) (intrans. § 19).

מַרְבֵּץ 3 *m., a stall, lair*; cstr. מִרְבַּץ. § 26.

רֹגֶז 2, *raging, turmoil.*

רֶגֶל 2 *f., a foot,* du., § 25. 3.

רָדַף *to pursue.*—Pi. *id.*

רוּחַ 2 *c., breath, wind, spirit.* Pl. *ôth*; cf. § 14, note to Voc.

רוּם *to be high, to rise up* (§ 30); Poʿlel, *to exalt*; Hiph. *to lift up*; Hoph. *pass.*

רָם 1 adj., *high, lofty.* § 31.

מָרוֹם 1 *m., height, high place.*

רוּץ *to run* (§ 30).

רָחַב *to be broad, wide* (*intrans.* § 19).

רֹחַב 2 *m., breadth*; רָחָב *broad, wide.*

רְחֹב 2 *f., broadway, street.* Pl. *ôth.*

רָחַם *to love* (§ 36).—Pi. רִחַם *to have pity, compassion, on.* Pu. *pass.*

רַחֲמִים *mercy, compassion*; רַחוּם *merciful, compassionate.*

רָחַץ *to wash* (§ 36).

רָחַק *to be distant, to withdraw* (§ 36).

רָחוֹק 1 adj., *distant.*

רִיב *to plead, contend* (§ 30).

רִיב 2 *m., contention, strife.* § 31.

מְרִיבָה *f., id.*

רֵיחַ *smell.*

רִיק 2 *m., emptiness, vanity.*

רֵק (רֵיק) *empty*; רֵיקָם *with empty hands, for nothing.*

רָכַב *to ride* (*intrans.*).—Hiph. *to set upon* a beast.

רְכוּשׁ *possessions.*

רֹמַח 2 *m., a lance, spear.*

רָמַשׂ *to creep.*

רֶמֶשׂ 2 *m., creeping things,* coll.

רִנָּה 4 *f., a ringing cry, complaint.*

רָעֵב *to be hungry* (*intrans.* § 19).

רָעֵב 1 adj., *hungry, famished.*

רָעָב 1 *m., hunger, famine.*

רָעָה *to feed, tend* (§ 32).—Ptc. רֹעֶה *a shepherd.*

רֵעֶה *m., a friend*; אִישׁ ... רֵעֵהוּ *one ... another.* § 33. 4.

רָעַע *to be evil* (§ 39, *intrans.*).—Hiph. הֵרַע *to afflict, injure.*

רַע 4 adj., *evil*; *f.* רָעָה *an evil.*

רָעַשׁ *to quake* (§ 36).—Hiph. *to shake.*

רַעַשׁ 2 *m., earthquake.*

רָפָא *to heal* (§ 38).—Niph. *pass.*

רָפָה Hiph. *to leave alone, to let be.*

רָקַב *to rot* (*intrans.* § 19).

רָקִיעַ 1 *m., firmament.*

רָשׁ (ptc. of רוּשׁ) *poor.*

רָשָׁע 1 adj., *wicked.*

רִשְׁעָה 1 *f., wickedness.*

שׂ

שָׂבַע *to be sated, satisfied* (*intrans.* § 36); with *acc.*—Hiph. *to satisfy*; *one with* —, *two acc.*

שָׂדֶה (שָׂדַי poet.) 1 *m., a field.* § 33. 3.

שֶׂה *a sheep* (*a goat*).

שָׂחַק *to laugh* (§ 36); Pi. *to play, sport.*

שֵׂיבָה *f., gray hairs.*

שִׂיחָה *f., meditation.*

שִׂים *to set, place* (§ 30).

שׂכל Hiph. *to prosper, to do wisely.*

שֶׂכֶל 2 *i. m., understanding.*

שָׂכַר *to hire*; שָׂכִיר *a hireling.*

שָׂמַח, שָׂמֵחַ *to rejoice, be glad* (§ 36).

שָׂמֵחַ adj. *glad, joyful.*

שִׂמְחָה 1 *f., gladness, joy.*

שָׂנֵא *to hate* (§ 38. *intrans.*); but Part. שֹׂנֵא.

שָׂפָה 1 *f., lip, edge, bank*; du. שְׂפָתַיִם. § 16. 2b.

שַׂק *sackcloth.*

שָׂרַף *to burn.*—Niph. *pass.*

שָׂרָף 1 *m., a seraph.*

שַׂר 1 *m., a prince, captain.* § 40.

ש

שָׁאַב *to draw* (water). § 36.

שָׁאַל *to ask* (§ 36); לְ *in reference to.*

שְׁאֵלָה *f., request.*

שְׁאוֹל *c., Sheol, the underworld.*

שָׁאוּל *Saul.*

שָׁאַר *to be left over, to remain.* Qal (rare) and Niph..—Hiph. *to leave over.*

שָׁבָה § 32f., *to take captive.*

שֵׁבֶט 2 *m., rod, sceptre, tribe.*

שֶׁבַע 2 *seven*; שְׁבִיעִי *seventh.* § 45.

שבע Qal not in use.—Niph. *to swear* (§ 36); Hiph. *to adjure.*

שָׁבַר *to break.*—Niph. *pass.* Ptc. נִשְׁבָּר *broken.*—Pi. *to break in pieces.*

שֶׁבֶר 2 *i.*, and שֵׁבֶר *breach, ruin.*

שָׁבַר *to buy* or *sell corn.*

שֶׁבֶר 2 *m., grain, corn.*

שָׁבַת *to rest, cease.*—Hiph. *to finish.*

שַׁבָּת 1 *c., rest, sabbath.*

שַׁדַּי *m.*, Shaddai (*mountaineer*) generally with אֵל *God.*

שׁוּב *to turn, return* (§ 30).—Hiph. *to restore, bring back*; תְּשׁוּבָה *return, answer.*

שׁוֹפָר 1 *c., a trumpet.* Pl. *ôth.*

שׁוֹר 2 *m*, *ox.* Pl. שְׁוָרִים. § 31.

שחה Hithpa‘lel *to prostrate oneself.* § 32. 4.

שָׁחַט *to slay, slaughter* (§36, Parad.)

שַׁחַר 2 *m., dawn.*

שחת Qal not in use.—Pi. שִׁחֵת *to destroy* (§ 36).—Hiph. *id.*; *to act corruptly, to corrupt.*—Niph *pass.*

שִׁיר 2 *m., a song*; *f. id.* § 31.

שִׁית *to set, place* (§ 30).

שָׁכַב *to lie down* (*intrans.* § 19).

שָׁכַח *to forget* (§ 36).—Niph. *pass.*

שכם Hiph. *to rise early.*

שְׁכֶם *m., shoulder.* Suff. שִׁכְמוֹ.

שָׁכַן *to dwell.*—Impf. יִשְׁכֹּן (§ 19. 2). Hiph. *to cause to dwell, place.*

מִשְׁכָּן 1 *m., dwelling, tabernacle.*

שָׁלַח *to send, stretch out.*—Pi. *send away*; *let go.*

שֻׁלְחָן 1 *c., a table.*

שלך Qal not in use.—Hiph. *to cast, cast off.*—Hoph. *pass.*

שָׁלָל 1, *spoil, plunder.*

שָׁלֵם *to be whole, sound* (*intrans.* § 19).—Pi. *to complete, perform, pay.*

שָׁלֵם 1 adj., *whole, sound.*

שָׁלוֹם 1 *m.*, *soundness, health, peace.*

שְׁלֹמֹה *Solomon.*

שָׁלֹשׁ 1 adj., *three.* § 45.

שָׁם adv., *there*; שָׁ֫מָּה *thither*; מִשָּׁם *from there, thence.*

שֵׁם 3 *m.*, *a name.* Pl. שֵׁמוֹת. § 26. 2.

שמד Qal not in use.—Hiph. *to destroy.*—Niph. *pass.*

שְׁמוּאֵל *Samuel.*

שָׁמַ֫יִם 1 pl. *heaven, heavens.* § 13. 6e.

שָׁמֵם *to be desolate* (§ 39). Impf. יֵשֹׁם, יָשֹׁם and יִשַּׁם.—Hiph. *to desolate.*—Niph. *pass.*

שָׁמַע *to hear*; שָׁמַע לְ, בְּ, אֶל־ *to listen to,* (§ 36).—Niph. *pass.*

שֵׁמַע 2 *m.*, שְׁמוּעָה 1 *f.*, *a report.*

שָׁמַר *to keep, watch.*—Niph. *to take heed, beware.*—Hithp. *to keep oneself.*

שֹׁמֵר 3 ptc., *watchman.*

מִשְׁמָר 1 *m.*, and מִשְׁמֶ֫רֶת *f.*, *ward, watch, observance.* § 25. 3.

שֶׁמֶשׁ 2 *c.*, *the sun.*

שִׁמְשׁוֹן *Samson.*

שָׁנָה 1 *f.*, *a year.* Pl. שָׁנִים (Poet. *ôth*).

שְׁנַיִם du., *two.* § 45.

שֵׁנִי 1 adj., *second.* § 45.

שען Qal not in use.—Niph. *to lean, rest on.*

שַׁ֫עַר 2 *c.*, *a gate.*

שִׁפְחָה 2 *f.*, *handmaid.*

שָׁפַט *to judge.*—Niph. *to litigate.*

שֹׁפֵט 3 ptc., *a judge.*

מִשְׁפָּט 1 *m.*, *judgment, justice.* § 18, note to Voc.

שָׁפַךְ *to pour out, spill.*—Niph. *pass.*

שָׁפֵל *to be low, abased* (*intrans.* § 19).

שָׁקַל *to weigh.*—Niph. *pass.*

שְׁרִירוּת *stubbornness.*

שָׁרַץ *to swarm*; with *acc.*

שֶׁ֫רֶץ 2 *m.*, *creeping things.*

שרת Qal not in use.—Pi. שֵׁרֵת *to serve, minister* (§ 36).

שקה See next word.

שָׁתָה *to drink* (§ 32).—Impf. apoc. יֵשְׁתְּ.—Niph. *pass.* — For Hiph. הִשְׁקָה *to give drink, to water.*

מַשְׁקֶה *m.* ptc., *a cupbearer, butler*; also *butlership.*

מִשְׁתֶּה *m.*, *a feast.*

ת

תֵּבָה 1 *f.*, *ark* (*e* firm), *basket.*

תּוֹדָה *f.*, *thanksgiving, thank-offering.*

תָּ֫וֶךְ 2 *m.*, *midst*; cstr. תּוֹךְ, § 31.

בְּתוֹכִי *within me.*

תּוֹלְדוֹת pl. *f.*, *generations, history* (see יָלַד).

תּוֹרָה *f., instruction, law* (ירה).
cf. § 14, note to Voc.

תְּחִנָּה
תַּחֲנוּנִים } *supplication(s)*.

תַּחַת prep., *under, beneath, instead of*.—Suff. תַּחְתַּי, § 36. 4a.

תָּמַם *to be complete, ended* (§ 39).—Impf. יִתֹּם.—Hiph. *to complete, finish*.

תָּם 4 adj., *complete, perfect* (§ 40).

תָּמִים 1 adj., *id*.

תָּמִיד adv., *continually*.

תָּמָר 2 *m., a palm tree*.

תָּעָה *to wander*.

תִּפְאָרָה and **תִּפְאֶרֶת** 2 *f., glory*.

תְּפִלָּה *prayer*.

תָּקַע *to strike, blow* (a trumpet).

תְּשׁוּבָה. See **שׁוּב**.

תְּשׁוּעָה. See **ישׁע**.

PARADIGMS OF VERBS, NOUNS AND PREPOSITIONS

THE REGULAR

		Qal			
		act.		*stat.*	Niph'al
Perf. Sing.	3 *m.*	קָטַל	כָּבֵד	קָטֹן	נִקְטַל
	3 *f.*	קָֽטְלָה	כָּֽבְדָה	קָֽטְנָה	נִקְטְלָה
	2 *m.*	קָטַ֫לְתָּ	כָּבַ֫דְתָּ	קָטֹ֫נְתָּ	נִקְטַ֫לְתָּ
	2 *f.*	קָטַלְתְּ	כָּבַדְתְּ	קָטֹנְתְּ	נִקְטַלְתְּ
	1 *c.*	קָטַ֫לְתִּי	כָּבַ֫דְתִּי	קָטֹ֫נְתִּי	נִקְטַ֫לְתִּי
Plur.	3 *c.*	קָֽטְלוּ	כָּֽבְדוּ	קָֽטְנוּ	נִקְטְלוּ
	2 *m.*	קְטַלְתֶּם	כְּבַדְתֶּם	קְטָנְתֶּם	נִקְטַלְתֶּם
	2 *f.*	קְטַלְתֶּן	כְּבַדְתֶּן	קְטָנְתֶּן	נִקְטַלְתֶּן
	1 *c.*	קָטַ֫לְנוּ	כָּבַ֫דְנוּ	קָטֹ֫נּוּ	נִקְטַ֫לְנוּ
Impf. Sing.	3 *m.*	יִקְטֹל	יִכְבַּד	יִקְטַן	יִקָּטֵל
	3 *f.*	תִּקְטֹל	תִּכְבַּד	&c. as	תִּקָּטֵל
	2 *m.*	תִּקְטֹל	תִּכְבַּד	with יִכְבַּד	תִּקָּטֵל
	2 *f.*	תִּקְטְלִי (ין)	תִּכְבְּדִי		תִּקָּֽטְלִי
	1 *c.*	אֶקְטֹל	אֶכְבַּד		אֶקָּטֵל (אִקָּטֵל)
Plur.	3 *m.*	יִקְטְלוּ (וּן)	יִכְבְּדוּ		יִקָּֽטְלוּ
	3 *f.*	תִּקְטֹ֫לְנָה	תִּכְבַּ֫דְנָה		תִּקָּטַ֫לְנָה
	2 *m.*	תִּקְטְלוּ (וּן)	תִּכְבְּדוּ		תִּקָּֽטְלוּ
	2 *f.*	תִּקְטֹ֫לְנָה	תִּכְבַּ֫דְנָה		תִּקָּטַ֫לְנָה
	1 *c.*	נִקְטֹל	נִכְבַּד		נִקָּטֵל
Imp. Sing.	2 *m.*	קְטֹל (קָטְלָה)	כְּבַד (כִּבְדָה)		הִקָּטֵל (הִקָּ֫טֶל)
	2 *f.*	קִטְלִי (קָטְלִי)	כִּבְדִי		הִקָּֽטְלִי
Plur.	2 *m.*	קִטְלוּ	כִּבְדוּ		הִקָּֽטְלוּ
	2 *f.*	קְטֹ֫לְנָה	כְּבַ֫דְנָה		הִקָּטַ֫לְנָה

Cont. on p. 266)

VERB—§§ 11, 17-24

Pi'ēl	Pu'al	Hithpa'ēl	Hiph'îl	Hoph'al
קִטֵּל (קִטַּל)	קֻטַּל	הִתְקַטֵּל (־קַטַּל)	הִקְטִיל	הָקְטַל
קִטְּלָה	קֻטְּלָה	הִתְקַטְּלָה	הִקְטִ֫ילָה	הָקְטְלָה
קִטַּ֫לְתָּ	קֻטַּ֫לְתָּ	הִתְקַטַּ֫לְתָּ	הִקְטַ֫לְתָּ	הָקְטַ֫לְתָּ
קִטַּלְתְּ	קֻטַּלְתְּ	הִתְקַטַּלְתְּ	הִקְטַלְתְּ	הָקְטַלְתְּ
קִטַּ֫לְתִּי	קֻטַּ֫לְתִּי	הִתְקַטַּ֫לְתִּי	הִקְטַ֫לְתִּי	הָקְטַ֫לְתִּי
קִטְּלוּ	קֻטְּלוּ	הִתְקַטְּלוּ	הִקְטִ֫ילוּ	הָקְטְלוּ
קִטַּלְתֶּם	קֻטַּלְתֶּם	הִתְקַטַּלְתֶּם	הִקְטַלְתֶּם	הָקְטַלְתֶּם
קִטַּלְתֶּן	קֻטַּלְתֶּן	הִתְקַטַּלְתֶּן	הִקְטַלְתֶּן	הָקְטַלְתֶּן
קִטַּ֫לְנוּ	קֻטַּ֫לְנוּ	הִתְקַטַּ֫לְנוּ	הִקְטַ֫לְנוּ	הָקְטַ֫לְנוּ
יְקַטֵּל	יְקֻטַּל	יִתְקַטֵּל	יַקְטִיל	יָקְטַל
תְּקַטֵּל	תְּקֻטַּל	תִּתְקַטֵּל	תַּקְטִיל	תָּקְטַל
תְּקַטֵּל	תְּקֻטַּל	תִּתְקַטֵּל	תַּקְטִיל	תָּקְטַל
תְּקַטְּלִי	תְּקֻטְּלִי	תִּתְקַטְּלִי	תַּקְטִ֫ילִי	תָּקְטְלִי
אֲקַטֵּל	אֲקֻטַּל	אֶתְקַטֵּל	אַקְטִיל	אָקְטַל
יְקַטְּלוּ	יְקֻטְּלוּ	יִתְקַטְּלוּ	יַקְטִ֫ילוּ	יָקְטְלוּ
תְּקַטֵּ֫לְנָה	תְּקֻטַּ֫לְנָה	תִּתְקַטֵּ֫לְנָה	תַּקְטֵ֫לְנָה	תָּקְטַ֫לְנָה
תְּקַטְּלוּ	תְּקֻטְּלוּ	תִּתְקַטְּלוּ	תַּקְטִ֫ילוּ	תָּקְטְלוּ
תְּקַטֵּ֫לְנָה	תְּקֻטַּ֫לְנָה	תִּתְקַטֵּ֫לְנָה	תַּקְטֵ֫לְנָה	תָּקְטַ֫לְנָה
נְקַטֵּל	נְקֻטַּל	נִתְקַטֵּל	נַקְטִיל	נָקְטַל
קַטֵּל		הִתְקַטֵּל	הַקְטֵל	
קַטְּלִי	wanting	הִתְקַטְּלִי	הַקְטִ֫ילִי	wanting
קַטְּלוּ		הִתְקַטְּלוּ	הַקְטִ֫ילוּ	
קַטֵּ֫לְנָה		הִתְקַטֵּ֫לְנָה	הַקְטֵ֫לְנָה	

(Cont. on p. 267

Continued

THE REGULAR

	Qal act.	Qal stat.		Niph'a[l]
Jussive 3 *sing.*	יִקְטֹל	יִכְבַּד		יִקָּטֵל (יִקָּ֫טֶל)
wāw cons. impf.	וַיִּקְטֹל	וַיִּכְבַּד		וַיִּקָּטֵל (וַיִּקָּ֫טֶל)
Cohort. 1 *sing.*	אֶקְטְלָה	אֶכְבְּדָה		אֶקָּטְלָה
wāw cons. perf.	וְקָטַלְתָּ֫	&c		
Inf. cstr.	קְטֹל	כְּבֹד (כְּבַד)		הִקָּטֵל
absol.	קָטוֹל	כָּבוֹד		הִקָּטֹל, נִקְטֹל
Part. act.	קֹטֵל	כָּבֵד	קָטֹן	
pass.	קָטוּל			נִקְטָל

VERB—§§ 11, 17-24

Pi'ēl	Pu'al	Hithpa'ēl	Hiph'îl	Hoph'al
יְקַטֵּל	יְקֻטַּל	יִתְקַטֵּל	יַקְטֵל	
וַיְקַטֵּל	וַיְקֻטַּל	וַיִּתְקַטֵּל	וַיַּקְטֵל	וַיָּקְטַל
אֲקַטְּלָה		אֶתְקַטְּלָה	אַקְטִ֫ילָה	
קַטֵּל	(קֻטַּל)	הִתְקַטֵּל	הַקְטִיל	(הָקְטַל)
קַטֵּל, קַטֹּל	קֻטֹּל	(הִתְקַטֵּל)	הַקְטֵל	(הָקְטֵל)
מְקַטֵּל		מִתְקַטֵּל	מַקְטִיל	
	מְקֻטָּל			מָקְטָל

THE VERBAL SUFFIXE

See also suffixes

Qal

Perf.	3 *s. m.*		3 *s. f.*	2 *s. m.*	2 *s. f.*
Suff.	קָטַל	כָּבֵד[1]	קָֽטְלָה	קָטַלְתָּ	טַלְתְּ
s. I *c.*	קְטָלַ֫נִי	כְּבֵדַ֫נִי	קְטָלַ֫תְנִי כְּבֵד׳	קְטַלְתַּ֫נִי	קְטַלְתִּ֫ינִי
2 *m.*	קְטָֽלְךָ	כְּבֵֽדְךָ	קְטָלַתְךָ	—	—
2 *f.*	קְטָלֵךְ ‑ָךְ	כְּבֵדֵךְ	קְטָלַ֫תֶךְ	—	—
3 *m.*	קְטָלוֹ	כְּבֵדוֹ	קְטָלַתְהוּ ‑ַתּוּ	קְטַלְתּוֹ ‑תָּהוּ	טַלְתִּ֫יהוּ
3 *f.*	קְטָלָהּ	כְּבֵדָהּ	קְטָלַ֫תָּה	קְטַלְתָּהּ	טַלְתִּ֫יהָ
pl I *c*	קְטָלָ֫נוּ	כְּבֵדָנוּ	קְטָלַ֫תְנוּ	קְטַלְתָּ֫נוּ	טַלְתִּ֫ינוּ
2 *m.*	קְטַלְכֶם	כְּבֵדְכֶם	wanting	—	—
2 *f.*	קְטַלְכֶן	כְּבֵדְכֶן		—	—
3 *m.*	קְטָלָם	כְּבֵדָם	קְטָלָ֫תַם	קְטַלְתָּם	טַלְתִּים
3 *f.*	קְטָלָן	כְּבֵדָן	קְטָלָ֫תַן	קְטַלְתָּן	טַלְתִּין

Impf.	3 *s. m.*		3 *pl. m.*	*Imper. s.*		*pl.*
Suff.	יִקְטֹל	יִכְבַּד	יִקְטְלוּ	קְטֹל	כְּבַד	טְלוּ
s. I *c.*	יִקְטְלֵ֫נִי	יְכַבְּדֵ֫נִי	יִקְטְל֫וּנִי יִכְבָּד׳	קָטְלֵ֫נִי[2]	כִּבְדָ׳	טְל֫וּנִי כִּבְדָ׳
2 *m.*	יִקְטָלְךָ	יְכַבֶּדְךָ	יִקְטְל֫וּךָ	—		—
2 *f.*	יִקְטְלֵךְ	&c.	יִקְטְלוּךְ	—		—
3 *m.*	יִקְטְלֵ֫הוּ		יִקְטְלֻ֫הוּ	קָטְלֵ֫הוּ		&c.
3 *f.*	יִקְטְלֶ֫הָ (‑ָהּ)		יִקְטְל֫וּהָ	קָטְלֶ֫הָ (‑ָהּ)		as in
pl. I *c.*	יִקְטְלֵ֫נוּ		יִקְטְלֻ֫נוּ	קָטְלֵ֫נוּ		imperf.
2 *m.*	יִקְטָלְכֶם	יִכְבַּדְ׳	יִקְטְלוּכֶם יִכְבּ׳	—		3rd plural —
2 *f.*	יִקְטָלְכֶן		יִקְטְלוּכֶן	—		—
3 *m.*	יִקְטְלֵם		יִקְטְלוּם	קָטְלֵם		
3 *f.*	יִקְטְלֵן		יִקְטְלוּן	קָטְלֵן		

And so all parts of impf. ending in a Consonant.

So 2 *pl. m.*, and 2, 3 *pl. f.* which becomes תִּקְטְלוּ.

[1] This column may be als written defectively, e.g. קְטַלְתִּנִי, &c. [2] The first syl throughout imperative is hal open, e.g. כָּתְבֵנִי, *koth•bhēn*

[1] כָּבֵד, which is used here to illustrate stative or intransitive verbs wit verbal suffixes, is, in actual fact, never found with such suffixes.

REGULAR VERB—§ 27

Lamedh He verbs, p. 278f.

Qal				Pi'ēl
1 *s. c.*	3 *pl. c.*	2 *pl. c.*	1 *pl. c.*	3 *s. m.*
קְטַלְתִּי	קְטָלוּ	קְטַלְתֶּם	קְטַלְנוּ	קִטֵּל
—	קְטָלוּנִי כִּבְּד׳	קְטַלְתּוּנִי	—	קִטְּלַנִי
קְטַלְתִּיךָ	קְטָלוּךָ	—	קְטַלְנוּךָ	קִטֶּלְךָ
קְטַלְתִּיךְ	קְטָלוּךְ	—	&c.	קִטְּלֵךְ
קְטַלְתִּיהוּ —יו	קְטָלֻהוּ	&c.	as 3 *pl.*	קִטְּלוֹ
קְטַלְתִּיהָ	קְטָלוּהָ	as 3 *pl.*		קִטְּלָהּ
—	קְטָלֻנוּ		—	קִטְּלָנוּ
קְטַלְתִּיכֶם	wanting	—		קִטֶּלְכֶם
קְטַלְתִּיכֶן		—		קִטֶּלְכֶן
קְטַלְתִּים	קְטָלוּם			קִטְּלָם
קְטַלְתִּין	קְטָלוּן			קִטְּלָן

Impf. and imper. with nûn energ.		*Infin. cstr.*		
		כַּבֵּד	קְטֹל	יְקַטֵּל
יְקַטְלֶנִּי יְכַבְּ׳	קָטְלֶנִּי כַּבְּ׳	כַּבְּדִי	קָטְלִי (—ֵנִי)	יְקַטְּלֵנִי
יְקַטְלֶךָּ		כַּבֶּדְךָ	קָטְלְךָ קְטָלְךָ	יְקַטֶּלְךָ
		כַּבְּדֵךְ	קָטְלֵךְ	יְקַטְּלֵךְ
יְקַטְלֶנּוּ	קָטְלֶנּוּ	&c.	קָטְלוֹ (ـֵהוּ)	יְקַטְּלֵהוּ
יְקַטְלֶנָּה	קָטְלֶנָּה		קָטְלָהּ	יְקַטְּלֶהָ
			קָטְלֵנוּ	יְקַטְּלֵנוּ
		כַּבֶּדְכֶם	קָטְלְכֶם[1]	יְקַטֶּלְכֶם
			קָטְלְכֶן[1]	יְקַטֶּלְכֶן
			קָטְלָם	יְקַטְּלֵם
			קָטְלָן	יְקַטְּלֵן

For the use and meaning of these suff. see § 27. 8a. The first syll. is half-open: e.g. כָּתְבוֹ, except before ךָ and כֶם, where it is closed, e.g. כָּתְבְךָ, כַּבֶּדְךָ; cf. § 27. 8a. [1] Or קְטָלְכֶם, קְטָלְכֶן.

PĒ YÔDH AND PĒ

Verbs פ״ו

			Qal		Niph.
Perf.	*Sing.* 3 *m.*	יָשַׁב	יָרֵא	יָרַשׁ	נוֹשַׁב
	3 *f.*	as	יָֽרְאָה	as	נוֹשְׁבָה
	2 *m.*	קָטַל	יָרֵאתָ	קָטַל	נוֹשַׁבְתָּ
	2 *f.*		יָרֵאת		&c.
	1 *c.*		יָרֵאתִי		
	Plur. 3 *c.*		יָֽרְאוּ		
	2 *m.*		יְרֵאתֶם		
	2 *f.*		יְרֵאתֶן		
	1 *c.*		יָרֵאנוּ		
Impf.	*Sing.* 3 *m.*	יֵשֵׁב	יִירָא	יִירַשׁ	יִוָּשֵׁב
	3 *f.*	תֵּשֵׁב	תִּירָא	תִּירַשׁ	תִּוָּשֵׁב
	2 *m.*	תֵּשֵׁב	תִּירָא	תִּירַשׁ	תִּוָּשֵׁב
	2 *f.*	תֵּשְׁבִי	תִּֽירְאִי	תִּֽירְשִׁי	תִּוָּֽשְׁבִי
	1 *c.*	אֵשֵׁב	אִירָא	אִירַשׁ	אִוָּשֵׁב
	Plur. 3 *m.*	יֵשְׁבוּ	יִֽירְאוּ	יִֽירְשׁוּ	יִוָּֽשְׁבוּ
	3 *f.*	תֵּשַׁבְנָה	תִּירֶאנָה	תִּירַשְׁנָה	תִּוָּשַׁבְנָה
	2 *m.*	תֵּשְׁבוּ	תִּֽירְאוּ	תִּֽירְשׁוּ	תִּוָּֽשְׁבוּ
	2 *f.*	תֵּשַׁבְנָה	תִּירֶאנָה	תִּירַשְׁנָה	תִּוָּשַׁבְנָה
	1 *c.*	נֵשֵׁב	נִירָא	נִירַשׁ	נִוָּשֵׁב
Imp.	*Sing.* 2 *m.*	שֵׁב (שְׁבָה)	יְרָא	רַשׁ (רֵשׁ)	הִוָּשֵׁב
	2 *f.*	שְׁבִי	יִרְאִי	רְשִׁי	הִוָּֽשְׁבִי
	Plur. 2 *m.*	שְׁבוּ	יִרְאוּ	רְשׁוּ	הִוָּֽשְׁבוּ
	2 *f.*	שֵׁבְנָה	יְרֶאנָה	רַשְׁנָה	הִוָּשַׁבְנָה

Cont. on p. 272)

WĀW VERBS—§ 29

		Verbs פ״י		Verbs assimilating		
Hiph.	Hoph.	Qal	Hiph.	Qal	Niph.	Hiph.
הוֹשִׁיב	הוּשַׁב	יָנַק	הֵינִיק	יָצַת	נִצַּת	הִצִּית
הוֹשִׁ֫יבָה	הוּשְׁבָה	as	הֵינִ֫יקָה	יָצַק		
הוֹשַׁ֫בְתָּ	הוּשַׁ֫בְתָּ	קָטַל	הֵינַ֫קְתָּ			
הוֹשַׁבְתְּ	&c.		הֵינַקְתְּ			
הוֹשַׁ֫בְתִּי			הֵינַ֫קְתִּי			
הוֹשִׁיבוּ			הֵינִיקוּ			
הוֹשַׁבְתֶּם			הֵינַקְתֶּם			
הוֹשַׁבְתֶּן			הֵינַקְתֶּן			
הוֹשַׁ֫בְנוּ			הֵינַ֫קְנוּ			
יוֹשִׁיב	יוּשַׁב	יִינַק	יֵינִיק	יִצַּת		יַצִּית
תּוֹשִׁיב	תּוּשַׁב	תִּינַק	תֵּינִיק	יִצֹּק		
תּוֹשִׁיב	תּוּשַׁב	תִּינַק	תֵּינִיק			
תּוֹשִׁ֫יבִי	תּוּשְׁבִי	תִּינְקִי	תֵּינִ֫יקִי			
אוֹשִׁיב	&c.	אִינַק	אֵינִיק			
יוֹשִׁיבוּ		יִינְקוּ	יֵינִ֫יקוּ			
תּוֹשֵׁ֫בְנָה		תִּינַ֫קְנָה	תֵּינַ֫קְנָה			
תּוֹשִׁיבוּ		תִּינְקוּ	תֵּינִ֫יקוּ			
תּוֹשֵׁ֫בְנָה		תִּינַ֫קְנָה	תֵּינַ֫קְנָה			
נוֹשִׁיב		נִינַק	נֵינִיק			
הוֹשֵׁב			הֵינֵק			
הוֹשִׁ֫יבִי			הֵינִ֫יקִי			
הוֹשִׁ֫יבוּ			הֵינִ֫יקוּ			
הוֹשֵׁ֫בְנָה			הֵינַ֫קְנָה			

(Cont. on p. 273

PĒ YODH AND PĒ

Continued Verbs. פ״י

	Qal			Niph.
Juss. 3 sing.				
wāw cons. impf.	וַיֵּ֫שֶׁב		וַיִּירַשׁ	
Cohort. 1 sing.	אֵֽשְׁבָה		אִֽירְשָׁה	
Impf. in a *with suff.*	יֵדָעֵ֫נִי	*Imper.* דָּעֵהוּ		
Infin. cstr.	שֶׁ֫בֶת	[1]יִרְאָה	רֶ֫שֶׁת	הִוָּשֵׁב
absol.	יָשׁוֹב		יָרוֹשׁ	
Part. act.	יֹשֵׁב	יָרֵא	יֹרֵשׁ	
pass.	יָשׁוּב		יָרוּשׁ	נוֹשָׁב

[1] Very rarely יְרֹא.

WĀW VERBS—§ 29

		Verbs. פ״י		Verbs assimilating		
Hiph.	Hoph.	Qal	Hiph.	Qal.	Niph.	Hiph.
יוֹשֵׁב			יֵינַק			יַצֵּת
וַיּ֫וֹשֶׁב			וַיֵּ֫ינֶק			
הוֹשִׁיב	הוּשַׁב		הֵינִיק			
הוֹשֵׁב			הֵינֵק			
מוֹשִׁיב		יוֹנֵק	מֵינִיק			מַצִּית
	מוּשָׁב	יָנוּק				

ʻ*AYIN WĀW* AND

Qal

	act.	*stat.*		
Perf. Sing. 3 *m.*	קָם	מֵת	בּוֹשׁ	בָּן
3 *f.*	קָמָה	מֵתָה	בּוֹשָׁה	בָּנָה
2 *m.*	קַמְתָּ	מַתָּה	בֹּשְׁתָּ	בַּנְתָּ
2 *f.*	קַמְתְּ	מַתְּ	בֹּשְׁתְּ	בַּנְתְּ
1 *c.*	קַמְתִּי	מַתִּי	בֹּשְׁתִּי	בָּנְתִּי
Plur. 3 *c.*	קָמוּ	מֵתוּ	בּוֹשׁוּ	בָּנוּ
2 *m.*	קַמְתֶּם	מַתֶּם	בָּשְׁתֶּם	בַּנְתֶּם
2 *f.*	קַמְתֶּן	מַתֶּן	בָּשְׁתֶּן	בַּנְתֶּן
1 *c.*	קַמְנוּ	מַתְנוּ	בֹּשְׁנוּ	בַּנּוּ
Impf. Sing. 3 *m.*	יָקוּם	יָמוּת	יֵבוֹשׁ	יָבִין
3 *f.*	תָּקוּם	תָּמוּת	תֵּבוֹשׁ	תָּבִין
2 *m.*	תָּקוּם	תָּמוּת	תֵּבוֹשׁ	תָּבִין
2 *f.*	תָּקוּמִי	תָּמוּתִי	תֵּבוֹשִׁי	תָּבִינִי
1 *c.*	אָקוּם	אָמוּת	אֵבוֹשׁ	אָבִין
Plur. 3 *m.*	יָקוּמוּ	יָמוּתוּ	יֵבוֹשׁוּ	יָבִינוּ
3 *f.*	תְּקוּמֶינָה	תְּמוּתֶינָה	תֵּבֹשְׁנָה	[1]תְּבִינֶינָה
2 *m.*	תָּקוּמוּ	תָּמוּתוּ	תֵּבוֹשׁוּ	תָּבִינוּ
2 *f.*	תְּקוּמֶינָה	תְּמוּתֶינָה	תֵּבֹשְׁנָה	[1]תְּבִינֶינָה
1 *c.*	נָקוּם	נָמוּת	נֵבוֹשׁ	נָבִין
Imp. Sing. 2 *m.*	קוּם קוּמָה	מוּת	בּוֹשׁ	בִּין
2 *f.*	קוּמִי	מוּתִי	בּוֹשִׁי	בִּינִי
Plur. 2 *m.*	קוּמוּ	מוּתוּ	בּוֹשׁוּ	בִּינוּ
2 *f.*	קֹמְנָה	מֹתְנָה	בֹּשְׁנָה	

[1] or תָּבֵנָּה.

Cont. on p. 276)

YO<u>DH</u> VERBS—§ 30

Niph.	Hiph.	Hoph.
נָקוֹם	הֵקִים	הוּקַם
נָק֫וֹמָה	הֵקִ֫ימָה	הוּקְמָה
נְקוּמֹ֫תָ	הֲקִימ֫וֹתָ	הוּקַ֫מְתָּ
נְקוּמֹת	הֲקִימוֹת	הוּקַמְתְּ
נְקוּמֹ֫תִי	הֲקִימ֫וֹתִי	הוּקַ֫מְתִּי
נָק֫וֹמוּ	הֵקִ֫ימוּ	הוּקְמוּ
[1]נְקוֹמֹתֶם	הֲקִימוֹתֶם	הוּקַמְתֶּם
נְקוֹמֹתֶן	הֲקִימוֹתֶן	הוּקַמְתֶּן
נְקוּמֹ֫נוּ	הֲקִימ֫וֹנוּ	הוּקַ֫מְנוּ
יִקּוֹם	יָקִים	יוּקַם
תִּקּוֹם	תָּקִים	תּוּקַם
תִּקּוֹם	תָּקִים	תּוּקַם
תִּקּ֫וֹמִי	תָּקִ֫ימִי	תּוּקְמִי
אֶקּוֹם	אָקִים	אוּקַם
יִקּ֫וֹמוּ	יָקִ֫ימוּ	יוּקְמוּ
	תְּקִימֶ֫ינָה, תָּקֵ֫מְנָה)	תּוּקַ֫מְנָה
תִּקּ֫וֹמוּ	תָּקִ֫ימוּ	תּוּקְמוּ
	תָּקֵ֫מְנָה	תּוּקַ֫מְנָה
נִקּוֹם	נָקִים	נוּקַם
הִקּוֹם	הָקֵם, הָקִ֫ימָה	
הִקּ֫וֹמִי	הָקִ֫ימִי	
הִקּ֫וֹמוּ	הָקִ֫ימוּ	
הִקּ֫מְנָה	הָקֵ֫מְנָה	

Forms of Intens.

Act.	*Pass.*	*Reflex.*
קַיֵּם		הִתְקַיֵּם
קוֹמֵם	קוֹמַם	הִתְקוֹמֵם
קִמְקֵם	קָמְקַם	הִתְקַמְקֵם

like *Piʻēl* &c. of the Regular Verb

[1] The only examples of 2 *pl.* have *ô*, not *û*.

(Cont. on p. 277

‘*AYIN WĀW* AND

	Qal			
	act.	*stat.*		
Juss. 3 *sing.*	יָקֹם	יָמֹת		יָבֵן
wāw cons. impf.	וַיָּ֫קָם	וַיָּ֫מָת		וַיָּ֫בֶן
Cohort. 1 *sing.*	אָקֽוּמָה	אָמ֫וּתָה		אָבִ֫ינָה
wāw cons. perf.	וְקַמְתָּ֫	וּמַתָּה		וּבַנְתָּ֫
Inf. cstr.	קוּם	מוּת	בּוֹשׁ	בִּין
absol.	קוֹם	מוֹת	בּוֹשׁ	בּוֹן
Part. act.	קָם קָמָה	מֵת	בּוֹשׁ	בָּן
pass.	קוּם קוּמָה			(בּוּן בִּין)

YÔ͟DH VERBS—§ 30

Niph.	Hiph.	Hoph.
	יָקֵם	
	וַיָּ֫קֶם	
	אָקִ֫ימָה	
	וַהֲקִימוֹתָ	
הִקּוֹם	הָקִים	הוּקַם
הִקּוֹם, נָקוֹם	הָקֵם	
	מֵקִים, מְקִימָה *f.*	
נָקוֹם, נְקוֹמָה *f.*		מוּקָם

LĀMEDH HĒ (LĀM. YÔDH

		Qal	Niph.	Pi'ēl	Pu'al
Perf. *Sing.*	3 *m.*	גָּלָה	נִגְלָה	גִּלָּה	גֻּלָּה
	3 *f.*	גָּֽלְתָה	נִגְלְתָה	גִּלְּתָה	גֻּלְּתָה
	2 *m.*	גָּלִ֫יתָ	נִגְלֵ֫יתָ	גִּלִּ֫יתָ ‑ֵ֫יתָ	גֻּלֵּ֫יתָ
	2 *f.*	גָּלִית	&c. נִגְלֵית	גִּלִּית	גֻּלֵּית
	1 *c.*	גָּלִ֫יתִי	נִגְלֵ֫יתִי	[2]גִּלִּ֫יתִי ‑ֵ֫יתִי	גֻּלֵּ֫יתִי
Plur.	3 *c.*	גָּלוּ	נִגְלוּ	גִּלּוּ	גֻּלּוּ
	2 *m.*	גְּלִיתֶם	נִגְלֵיתֶם	גִּלִּיתֶם	גֻּלֵּיתֶם
	2 *f.*	גְּלִיתֶן	נִגְלֵיתֶן	גִּלִּיתֶן	גֻּלֵּיתֶן
	1 *c.*	גָּלִ֫ינוּ	[1]נִגְלִ֫ינוּ	גִּלִּ֫ינוּ	גֻּלֵּ֫ינוּ
Impf. *Sing.*	3 *m.*	יִגְלֶה	יִגָּלֶה	יְגַלֶּה	יְגֻלֶּה
	3 *f.*	תִּגְלֶה	תִּגָּלֶה	תְּגַלֶּה	תְּגֻלֶּה
	2 *m.*	תִּגְלֶה	תִּגָּלֶה	תְּגַלֶּה	תְּגֻלֶּה
	2 *f.*	תִּגְלִי	תִּגָּלִי	תְּגַלִּי	תְּגֻלִּי
	1 *c.*	אֶגְלֶה	אֶגָּלֶה (אִגָּלֶה)	אֲגַלֶּה	אֲגֻלֶּה
Plur.	3 *m.*	יִגְלוּ	יִגָּלוּ	יְגַלּוּ	יְגֻלּוּ
	3 *f.*	תִּגְלֶ֫ינָה	תִּגָּלֶ֫ינָה	תְּגַלֶּ֫ינָה	תְּגֻלֶּ֫ינָה
	2 *m.*	תִּגְלוּ	תִּגָּלוּ	תְּגַלּוּ	תְּגֻלּוּ
	2 *f.*	תִּגְלֶ֫ינָה	תִּגָּלֶ֫ינָה	תְּגַלֶּ֫ינָה	תְּגֻלֶּ֫ינָה
	1 *c.*	נִגְלֶה	נִגָּלֶה	נְגַלֶּה	נְגֻלֶּה
Imp. *Sing.*	2 *m.*	גְּלֵה	הִגָּלֵה הִגָּל	גַּלֵּה גַּל	
	2 *f.*	גְּלִי	הִגָּלִי	גַּלִּי	
Plur.	2 *m.*	גְּלוּ	הִגָּלוּ	גַּלּוּ	
	2 *f.*	גְּלֶ֫ינָה	הִגָּלֶ֫ינָה	גַּלֶּ֫ינָה	

[1] 1 pl. Niph. always *î*.

Cont. on p. 280)

AND *WĀW*) VERBS—§ 32

Hithp.	Hiph.	Hoph.
הִתְגַּלָּה	הִגְלָה	הָגְלָה
הִתְגַּלְּתָה	הִגְלְתָה	הָגְלְתָה
הִתְגַּלִּ֫יתָ ‑ֵ֫יתָ	הִגְלִ֫יתָ ‑ֵ֫יתָ	הָגְלֵ֫יתָ
הִתְגַּלִּית ‑ֵית	הִגְלִית ‑ֵית	הָגְלֵית
הִתְגַּלִּ֫יתִי[2]	הִגְלִ֫יתִי[2] ‑ֵ֫יתִי	הָגְלֵ֫יתִי
הִתְגַּלּוּ	הִגְלוּ	הָגְלוּ
הִתְגַּלִּיתֶם	הִגְלִיתֶם	הָגְלֵיתֶם
הִתְגַּלִּיתֶן	הִגְלִיתֶן	הָגְלֵיתֶן
הִתְגַּלִּ֫ינוּ	הִגְלִ֫ינוּ	הָגְלֵ֫ינוּ
יִתְגַּלֶּה	יַגְלֶה	יָגְלֶה
תִּתְגַּלֶּה	תַּגְלֶה	תָּגְלֶה
תִּתְגַּלֶּה	תַּגְלֶה	תָּגְלֶה
תִּתְגַּלִּי	תַּגְלִי	תָּגְלִי
אֶתְגַּלֶּה	אַגְלֶה	אָגְלֶה
יִתְגַּלּוּ	יַגְלוּ	יָגְלוּ
תִּתְגַּלֶּ֫ינָה	תַּגְלֶ֫ינָה	תָּגְלֶ֫ינָה
תִּתְגַּלּוּ	תַּגְלוּ	תָּגְלוּ
תִּתְגַּלֶּ֫ינָה	תַּגְלֶ֫ינָה	תָּגְלֶ֫ינָה
נִתְגַּלֶּה	נַגְלֶה	נָגְלֶה
הִתְגַּלֵּה ‑גַּל	הַגְלֵה הֶגֶל	
הִתְגַּלִּי	הַגְלִי	
הִתְגַּלּוּ	הַגְלוּ	
הִתְגַּלֶּ֫ינָה	הַגְלֶ֫ינָה	

Suffixes		
Perf. Qal Sing.	1 *c.*	גָּלַ֫נִי ‑ַ֫נִי
	2 *m.*	גָּלְךָ
	2 *f.*	גָּלָךְ
	3 *m.*	גָּלָ֫הוּ
	3 *f.*	גָּלָהּ
Plur.	1 *c.*	גָּלָנוּ
	2 *m.*	
	2 *f.*	
	3 *m.*	גָּלָם
	3 *f.*	
Impf. Sing.	1 *c.*	יִגְלֵ֫נִי
	2 *m.*	יִגְלְךָ
	2 *f.*	יִגְלֵךְ
	3 *m.*	יִגְלֵ֫הוּ
	3 *f.*	יִגְלֶ֫הָ
Plur.	1 *c.*	יִגְלֵ֫נוּ
	2 *m.*	
	2 *f.*	
	3 *m.*	יִגְלֵם
	3 *f.*	
Imp. Sing.	1 *c.*	גְּלֵ֫נִי
	3 *m.*	גְּלֵ֫הוּ
	3 *f.*	גְּלֶ֫הָ
Plur.	1 *c.*	גְּלֵ֫נוּ
	3 *m.*	גְּלֵ֫ם

[2] 1 sing. Pi. Hiph. Hithp. usually *ê*, probably to avoid the twofold *î*; e.g. גִּלֵּיתִי.

(Cont. on p. 281

LĀMEDH HĒ (LĀM. YÔDH

		Qal	Niph.	Pi‘ēl	Pu‘al
Juss. 3 sing. m.	&c.	יִ֫גֶל	יִגָּל	יְגַל	
wāw cons. impf.	&c.	וַיִּ֫גֶל	וַיִּגָּל	וַיְגַל	
wāw cons. perf.		וְגָלִ֫יתָ	וְנִגְלֵ֫יתָ	וְגִלִּ֫יתָ	
Inf. cstr.		גְּלוֹת	הִגָּלוֹת	גַּלּוֹת	גֻּלּוֹת
absol.		גָּלֹה	נִגְלֹה	גַּלֵּה	גֻּלֹּה
Part. act.		גֹּלֶה —לָה *f.*		מְגַלֶּה	
pass.		גָּלוּי גְּלוּיָה	נִגְלֶה		מְגֻלֶּה
intrans.		קָשֶׁה —שָׁה			

AND *WĀW* VERBS—§ 32

Hithp.	Hiph.	Hoph.
יִתְגַּל	יֶ֫גֶל	
וַיִּתְגַּל	וַיֶּ֫גֶל	
הִתְגַּלּוֹת	הַגְלוֹת	הָגְלוֹת
הִתְגַּלֵּה	הַגְלֵה	הָגְלֵה
מִתְגַּלֶּה	מַגְלֶה	
		מָגְלֶה

PĒ NÛN VERB—§ 34

	Qal		Niph.	Hiph.	Hoph.
Perf. Sing. 3 *m.*	(נָגַשׁ)	נָפַל	נִגַּשׁ	הִגִּישׁ	הֻגַּשׁ
3 *f.*	(נָֽגְשָׁה)	נָֽפְלָה	נִגְּשָׁה	הִגִּישָׁה	הֻגְּשָׁה
2 *m.*	(נָגַשְׁתָּ)	נָפַלְתָּ	נִגַּשְׁתָּ	הִגַּשְׁתָּ	הֻגַּשְׁתָּ
	&c.	&c.	&c.	&c.	&c.
Impf. Sing. 3 *m.*	יִגַּשׁ	יִפֹּל	יִנָּגֵשׁ	יַגִּישׁ	יֻגַּשׁ
3 *f.*	תִּגַּשׁ	תִּפֹּל	תִּנָּגֵשׁ	תַּגִּישׁ	&c.
2 *m.*	תִּגַּשׁ	תִּפֹּל	תִּנָּגֵשׁ	תַּגִּישׁ	
2 *f.*	תִּגְּשִׁי	תִּפְּלִי	תִּנָּֽגְשִׁי	תַּגִּישִׁי	
1 *c.*	אֶגַּשׁ	אֶפֹּל	אֶנָּגֵשׁ	אַגִּישׁ	
Plur. 3 *m.*	יִגְּשׁוּ	יִפְּלוּ	יִנָּֽגְשׁוּ	יַגִּישׁוּ	
3 *f.*	תִּגַּשְׁנָה	תִּפֹּלְנָה	תִּנָּגַשְׁנָה	תַּגֵּשְׁנָה	
2 *m.*	תִּגְּשׁוּ	תִּפְּלוּ	תִּנָּֽגְשׁוּ	תַּגִּישׁוּ	
2 *f.*	תִּגַּשְׁנָה	תִּפֹּלְנָה	תִּנָּגַשְׁנָה	תַּגֵּשְׁנָה	
1 *c.*	נִגַּשׁ	נִפֹּל	נִנָּגֵשׁ	נַגִּישׁ	
Imp. Sing. 2 *m.*	גַּשׁ (גְּשָׁה)	נְפֹל	הִנָּגֵשׁ	הַגֵּשׁ	
2 *f.*	גְּשִׁי	נִפְלִי	הִנָּֽגְשִׁי	הַגִּישִׁי	wanting
Plur. 2 *m.*	גְּשׁוּ	נִפְלוּ	הִנָּֽגְשׁוּ	הַגִּישׁוּ	
2 *f*	גַּשְׁנָה	נְפֹלְנָה	הִנָּגַשְׁנָה	הַגֵּשְׁנָה	
Juss. 3 *sing.*		יִפֹּל		יַגֵּשׁ	
wāw cons. impf.		וַיִּפֹּל		וַיַּגֵּשׁ	
Cohort. 1 *sing.*	אֶגְּשָׁה	אֶפְּלָה		אַגִּישָׁה	
wāw cons. perf.	וְנָֽגַשְׁתָּ֫	וְנָֽפַלְתָּ֫			
Inf. cstr.	גֶּשֶׁת	נְפֹל	הִנָּגֵשׁ	הַגִּישׁ	הֻגַּשׁ
absol.	נָגוֹשׁ	נָפוֹל	הִנָּגֵשׁ	הַגֵּשׁ	הֻגֵּשׁ
Part. act.	נֹגֵשׁ	נֹפֵל		מַגִּישׁ	
pass.	נָגוּשׁ	—	נִגָּשׁ		מֻגָּשׁ

PĒ NÛN VERB—§ 34

	Qal		Niph.	Pass. Qal
Perf. Sing. 3 *m.*	נָתַן	לָקַח	נִלְקַח, נִתַּן	לֻקַּח
3 *f.*	נָתְנָה	לָקְחָה	נִלְקְחָה, נִתְּנָה	לֻקְּחָה
2 *m.*	נָתַ֫תָּ ־תָּה	לָקַ֫חְתָּ	נִלְקַ֫חְתָּ, נִתַּ֫תָּ	לֻקַּ֫חְתָּ
2 *f.*	נָתַתְּ	&c.	נִלְקַחְתְּ, נִתַּתְּ	לֻקַּחְתְּ
1 *c.*	נָתַ֫תִּי		נִלְקַ֫חְתִּי, נִתַּ֫תִּי	לֻקַּ֫חְתִּי
Plur. 3 *c.*	נָתְנוּ		נִלְקְחוּ, נִתְּנוּ	לֻקְּחוּ
2 *m.*	נְתַתֶּם		נִלְקַחְתֶּם, נִתַּתֶּם	לֻקַּחְתֶּם
2 *f.*				
1 *c.*	נָתַנּוּ		נִלְקַ֫חְנוּ, נִתַּ֫נּוּ	לֻקַּ֫חְנוּ
Impf. Sing. 3 *m.*	יִתֵּן	יִקַּח	יִלָּקַח, יִנָּתֵן	יֻקַּח, יֻתַּן
3 *f.*	תִּתֵּן	תִּקַּח	תִּלָּקַח, תִּנָּתֵן	תֻּקַּח, תֻּתַּן
2 *m.*	תִּתֵּן	תִּקַּח	תִּלָּקַח, תִּנָּתֵן	תֻּקַּח, תֻּתַּן
2 *f.*	תִּתְּנִי	תִּקְחִי	תִּלָּקְחִי, תִּנָּתְנִי	תֻּקְחִי, תֻּתְּנִי
1 *c.*	אֶתֵּן ־תְּנָה	אֶקַּח	אֶלָּקַח, אֶנָּתֵן	אֻקַּח, אֻתַּן
Plur. 3 *m.*	יִתְּנוּ	יִקְחוּ	יִלָּקְחוּ, יִנָּתְנוּ	יֻקְחוּ, יֻתְּנוּ
3 *f.*				
2 *m.*	תִּתְּנוּ	תִּקְחוּ	תִּלָּקְחוּ,תִּנָּתְנוּ	תֻּקְחוּ, תֻּתְּנוּ
2 *f.*				
1 *c.*	נִתֵּן	נִקַּח	נִלָּקַח, נִנָּתֵן	נֻקַּח, נֻתַּן
Imp. Sing. 2 *m.*	תֵּן, תְּנָה	קַח, קְחָה	הִלָּקַח, הִנָּתֵן	wanting
2 *f.*	תְּנִי	קְחִי	הִלָּקְחִי, הִנָּתְנִי	
Plur. 2 *m.*	תְּנוּ	קְחוּ	הִלָּקְחוּ, הִנָּתְנוּ	
2 *f.*				
Juss. 3 *sing.*	יִתֵּן	יִקַּח		
wāw cons. impf.	וַיִּתֵּן	וַיִּקַּח		
Inf. cstr.	תֵּת, תִּתִּי (נְתֹן)	קַ֫חַת, קַחְתִּי	הִלָּקַח, הִנָּתֵן	
abs.	נָתוֹן	לָקוֹחַ	הִנָּתֹן	
Part. act.	נֹתֵן	לֹקֵחַ		
pass.	נָתוּן	לָקוּחַ	נִלְקָח נִתָּן	

PĒ GUTTURAL

		Qal *act.*		Qal *intrans.*		Niph.
Perf.	*Sing.* 3 *m.*	חָתַם	עָמַד	חָכַם	חָזֵק	נֶעֱמַד נֶחְתַּם[1]
	3 *f.*	&c.	עָמְדָה	&c.	or חָזַק	נֶעֶמְדָה
	2 *m.*		עָמַדְתָּ		&c.	נֶעֱמַדְתָּ
	2 *f.*		עָמַדְתְּ			נֶעֱמַדְתְּ
	1 *c.*		עָמַדְתִּי			נֶעֱמַדְתִּי
	Plur. 3 *c.*		עָמְדוּ			נֶעֶמְדוּ
	2 *m.*		עֲמַדְתֶּם			נֶעֱמַדְתֶּם
	2 *f.*		עֲמַדְתֶּן			נֶעֱמַדְתֶּן
	1 *c.*		עָמַדְנוּ			נֶעֱמַדְנוּ
Impf.	*Sing.* 3 *m.*	יַחְתֹּם	יַעֲמֹד	יֶחְכַּם	יֶחֱזַק	יֵעָמֵד
	3 *f.*	&c.	תַּעֲמֹד	&c.	תֶּחֱזַק	תֵּעָמֵד
	2 *m.*		תַּעֲמֹד		תֶּחֱזַק	תֵּעָמֵד
	2 *f.*		תַּעַמְדִי		תֶּחֶזְקִי	תֵּעָמְדִי
	1 *c.*		אֶעֱמֹד		אֶחֱזַק	אֵעָמֵד
	Plur. 3 *m.*		יַעַמְדוּ		יֶחֶזְקוּ	יֵעָמְדוּ
	3 *f.*		תַּעֲמֹדְנָה		תֶּחֱזַקְנָה	תֵּעָמַדְנָה
	2 *m.*		תַּעַמְדוּ		תֶּחֶזְקוּ	תֵּעָמְדוּ
	2 *f.*		תַּעֲמֹדְנָה		תֶּחֱזַקְנָה	תֵּעָמַדְנָה
	1 *c.*		נַעֲמֹד		נֶחֱזַק	נֵעָמֵד
Imp.	*Sing.* 2 *m.*	חֲתֹם	עֲמֹד	חֲכַם	חֲזַק	הֵעָמֵד
	2 *f.*	&c.	עִמְדִי	&c.	חִזְקִי	הֵעָמְדִי
	Plur. 2 *m.*		עִמְדוּ		חִזְקוּ	הֵעָמְדוּ
	2 *f.*		עֲמֹדְנָה		חֲזַקְנָה	הֵעָמַדְנָה

[1] No Niph. of **עָמַד** is actually found in use.

Cont. on p. 286)

VERB—§ 35 *PĒ ’ĀLEPH*—§ 37

Hiph.		Hoph.		Qal
הֶחְתִּים	הֶֽעֱמִיד	הָחְתַּם	הָֽעֳמַד	אָכַל
	הֶֽעֱמִידָה		הָֽעָמְדָה	&c.
	הֶֽעֱמַ֫דְתָּ		הָֽעֳמַ֫דְתָּ	
	הֶֽעֱמַדְתְּ		הָֽעֳמַדְתְּ	
	הֶֽעֱמַ֫דְתִּי		הָֽעֳמַ֫דְתִּי	
	הֶֽעֱמִ֫ידוּ		הָֽעָמְדוּ	
	הֶֽעֱמַדְתֶּם		הָֽעֳמַדְתֶּם	
	הֶֽעֱמַדְתֶּן		הָֽעֳמַדְתֶּן	
	הֶֽעֱמַ֫דְנוּ		הָֽעֳמַ֫דְנוּ	
	יַֽעֲמִיד		יָֽעֳמַד	יֹאכַל
	תַּֽעֲמִיד		תָּֽעֳמַד	תֹּאכַל
	תַּֽעֲמִיד		תָּֽעֳמַד	תֹּאכַל
	תַּֽעֲמִ֫ידִי		תָּֽעָמְדִי	תֹּֽאכְלִי
	אַֽעֲמִיד		אָֽעֳמַד	אֹכַל
	יַֽעֲמִ֫ידוּ		יָֽעָמְדוּ	יֹֽאכְלוּ
	תַּֽעֲמֵ֫דְנָה		תָּֽעֳמַ֫דְנָה	תֹּאכַ֫לְנָה
	תַּֽעֲמִ֫ידוּ		תָּֽעָמְדוּ	תֹּֽאכְלוּ
	תַּֽעֲמֵ֫דְנָה		תָּֽעֳמַ֫דְנָה	תֹּאכַ֫לְנָה
	נַֽעֲמִיד		נָֽעֳמַד	נֹאכַל
	הַֽעֲמֵד			אֱכֹל
	הַֽעֲמִ֫ידִי			אִכְלִי
	הַֽעֲמִ֫ידוּ		wanting	אִכְלוּ
	הַֽעֲמֵ֫דְנָה			אֱכֹ֫לְנָה

(Cont. on p. 287

PĒ GUTTURAL

Continued

	Qal *act.*		Qal *intrans.*		Niph.
Juss. 3 sing.	יַחְתֹּם	יַעֲמֹד	יֶחְכַּם	יֶחֱזַק	
wāw cons. impf.	וַיַּחְתֹּם	וַיַּעֲמֹד	וַיֶּחְכַּם	וַיֶּחֱזַק	
Cohort. 1 sing.		אֶעֶמְדָה			
wāw cons. perf.		וְעָמַדְתָּ			
Inf. cstr.	חֲתֹם	עֲמֹד			הֵעָמֵד
absol.	חָתוֹם	עָמוֹד			נַעֲמוֹד נַחְתּוֹם
Part. act.	חֹתֵם	עֹמֵד		חָזֵק	
pass.	חָתוּם	עָמוּד			נֶעֱמָד נֶחְתָּם

Hiph.	Hoph.	Qal
יַעֲמֵד		
וַיַּעֲמֵד		וַיֹּאכַל (וַיֹּאמֶר)
אַעֲמִידָה		אֹכְלָה
וְהַעֲמַדְתָּ		
הַעֲמִיד		אֱכֹל
הַעֲמֵד	הָעֳמֵד	אָכוֹל
מַעֲמִיד		אֹכֵל
	מָעֳמָד	אָכוּל

ʿ*ĀYIN* GUTTURAL

	Qal	Niphʿal
Perf. *Sing.* 3 *m.*	שָׁחַט (נָחַם)	נִחַם נִשְׁחַט
3 *f.*	שָֽׁחֲטָה	נִשְׁחֲטָה
2 *m.*	שָׁחַ֫טְתָּ	נִשְׁחַ֫טְתָּ
2 *f.*	שָׁחַטְתְּ	נִשְׁחַטְתְּ
1 *c.*	שָׁחַ֫טְתִּי	נִשְׁחַ֫טְתִּי
Plur. 3 *c.*	שָֽׁחֲטוּ	נִשְׁחֲטוּ
2 *m.*	שְׁחַטְתֶּם	נִשְׁחַטְתֶּם
2 *f.*	שְׁחַטְתֶּן	נִשְׁחַטְתֶּן
1 *c.*	שָׁחַ֫טְנוּ	נִשְׁחַ֫טְנוּ
Impf. *Sing.* 3 *m.*	יִשְׁחַט	יִנָּחֵם יִשָּׁחֵט
3 *f.*	תִּשְׁחַט	תִּשָּׁחֵט
2 *m.*	תִּשְׁחַט	תִּשָּׁחֵט
2 *f.*	תִּשְׁחֲטִי	תִּשָּֽׁחֲטִי
1 *c.*	אֶשְׁחַט	אֶשָּׁחֵט
Plur. 3 *m.*	יִשְׁחֲטוּ	יִשָּֽׁחֲטוּ
3 *f*	תִּשְׁחַ֫טְנָה	תִּשָּׁחַ֫טְנָה
2 *m.*	תִּשְׁחֲטוּ	תִּשָּֽׁחֲטוּ
2 *f.*	תִּשְׁחַ֫טְנָה	תִּשָּׁחַ֫טְנָה
1 *c.*	נִשְׁחַט	נִשָּׁחֵט
Imp. *Sing.* 2 *m.*	שְׁחַט	הִנָּחֵם הִשָּׁחֵט
2 *f.*	שַֽׁחֲטִי	הִשָּֽׁחֲטִי
Plur. 2 *m.*	שַֽׁחֲטוּ	הִשָּֽׁחֲטוּ
2 *f.*	שְׁחַ֫טְנָה	הִשָּׁחַ֫טְנָה

Cont. on p. 290)

VERBS—§ 36

Pi‘ēl		Pu‘al		Hithp.	
בֵּרֵךְ	נִחַם	בֹּרַךְ	נֻחַם	הִתְבָּרֵךְ	הִתְנַחֵם
בֵּרֲכָה, בֵּרְכָה		בֹּרְכָה		הִתְבָּרֲכָה	
בֵּרַכְתָּ		בֹּרַכְתָּ		הִתְבָּרַכְתָּ	
בֵּרַכְתְּ		בֹּרַכְתְּ		הִתְבָּרַכְתְּ	
בֵּרַכְתִּי		בֹּרַכְתִּי		הִתְבָּרַכְתִּי	
בֵּרֲכוּ, בֵּרְכוּ		בֹּרְכוּ		הִתְבָּרֲכוּ	
בֵּרַכְתֶּם		בֹּרַכְתֶּם		הִתְבָּרַכְתֶּם	
בֵּרַכְתֶּן		בֹּרַכְתֶּן		הִתְבָּרַכְתֶּן	
בֵּרַכְנוּ		בֹּרַכְנוּ		הִתְבָּרַכְנוּ	
יְבָרֵךְ	יְנַחֵם	יְבֹרַךְ	יְנֻחַם	יִתְבָּרֵךְ	יִתְנַחֵם
תְּבָרֵךְ		תְּבֹרַךְ		תִּתְבָּרֵךְ	
תְּבָרֵךְ		תְּבֹרַךְ		תִּתְבָּרֵךְ	
תְּבָרֲכִי, תְּבָרְכִי		תְּבֹרְכִי		תִּתְבָּרֲכִי	
אֲבָרֵךְ		אֲבֹרַךְ		אֶתְבָּרֵךְ	
יְבָרֲכוּ, יְבָרְכוּ		יְבֹרְכוּ		יִתְבָּרֲכוּ	
תְּבָרַכְנָה		תְּבֹרַכְנָה		תִּתְבָּרַכְנָה	
תְּבָרֲכוּ, תְּבָרְכוּ		תְּבֹרְכוּ		תִּתְבָּרֲכוּ	
תְּבָרַכְנָה		תְּבֹרַכְנָה		תִּתְבָּרַכְנָה	
נְבָרֵךְ		נְבֹרַךְ		נִתְבָּרֵךְ	
בָּרֵךְ	נַחֵם	–		הִתְבָּרֵךְ	הִתְנַחֵם
בָּרֲכִי, בָּרְכִי		–		הִתְבָּרֲכִי	
בָּרֲכוּ, בָּרְכוּ		–		הִתְבָּרֲכוּ	
בָּרַכְנָה		–		הִתְבָּרַכְנָה	

Continued ʿAYIN GUTTURAL

	Qal	Niphʿal
Juss. 3 sing.	יִשְׁחַט	יִשָּׁחֵט
wāw cons. impf.	וַיִּשְׁחַט	וַיִּשָּׁחֵט
impf. with suff.	יִשְׁחָטֵנִי	
Inf. cstr.	שְׁחֹט	הִנָּחֵם הִשָּׁחֵט
absol.	שָׁחוֹט	נִשְׁחוֹט
Part. act.	שֹׁחֵט	
pass.	שָׁחוּט	נִחָם נִשְׁחָט

VERBS—§ 36

Pi'ēl	Pu'al	Hithp.
נַחֵם בָּרֵךְ	נֻחַם בֹּרַךְ	הִתְנַחֵם הִתְבָּרֵךְ
בָּרֵךְ		
מְנַחֵם מְבָרֵךְ		מִתְנַחֵם מִתְבָּרֵךְ
	מְנֻחָם מְבֹרָךְ	

LĀMEDH GUTTURAL

	Qal	Niph.	Piʿēl
Perf. *Sing.* 3 *m.*	שָׁלַח	נִשְׁלַח	שִׁלַּח
3 *f.*	שָֽׁלְחָה	נִשְׁלְחָה	שִׁלְּחָה
2 *m.*	שָׁלַ֫חְתָּ	נִשְׁלַ֫חְתָּ	שִׁלַּ֫חְתָּ
2 *f.*	שָׁלַ֫חַתְּ	נִשְׁלַ֫חַתְּ	שִׁלַּ֫חַתְּ
1 *c.*	שָׁלַ֫חְתִּי	נִשְׁלַ֫חְתִּי	שִׁלַּ֫חְתִּי
Plur. 3 *c.*	שָֽׁלְחוּ	נִשְׁלְחוּ	שִׁלְּחוּ
2 *m.*	שְׁלַחְתֶּם	נִשְׁלַחְתֶּם	שִׁלַּחְתֶּם
2 *f.*	שְׁלַחְתֶּן	נִשְׁלַחְתֶּן	שִׁלַּחְתֶּן
1 *c.*	שָׁלַ֫חְנוּ	נִשְׁלַ֫חְנוּ	שִׁלַּ֫חְנוּ
Impf. *Sing.* 3 *m.*	יִשְׁלַח	יִשָּׁלַח	יְשַׁלַּח
3 *f.*	תִּשְׁלַח	תִּשָּׁלַח	תְּשַׁלַּח
2 *m.*	תִּשְׁלַח	תִּשָּׁלַח	תְּשַׁלַּח
2 *f.*	תִּשְׁלְחִי	תִּשָּֽׁלְחִי	תְּשַׁלְּחִי
1 *c.*	אֶשְׁלַח	אֶשָּׁלַח	אֲשַׁלַּח
Plur. 3 *m.*	יִשְׁלְחוּ	יִשָּֽׁלְחוּ	יְשַׁלְּחוּ
3 *f.*	תִּשְׁלַ֫חְנָה	תִּשָּׁלַ֫חְנָה	תְּשַׁלַּ֫חְנָה
2 *m.*	תִּשְׁלְחוּ	תִּשָּֽׁלְחוּ	תְּשַׁלְּחוּ
2 *f.*	תִּשְׁלַ֫חְנָה	תִּשָּׁלַ֫חְנָה	תְּשַׁלַּ֫חְנָה
1 *c.*	נִשְׁלַח	נִשָּׁלַח	נְשַׁלַּח
Imp. *Sing.* 2 *m.*	שְׁלַח	הִשָּׁלַח	שַׁלַּח
2 *f.*	שִׁלְחִי	הִשָּֽׁלְחִי	שַׁלְּחִי
Plur. 2 *m.*	שִׁלְחוּ	הִשָּֽׁלְחוּ	שַׁלְּחוּ
2 *f.*	שְׁלַ֫חְנָה	הִשָּׁלַ֫חְנָה	שַׁלַּ֫חְנָה

Cont. on p. 294)

VERBS—§ 36

Puʿal	Hithp.	Hiph.	Hoph.
שֻׁלַּח	הִשְׁתַּלַּח	הִשְׁלִיחַ	הָשְׁלַח
שֻׁלְּחָה	הִשְׁתַּלְּחָה	הִשְׁלִ֫יחָה	הָשְׁלְחָה
שֻׁלַּ֫חְתָּ	הִשְׁתַּלַּ֫חְתָּ	הִשְׁלַ֫חְתָּ	הָשְׁלַ֫חְתָּ
שֻׁלַּ֫חַתְּ	הִשְׁתַּלַּ֫חַתְּ	הִשְׁלַ֫חַתְּ	הָשְׁלַ֫חַתְּ
שֻׁלַּ֫חְתִּי	הִשְׁתַּלַּ֫חְתִּי	הִשְׁלַ֫חְתִּי	הָשְׁלַ֫חְתִּי
שֻׁלְּחוּ	הִשְׁתַּלְּחוּ	הִשְׁלִ֫יחוּ	הָשְׁלְחוּ
שֻׁלַּחְתֶּם	הִשְׁתַּלַּחְתֶּם	הִשְׁלַחְתֶּם	הָשְׁלַחְתֶּם
שֻׁלַּחְתֶּן	הִשְׁתַּלַּחְתֶּן	הִשְׁלַחְתֶּן	הָשְׁלַחְתֶּן
שֻׁלַּ֫חְנוּ	הִשְׁתַּלַּ֫חְנוּ	הִשְׁלַ֫חְנוּ	הָשְׁלַ֫חְנוּ
יְשֻׁלַּח	יִשְׁתַּלַּח	יַשְׁלִיחַ	יָשְׁלַח
תְּשֻׁלַּח	תִּשְׁתַּלַּח	תַּשְׁלִיחַ	תָּשְׁלַח
תְּשֻׁלַּח	תִּשְׁתַּלַּח	תַּשְׁלִיחַ	תָּשְׁלַח
תְּשֻׁלְּחִי	תִּשְׁתַּלְּחִי	תַּשְׁלִ֫יחִי	תָּשְׁלְחִי
אֲשֻׁלַּח	אֶשְׁתַּלַּח	אַשְׁלִיחַ	אָשְׁלַח
יְשֻׁלְּחוּ	יִשְׁתַּלְּחוּ	יַשְׁלִ֫יחוּ	יָשְׁלְחוּ
תְּשֻׁלַּ֫חְנָה	תִּשְׁתַּלַּ֫חְנָה	תַּשְׁלַ֫חְנָה	תָּשְׁלַ֫חְנָה
תְּשֻׁלְּחוּ	תִּשְׁתַּלְּחוּ	תַּשְׁלִ֫יחוּ	תָּשְׁלְחוּ
תְּשֻׁלַּ֫חְנָה	תִּשְׁתַּלַּ֫חְנָה	תַּשְׁלַ֫חְנָה	תָּשְׁלַ֫חְנָה
נְשֻׁלַּח	נִשְׁתַּלַּח	נַשְׁלִיחַ	נָשְׁלַח
	הִשְׁתַּלַּח	הַשְׁלַח	
wanting	הִשְׁתַּלְּחִי	הַשְׁלִ֫יחִי	wanting
	הִשְׁתַּלְּחוּ	הַשְׁלִ֫יחוּ	
	הִשְׁתַּלַּ֫חְנָה	הַשְׁלַ֫חְנָה	

(Cont. on p. 295

Continued LĀMEDH GUTTURAL

	Qal	Niph.	Pi'ēl
Juss. 3 sing.	יִשְׁלַח	יִשָּׁלַח	יְשַׁלַּח
wāw cons. impf.	וַיִּשְׁלַח	וַיִּשָּׁלַח	וַיְשַׁלַּח
impf. with suff.	יִשְׁלָחֵ֫נִי	&c.	
Inf. cstr.	שְׁלֹחַ	הִשָּׁלַח	שַׁלַּח
absol.	שָׁלוֹחַ	נִשְׁלֹחַ	שַׁלֵּחַ
Part. act.	שֹׁלֵחַ		מְשַׁלֵּחַ
pass.	שָׁלוּחַ	נִשְׁלָח	

VERBS—§ 36

Puʿal	Hithp.	Hiph.	Hoph.
	יִשְׁתַּלַּח	יַשְׁלַח	
	וַיִּשְׁתַּלַּח	וַיַּשְׁלַח	
	הִשְׁתַּלַּח	הַשְׁלִיחַ	
		הַשְׁלֵחַ	הָשְׁלֵחַ
	מִשְׁתַּלֵּחַ	מַשְׁלִיחַ	
מְשֻׁלָּח			מָשְׁלָח

LĀMEDH ʾĀLEPH

	Qal		Niph.
Perf. Sing. 3 *m.*	מָצָא	מָלֵא	נִמְצָא
3 *f.*	מָֽצְאָה	מָֽלְאָה	נִמְצְאָה
2 *m.*	מָצָ֫אתָ	מָלֵ֫אתָ	נִמְצֵ֫אתָ
2 *f.*	מָצָאת	מָלֵאת	נִמְצֵאת
1 *c.*	מָצָ֫אתִי	מָלֵ֫אתִי	נִמְצֵ֫אתִי
Plur. 3 *c.*	מָֽצְאוּ	מָֽלְאוּ	נִמְצְאוּ
2 *m.*	מְצָאתֶם	מְלֵאתֶם	נִמְצֵאתֶם
2 *f.*	מְצָאתֶן	מְלֵאתֶן	נִמְצֵאתֶן
1 *c.*	מָצָ֫אנוּ	מָלֵ֫אנוּ	נִמְצֵ֫אנוּ
Impf. Sing. 3 *m.*	יִמְצָא	יִמְלָא	יִמָּצֵא
3 *f.*	תִּמְצָא	תִּמְלָא	תִּמָּצֵא
2 *m.*	תִּמְצָא	תִּמְלָא	תִּמָּצֵא
2 *f.*	תִּמְצְאִי	תִּמְלְאִי	תִּמָּֽצְאִי
1 *c.*	אֶמְצָא	אֶמְלָא	אֶמָּצֵא
Plur. 3 *m.*	יִמְצְאוּ	יִמְלְאוּ	יִמָּֽצְאוּ
3 *f.*	תִּמְצֶ֫אנָה	תִּמְלֶ֫אנָה	תִּמָּצֶ֫אנָה
2 *m.*	תִּמְצְאוּ	תִּמְלְאוּ	תִּמָּֽצְאוּ
2 *f.*	תִּמְצֶ֫אנָה	תִּמְלֶ֫אנָה	תִּמָּצֶ֫אנָה
1 *c.*	נִמְצָא	נִמְלָא	נִמָּצֵא
Imp. Sing. 2 *m.*	מְצָא	מְלָא	הִמָּצֵא
2 *f.*	מִצְאִי	מִלְאִי	הִמָּֽצְאִי
Plur. 2 *m.*	מִצְאוּ	מִלְאוּ	הִמָּֽצְאוּ
2 *f.*	מְצֶ֫אנָה	מְלֶ֫אנָה	הִמָּצֶ֫אנָה

Cont. on p. 298)

VERBS—§ 38

Piʿēl	Puʿal	Hithp.	Hiph.	Hoph.
מִצֵּא	מֻצָּא	הִתְמַצֵּא	הִמְצִיא	הֻמְצָא
מִצְּאָה	מֻצְּאָה	as	הִמְצִ֫יאָה	הֻמְצְאָה
מִצֵּ֫אתָ	מֻצֵּ֫אתָ [1]	*Pi.*	הִמְצֵ֫אתָ	הֻמְצֵ֫אתָ [1]
מִצֵּאת	מֻצֵּאת		הִמְצֵאת	as
מִצֵּ֫אתִי	מֻצֵּ֫אתִי		הִמְצֵ֫אתִי	*Pu.*
מִצְּאוּ	מֻצְּאוּ		הִמְצִ֫יאוּ	
מִצֵּאתֶם	מֻצֵּאתֶם		הִמְצֵאתֶם	
מִצֵּאתֶן	מֻצֵּאתֶן		הִמְצֵאתֶן	
מִצֵּ֫אנוּ	מֻצֵּ֫אנוּ		הִמְצֵ֫אנוּ	
יְמַצֵּא	יְמֻצָּא	יִתְמַצֵּא	יַמְצִיא	יֻמְצָא
תְּמַצֵּא	as	as	תַּמְצִיא	as
תְּמַצֵּא	*Qal*	*Pi.*	תַּמְצִיא	*Qal*
תְּמַצְּאִי			תַּמְצִ֫יאִי	
אֲמַצֵּא			אַמְצִיא	
יְמַצְּאוּ			יַמְצִ֫יאוּ	
תְּמַצֶּ֫אנָה			תַּמְצֶ֫אנָה	
תְּמַצְּאוּ			תַּמְצִ֫יאוּ	
תְּמַצֶּ֫אנָה			תַּמְצֶ֫אנָה	
נְמַצֵּא			נַמְצִיא	
מַצֵּא		הִתְמַצֵּא	הַמְצֵא	
מַצְּאִי	wanting		הַמְצִ֫יאִי	wanting
מַצְּאוּ			הַמְצִ֫יאוּ	
מַצֶּ֫אנָה			הַמְצֶ֫אנָה	

[1] Or possibly הֻמְצָאתָ, מֻצָּאתָ, &c. The only existing example of a pf. pass. inflected in a manner to indicate its vowel, is pointed *ā* not *ē*. (Ez. 40. 4.)

(Cont. on p. 299

LĀMEDH ʾĀLEPH

Continued	Qal		Niph.
Juss. 3 sing.	יִמְצָא	יִמְלָא	יִמָּצֵא
wāw cons. impf.	וַיִּמְצָא	וַיִּמְלָא	וַיִּמָּצֵא
wāw cons. perf.	וּמָצָאתָ	וּמָלֵ֫אתָ	וְנִמְצֵ֫אתָ
impf. with suff.	יִמְצָאֵנִי	יִמְלָאֵנִי	
Inf. cstr.	מְצֹא	מְלֹא	הִמָּצֵא
absol.	מָצוֹא	מָלוֹא	נִמְצֹא
Part. act.	מֹצֵא	מָלֵא	נִמְצָא
pass.	מָצוּא		

VERBS—§ 38

Pi'ēl	Pu'al	Hithp.	Hiph.	Hoph.
			יַמְצֵא	
			וַיַּמְצֵא	
וּמִצֵּאתָ				
יְמַצְּאֵנִי			יַמְצִיאֵנִי	
מַצֵּא		הִתְמַצֵּא	הַמְצִיא	הָמְצָא
מַצֹּא			הַמְצֵא	
מְמַצֵּא		מִתְמַצֵּא	מַמְצִיא	
	מְמֻצָּא			מָמְצָא

VERBS DOUBLE

			Qal			
			act.		*intrans.*	
Perf.	*Sing.*	3 *m.*	(סַב) סָבַב		קַל	מַל
		3 *f.*	(סַבָּה) סָבְבָה		קַלָּה	&c.
		2 *m.*	סַבּוֹתָ		קַלּוֹתָ	
		2 *f.*	סַבּוֹת		קַלּוֹת	
		1 *c.*	סַבּוֹתִי		קַלּוֹתִי	
	Plur.	3 *c.*	(סַבּוּ) סָבְבוּ		קַלּוּ	
		2 *m.*	סַבּוֹתֶם		קַלּוֹתֶם	
		2 *f.*	סַבּוֹתֶן		קַלּוֹתֶן	
		1 *c.*	סַבּוֹנוּ		קַלּוֹנוּ	
Impf.	*Sing.*	3 *m.*	יָסֹב	יִסֹּב	יֵקַל	יִמַּל
		3 *f.*	תָּסֹב	תִּסֹּב	תֵּקַל	תִּמַּל
		2 *m.*	תָּסֹב	תִּסֹּב	תֵּקַל	תִּמַּל
		2 *f.*	תָּסֹבִּי	תִּסְּבִי	תֵּקַלִּי	תִּמְּלִי
		1 *c.*	אָסֹב	אֶסֹּב	אֵקַל	אֶמַּל
	Plur.	3 *m.*	יָסֹבּוּ	יִסְּבוּ	יֵקַלּוּ	יִמְּלוּ
		3 *f.*	תְּסֻבֶּינָה	תִּסֹּבְנָה	תְּקַלֶּינָה	תִּמַּלְנָה
		2 *m.*	תָּסֹבּוּ	תִּסְּבוּ	תֵּקַלּוּ	תִּמְּלוּ
		2 *f.*	תְּסֻבֶּינָה	תִּסֹּבְנָה	תְּקַלֶּינָה	תִּמַּלְנָה
		1 *c.*	נָסֹב	נִסֹּב	נֵקַל	נִמַּל
Imp.	*Sing.*	2 *m.*	סֹב			
		2 *f.*	סֹבִּי			
	Plur.	2 *m.*	סֹבּוּ			
		2 *f.*	סֻבֶּינָה			

Cont. on p. 302)

‘AYIN—§ 39

Niph.	Hiph.	Hoph.
נָסַב	הֵסֵב	הוּסַב
נָסַ֫בָּה	הֵסֵ֫בָּה	הוּסַ֫בָּה
נְסַבּ֫וֹתָ	הֲסִבּ֫וֹתָ	הוּסַבּ֫וֹתָ
נְסַבּוֹת	הֲסִבּוֹת	&c.
נְסַבּ֫וֹתִי	הֲסִבּוֹתִי	
נָסַבּוּ	הֵסַבּוּ	
נְסַבּוֹתֶם	הֲסִבּוֹתֶם	
נְסַבּוֹתֶן	הֲסִבּוֹתֶן	
נְסַבּ֫וֹנוּ	הֲסִבּוֹנוּ	
יִסַּב	יָסֵב יַסֵּב	יוּסַב יֻסַּב
תִּסַּב	תָּסֵב	&c.
תִּסַּב	תָּסֵב	
תִּסַּ֫בִּי	תָּסֵ֫בִּי	
אֶסַּב	אָסֵב	
יִסַּ֫בּוּ	יָסֵ֫בּוּ	
תִּסַּבֶּ֫ינָה	תְּסִבֶּ֫ינָה	
תִּסַּ֫בּוּ	תָּסֵ֫בּוּ	
תִּסַּבֶּ֫ינָה	תְּסִבֶּ֫ינָה	
נִסַּב	נָסֵב	
הִסַּב	הָסֵב	
הִסַּ֫בִּי	הָסֵ֫בִּי	
הִסַּ֫בּוּ	הָסֵ֫בּוּ	
הִסַּבֶּ֫ינָה	הֲסִבֶּ֫ינָה	

Forms of Intens.

Act.	*Pass.*	*Reflex.*
קִלֵּל	קֻלַּל	הִתְקַלֵּל
קוֹלֵל	קוֹלַל	הִתְקוֹלֵל
קִלְקֵל	קָלְקַל	הִתְקַלְקֵל

like *Pi‘ēl* &c. in the Regular Verb

(Cont. on p. 303

VERBS DOUBLE

Continued	Qal			
		act.		*intrans.*
Juss. 3 *sing.*	יָסֹב	יִסֹּב	יֵקַל	יִמַּל
wāw cons. impf.	וַיָּסָב	וַיִּסֹּב	וַיֵּקַל	וַיִּמַּל
Cohort. 1 *sing.*	אָסֹ֫בָּה	אֶסְּבָה	אֵקַ֫לָּה	אֶמְּלָה
wāw cons. perf.	וְסַבּוֹתָ			
Inf. cstr.		סֹב	קֹל קַל	
absol.		סָבוֹב	קָלוֹל	
Part. act.		סוֹבֵב	קַל קַלָּה	
pass.		סָבוּב		

ʿAYIN—§ 39

Niph.	Hiph.	Hoph.
	יָסֵב	
	וַיָּ֫סֶב	
הִסַּב	הָסֵב	הוּסַב
הִסּוֹב	הָסֵב	
	מֵסֵב מְסִבָּה	
נָסָב נְסַבָּה		מוּסָב

NOUNS

FIRST DECLENSION—§§ 15, &c.

MASC.	*word*	*old man*	*star*	*desert*	*hand*	*blood*	*ri*
Sing. abs.	דָּבָר	זָקֵן	כּוֹכָב	מִדְבָּר	יָד	דָּם	ר
cstr.	דְּבַר	זְקַן	כּוֹכַב	מִדְבַּר	יַד	דַּם	ר
w. 1 *s.suf.*	דְּבָרִי	זְקֵנִי	כּוֹכָבִי	מִדְבָּרִי	יָדִי	דָּמִי	רִי
2. *s.m.*	דְּבָרְךָ	זְקֵנְךָ	כּוֹכָבְךָ	מִדְבָּרְךָ	יָדְךָ	דָּמְךָ	רְךָ
2 *pl.m.*	דְּבַרְכֶם	זְקַנְכֶם	כּוֹכַבְכֶם	מִדְבַּרְכֶם	יֶדְכֶם	דַּמְכֶם	רְכֶם
Plur. abs.	דְּבָרִים	זְקֵנִים	כּוֹכָבִים	מִדְבָּרִים	יָדוֹת	דָּמִים	רִים
cstr.	דִּבְרֵי	זִקְנֵי	כּוֹכְבֵי	מִדְבְּרֵי	יְדוֹת	דְּמֵי	רֵי
w. 1 *s.suf.*	דְּבָרַי	זְקֵנַי	כּוֹכָבַי	מִדְבָּרַי	יְדֹתַי	דָּמַי	רַי
2 *s.m.*	דְּבָרֶיךָ	זְקֵנֶיךָ	כּוֹכָבֶיךָ	מִדְבָּרֶיךָ	יְדֹתֶיךָ	דָּמֶיךָ	רֶיךָ
2. *pl.m.*	דִּבְרֵיכֶם	זִקְנֵיכֶם	כּוֹכְבֵיכֶם	מִדְבְּרֵיכֶם	יְדֹתֵיכֶם	דְּמֵיכֶם	רֵיכֶם

---

	wicked	*joyful*	*army*	*rising*	*dead*	*leaf*	*field*	*beau*
Sing. abs.	רָשָׁע	שָׂמֵחַ	צָבָא	קָם	מֵת	עָלֶה	שָׂדֶה	
cstr.	רְשַׁע	שְׂמַח	צְבָא	קָם	מֵת	עֲלֵה	שְׂדֵה	
w. 1. *s.suf.*	רְשָׁעִי	שְׂמֵחִי	צְבָאִי	קָמִי	מֵתִי	עָלִי	שָׂדִי	
2 *s.m.*	רְשָׁעֲךָ	שְׂמֵחֲךָ	צְבָאֲךָ	קָמְךָ	מֵתְךָ	עָלְךָ	שָׂדְךָ	)
2 *pl.m.*	רְשַׁעֲכֶם	שְׂמַחֲכֶם	צְבַאֲכֶם	קָמְכֶם	מֵתְכֶם	עַלְכֶם	שַׂדְכֶם	ם)
Plur. abs.	רְשָׁעִים	שְׂמֵחִים	צְבָאוֹת	קָמִים	מֵתִים	עָלִים	שָׂדוֹת	
cstr.	רִשְׁעֵי	שִׂמְחֵי / שְׂמֵחֵי	צִבְאוֹת	קָמֵי	מֵתֵי	עֲלֵי	שְׂדוֹת	
w. 1. *s.suf.*	רְשָׁעַי	שְׂמֵחַי	צִבְאֹתַי	קָמַי	מֵתַי	עָלַי	שְׂדֹתַי	
2. *s.m.*	רְשָׁעֶיךָ	שְׂמֵחֶיךָ	צִבְאֹתֶיךָ	קָמֶיךָ	מֵתֶיךָ	עָלֶיךָ	שְׂדֹתֶיךָ	ךָ)
2. *pl.m.*	רִשְׁעֵיכֶם	שְׂמֵחֵיכֶם	צִבְאֹתֵיכֶם	קָמֵיכֶם	מֵתֵיכֶם	עֲלֵיכֶם	שְׂדֹתֵיכֶם	כֶם)

EM.	*righteousness*	*corpse*	*fish*	*rising*	*dead*	*beautiful*
ing. abs.	צְדָקָה	נְבֵלָה	דָּגָה	קָמָ֫ה	מֵתָ֫ה	יָפָה
cstr.	צִדְקַת	נִבְלַת	דְּגַת	קָמַת	מֵתַת	יְפַת
. 1. *s.suf.*	צִדְקָתִי	נִבְלָתִי	דְּגָתִי	קָמָתִי	מֵתָתִי	(יְפָתִי)
2. *s.m.*	צִדְקָֽתְךָ	נִבְלָֽתְךָ	דְּגָֽתְךָ	קָמָֽתְךָ	מֵתָֽתְךָ	(יְפָֽתְךָ)
2. *pl.m.*	צִדְקַתְכֶם	נִבְלַתְכֶם	דְּגַתְכֶם	קָמַתְכֶם	מֵתַתְכֶם	(יְפַתְכֶם)
ur. abs.	צְדָקוֹת	נְבֵלוֹת	דָּגוֹת	קָמוֹת	מֵתוֹת	יָפוֹת
cstr.	צִדְקוֹת	נִבְלוֹת	דְּגוֹת	קָמוֹת	מֵתוֹת	יְפוֹת
. 1. *s.suf.*	צִדְקֹתַי	נִבְלֹתַי	דְּגֹתַי	קָמֹתַי	מֵתֹתַי	(יְפֹתַי)
2. *s.m.*	צִדְקֹתֶיךָ	נִבְלֹתֶיךָ	דְּגֹתֶיךָ	קָמֹתֶיךָ	מֵתֹתֶיךָ	(יְפֹתֶיךָ)
2. *pl.m.*	צִדְקֹתֵיכֶם	נִבְלֹתֵיכֶם	דְּגֹתֵיכֶם	קָמֹתֵיכֶם	מֵתֹתֵיכֶם	(יְפֹתֵיכֶם)

DUAL.	*hands*	*lips*
Abs.	יָדַיִם	שְׂפָתַיִם
cstr.	יְדֵי	שִׂפְתֵי
w. 1. *s.suf.*	יָדַי	שְׂפָתַי
2. *s.m.*	יָדֶיךָ	שְׂפָתֶיךָ
2. *pl. m.*	יְדֵיכֶם	שִׂפְתֵיכֶם

SECOND DECLENSION—§§ 25, &c.

MASC.	*king*	*book*	*morning*	*young man*	*terror*	*breadt*
Sing. abs.	מֶ֫לֶךְ	סֵ֫פֶר	בֹּ֫קֶר	נַ֫עַר	פַּ֫חַד	חַב
cstr.	מֶ֫לֶךְ	סֵפֶר	בֹּקֶר	נַעַר	פַּחַד	חַב
w. 1. *s.suf.*	מַלְכִּי	סִפְרִי	בָּקְרִי	נַעֲרִי	פַּחְדִּי	חְבִּי
2. *s.m.*	מַלְכְּךָ	סִפְרְךָ	בָּקְרְךָ	נַעַרְךָ	פַּחְדְּךָ	חְבְּךָ
2. *pl.m.*	מַלְכְּכֶם	סִפְרְכֶם	בָּקְרְכֶם	נַעַרְכֶם	פַּחְדְּכֶם	חְבְּכֶם
Plur. abs.	מְלָכִים	סְפָרִים	בְּקָרִים	נְעָרִים	פְּחָדִים	חָבִים)
cstr.	מַלְכֵי	סִפְרֵי	בָּקְרֵי	נַעֲרֵי	פַּחֲדֵי	חֲבֵי)
w. 1. *s.suf.*	מְלָכַי	סְפָרַי	בְּקָרַי	נְעָרַי	פְּחָדַי	חָבַי)
2. *s.m.*	מְלָכֶיךָ	סְפָרֶיךָ	בְּקָרֶיךָ	נְעָרֶיךָ	פְּחָדֶיךָ	חָבֶיךָ)
2. *pl.m.*	מַלְכֵיכֶם	סִפְרֵיכֶם	בָּקְרֵיכֶם	נַעֲרֵיכֶם	פַּחֲדֵיכֶם	חֲבֵיכֶם)

	seed	*spear*	*sin*	*death*	*olive-tree*	*army* *pow*
Sing. abs.	זֶ֫רַע	רֹמַח	חֵטְא	מָוֶת	זַ֫יִת	יִל
cstr.	זֶרַע	רֹמַח	חֵטְא	מוֹת	זֵית	יל
w. 1. *s.suf.*	זַרְעִי	רָמְחִי	חֶטְאִי	מוֹתִי	זֵיתִי	ילִי
2. *s.m.*	זַרְעֲךָ	רָמְחֲךָ	חֶטְאֲךָ	מוֹתְךָ	זֵיתְךָ	ילְךָ
2. *pl.m.*	זַרְעֲכֶם	רָמְחֲכֶם	חֶטְאֲכֶם	מוֹתְכֶם	זֵיתְכֶם	ילְכֶם
Plur. abs.	זְרָעִים	רְמָחִים	חֲטָאִים	מוֹתִים	זֵיתִים	יָלִים
cstr.	זַרְעֵי	רָמְחֵי	חֲטָאֵי	מוֹתֵי	זֵיתֵי	ילֵי
w. 1. *s.suf.*	זְרָעַי	רְמָחַי	חֲטָאַי	מוֹתַי	זֵיתַי	יָלַי)
2. *s.m.*	זְרָעֶיךָ	רְמָחֶיךָ	חֲטָאֶיךָ	מוֹתֶיךָ	זֵיתֶיךָ	יָלֶיךָ)
2. *pl.m.*	זַרְעֵיכֶם	רָמְחֵיכֶם	חַטְאֵיכֶם	מוֹתֵיכֶם	זֵיתֵיכֶם	ילֵיכֶם

	honey	*stench*	*fruit*	*half*	*sickness*
Sing. abs.	דְּבַשׁ	בְּאשׁ	פְּרִי	חֲצִי	חֳלִי
cstr.	דְּבַשׁ	בְּאשׁ	פְּרִי	חֲצִי	חֳלִי
w. I. *s.suf.*	דִּבְשִׁי	בָּאְשִׁי	פִּרְיִי	חֶצְיִי	חָלְיִי
2. *s.m.*	דִּבְשְׁךָ	בָּאְשְׁךָ	פִּרְיְךָ	חֶצְיְךָ	חָלְיְךָ
2. *pl.m.*	דִּבְשְׁכֶם	בָּאְשְׁכֶם	פִּרְיְכֶם	חֶצְיְכֶם	חָלְיְכֶם
Plur. abs.					חֳלָיִים
cstr.					חָלְיֵי
w. I. *s.suf.*					(חֳלָיַי)
2. *s.m.*					(חֳלָיֶיךָ)
2. *pl.m.*					(חָלְיֵיכֶם)

	queen	*ewe-lamb*	*desert*	*kingdom*	*nurse*	*tunic*
abs.	מַלְכָּה	כִּבְשָׂה	חָרְבָּה	מַמְלָכָה	מֵינֶקֶת	כְּתֹנֶת, כֻּתֹּנֶת
cstr.	מַלְכַּת	כִּבְשַׂת	חָרְבַּת	מַמְלֶכֶת	מֵינֶקֶת	כְּתֹנֶת
s.suf.	מַלְכָּתִי	כִּבְשָׂתִי	חָרְבָּתִי	מַמְלַכְתִּי	מֵינִקְתִּי	כֻּתָּנְתִּי
s.m.	מַלְכָּתְךָ	כִּבְשָׂתְךָ	חָרְבָּתְךָ	מַמְלַכְתְּךָ	מֵינִקְתְּךָ	כֻּתָּנְתְּךָ
pl.m.	מַלְכַּתְכֶם	כִּבְשַׂתְכֶם	חָרְבַּתְכֶם	מַמְלַכְתְּכֶם	מֵינִקְתְּכֶם	כֻּתָּנְתְּכֶם
abs.	מְלָכוֹת	כְּבָשׂוֹת	חֳרָבוֹת	מַמְלָכוֹת	מֵינִיקוֹת	כֻּתֳּנוֹת
cstr.	מַלְכוֹת	כִּבְשׂוֹת	חָרְבוֹת	מַמְלְכוֹת	מֵינִיקוֹת	כָּתְנוֹת
s.suf.	מַלְכוֹתַי	כִּבְשׂוֹתַי	חָרְבוֹתַי	מַמְלְכוֹתַי	מֵינִיקוֹתַי	כֻּתֳּנוֹתַי
s.m.	מַלְכֹתֶיךָ	כִּבְשֹׂתֶיךָ	חָרְבֹתֶיךָ	מַמְלְכֹתֶיךָ	מֵינִיקֹתֶיךָ	כֻּתֳּנֹתֶיךָ
pl.m.	מַלְכֹתֵיכֶם	כִּבְשֹׂתֵיכֶם	חָרְבֹתֵיכֶם	מַמְלְכֹתֵיכֶם	מֵינִיקֹתֵיכֶם	כֻּתֳּנֹתֵיכֶם

DUAL.	*feet*	*knees*	*ears*	*sides*
Absol.	רַגְלַיִם	בִּרְכַּיִם	אָזְנַיִם	יַרְכָתַיִם
Cstr.	רַגְלֵי	בִּרְכֵּי	אָזְנֵי	יַרְכְּתֵי
w. I. *s.suf.*	רַגְלַי	בִּרְכַּי	אָזְנַי	(יַרְכָתַי)
2. *s.m.*	רַגְלֶיךָ	בִּרְכֶּיךָ	אָזְנֶיךָ	(יַרְכָתֶיךָ)
pl. 2. *m.*	רַגְלֵיכֶם	בִּרְכֵּיכֶם	אָזְנֵיכֶם	(יַרְכְּתֵיכֶם)

THIRD DECLENSION—§§ 26, &c.

	killing	*staff*	*name*	*priest*	*altar*	*possessor*
Sing. abs.	קֹטֵל	מַקֵּל	שֵׁם	כֹּהֵן	מִזְבֵּחַ	קֹנֶה
cstr.	קֹטֵל	מַקֵּל	שֵׁם	כֹּהֵן	מִזְבַּח	קֹנֵה
w. 1. *s.suf.*	קֹטְלִי	מַקְלִי	שְׁמִי	כֹּהֲנִי	מִזְבְּחִי	קֹנִי
2. *s.m.*	קֹטֶלְךָ	מַקֶּלְךָ	שִׁמְךָ	כֹּהַנְךָ	מִזְבַּחֲךָ	קֹנְךָ
2. *pl.m.*	קֹטֶלְכֶם	מַקֶּלְכֶם	שִׁמְכֶם	כֹּהַנְכֶם	מִזְבַּחֲכֶם	קֹנְכֶם
Plur. abs.	קֹטְלִים	מַקְלוֹת	שֵׁמוֹת	כֹּהֲנִים	מִזְבְּחוֹת	קֹנִים
cstr.	קֹטְלֵי	מַקְלוֹת	שְׁמוֹת	כֹּהֲנֵי	מִזְבְּחוֹת	קֹנֵי
w. 1. *s.suf.*	קֹטְלַי	מַקְלוֹתַי	שְׁמוֹתַי	כֹּהֲנַי	מִזְבְּחוֹתַי	קֹנַי
2. *s.m.*	קֹטְלֶיךָ	מַקְלֹתֶיךָ	שְׁמֹתֶיךָ	כֹּהֲנֶיךָ	מִזְבְּחֹתֶיךָ	קֹנֶיךָ
2. *pl.m.*	קֹטְלֵיכֶם	מַקְלֹתֵיכֶם	שְׁמֹתֵיכֶם	כֹּהֲנֵיכֶם	מִזְבְּחֹתֵיכֶם	קֹנֵיכֶם

FOURTH DECLENSION—§ 40

MASC.	*people*	*mountain*	*arrow*	*statute*	*small*	*nose, nostrils*
Sing. abs.	עַם	הַר	חֵץ	חֹק	קָטָן	אַף
cstr.	עַם	הַר	חֵץ	חָק־	קְטַן	אַף
w. 1. s.suf.	עַמִּי	הָרִי	חִצִּי	חֻקִּי	קְטַנִּי	אַפִּי
2. s.m.	עַמְּךָ	הָרְךָ	חִצְּךָ	חֻקְּךָ	קְטַנְּךָ	אַפְּךָ
2. pl.m.	עַמְּכֶם	הָרְכֶם	חִצְּכֶם	חֻקְּכֶם	קְטַנְּכֶם	אַפְּכֶם
						DUAL
Plur. abs.	עַמִּים	הָרִים	חִצִּים	חֻקִּים	קְטַנִּים	אַפַּיִם
cstr.	עַמֵּי	הָרֵי	חִצֵּי	חֻקֵּי	קְטַנֵּי	אַפֵּי
w. 1. s.suf.	עַמַּי	הָרַי	חִצַּי	חֻקַּי	קְטַנַּי	אַפַּי
2. s.m.	עַמֶּיךָ	הָרֶיךָ	חִצֶּיךָ	חֻקֶּיךָ	קְטַנֶּיךָ	אַפֶּיךָ
2. pl.m.	עַמֵּיכֶם	הָרֵיכֶם	חִצֵּיכֶם	חֻקֵּיכֶם	קְטַנֵּיכֶם	אַפֵּיכֶם

EM.	*mother*	*desolation*	*measure*	*statute*	*evil*	*small*
ing. abs.	אֵם	שַׁמָּה	מִדָּה	חֻקָּה	רָעָה	קְטַנָּה
cstr.	אֵם	שַׁמַּת	מִדַּת	חֻקַּת	רָעַת	קְטַנַּת
. 1. s.m.	אִמִּי	שַׁמָּתִי	מִדָּתִי	חֻקָּתִי	רָעָתִי	קְטַנָּתִי
2. s.suf.	אִמְּךָ	שַׁמָּתְךָ	מִדָּתְךָ	חֻקָּתְךָ	רָעָתְךָ	קְטַנָּתְךָ
2. pl.m.	אִמְּכֶם	שַׁמַּתְכֶם	מִדַּתְכֶם	חֻקַּתְכֶם	רָעַתְכֶם	קְטַנַּתְכֶם
lur. abs.	אִמּוֹת	שַׁמּוֹת	מִדּוֹת	חֻקּוֹת	רָעוֹת	קְטַנּוֹת
cstr.	אִמּוֹת	שַׁמּוֹת	מִדּוֹת	חֻקּוֹת	רָעוֹת	קְטַנּוֹת
. 1. s.suf.	אִמּוֹתַי	שַׁמּוֹתַי	מִדּוֹתַי	חֻקּוֹתַי	רָעוֹתַי	קְטַנּוֹתַי
2. s.m.	אִמֹּתֶיךָ	שַׁמֹּתֶיךָ	מִדֹּתֶיךָ	חֻקֹּתֶיךָ	רָעֹתֶיךָ	קְטַנֹּתֶיךָ
2. pl.m.	אִמֹּתֵיכֶם	שַׁמֹּתֵיכֶם	מִדֹּתֵיכֶם	חֻקֹּתֵיכֶם	רָעֹתֵיכֶם	קְטַנֹּתֵיכֶם

PREPOSITIONS—§§ 12, 16, 36, 40

	in, by, with	*to, at, for*	*like*	*after*	*into*	*upon, beside*
	בְּ	לְ	כְּ	אַחֲרֵי	אֶל־	עַל
With 1. *s.suf.*	בִּי	לִי	כָּמוֹנִי	אַחֲרַי	אֵלַי	עָלַי
2. *s.m.*	בְּךָ	לְךָ	כָּמוֹךָ	אַחֲרֶיךָ	אֵלֶיךָ	עָלֶיךָ
2. *s.f.*	בָּךְ	לָךְ	כָּמוֹךְ	אַחֲרַיִךְ	אֵלַיִךְ	עָלַיִךְ
3. *s.m.*	בּוֹ	לוֹ	כָּמוֹהוּ	אַחֲרָיו	אֵלָיו	עָלָיו
3. *s.f.*	בָּהּ	לָהּ	כָּמוֹהָ	אַחֲרֶיהָ	אֵלֶיהָ	עָלֶיהָ
1. *pl.c.*	בָּנוּ	לָנוּ	כָּמוֹנוּ	אַחֲרֵינוּ	אֵלֵינוּ	עָלֵינוּ
2. *pl.m.*	בָּכֶם	לָכֶם	כָּכֶם	אַחֲרֵיכֶם	אֲלֵיכֶם	עֲלֵיכֶם
2. *pl.f.*	בָּכֶן	לָכֶן	כָּכֶן	אַחֲרֵיכֶן	אֲלֵיכֶן	עֲלֵיכֶן
3. *pl.m.*	בָּהֶם, בָּם	לָהֶם	כָּהֵם[1]	אַחֲרֵיהֶם	אֲלֵיהֶם	עֲלֵיהֶם
3. *pl.f.*	בָּהֶן	לָהֶן	כָּהֵן[1]	אַחֲרֵיהֶן	אֲלֵיהֶן	עֲלֵיהֶן

	up to, as far as	*under*	*from*	*with*			*between*
	עַד	תַּחַת	מִן	אֵת	עִם		בֵּין
With 1. *s.suf.*	עָדַי	תַּחְתַּי	מִמֶּנִּי	אִתִּי	עִמִּי	(עִמָּדִי)	בֵּינִי
2. *s.m.*	עָדֶיךָ	תַּחְתֶּיךָ	מִמְּךָ	אִתְּךָ	עִמְּךָ		בֵּינְךָ
2. *s.f.*	עָדַיִךְ	תַּחְתַּיִךְ	מִמֵּךְ	אִתָּךְ	עִמָּךְ		בֵּינֵךְ
3. *s.m.*	עָדָיו	תַּחְתָּיו	מִמֶּנּוּ	אִתּוֹ	עִמּוֹ		בֵּינוֹ
3. *s.f.*	עָדֶיהָ	תַּחְתֶּיהָ	מִמֶּנָּה	אִתָּהּ	עִמָּהּ		בֵּינָהּ
1. *pl.c.*	עָדֵינוּ	תַּחְתֵּינוּ	מִמֶּנּוּ	אִתָּנוּ	עִמָּנוּ		בֵּינֵינוּ
2. *pl.m.*	עֲדֵיכֶם	תַּחְתֵּיכֶם	מִכֶּם	אִתְּכֶם	עִמָּכֶם		בֵּינֵיכֶם
2. *pl.f.*	עֲדֵיכֶן	תַּחְתֵּיכֶן	מִכֶּן	אִתְּכֶן	עִמָּכֶן		בֵּינֵיכֶן
3. *pl.m.*	עֲדֵיהֶם	תַּחְתֵּיהֶם	מֵהֶם	אִתָּם	עִמָּם		בֵּינֵיהֶם
3. *pl.f.*	עֲדֵיהֶן	תַּחְתֵּיהֶן	מֵהֶן	אִתָּן	עִמָּן		בֵּינֵיהֶן

[1] Alternatively כָּהֶם or כָּהֵ֫מָּה and כָּהֵ֫נָּה

INDEX OF SUBJECTS

SUMMARY OF §§ 2–7

I. *Vowels in Hebrew* (§§ 2, 3).

The Hebrew Alphabet is consonantal; but three of the consonants are also used as vowels:

ה = generally pure long *a* (but sometimes *e* and *o*)

ו = pure long *o, u*

י = pure long *e, i*

This primary vocalic system became increasingly used from the time of Ezra and Nehemiah because of the decreasing knowledge of Hebrew among the Jews, and its use was extended to indicate tone long and even short vowels as well as pure-long ones.

When these letters occur at the beginning of a syllable, they are consonantal; e.g. יום *yôm*, ושיר *wᵉšîr*, הוד *hôḏh*. When ו and י occur within a syllable (as the *wāw* does in יום and הוד and the *yôḏh* in שיר) or at the end of it, they are vocalic; e.g. לין *lîn*, קום *qûm*, לי *lî*, לו *lô*. ה is vocalic only at the end of a final syllable, and even in that position it can be used as a consonant (§ 6. 8).

By the seventh century A.D. Hebrew had become a 'dead' language. Therefore the Massoretes (*massōra* = 'tradition', i.e. of the correct pronunciation) developed a system of dots and dashes to convey the traditional sounds of the vowels. What are the classes of vowels for which signs had to be devised?—

(a) pure-long vowels, i.e. those unchangeable by nature.

(b) vowels which are long only because of their relation to the tone and are modified when the relation undergoes change (Hebrew is a strongly accented language with the accent coming, generally speaking, at the end of the word).

(c) short vowels.

(d) hurriedly pronounced, hence indistinct vowels. This class is not peculiar to Hebrew, but in many languages the vowels of this class are not marked by distinctive signs (cf. the first *e* in *bereft* and the first *i* in *divine*).

For the signs the Massoretes used and the names of them, see table p. 18. Summary:

<table>
<tr><th></th><th>a</th><th>e</th><th>i</th><th>o</th><th>u</th></tr>
<tr><td>Long</td><td>טָ(טָה)</td><td>טֵ(טֵי)</td><td>טִ(טִי)</td><td>טֹ(טוֹ)</td><td>טֻ(טוּ)</td></tr>
<tr><td>Short</td><td>טַ</td><td>טֶ</td><td>טִ</td><td>טָ</td><td>טֻ</td></tr>
<tr><td>Indistinct with consonants other than gutturals</td><td>טְ</td><td colspan="2">טְ</td><td colspan="2">טְ</td></tr>
<tr><td>Indistinct with gutturals (i.e. אהחע)</td><td>עֲ</td><td colspan="2">אֱ</td><td colspan="2">חֳ</td></tr>
</table>

II. *External Vowel Signs.*

1. Since it was a complete system of vocalic signs which the Massoretes developed, pure long vowels may, in consequence, be doubly marked, e.g. מי may be read *mî* or *mê*, while מֵ is read as *mē* and מִ as *mī*. Therefore, in the forms מֵי and מִי the vowel is symbolized in two ways. Commonly the vocalic consonants are used for pure-long vowels, while the massoretic signs for long vowels, when used alone, indicate tone long vowels; but this use is not invariable.

2. The *shᵉwa* sign has two uses (a) as *vocalic shᵉwa* it indicates an indistinct vowel; (b) as *silent shᵉwa* it is placed under unvowelled consonants at the end of non-final syllables; (but it can be used with final ך, thus ךְ).

3. The vowel signs ַ and ֶ which represent the short vowels *a* and *e* are found sometimes under the tone (נַ֫עַר, מֶ֫לֶךְ).

4. Both long and short *i* are expressed by the same sign.

5. Long *a* and short *o* are expressed by the same sign.

6. The vowel points are placed under the consonants after which they are pronounced, except the sign for long *o*.

III. *Features of the Syllable* (§ 4).

1. A syllable must begin with a consonant followed by a vowel.

2. A consonant followed by vocal sh^ewa, such as *q*^e in קְטֹל (*q*^e *ṭōl*) is best understood as a preclitic element, so that *q*^e*ṭōl* is virtually one syllable.

3. A syllable may be *open*, composed of consonant and vowel only, or *shut*, composed of consonant, vowel and consonant, e.g. in דָּבָר the first syllable דָּ *dā* is open and the second בָר *bhār* is shut. Only a final syllable can end on two consonants and this is rare.

IV. *The Tone Syllable in Hebrew* (§ 5).

The rules given here apply particularly to substantives of the first declension.

1. The accent falls generally on the last syllable of a word: e.g. דָּבָ֫ר *dā-bhā́r*. As a consequence the vowel of such a syllable is long.

2. In דָּבָר the vowel of the *open* pre-tonic syllable (דָּ) is long. This is common practice in substantives of this declension.

3. When the pre-tonic syllable is shut, its short vowel remains unchanged (מִשְׁפָּט *mis-pā́ṭ*, מַלְאָךְ *mal-'ā́kh*).

4. Vowels further from the tone tend to be shortened as much as possible:

(a) In דְּבָרִים *d*^e*bhā-rîm*, the vowel of the first syllable, basically *dā* (cf. דָּבָר above) becomes a hurriedly pronounced vocal sh^ewa. But when the basic vowel in such a case is pure-long, no such shortening can take place and the vowel remains unchanged (cf. כּוֹכָבִים).

(b) two hurriedly-pronounced vowels cannot be found together; the first becomes most frequently *ḥîreq*: e.g. a form derived from דָּבָר is, in the first instance, דְּבְרֵי which is modified to דִּבְרֵי.

5. The principles stated above refer to a considerable extent to verbal forms as well as to substantival forms; but

(a) *pathaḥ*, not *qāmeṣ*, is found in verbal forms under the tone in the final syllable, e.g. קָטַ֫ל (not קָטָ֫ל); cf. IV. 1 above.

(b) contrary to IV. 2 above, the sh^{e}wa in verbal forms does not stand in the second place from the tone but immediately before it: קָטְלָה (feminine of verb קָטַל); but הֲדָרָה (feminine form of substantive הָדָר).

V. *Daghesh and Mappîq* (§ 6).

1. By means of a point in the bosom of letters the Massoretes preserved other features of pronunciation:

(a) *Daghesh lene.* Its use is confined to six letters, בגדכפת, the so-called *B*^{e}*ghadhk*^{e}*phath* letters. When one of these letters follows the vowel of an open syllable (for this purpose *vocalic sh*^{e}*wa* has the effect of a vowel), it has its aspirated pronunciation; when it is preceded by a closed syllable, it has its hard pronunciation and is marked with a point in its bosom called *Daghesh lene* (e.g. כָּבוֹד *kā-bhôdh*; זְכֹר *z*^{e}*khōr*; מִשְׁפָּט *miš-pāṭ*).

(b) *Daghesh forte* may be used with all letters except the gutturals and *rêš*; its effect is to strengthen or double a letter. It is not used in final letters; thus the sing. of עַמִּים (ים. being a plur. ending) is written as עַם.

(c) As an aid to distinguishing *Daghesh lene* and *Daghesh forte* in use, it may be said that the former cannot be used in a *B*^{e}*ghadhk*^{e}*phath* letter after a vowel, while the latter can occur only after a vowel.

(d) Other uses such as *Daghesh forte dirimens* and *Daghesh forte conjunctivum* can be learned as they are exemplified in use (§ 6. 6).

2. *Mappîq* is a point inserted in a final ה to indicate that it has consonantal value and is not merely a vowel letter.

VI. *The Gutturals* (§ 7).

The four guttural letters are **אהחע**. The following distinctive features of their use should be noted:

1. (a) Gutturals tend to have *a* vowels associated with them; e.g. נַעַר (type מֶלֶךְ); כֹּהֲנִים (type קֹטְלִים); שָׁחֲטָה (type קָטְלָה.)

(b) If a final guttural is preceded

i. by a short vowel other than *pat͟haḥ*, the short vowel is modified to *pat͟haḥ*; e.g. מֶלַח (type מֶלֶךְ);

ii. by a tone-long vowel, that vowel often becomes *pat͟haḥ*; e.g. יִשְׁלַח (type יִשְׁמֹר);

iii. by a pure-long vowel other than *qāmeṣ*, there slips in, between the vowel and the final guttural, a so-called *pat͟haḥ furtive*; e.g. הִשְׁלִיחַ *hiš-lîaḥ* (type הִקְטִיל).

2. A short *i* falling before a guttural in a closed, non-final syllable is usually depressed to *e*; e.g. יֶחְדַּל (type יִכְבַּד).

3. Gutturals take composite sh^{e}wa in place of simple sh^{e}wa vocal; e.g. עֲבֹר (type קְטֹל); but אֱמֹר.

4. A guttural falling at the end of a non-final syllable often is written with a helping vowel, which is the *ḥaṭep͟h* corresponding to the preceding short vowel; e.g. הִעְמִיד > הֶעְמִיד (cf. 2 above) > הֶעֱמִיד. This is most common with **א** and **ה**, frequent with **ע**, and used least with **ח** (cf. יֶחְדַּל, יֶחְכַּם, etc.).

5. If, in the process of inflection, a composite sh^{e}wa is preceded by a simple vocal sh^{e}wa, the simple sh^{e}wa becomes the short vowel corresponding to the composite sh^{e}wa (לְעֲבֹר *l^{e}ʿ^{a}b͟hōr* becomes לַעֲבֹר *laʿ^{a}b͟hōr*).

6. If, in the process of inflection, a composite sh^{e}wa precedes a simple vocal sh^{e}wa, the composite sh^{e}wa is raised to become its component short vowel (חֲכְמֵי *ḥ^{a}k͟h^{e}mê* becomes חַכְמֵי *ḥak͟h^{e}mê*.

7. Gutturals cannot be written with *Daghesh forte*. (This is true also of **ר**.) Wherever **א**, **ע** (or **ר**) occurs in a position in which a non-guttural consonant would be doubled, a short

vowel immediately preceding it is permanently lengthened in compensation: e.g. מֵאֵן (type קִטֵּל); הֵעָבֵד (type הִקָּטֵל). Where ה or ח occurs in such a position, a short vowel before it remains short and the guttural is said to take an implicit *Daghesh forte*.

8. א and ה should be particularly noted:

(a) At the end of a non-final syllable ה is consonantal but א is usually quiescent (hence without *silent shᵉwa* written to it).

(b) At the end of a final syllable א is always quiescent and ה is commonly vocalic (often with a lengthening of the vowel in the open final syllable: e.g. מָצָא, בָּלָה (type קָטַל)).